AF600447

OBJECTS OBSERVED

Objects Observed

The Poetry of Things in Twentieth-Century France and America

JOHN C. STOUT

UNIVERSITY OF TORONTO PRESS
Toronto Buffalo London

© University of Toronto Press 2018
Toronto Buffalo London
utorontopress.com

ISBN 978-1-4875-0157-0 (cloth)

University of Toronto Romance Series

Library and Archives Canada Cataloguing in Publication

Stout, John Cameron, author
Objects observed : the poetry of things in twentieth-century France and America / John C. Stout.

Includes bibliographical references and index.
ISBN 978-1-4875-0157-0 (hardcover)

1. Art objects in literature. 2. Object (Aesthetics) in literature. 3. American poetry – 20th century – History and criticism. 4. French poetry – 20th century – History and criticism. 5. Poetry, Modern – 20th century – History and criticism. I. Title.

PQ443.S78 2018 811'.509357 C2017-906714-1

George Oppen, "Discrete Series 1: 'White. From the'" is from NEW COLLECTED POEMS, copyright © 1934 by The Objectivist Press. Reprinted by permission of New Directions Publishing Corp. and by permission of Carcanet Press.

William Carlos Williams, "The Great Figure," and "The Red Wheelbarrow" are from THE COLLECTED POEMS: Volume I, 1909–1939, copyright © 1938 by New Directions Publishing Corp. and by Carcanet Press. Reprinted with permission.

All reasonable efforts have been made to contact copyright holders. Those who believe they have not been properly acknowledged are invited to contact University of Toronto Press.

University of Toronto Press acknowledges the financial assistance to its publishing program of the Canada Council for the Arts and the Ontario Arts Council, an agency of the Government of Ontario.

Canada Council for the Arts Conseil des Arts du Canada

Funded by the Government of Canada Financé par le gouvernement du Canada

To Suzanne Nash
And
To Lynn Wood
And
To Mildred Wood

Contents

Acknowledgments

A number of people have been helpful and inspirational to me during the long process of research and writing through which this book was completed. I would like, especially, to thank Professor Suzanne Nash of Princeton University, in whose course on twentieth-century French poets' dialogue with the visual arts I first encountered the work of Apollinaire, Reverdy and Ponge. After studying these poets with her in the early 1980s, I soon developed the desire to work on their texts in depth. Reading Suzanne's critical articles and interview with Jean Tortel later led me to include a chapter on Tortel in the present book.

I also wish to thank the many specialists in twentieth-century French poetry on both sides of the Atlantic whom I have had the opportunity to meet over the years. Reading their scholarship, hearing their conference papers and speaking with them on the various occasions when we have met has been a constant source of support and encouragement. Many thanks, in particular, to the participants in the 1999 conference "Poétiques de l'objet en France," which took place at Queen's University.

Thanks also to Dr Ira B. Nadel and Dr Ross Labrie of the UBC English Department, both excellent teachers. I first studied modern American poetry with them.

Many thanks to Richard Ratzlaff for his expert advice and guidance during the final stages of the writing of *Objects Observed*.

Finally, my thanks to Kenneth Hand for his expert typing of the manuscript of *Objects Observed*.

A shorter version of chapter 3 appeared as "The Text as Object: Francis Ponge's Verbal Still Lifes" in *Symposium* Vol. XLVII, No. 1 (Spring 1993): 50–63. A shorter version of chapter 5 appeared, in French, as "Objets et figures maternelles" in S. Villani, P. Perron and P. Michelucci, eds.

Lectures de Guillevic: approches critiques (New York: Legas, 2002): 273–84. A slightly shorter version of one section of chapter 7 appeared as "Le Blason contemporain: On Women Poets' Objectifying of the Male Body" in *Romance Notes* Vol. 21, No. 1 (March 2003): 53–69 (http://taylorandfrancis.com). Another section of chapter 7 appeared as "The Revival of Still Life in Contemporary French Poetry: Paul Louis Rossi's *Cose naturali* and Tita Reut's *Vis cachées*" in *Sites* Vol. 7, No. 1 (Spring 2003): 98–118. My thanks to all of these journals and to Sergio Villani for allowing me to reprint material from these earlier pieces.

Abbreviations

Chapter 1
Ezra Pound. *Selected Poems*: SP
William Carlos Williams. *Collected Poems*: CP
Marianne Moore. *Complete Poems*: CP
Wallace Stevens. *Collected Poems*: CP
Gertrude Stein. *Tender Buttons*: TB
George Oppen. *New Collected Poems*: NCP
George Oppen. *Selected Letters*: SL
Rainer Maria Rilke. *New Poems*: NP
André Breton. *Œuvres complètes*: OC
Victor Segalen. *Trahison fidèle*. Victor Segalen, Henry Manceron, Correspondance 1907–1918: VS / HM

Chapter 2
Cette émotion appelée poésie: *CEP*
Œuvres complètes Tome I: *OC Tome I*
Œuvres complètes Tome II: *OC Tome II*

Chapter 3
Œuvres complètes: OC
Comment une figue de paroles et pourquoi: CFPP

Chapter 4
Tout instant: TI
L'Épicerie d'enfance: EE
Exister/Territoires: ET

Agendas: A
D'après tout: DT

Chapter 5
Terraqué: T
Vivre en poésie: VP
Carnac: C
Ville: V
Paroi: P
Du domaine: DD
Euclidiennes: E

OBJECTS OBSERVED

Introduction

This book explores the encounter with the object which has been a recurring feature of twentieth-century French and American poetry and poetics. On both sides of the Atlantic, the object has been a catalyst for making and (re)thinking poetry from the years of high modernism, shortly after 1900 to the early 1930s, to more recent times, especially in France.

Why are poets so fascinated by objects? What do they seek in evoking, naming, and describing objects? Pierre Laszlo's article "*La Leçon de choses*, or Lessons from Things" suggests some possible reasons for their attention to things by tracing the influence of the *leçon de choses* given in class to the generations of French writers who attended elementary school during the Third Republic, between 1870 and 1940. The *leçon de choses* was a regular feature of the curriculum then. It was a pedagogical exercise in which children closely examined ordinary things from the natural world, such as plants. The lesson had a set format:

> Each of the lectures had three parts. In the first, the gospel for the day, so to speak, was announced. The teacher would write the topic on the blackboard, and show the actual object or a picture of it, and gather remarks from the class. This observation stage was followed by a stage of formalization. The spontaneous speech of the pupils was replaced by scholarly language, or at least by correct French; a lexically rich and difficult vocabulary was introduced. The teacher would then tell the pupils what they had seen, but also how they were supposed to describe it. Finally, he would write on the board or dictate a summary. They were supposed to learn it by rote for the next day's class. (280)

This slow and attentive study of objects provided pupils with an initiation into the art of observation and description, while acquainting them with the functioning of elements of the natural world. Laszlo asserts that these lessons formed a crucial influence on French writers between 1900 and 1950, such as Jules Renard, Colette, and Valery Larbaud, whose work displays peculiarly intense descriptions of nature. Laszlo observes that "these writers use language to store their sensual attraction to an object. They are intent upon recording clinically their perceptions in their most intimate, diminutive and fleeting aspects" (274). The experience of the *leçon de choses* has taught them that "[l]ooked at closely, a banal object may be a splendid spectacle" (275). The French and American poets whose work will be studied here foreground this profound concern for things, initiating their readers into a deeper and different awareness of the world around them.

Even more than the *leçon de choses*, the key genre for understanding the aims and importance of object poetry is the art historical genre of the still life. Several of the poets whose work I will examine pay homage to the still life, often making reference to it explicitly as an aesthetic model. As we shall see, poems by William Carlos Williams, Wallace Stevens, Rainer Maria Rilke, Pierre Reverdy, Francis Ponge, and Paul Louis Rossi develop complex strategies for transcribing the still life to transform it into a poetic genre.

It was in the mid-seventeenth century that the term "still life" (or "Stilleven" in Dutch) began to be used. In France, in the eighteenth century, the expression "nature morte" was coined.[1] The still life is an art of description which eschews narration. It typically presents an arrangement of domestic objects (foodstuffs, cutlery, pipes, watches, musical instruments, flowers, and so on) on a tabletop. Human figures are absent, represented only by proxy through illusionistic realism, as Norbert Schneider observes in his study of the genre:

> It is a noticeable feature of these early paintings that objects and their physical properties have been studied with almost obsessive precision, and that these properties are sometimes rendered with an excessive degree of exactitude. The artists were particularly interested in the effect of light and colour on the objects, which changed considerably according to the time of day. Temporality, variability and chance were a matter of real day-to-day experiences which influenced these paintings and, subsequently, also the entire genre of still lifes. (16)

However, as Schneider also notes, the deceptively realistic rendering of the objects on the table represents only one side of a classic still life painting. Along with the impression of literalness and of a faithful reproduction of everyday reality that these pictures convey, various symbolic meanings also lie concealed. Seventeenth-century still lifes offer a hidden moral lesson for the viewer to see (or not see, if he or she does not examine the picture closely enough). The remains of a meal on the table, flowers that will soon wilt, or a timepiece ticking away the hours can be read as reminders of our mortality as much as signs of sensuous pleasure and of plenty. This ambivalence or split focus characteristic of the still life genre is echoed in many works by the poets studied in this book.

Despite their air of naturalness and simplicity, still life paintings are meticulously ordered and manipulated, as Glen D. Lowry notes: "For still lifes by their very nature are highly contrived assemblages …, carefully constructed to amplify the quotidian by refracting and magnifying it, turning the commonplace into an object of desire" (7). In her study of the modern still life entitled *Objects of Desire*, Margit Rowell underscores the artificiality and codedness that are dominant within the genre. She reminds us that, contrary to appearances, a still life artist does not simply stumble upon a chance arrangement of objects which he or she merely records spontaneously: "[a] still life … often does not exist until the artist decides to constitute the model" (9). In other words, a still life is created after the artist has deliberately organized objects into a careful, consciously contrived pattern. Rowell argues that the still life genre is based mainly on a trick or illusion: "the objects of a still life, although they appear accessible, are actually inaccessible, fictional, created" (10). Accordingly, she interprets still life as "a fictional system corresponding to a structure of desire" (13). The genre tantalizes and frustrates the viewer, as it is "based on a yearning for possession of the real that, supplanted by a fiction, is perpetually deferred or denied" (17).

As an art of description, still life (whether verbal or visual) poses unique problems. In his introduction to a 1981 special issue of *Yale French Studies* on description, Jeffrey Kittay draws attention, first, to the traditional tendency to deemphasize the importance of description in favour of narration:

> We still operate very much within the Aristotelian concept of action, which suggests that description be viewed as secondary, and purely functional,

> or merely decorative. Consequently, description is seen as something which must be kept in its place, functioning to fill in or set up, and having a certain marginality or accidence, making it detachable or skippable; otherwise, if it does claim a larger *droit de cité* (as in descriptive poetry of the eighteenth century), it is seen to be uncontrolled or excessive or boring. (1)

Several different models or metaphors for the poetry of things have been selected and privileged by both French and American poets: the collection, the *blason*, the *leçon de choses*, and the fetish, among others. Each of these models will receive significant attention in this book. However, I will pay particularly close attention to the still life, which has a synecdochal relationship to the entire corpus of object-centred poetry, from Apollinaire and Reverdy, Williams and Stevens, to the work of contemporary poets such as Paul Louis Rossi and Tita Reut.

Of course, my own adaptation of an art-historical genre as a model for understanding the work of some of the key French poets of the twentieth century may be questioned at the outset, as it depends on a bringing together of visual and verbal art forms which many critics would regard as fundamentally different, even incompatible. The inter-arts comparison on which the present study depends is not, I agree, without difficulties. However, Modernist poetry in France and America developed through a *rapprochement* between poetry and the visual arts. Close friendships, and artistic collaboration and mutual influences among visual artists and poets, are a defining feature of the development of poetry in both contexts, from the Cubist years early in the century to the contemporary period. Many of the most important poets (Apollinaire, Reverdy, Ponge, André Breton, Yves Bonnefoy, Jacques Dupin, Paul Louis Rossi, and a host of others) have made celebrated contributions to art criticism. Their awareness of the work of visual artists – especially painters – has played a fundamental role in the evolution of their own creativity. Some well-known poems by Williams and Stevens are – or include descriptions of – paintings. Without engaging with this close affiliation between poetry and the visual arts, one cannot understand the complex achievement of these poets.

The poetry of the object foregrounds the description of objects from everyday life, adhering closely to the surface of experience, much as does its model from the visual arts, the still life. Nevertheless, in these poems – as in still life paintings – it is through the study of the interplay between surface signs and a half-hidden deeper meaning that the reader or beholder is able to come to grips with the complexity of the work.

I begin chapter 1 with a general discussion of two object-centred aesthetic movements which have shaped the development of twentieth-century American poetry in decisive ways: Imagism and Objectivism. Between 1913, when Ezra Pound's "A Few Don'ts by an Imagiste" appeared, and 1931, when *Poetry* magazine published a special issue on the Objectivists, a rich variety of object-focused poetry was produced by some of the leading modernist American poets: William Carlos Williams, Marianne Moore, Wallace Stevens, Gertrude Stein, Louis Zukofsky, and George Oppen being the most prominent. Their turn to the object was prompted in part by a rejection of the Romantic and Symbolist aesthetics of the nineteenth century which accorded exceptional powers to the imagination and the poet's subjectivity as they transformed reality in words. Reacting against this idealism of their predecessors, these American poets took inspiration from objects, from facts, from the material reality around them. Each poet's approach to the object is distinctive. Where Williams grants primacy to the transcription of everyday reality, Stevens registers an irresolvable ambivalence regarding the relationship between ideas and things. The Objectivists develop a more overtly political focus on the objects.

The second section of chapter 1 turns to modernist French poets' engagements with the object. These poets celebrate and problematize the object from varying points of view. Guillaume Apollinaire's *Calligrammes* (1918) features shaped poems in which the words on the page serve also as a "drawing" of the things they reference. Apollinaire combines traditional still life themes with an innovative modernist textuality. In Max Jacob's preface to his 1916 collection *Le Cornet à dés* (*The Dice Cup*), the poet presents his aesthetic theory of impersonality via a focus on the object. Chapter 1 also includes a consideration of Surrealist art and poetry, highlighting the Surrealists' fascination with the object as a conduit for the marvellous. I then discuss Victor Segalen's appropriation of Chinese steles to create the poem-steles of his 1916 collection *Stèles*. Chapter 1 concludes with an examination of Rainer Maria Rilke's *Dinggedichte* (or "thing poems") which he wrote during his years in Paris, in response to the influence on his aesthetics of the work of Auguste Rodin and Paul Cézanne.

Chapters 2 to 6 all study in detail the evolving functions of the object in the work of the five twentieth-century French poets most often designated as "poètes de l'objet": Pierre Reverdy, Francis Ponge, Jean Follain, Eugène Guillevic, and Jean Tortel.

Chapter 2 traces the place of the object in the poetry of Reverdy. Reverdy's poems written during the first decades of the twentieth century are strongly influenced by Cubist art. He shares this Cubist perspective with Gertrude Stein, William Carlos Williams, Max Jacob and Apollinaire; however, each of the five poets responds very differently to Cubism. Rejecting mimesis, Reverdy valorizes the breaking down of everyday reality and the recombining of its elements into a different kind of order. In the still life prose poems of *Au soleil du plafond* (*At the Ceiling's Sun*) he plays upon verbal ambiguity in a manner similar to Cubist painter Juan Gris's uses of visual ambiguity. In Reverdy's later work, the human subject, who was largely absent previously, now becomes dominant.

Chapter 3 explores the work of France's best-known poet of objects, Francis Ponge. I begin by suggesting comparisons between Ponge's poems and the still life, as both engage in a defamiliarization of the commonplace. I highlight the ways in which Ponge's "definitions-descriptions" bring things to life in words, yet also – troublingly – annihilate them by replacing things with a verbal equivalent. The chapter then moves to a discussion of Ponge's view of language and his adoption of open-ended textualities in his later work. The later texts present an unfinished, fragmented representation of the object; in a sense, they radicalize the still life model. The chapter also proposes a comparison between Ponge's text-objects and the object sculptures of American artist Claes Oldenburg. A brief look at the signature adds a final twist to the relationship between subject and object in Ponge's work.

Chapter 4 is concerned with the poetry of Jean Follain. A Follain poem is typically organized around a scene from everyday life, set in the past. The silent presence of objects is a constant in these poems. The object serves as a container for the passage of time in the poems. Although Follain's work appears at first glance to be modest and limited in scope, I underscore its originality by situating the poet in relationship to his great modernist precursors, Reverdy and Jacob. Later, I study an idiosyncratic Follain text, *L'Epicerie d'enfance* (*The Childhood Grocery Store*), in the context of theories of collecting. Chapter 5 focuses on the poetry of Eugène Guillevic, whose œuvre moves through three distinct phases. His early poems, collected in *Terraqué* (*Of Earth and Water*) (1942), place the object in rooms and landscapes coloured by fear and anxiety. Using the psychoanalytic theories of Melanie Klein, I explore the links between these early poems and a maternal presence / absence which generates recurring unconscious phantasies in the poems. In a second creative period, represented by *Carnac* (1960), the poet returns to his childhood Brittany, working towards a reconciliation with "la mèr(e)." Finally, Guillevic's later poems reflect what Jean Pierrot calls "la sérénite gagnée" ("serenity achieved"). I pay particular attention to two late collections of poems: *Du Domaine* (*Of the Estate*) (1977) and *Euclidiennes* (*Euclidian Poems*) (1967).

Chapter 6 considers the poetry of Jean Tortel, a contemporary of Ponge and Guillevic who has also been a mentor for a younger generation of French poets. The chapter begins with Tortel's poetics of the gaze in his garden poetry. I note how he represents and problematizes the relationship between perception and the seizing of the object in writing. In his final, minimalist poems this difficult act of transcription of reality is taken to its limits. The chapter closes with a discussion of the connection between the object and the feminine, which is central both to Tortel's reading of Maurice Scève's sixteenth-century collection of poems *Délie* and to Tortel's own poetics. Scève stages the feminization of the object and its otherness and ungraspability – a topic that also fascinates Ponge and Williams.

Chapter 7 focuses on several contemporary postmodern French texts which discover new possibilities for the object. Using the playing board (go-ban) of the Japanese game of go as a model, the Oulipo poet Jacques Roubaud revitalizes the art of the sonnet in his text ∈ *(Signe d'appartenance)* (*Sign of Belonging*). I also look at *Blasons du corps masculin* (*Blasons of the Male Body*), a 1990 collection in which several contemporary women poets write (on) the male body, reversing the gender dynamics of the Renaissance *blazon* – that is, poems in which a male speaker praised or blamed an individual part of the female body. In the third section of chapter 7, I return to the still life, this time as it is appropriated by Paul Louis Rossi and Tita Reut. Rossi's *Cose naturali* (*Natural Things*) creates textual equivalents to still life paintings which the poet has contemplated. Reut's *Vis cachées* (*Hidden Screws/Flaws*) features elaborate descriptions of individual tools. Her playful poems are in dialogue with works by French artists Arman and César, whose approach to things is as eccentric as Reut's own. Chapter 8 concludes with a passage on the experimental texts of Christophe Tarkos and Nathalie Quintane, poets born in the mid-nineteen sixties. Their texts prove that the object continues to morph into new literary forms today. Tarkos's *calligrammes* seem, at first, completely unconnected to those of his precursor Apollinaire, but a closer comparison of their texts reveals unexpected affinities. Quintane's *Chaussure* (*Shoe*) is anti-lyrical, an example of the sort of text critic Jean-Marie Gleize has called "La post-poésie" ("post-poetry").

Male poets' feminization of the object which they manipulate and textualize is a recurring preoccupation within the tradition I will be exploring. For this reason, I will frequently appeal to feminist criticism to elucidate the gender politics at work behind the surface in many object poems. In her landmark 1949 study *Le Deuxième sexe* (*The Second Sex*), Simone de Beauvoir explores the manifold ways in which woman is placed in a subordinate position in patriarchal culture. Considered mainly (or only) man's "other," she is diminished and distorted, turned into an image or cliché: "on l'appelle 'le sexe' voulant dire par là qu'elle apparaît essentiellement au mâle comme un être sexué ... Elle se détermine et se différencie par rapport à l'homme et non celui-ci par rapport à elle ; elle est l'inessentiel en face de l'essentiel. Il est le Sujet, il est l'Absolu: elle est l'Autre" (16) ("she is called 'the sex', meaning that she appears to men essentially as a sexed being ... She is determined and differentiated with respect to man and not the other way around; she is what is inessential placed opposite to what is essential. He is the Subject, he is the Absolute: she is the Other"). Beauvoir undertakes a detailed account of the ways in which women have been marginalized historically while *myths* of "Woman" have replaced them, making them into the object of male fantasies and fears:

> Dalila et Judith, Aspasie et Lucrèce, Pandore et Athéné, la femme est à la fois Ève et la Vierge Marie. Elle est une idole, une servante, la source de la vie, une puissance des ténèbres; elle est le silence élémentaire de la vérité, elle est artifice, bavardage et mensonge; elle est la guérisseuse et la sorcière; elle est la proie de l'homme, elle est sa perte, elle est tout ce qu'il n'est pas et qu'il veut avoir, sa négation et sa raison d'être (193).
>
> (Delilah and Judith, Aspasia and Lucrezia, Pandora and Athena, woman is both Eve and the Virgin Mary. She is an idol, a servant, the source of life, a dark power; she is the elementary silence of truth, she is artifice, chatter, and lies; she is the healer and the sorceress; she is man's prey, she is his doom, she is everything he is not and which he longs to have, his negation and his reason for being.)

As we shall see in the chapters on Williams, Ponge, Follain, Guillevic, and Tortel, these male poets' fascination with the object as subject matter and *raison d'être* for their poetry stems in part from metaphorical connections between the object and the feminine. The recurrence of this theme of the feminized object must be interrogated. If woman is replaced by an object which the male poet manipulates – describing it, playing with it, controlling it – then the sexual politics of this type of poetry becomes disquieting, potentially misogynist. In order for the male poet's subjectivity and voice to be realized, the woman / object must be controlled (and often distorted) by the figural network into which he places her. She, and her difference, are sacrificed so that he may achieve mastery. The questioning of the gender politics implicit in many object poems will be an ongoing task in my critical study of object poetics.

An additional note: In his essay "Thing Theory," Bill Brown proposes a useful distinction between "objects" and "things." For Brown, the object is defined by its relation to a subject; it is used by the subject. (A car or a drill are examples he cites of "objects" in this sense). The thing, on the other hand, proves more elusive. "As they circulate through our lives," Brown writes, "we look *through* objects (to see what they disclose about history, society, nature, or culture – above all, what they disclose about *us*), but we only catch a glimpse of things" (4). "We begin to confront the thingness of objects when they stop working for us," he continues, "when the drill breaks, when the car stalls" (4). Brown asserts that the term "things" "designates an amorphous characteristic or a frankly irresolvable enigma" (5). The thing becomes, then, a latency or an excess concealed in objects: "You could imagine things … as what is excessive in objects, as what exceeds their mere materialization as objects – their force as a sensuous presence or as a metaphysical presence, the magic by which objects become values, fetishes, idols, and totems" (5).[2]

Generally, I will be using the term "object" to refer to a situation in which a subject is perceiving and describing the object before him / her. "Things" I will use in a more generic sense, but occasionally I will appeal to the more amorphous and mysterious side of "things" which Martin Heidegger and Brown both evoke.

Please note that all translations from the French are mine, unless otherwise indicated.

1 The Object in Modernism in the United States and France

In this book I will argue that an encounter with the object is of inestimable importance for the development of modernism, on both sides of the Atlantic. For a number of the poets whose work is most representative of modernist poetics – Pound, Williams, Moore, Stein, Zukofsky, Oppen, and Stevens in the United States; Mallarmé, Rimbaud, Apollinaire, Reverdy, Jacob, the Surrealists, Segalen, and Rilke in France – the object acted as a major focus of attention and a creative catalyst. Several factors help to explain this overarching fascination with the object in modernism. I will study how the object is integrated into a broad range of different poetries motivated by the call famously made by Ezra Pound to "Make it new" during the early decades of the twentieth century. It is the poets' double focus in their use of the object which interests me: the object provides them with subject matter with which to build poems; at the same time, it performs a crucial metapoetic function, as it is part of the basis for a new view of language and form. The frequency with which the object recurs in both these capacities throughout the years of high modernism in the teens, the twenties, and the thirties is extraordinary. This fact needs to be highlighted more in histories of modernism.

In this chapter I will begin with a discussion of modernism and the object in the United States. The discussion will then move to French poetry. A number of parallel concerns in the value and treatment of the object link these two different, and equally vital, areas of modernism.

Imagism ranks as one of the major avant-garde movements in early twentieth-century poetry. The term "Imagism" was coined by Ezra Pound in 1912 when, sitting in a café with poets Hilda Doolittle and Richard Aldington, he took a page of poetry by Doolittle (H.D.), made some edits to the poem, and wrote "H.D., Imagiste" at the bottom of the page. The best-known definition of Imagism was proposed by Pound in the February 1913 issue of *Poetry* magazine in "A Few Don'ts by an Imagiste." F.S. Flint reports in that piece, Pound underscores three main points concerning Imagism:

1. Direct treatment of the "thing," whether subjective or objective.
2. To use absolutely no word that did not contribute to the presentation.
3. As regarding rhythm: to compose in sequence of the musical phrase, not in sequence of the metronome.[1]

Romantic and Symbolist poetry – the tradition which the Imagists inherited – had generally been dominated by the subjectivity of the poem's first-person speaker, the "I" who was harnessing the power of the Imagination to transform the real. The object in these poetries was appropriated by the subject and subsumed into his visions. The object became a metaphor or a pretext. Taken from the natural world, it took on an abstract meaning within the poetic process. Imagism reverses this earlier trend by concentrating on the object itself to create a new kind of realism. Pound calls for an elimination of verbiage and excess detail. He also exhorts poets to avoid traditional metre. "Foremost in his mind," writes Charles Altieri, "was the need for poetry to avoid both sentimentality and rhetoric while coming to compete with the precision and elegance of prose writers like James and Flaubert."[2] In a sense, Imagism was a short-lived movement. By 1915, two years after publishing his piece in *Poetry*, Pound had moved on to a different model for his new poetics, which he called "Vorticism." Dissatisfied with the static and unstructured nature of the Imagist poem, he now advocated the notion of the image as "a vortex or cluster of fused ideas … endowed with energy" (Pound, SP 375). Imagism's intense focus on the object has a broad application to modernist American poetry, as we shall see.

The object returns as a central preoccupation, to generate a new poetics with the advent of the Objectivists in the 1930s. This later generation of modernists shared their predecessors' interest in a poetics of concreteness, realism and muted lyricism. However, the Objectivists' poetics was somewhat different in focus. In 1931, *Poetry* magazine published a special issue on Objectivist poetry in which Louis Zukofsky (1904–78), who acted as the main spokesman for the group, proposed the term "Objectivists." Zukofsky begins his short, manifesto-like essay "An Objective" (1930, 1931) with a compelling definition of the goals of his group's poetics:

> An Objective: (Optics) – The lens bringing the rays from an object to a focus. That which is aimed at. (Use extended to poetry) – Desire for what is objectively perfect, inextricably the direction of historic and contemporary particulars[3]

Zukofsky's elegant definition combines the need for acute perception and precise technical means required to produce the poem with a taste for realism ("historic and contemporary particulars").

William Carlos Williams (1883–1963) is perhaps the best-known poet of objects in American literature. Although closely connected to both Pound and Zukofsky – and, hence, to Imagism and Objectivism – Williams forged his own personal aesthetic, which changed over time. As a young man, he began to develop a distinctive view of the poem and practice of poetry. *Spring and All* (1923), his most famous collection, presents a radically new poetics and, with its mix of poems and pages of prose statements on poetics, *Spring and All* has an almost manifesto-like force. In his characteristic poems from the early 1920s, Williams focuses on individual objects in detail. As in the earlier poetry of Pierre Reverdy (see chapter 2), the human subject here is apparently absent, or rather, is present as a sharply focused gaze which isolates the salient features of the object to transcribe them onto the page. Williams's use of the line makes the object appear slowly, through carefully selected features, as in his famous poem "The Red Wheelbarrow":

> so much depends
> upon
>
> a red wheel
> barrow
>
> glazed with rain
> water
>
> beside the white
> chickens (CP 224) (Litz and McGowan, eds.)

Williams's oft-quoted declaration "No ideas but in things" (CP 263) is both helpful and misleading for a reader encountering his work. Critics were slow to accord his work the central importance it now has because they often read his poetry as anti-intellectual or naive.[4] However,

Williams never called for a poetry without ideas; on the contrary, a complex poetics grounds his work. What he insists on is that the ideas always be embedded in concrete particulars: things and places.

At first glance, Williams's early poems may seem to evoke things seen in a passive way, as though he were committed to a simplistic realism. Consider, for instance, his poem "The Great Figure" (1921):

Among the rain
and lights
I saw the figure 5
in gold
on a red
firetruck
moving
tense
unheeded
to gong clangs
siren howls
and wheels rumbling
through the dark city. (CP 174)

Williams never advocated a copying of reality. Instead, he spoke of an art of "imitation," which, to him, requires an active response to reality, not passivity. He writes in *Spring and All*: "Imagination is not to avoid reality, nor is it description nor an evocation of objects or situations, it is to say that poetry does not tamper with the world but moves it – It affirms reality most powerfully and therefore, since reality needs no personal support but exists free from human action, as proven by science and the indestructibility of matter and of force, it creates a new object, a play, a dance which is not a mirror up to nature but –" (CP 234–5). Williams's goal here – like that of so many of the poets I will be considering – is the creation of a poem that is itself a kind of object. The poem is to have the solidity, the concreteness, the particularity of a natural or manmade object. Avoiding metaphorization, Williams seeks to present the object through what Francis Ponge will call its "differential quality," which distinguishes it from all others: "Although it is a quality of the imagination that it seeks to place together those things which have a common relationship," Williams writes, "yet the coining of similes is a pastime of very low order, depending as it does upon a nearly vegetable coincidence. Much more keen [than metaphor or simile] is that power which discovers in things those inimitable particles of dissimilarity to all other things which are the peculiar perfections of the thing in question" (Williams, *Selected Essays* 16).

Many of the major critical studies of Williams's poetry (Dijkstra 1969, McGowan 1984, Diggory 1991, Halter 1994) underscore the vital connection between Williams's evolving aesthetics and the influence of the visual arts. From the 1913 Armory Show in New York, to Alfred Stieglitz's 291 Gallery, to Williams's friendships with artists such as Charles Demuth and Marsden Hartley, the visual arts play a large part in his poetics. In the preface to his *Selected Essays*, Williams writes that: "[t]he painters especially have been prominent among my friends. In fact, I almost became a painter, as my mother had before me" (xiv). Around the time he was writing the poems of *Spring and All* and *Sour Grapes* (1921), Cubist artist Juan Gris was Williams's favourite painter. As Gris painted many still lifes while cultivating a distinctive aesthetic, his work is clearly connected to modernist object poetry. Gris had important links to Gertrude Stein and to Pierre Reverdy and to their elaboration of a new poetics under the influence of Cubist art.

In what ways did Gris provide Williams with a model or inspiration? What is particular to Williams's interest in Gris is, in part, their similar views of art. Indeed, Williams actually transposed a Gris painting into one of the poems of *Spring and All*, "The Rose" (CP 195–6). Gris's paintings are comparable to Williams's poems of the 1920s and 1930s in their blend of realism and experimentalism. Gris's work corresponds mainly to the period in Cubism referred to as Synthetic Cubism. Whereas the earlier Analytic Cubism had been more concerned with breaking the image down into fragments, in the later, Synthetic period, still recognizable objects are presented in overlapping, interpenetrating planes. Likewise, Williams's poems are focused on presenting things as they are, while using unexpected line breaks to interrupt and change the reader's way of apprehending reality.

Flowers are a notable subject in Williams's poems of the early 1920s. *Sour Grapes* includes four flower poems, which Williams thought of as still lifes: "Daisy," "Primrose," "Queen-Anne's-Lace," and "Great Mullen" (CP 160–3). These poems propose a direct transcription of reality through colour and detail. "Primrose" begins with these lines:

Yellow, yellow, yellow, yellow!
It is not a color.
It is summer!

It is the wind on a willow,
the lap of waves, the shadow
under a bush, a bird, a bluebird,
three herons, a dead hawk
rotting on a pole –
Clear yellow! (CP 161)

The next poem, "Queen-Anne's-Lace" (CP 162), fuses together a woman's body and a flower, describing both simultaneously. This poem brings us to an interesting, but potentially problematic, aspect of Williams's work: his insistent gendering of his poetics and his fascination with the feminized object. As Celia Carlson notes, "much of Williams's energy in his lyric poetry comes from his attempts to harness what he viewed in rather traditional terms as the feminine power of the body" (27). Carlson draws attention to the frequent presence of girls, women, and feminized objects in his poetry, stating that "[s]uch icons both capture and 'express' desire" (34) and, rather troublingly, that "Williams's desire is often not separate from misogyny" (45). Certainly, the poet himself readily acknowledged the importance of eroticism in his aesthetics. As Terence Diggory explains, there is a tension running through his work and "[a]ll tension, in Williams's view, is fundamentally sexual. Accordingly, 'sex is at the bottom of all art ... because art seeks to accomplish simultaneity' for which 'we must have had two, multiplicity, the male and the female, man and woman – acting together, the fecundating principle'" (65). Christopher MacGowan adds that for Williams, "[t]he male art becomes itself a reality by being infused with the special qualities of female nature. The union is not a capitulation to that nature, but an infusion of its energies to the poet's own purpose, with the result that the poem achieves a life of its own" (29).

Williams shares this attraction to the feminized object with some other male object poets – in particular, with Francis Ponge and Jean Tortel. In each case, the gendering of the object introduces an erotic subtext to the poems, heightening their play with language and form yet also complicating our sense of what an object poem is. If the male poet's gesture aims primarily to possess woman / the feminine, to turn her into a stereotype, or even to manhandle her, then the gender politics which the poem encodes are open to condemnation. Reading such poems requires a critical balancing act. For instance, the final poem of *Spring and All* ends with the lines: "But you / are rich / in savagery

– // Arab / Indian / dark woman" (CP 236). These lines could be taken as blatant stereotyping of "the muse" but, in her study *Poetics of the Feminine: Authority and Literary Tradition in William Carlos Williams, Mina Loy, Denise Levertov, and Kathleen Fraser*, Linda A. Kinnahan provides a very useful and thoughtful corrective to this view of a misogynist Williams by placing him convincingly in a genealogy of women poets who have been inspired by his work, seeing it as an alternative to the highly masculist poetics of the later Pound, for example.

Williams's engagement with the object as a – or the – central feature of his poems continued into the 1930s. In time, though, like a number of other American modernist poets, he moved away from a focus on the object, as this focus came to seem a limitation. The writing of his five-volume epic *Paterson* (1946–51) would take him in a different direction.

A major American poet linked to Williams who also gives pride of place to objects is Marianne Moore (1887–1972). Moore began publishing her experimental poetry in 1915. Her work came to be praised by Williams, Pound, Wallace Stevens, T.S. Eliot, and other leading modern poets. The adjective which best describes Moore's poetry when one first encounters it is "eccentric." Both in her unconventional use of form and metre and in her quirky choice of subject matter, she is very much an American original. Like Williams and the Objectivists, she generally emphasizes things in her poems. Animals, especially exotic animals, such as the pangolin or jerboa or plumet basilisk, are the focus of many of her best-known poems. She blends highly precise and factual description of her animals and objects with a meditation on what sorts of virtues characterize them, what sorts of lessons one can extract from observing them. Moore finds exemplary qualities like humility, restraint, and modesty in the various creatures she observes, and her association of these animals with abstract virtues has led critics to place her poems in the tradition of the emblem and the medieval bestiary. However, whereas in these earlier traditions, the animal itself is displaced by its value as a symbol, in Moore the animal or object is only partially transformed by the imagination. Her sense of ethics requires her to maintain a certain distance from the animal or object she describes. Indeed, one of her themes is the resistance of the animal or thing to being possessed in language. Although she feels a kinship with her creatures, whose activities and way of being are often likened to those of the artist, she is also aware that she cannot produce an exact equivalent of each animal in words.

Like Williams, Moore keeps her, and her reader's, attention focused on the thing being described. The first-person lyrical subject is absent or subsumed into a gaze. She reinforces this emphasis on impersonality by a liberal incorporation of quotations into her poems. The quotations function as factual statements from voices of authority, yet their authority is not absolute, as Moore's recontextualization of her quotations adds fresh nuances to their significance. They bring further points of view into the poem, complicating its meaning, for the consideration of the thing from numerous points of view is important for her, as she told Donald Hall: "It is by the approach through a variety of perspectives that we establish a character's reality. If we are in doubt as to what an object is, for instance, we deliberately try to consider it in as many different terms as its nature permits: lifting, smelling, tasting, tapping, holding in different lights, subjecting to different pressures, dividing, matching, contrasting, etc."[5]

Characteristically, Moore blends reflection on the thing with description of the thing, weaving back and forth between these two approaches as the poem progresses. Thus, in "The Paper Nautilus" (CP 121–2), she describes the paper nautilus's exterior appearance – its "thin glass shell … a dull / white outside and smooth- / edged inner surface" – and what, for her, is its defining activity: its devotion to the eggs it holds within its protective shell: "she scarcely // eats until the eggs are hatched." The creature finally leads us to the insight, by the end of the poem, that "love / is the only fortress / strong enough to trust to," without losing any of its physicality or concreteness. Similarly, in "The Pangolin," Moore offers an extremely careful visual portrait of the animal as the poem begins:

> Another armored animal – scale
>   lapping scale with spruce-cone regularity until they
> form the uninterrupted central
>   tail-row! This near artichoke with head and legs and
>   grit-equipped gizzard (CP 117)

She maintains her focus on the object while, unexpectedly, moving off into digressions as the pangolin's appearance and behaviour suggest virtues to which the poet is signally attracted: grace and fortitude: "Unignorant, / modest and unemotional, and all emotion, / he has everlasting vigor, / power to grow" (CP 119).

French poet Francis Ponge, who is also drawn to using animals as subject matter along with things, may be read as favouring language over things, as he uses words to cover and replace the things he describes. Moore, by contrast, observes a respectful distance, as Bonnie Costello notes: "pursued objects become oblique mirrors of the pursuer in Moore but retain their position as objects" (*Imaginary Possessions* 33). The object's otherness fascinates Ponge but also seems threatening to him; Moore registers praise and admiration as the goals of her quirky, complex acts of description. "Moore's ambivalence about conquest" (Costello 1981: 131) makes her wary of using language to colonize the thing. Thus she strikes a balance between the showy linguistic brilliance of her descriptions of animals and objects and a tendency to self-effacement before what is being described. Her love of real things is a quality she shares with Henry James, one of her favourite precursors: "Things for Henry James glow, flush, glimmer, vibrate, shine, hum, bristle, reverberate" (*Predilections* 23). Her poems celebrate reality and the imagination in a harmonious and unique vision.

Moore's overarching concern to create a just link between reality and the imagination creates a significant bond between her and Wallace Stevens (1879–1955), another of her illustrious contemporaries. Her poetry combines the Imagists' taste for "direct presentation of the thing" with a strong belief in the importance and efficacy of the imagination. Stevens, who admired her work, is also interested in the object world and its relationship to the imagination, but the focus of his poetry is quite different from Moore's. From his first collection of poems, *Harmonium* (1923), to his final collection, *The Rock* (1954), Stevens's approach to the representation of the tension between reality and the imagination is a constant of his work, yet his framing of this issue varies considerably, often even within the same collection of poems. His point of view on the issue keeps evolving over time but he never reaches an ultimate resolution of the problem. Stevens is, certainly, highly conscious of having inherited an exalted view of the powers of the imagination from the Romantics, from Coleridge in particular. However, he is also concerned with including the natural object in his poetry. He shares something of Williams's preoccupation with concrete particulars, yet where Williams seeks to incorporate the natural object into his poems with little, if any, interference from a subjective consciousness, Stevens cannot separate the perception and naming of the object from an equal focus on subjectivity. He is always aware of "the impossibility of seeing without the deformations of subjectivity" because in his epistemology, "any perception is always part fiction for the perceiver" (Mao 225).

Stevens engages in a profound exploration of the still life in his 1942 collection of poems *Parts of a World*. (As Bonnie Costello points out, prior to *Parts of a World* he is mainly concerned with landscape, even in a poem such as "Anecdote of the Jar" (CP 76), which ostensibly focuses on an object [Costello 2008: 30]). Seven or eight of the poems in *Parts of a World* appeal to the still life as a model, yet the poet's approach to still life is not unambiguous. In "Study of Two Pears" (CP 196–7), he valorizes precise description of the object, with no distortion: "The pears are not viols, / Nudes or bottles. / They resemble nothing else. // They are yellow forms / Composed of curves / Bulging toward the base." The poem concludes with the lines: "The pears are not seen / As the observer wills." Here, Stevens comes close to a poetics of the object similar to that of Williams, with whom he carried on a long debate concerning poetics over many years. Nevertheless, in another poem from the same collection, "The Poems of Our Climate" (CP 193–4), even as Stevens again offers a careful, precise description of a still life, this time he underscores the gap between the presence of the object apprehended by the gaze and the gazing subject's desire, which the object cannot satisfy: "Clear water in a brilliant bowl, / Pink and white carnations. / … Pink and white carnations – one desires / So much more than that." Regardless of the sense of beauty or plenitude suggested by the object in this case, "Still one would want more, one would need more," the poem's speaker declares.

Parts of a World, unlike the other collections of poems discussed in this chapter, remains poised between a recurring appeal to the object, taken as privileged subject matter, and a repeated discovery of the insufficiency of the object before the imagination's thirst for knowledge and desire. Thus, "Stevens presents a curious case in the story of modernist obsessions with objects" (Costello 2008: 27). He both confirms and undermines the value accorded to the object by other modernist poets.

One of the most notoriously difficult and fascinating modernist texts is Gertrude Stein's *Tender Buttons* (1914). Stein (1874–1946), an expatriate American living in Paris, wrote *Tender Buttons* during a trip to Spain in 1912. She knew Picasso well and had an extensive collection of modernist paintings in her apartment where she and her partner, Alice Toklas, had a salon. She was profoundly engaged in literary experimentation in the years when she composed *Tender Buttons*. Because of her strong connection to Cubist painting, the text has often been read as a Cubist work. It does, obviously, present an unprecedented kind of writing, mixing prose and poetic effects, challenging conventional modes of representation and understanding. The text is divided into three separate sections: "Objects," "Food," and "Rooms." Stein's text continues to influence experimental writing today. As poet Charles Bernstein comments in his book cover blurb to the 2014 centenary edition, edited by Seth Perlow, "*Tender Buttons* is the touchstone work of radical modernist poetry, the fullest realization of 'wordness,' where word and object are merged."

The reception of *Tender Buttons* has gone from, mostly, incomprehension and even mockery in the first decades following its publication to a serious engagement with its aesthetics, especially since the 1970s. Edmund Wilson, one of the first critics to take the work seriously, likens the poems of *Tender Buttons* to Cubist still lifes, while also sensing the presence of a disguised subtext encoding lesbian sexuality (see Hoffmann, ed., 58–62, 85–8). Wilson's insights have been further developed and nuanced by later critics. Marianne DeKoven, for instance, acknowledges the influence of Cubism on Stein: "Stein's pre-World War I work *is* very similar to Cubist painting of the same period. They share an orientation toward the linguistic or pictorial surface, a movement in and out of recognizable representation; both shatter or fragment perception and the sentence (canvas), and both render multiple perspectives" (171). However, she also finds the idea of Cubism inadequate for understanding the "specific linguistic shapes" Stein creates.[6] Several feminist critics – including DeKoven 1983, Lisa Ruddick 1984, and Catharine R. Stimpson – have characterized Stein's writing as challenging conventional (patriarchal) language and forms in order to radicalize language to present female and lesbian sexuality.

The texts included in *Tender Buttons* vary in length; many are only two or three lines long. The texts evoke domestic objects and actions through indirection and non sequitur – never through conventional description. While writing these eccentric still lifes, Stein frequently includes phrases of metapoetic commentary, such as "The difference is spreading" (TB 11) or "Act so that there is no use in a center" (TB 63). Her emphasis on the idea of change in many of these short pieces reinforces her foregrounding of literary innovation. The recurrent references to cleaning things that have become dirty also signals to the reader that Stein's text plays on separate levels of sense: cleaning domestic objects that have become dirty, a sexual subtext, a concern with renewing language and form.

The prose poems in *Tender Buttons* are composed of short sentences which make statements. However, these brief pieces never actually define or describe the object named in the title of the piece. Rather, the object is approached indirectly (and, in some cases, not approached at all). Stein radically disrupts the relationship between language and things. Because of its fairly limited and predictable subject matter, still life helps her to achieve this realization of a new kind of writing. Since the content or subject matter of these poems is conventional, she can focus entirely on the elaboration of distortionary techniques. The process of writing itself replaces the actual subject matter.

In the twenty-first century, *Tender Buttons* continues to provide a productive model for experimental writing. Instead of its parodies by some of Stein's contemporaries and near-contemporaries, writers now pay homage to Stein's example while reframing its language.[7]

George Oppen (1908–84) is one of the best-known Objectivist poets. His *Discrete Series* (1934) provides one of the most striking examples of Objectivist poetics. As indicated earlier, Louis Zukofsky's essays, such as "An Objective" (1930–1) and "Sincerity and Objectification" (1931), constitute the clearest and most authoritative statement of Objectivist principles. In them, Zukofsky calls for a poetics grounded in the notions of sincerity and objectification. A commitment to sincerity in Zukofsky's sense requires the poet to focus on the object, on material reality, in order to transcribe it as directly as possible. If the poet respects this necessity of sincerity, then, says Zukofsky, "[w]riting occurs which is the detail, not mirage, of seeing, of thinking with the things as they exist, and of directing them along a line of melody. Shapes suggest themselves, and the mind senses and receives awareness."[8] The goal of the poet's efforts is the achievement of what Zukofsky calls "rested totality" by which the completed poem stands as a sort of object: "This rested totality may be called objectification – the apprehension satisfied completely as to the appearance of the art form as an object" (13). An attention to "historic and contemporary particulars" (12) is an essential component of the process of writing poetry, he believes. The poet must also consider the individual word as a sort of thing. Concrete detail has paramount importance: "Emphasize detail 130 times over – or there will be no poetic object" (17). An Objectivist stance combines ethics and aesthetics to an unusual degree. Both Zukofsky and Oppen were committed Marxists in the 1930s, the years of the Great Depression in

America. Although their poems rarely evince any direct political statements or affiliations, a critique of the contemporary capitalist reality in which they lived and then wrote is implicit in much of their poetry. As Sandra Kumamoto Stanley explains, "Zukofsky effected his own proletarian 'revolution of the word' by highlighting the materiality of language and refusing to reduce language to a commodity controlled by an authorial / authoritarian self" (3).

In his essay "The Mind's Own Place" (1963), Oppen presents the fundamental components of his own Objectivist aesthetic. He declares that "[m]odern American poetry begins with the determination to find the image, the thing encountered, the thing seen each day whose meaning has become the meaning of our lives. Verse, which had become a rhetoric of exaggeration, of inflation, was to the modernists a skill of accuracy, of precision, a test of truth" (30). Oppen echoes Zukofsky's belief in a poetics of sincerity as the basis for writing: "It is possible to find a metaphor for anything, an analogue: but the image is encountered, not found; it is an account of the poet's perception, the act of perception; it is a test of sincerity, a test of conviction, the rare poetic quality of truthfulness" (31). He sums up his view of modernism in stating that "the core of what 'modernism' restored to poetry [is] the sense of the poet's self among things. So much depends upon the red wheelbarrow" (32).[9]

The poems presented in *Discrete Series* are elliptical and minimalist. Each poem names only a few salient features of an object as the subject perceives it. Oppen's commitment to realism in these poems is clear, for they are always rooted in everyday life. Yet each poem generates an impression of strangeness and unfamiliarity. One of the first poems in the collection offers this image:

White. From the
Under arm of T

The red globe.

Up
Down. Round
Shiny fixed
Alternatives

From the quiet
Stone floor ... (NCP 6)

Whereas Williams presents more easily recognizable objects in his poems, while using the syntax (mostly) of everyday speech, Oppen here constructs a more fragmented vision. The object he is describing is an elevator but, since he has selected just a few features from it, the reader must struggle to learn to resee reality here, to view it differently. In other poems of the collection, Oppen describes a soda fountain (NCP 7), a car (NCP 13), a tugboat (NCP 19), a civil war photo (NCP 21), a town (NCP 25), and other objects in unexpected ways. His commitment to sincerity requires that he transcribe what is seen while eschewing metaphorization. His choice of title, *Discrete Series*, reflects this commitment. The poet has explained that "[e]ach term of a purely mathematical series is derived by a rule or a convention from the preceding term. A discrete series, to the mathematician, is a series of which each term is empirically true. The problem of poetry, circa 1929-1933, was, I thought, the problem of honesty and of intelligence: and to construct *meaning*, an adequate vision."[10] In *Discrete Series* he is fully engaged in exploring the contemporary reality of America in the 1930s. Several times he chooses an object produced by modern technology for scrutiny, and the political force of his descriptions is slowly revealed. As Kathleen D'Angelo observes, "In *Discrete Series* Oppen deconstructs objects that have come to define modern existence and, in that process, exposes the belief systems lurking within them that shape – and often limit – the subject's knowledge of its own conditions. Thus, Oppen takes apart the object to reveal what gets hidden within it" (160). Although Oppen and his wife Mary did not actually join the Communist Party until 1935, a Marxist critique of capitalist society is implicit in these poems, as Oppen himself later acknowledged: "FROM *DISCRETE SERIES* TO THE MARXISM WAS NOT A 'BREAK' – BY ANY MEANS" (Oppen, SL 255). He also noted that "[t]he 'Marxism' of *Discrete Series* is, was felt as, the struggle against the loss of the commonplace" (Oppen SL 254). To underscore the political aims grounding his descriptions of reality, Oppen distorts syntax and deliberately makes reality unfamiliar. He also works strategically with the white space of the page, incorporating blank spaces into the poems. Rachel Blau DuPlessis has argued that these silences and blank spaces become part of the prosody of the poems. After publishing *Discrete Series*, Oppen published no more poetry until 1962.

French modernist poets demonstrate a fascination with the object as subject matter and as a catalyst for a new poetics with a commitment equal to that of the American poets. The twentieth-century French poets' engagements with the object follow, in part, from the aesthetics of their nineteenth-century precursors. The mid-nineteenth-century Parnassian poets had practised a poetry of precise description of reality. Théophile Gautier and José-Maria de Hérédia had written collections of poems using the object as a model and metaphor: *Émaux et camées* (*Enamels and Cameos*) and *Les Trophées* (*The Trophies*). However, it is the great modernist precursors Stéphane Mallarmé and Arthur Rimbaud who developed the most complex and seminal poetics of the object in nineteenth-century France.

Mallarmé and Rimbaud: The Beginnings of Modernism and the Object

Stéphane Mallarmé (1842–98) developed a poetics of impersonality which has had a lasting influence on the modernist and post-modernist poetics of the twentieth century. The role of the object within Mallarmé's poetics is crucial. He engages with objects in several different ways. One of the places in which the object enters into his thought is through its participation in the aesthetics of "suggestion," which he was formulating from 1891 forwards. Suggestion, rather than outright representation, should be poetry's goal, he believed. Mallarmé's approach to the object, in this sense, is odd and paradoxical. The object is an indispensable component of his poetics, even though it is barely present, veiled. His aesthetic aim, as he expressed it in "Magie" ("Magic") is as follows: "Évoquer, dans une ombre exprès, l'objet tu, par des mots allusifs, jamais directs, se réduisant à du silence égal, comporte tentative proche de créer" ("To evoke, with deliberate obscurity, the silenced object, by means of allusion, never directly, as though by silence, brings with it an attempt at [literary] creation").[11] Accordingly, many of Mallarmé's famous sonnets are organized around the evocation of an object which remains mysterious, out of reach, or impossible. So, to take a famous example, in the "Sonnet du 'ptyx'" (also known as "Sonnet allégorique de lui-même" ["Self-allegorizing Sonnet"]), the "ptyx" (i.e., the mysterious thing upon which the poem focuses) may not exist at all. The poem's speaker implies that the "ptyx" may be unreal, naming it as an "aboli bibelot d'inanité sonore" ("abolished bibelot of sonorous inanity"). As scholars have puzzled over the meaning and origin of the word "ptyx," it has been interpreted as a seashell, a writing tablet, a fold, or a receptacle, among other possibilities. In her article "Mallarmé's 'Sonnet en *yx*': The Ambiguities of Speculation," Ellen S. Burt argues that "so many senses are hidden in this word ['ptyx'] that, taken together, they would make no sense" (71). Ultimately, she concludes, "the *ptyx* reflects nothing more than itself. It is fully adequate to itself in that its only referent is itself, in that the signifier and the signified are one and the same, in that what it names is exactly itself" (72).

While appealing to the object as a key feature of the highly abstract Symbolist poetics which he was developing, Mallarmé also exhibited a curious fascination for decorative and trivial objects: hats, fans, objects of fashion. That a poet as serious and cerebral as Mallarmé could be fascinated by trivial objects associated with domesticity, or by fashion, is surprising. Yet this fascination with things such as bibelots or fans is not gratuitous, as Yves-Alain Favre notes in his introduction to an edition of Mallarmé's *Œuvres*:

> On s'étonne parfois qu'un poète dont la métaphysique est si hardie et les ambitions si hautes, affectionne tant les bibelots: tasses de Sèvres, tasses chinoises, éventails, crédences, lampes, miroirs … Le bibelot sert finalement de protection; il nous rassure et nous détourne de toute recherche d'absolu. Entre le néant fondamental et lui-même, l'homme interpose de menus objets qui le garantissent du vertige. (L)
>
> (Readers are sometimes surprised that a poet [like Mallarmé] whose metaphysics is so bold and whose ambitions are so elevated, has such a great liking for bibelots: Sèvres teacups, Chinese cups, fans, credenzas, lamps, mirrors … The bibelot is, in the end, a kind of protection; it comforts us and makes us turn away from any search for the absolute. Between a fundamental nothingness and himself, man interposes small objects which safeguard him from vertigo.)

Mallarmé's fan poems are among his most interesting treatments of the object. He wrote eighteen short occasional pieces which he names "Fans" ("Éventails"). These poems were written directly onto the fans themselves, and offered as gifts. Thus, object and language are brought into unusually close proximity. Mallarmé dedicated three of these "Éventails" to the women to whom he had the deepest ties: his wife ("Éventail de Madame Mallarmé"), his daughter ("Éventail de Mademoiselle Mallarmé"), and Méry Laurent, a woman with whom he was infatuated. F.C. St Aubyn reports that "[t]he 'Éventail' of Madame Mallarmé was written in red ink on a fan of silvery paper decorated with white daisies, and first published in 1891." He adds that

"Mallarmé wrote the 'Éventail' for Méry Laurent in 1890 in white ink on a fan of gilt paper decorated with roses" (81, 83). The fan becomes a sort of metaphor or model for the Mallarmé poem.

Arthur Rimbaud (1854–91) arguably inaugurated modernist aesthetics more than any other poet of the nineteenth century. Several avant-garde movements have regarded Rimbaud as a key precursor and ancestor. The Surrealists and the radical students of the May 1968 demonstrations in France, as well as the Beat poets in the USA in the 1950s, saw themselves as continuing a struggle for social change, free love, and for a radically new aesthetics which Rimbaud had previously called for in such famous statements as "Trouver une langue" ("To find a language") and "L'amour est à réinventer" ("Love must be reinvented").

In his celebrated "Lettres du voyant" ("Letters of the Seer") of 13 and 15 May 1871, Rimbaud spoke of his project to renew poetry (and, simultaneously, society and subjectivity) by means of a poetics of *voyance*. This metaphor of the poet as seer had, of course, existed long before Rimbaud made it the focus of his own poetics; nevertheless, his particular notion of the poet as *voyant* is ground-breaking. In the 13 May letter to his former teacher Georges Izambard, he called for a redefining of subjectivity and objectivity in poetry in the following passage, which occurs towards the end of the letter:

> Je veux être poète, et je travaille à me
> rendre *Voyant* ... Il s'agit d'arriver à
> l'inconnu par le dérèglement de *tous*
> *les sens* ... C'est faux de dire: Je pense:
> on devrait dire on me pense. – Pardon du
> jeu de mots. –
> JE est un autre. Tant pis pour le bois
> qui se trouve violon, et Nargue aux inconscients,
> qui ergotent sur ce qu'ils ignorent tout à fait! (90)

> (I wish to be a poet and I am working to make
> myself into a *Seer* ... I need to reach what is
> unknown by means of the derangement of *all*
> *the senses* ... It is false to
> say: I think: one should say I am thought. –
> Excuse the play on words. –

I is an other. Too bad for the wood that finds
itself turned into a violin, Fie on those Oblivious
ones who quibble about what they know nothing of!)

Most of the commentary on this letter has drawn attention to the poet's use of the term "voyant" and his incitement of himself (and, implicitly, others who would attempt to become poets) to a "dérèglement de tous les sens" ("derangement of all senses") as well as his statement "JE est un autre" ("I is an other"). Commentators on this letter generally, though, do not point out that the element explicitly given here as the arch-example of this new poetics is the image of the transformation of an everyday thing – wood – into the new poetics. Similarly, in his 15 May 1871 letter, Rimbaud again uses the metamorphosis of an object into something else to illustrate the revolution in subjectivity which his project requires: "Car Je est un autre. Si le cuivre s'éveille clarion, il n'y a rien de sa faute" ("For I is an other. If copper wakes up to find itself a trumpet, that is not its fault").

Rimbaud's unexpected – even jarring – appeal to the object in these letters is striking. His invocation of the object is not a minor detail of these texts; rather, it serves as the fulcrum for his new poetic vision.[12]

During his brief and intense years as a poet, Rimbaud forged a challenging, unprecedented textuality, which the poems of his *Illuminations*, in particular, exemplify. Poetic subjectivity is profoundly altered in these poems, as Susan Harrow explains: "In Rimbaud's dazzling mix of thematic capaciousness and verbal concentration, the self emerges at once fractured and extendible, fissiparous and boundless, quivering and blasting: this radically uncentered subjectivity, formed in the pressured and pleasurable displacements of language, reminds us why 'JE est un autre' has become a rallying cry for modernism" (11). Elaborating, then, on the polyvalent significance of this phrase "JE est un autre," Harrow locates its force primarily in a process of "self-objectification" through which the textuality of *Illuminations* operates: "the construction of thought as a perceptual event experienced from the outside performs stylistically the self-objectification to which 'JE est un autre' alludes, and which comes forth in Rimbaud's poetry in representations of the body, sensation, colour, atmosphere, nature, objects, and debris" (12).

The theorization and practice of a new poetics based on an engagement with the object which we have observed in Mallarmé and

Rimbaud continues in the work of several major twentieth-century French poets and avant-garde movements, whose contribution to the creation of a poetics of the object will now be explored.

Twentieth-Century Examples

A continuing fascination with objects has influenced the development of poetry as a genre in twentieth-century France. Many major French poets of the past century focus on the exploration of the world of objects while underscoring their sense of the poem itself as a sort of object. Collections like Apollinaire's *Calligrammes* (1918), Max Jacob's *Le Cornet à dés* (1916), or Victor Segalen's *Stèles* (1912) offer compelling and innovative practices of the "poème-objet." These modernist texts bear witness to the poets' quest to rethink what a poem is, how it should be read, expanding the boundaries of poetry via the influence of the object. This focus on objects is a catalyst for new aesthetic theories. Cubist poets, Surrealist poets, Oulipian poets and other adherents of the twentieth-century avant-garde have turned to objects as a pre-text and muse inspiring their work.

Apollinaire's *Calligrammes*

Calligrammes (*Calligrams*), Guillaume Apollinaire's second major collection of poetry, published in 1918, is generally considered one of the key expressions of the new, modernist aesthetic. Apollinaire (1880–1918) wrote the first poems of *Calligrammes* in December 1912 and early 1913, after completing his earlier collection, *Alcools* (*Spirits*). Whereas the poems of *Alcools* still reveal the influence of the Symbolist aesthetics which had dominated French poetry during the late nineteenth century and the beginning of the new century, with *Calligrammes* Apollinaire foregrounds innovative aesthetic strategies that critics have read as emblematic of the advent of modernist poetics. As S.I. Lockerbie notes, the poets and artists of Apollinaire's generation were motivated by a strong sense of living in a new world: "It was a change of mood that stemmed ultimately from the rapid advances of the early years of the twentieth century and the general widening of horizons brought about by such inventions as the motorcar, the airplane, radiography, cinematography, and radio communications" (2–3). At the same time that these exciting technological advances were reshaping everyday life, the Cubist artists Georges Braque and Pablo Picasso (a close friend of Apollinaire) were creating paintings that challenged and recast traditional representations of space and time. This new art of dislocation, fragmentation, and unexpected combinations of elements abstracted from reality was to prove extremely influential on the poetry of Apollinaire, Max Jacob, and Pierre Reverdy, in particular, between 1909 and 1918.

Responding to the changes in vision and consciousness prompted by innovations in art and technologies, Apollinaire developed what he called an aesthetic of simultaneity. As Lockerbie explains, this entailed "a type of structure that would give the impression of a full and instant awareness within one moment of space-time" (3). Poems from *Calligrammes* such as "Lundi rue Christine" ("Monday on Christine Street") are composed of juxtapositions of fragments of speech and objects from everyday life using a collage technique. The reader initially experiences a sense of disorder upon encountering this poem. This sense of confusion fades as one realizes that the poet has consciously shaped and ordered the fragments making up "Lundi rue Christine" so that the poem becomes an autonomous object possessing its own unconventional structure.

Apollinaire engenders a feeling of decentered subjectivity, spatio-temporal dislocation, and simultaneity in the opening sequence of poems in *Calligrammes.* He also highlights the role of ordinary objects in these poems. As Susan Harrow observes in her important study of *Calligrammes,* in the poems from "Ondes" ("Waves") "[b]anal things are presented in the 'raw,' directly incorporated in spare, precise language. While the dull familiarity of old shoes, a pocket watch, a white tie, half a dozen mirrors, sawdust, hashish, a barrel organ, a malachite ring, gas burners, a postcard, a pile of plates, a railway waiting room, and grubby floor rugs provides something of a reality effect, the persistence of trivial objects exceeds the narrow scope of local colour … The fascinated gaze that Apollinaire directs at the small-scale objects of everyday consumption, via concise notations, reveals a profoundly human-informed reality and a material counterweight to the overwhelming technological entities that are the epic expression of the modern age [in *Calligrammes*]" (72). Thus, the focus on ordinary objects keeps these poems anchored in the material world even as radical distortionary techniques which the poems use lead to an abstract and unsettling vision.

The most famous texts in *Calligrammes* are the shaped poems that give the collection its title. Apollinaire coined the term "calligramme" by combining "calligraphy" and "ideogramme." As Jean-Gérard Lapacherie notes, each of these two terms refers to practices of writing: "l'écriture, comme série de gestes, produits par la main, qui tracent des figures sur un support ... l'écriture comme geste et trace, l'écriture comme principe qui organise la page" ("writing, as a series of gestures, produced by the hand which traces figures onto a support ... writing as gesture and trace, writing as the principle organizing the page") (195). Only a relatively small number of the poems in the collection are true *calligrammes*, produced through a fusion of writing and drawing in which the visual image doubles the object(s) described in the poem. Nevertheless, Apollinaire's decision to use *Calligrammes* as the title of the entire collection accords pride of place to these particular poems, emphasizing their importance for him as he elaborates a radically new, modernist aesthetic.

The poet had originally planned to publish a slim volume of what he terms "idéogrammes lyriques" to be called *Et moi aussi je suis peintre* (*And I Too Am a Painter*) in August 1914. (The publication of the volume was made impossible because of the outbreak of the First World War, in which Apollinaire served; the poems from the volume were later included in the much larger collection of *Calligrammes*). As Per Nykrog argues, this 1914 volume grouping together five of Apollinaire's best-known object-poems – "Voyage" ("Voyage"), "Paysage animé" ("Animated Landscape"), "Coeur, couronne et miroir" ("Heart, Crown and Mirror") "Lettre-océan" ("Ocean-Letter") and "La Cravate et la montre" ("The Tie and the Watch") – under the rubric "idéogrammes lyriques" is a decisive gesture in the evolution of the poet's ideas about art and writing. Nykrog finds that "idéogramme" may be a more apt term for Apollinaire's project here than "calligramme": "Or, 'idéogramme' et 'calligramme' ne sont pas la même chose. Les cinq 'idéogrammes' sont bien des 'calligrammes,' mais les 'calligrammes' faits après 1914 ne sont pas de[s] idéogrammes.' Un 'bel écrit' – calligramme – est un écrit qui forme ornement devant le sens de la vue; un 'idéogramme' est, par contre, une configuration qui communique une *idée* sous la forme d'un dessin – à travers la perception visuelle il fait appel à l'intellect" ("Yet, 'ideogram' and 'calligram' are not the same thing. The five 'ideograms' are certainly 'calligrams' but the 'calligrams' made after 1914 are not 'ideograms.' A 'beautiful written thing [écrit]' – calligram – is a written thing which forms a visually appealing ornament; an 'ideogram' is, on the other hand, a verbal configuration which communicates an *idea* in the form of a drawing – by means of visual perception it appeals to the intellect") (112). Nykrog is right to draw our attention to the original conception of Apollinaire's concrete poems as conveying a complex *idea* through both words and visual images, as the *calligrammes* were initially often dismissed as frivolous, childish exercises without serious literary value. They were seen as the result of a "jeu inoffensif," "assez puérile," or as an "absurdité visuelle" ("harmless game," "rather childish," "visual absurdity").[13] However, the more closely one reads – and rereads – these poems, the more one perceives the subtle and brilliant artistry behind them, as we shall see.

In fact, reading the *calligrammes* of Apollinaire involves an unusual challenge, for these poems need to be studied simultaneously on a visual and a verbal level. As Jean-Pierre Goldenstein observes in his essay "Pour une sémiologie du calligramme" ("Towards a Semiology of the Calligram"), "[l]es calligrammes, objets complexes, à la fois linguistiques et iconiques, s'offrent à nous comme un travail essentiellement ambigu" ("[t]he calligrams, which are complex objects, both linguistic and iconic, present themselves to us in an essentially ambiguous manner") (1). These shaped poems by Apollinaire are so ambiguous, in part, because it is not always clear whether the image on the page is reiterating what the words of the poem say or whether there is a (potential) disjunction between the visual and verbal levels of the poem. The type of doubly focused reading which these poems call for leads us to question and reformulate conventional reading practices. The *calligramme*, as Goldenstein says, "se situe au carrefour de la *lisibilité* et de la *visibilité*" ("is situated at the crossraods of *readability* and *visibility*") (4). As they breach the standard boundary between visual and verbal sign systems, these poems initiate the reader into a reconsideration of what poetry can be and how it can function. "Une des fonctions majeures des calligrammes, leur 'travail' spécifique," asserts Goldenstein, "serait d'empêcher le lecteur de décrire / déchiffrer un sens déjà-là … pour lui proposer, à travers l'aventure de l'écriture, l'aventure de la lecture" ("One of the major functions of the calligrams, their specific 'task', would be to prevent the reader from describing / deciphering a meaning which is already there … in order to invite him, through the adventure of writing, to pursue the adventure of reading" (6).

Furthermore, one must note from the outset that there are widely different categories of poems included within the term "*calligrammes*." Many of these small texts, such as "La Cravate et la montre" or "Coeur, couronne et miroir" feature drawings of objects via the words that comment upon them. These particular poems resemble still-life paintings, and pay homage to central themes from the still-life tradition, such as time, mortality, and the *carpe diem* motif. Other *calligrammes* seem closer to the landscape tradition in painting; here Apollinaire positions the drawn objects in a symbolic relation to one another, using a spatial relationship on the page to intensify the poem's meaning. "Voyage" and "Lettre-Océan" are two of the representative poems in this category. In still other poems in the collection, such as "2e cannonier conducteur" ("2nd Lead Gunner") or "La petite voiture" ("The Little Car") the visual image is incorporated into a verse poem so that the drawing is one part of the text, rather than constituting the whole poem. Through these varied practices of writing and drawing, the poet extends his exploration of visual poetics beyond the limits of a merely decorative or amusing game.

A closer examination of one or two of the more famous concrete poems from *Calligrammes* will reveal the seriousness and ambitiousness of Apollinaire's contribution to the modernist aesthetic and to the revitalization of concrete poetry in the twentieth century. Although examples of concrete poetry had existed for centuries before *Calligrammes* appeared, Apollinaire declared that his own drawing-poems were a departure from works of the past, such as Rabelais's verbal drawing of the "Dive Bouteille" ("Divine Bottle") or Panard's verbal drawing of a glass from the sixteenth century. He wrote that "[l]es figures uniques de Rabelais et de Panard sont inexpressives comme les autres dessins typographiques, tandis que les rapports qu'il y a entre les figures juxtaposées de mes poèmes sont tout aussi expressifs que les mots qui les composent" ("[t]he unique figures of Rabelais and Panard are mute, like other typographical drawings, whereas the relationships among the juxtaposed figures in my poems are just as expressive as the words which compose them").

"La Cravate et la montre" features a juxtaposition of two poems / drawings. One object-poem (the watch) is much larger and dominates the page; the tie, set in the upper right-hand corner of the page, is much smaller. Through this striking difference in positioning and size, the poet already offers an implicit comment on time and mortality, those repeated leitmotivs from the still-life tradition towards which the poem gestures. The poem was reportedly inspired by Apollinaire's removing his tie and placing it next to a pocket watch one day during a visit to the offices of the paper *Les Soirées de Paris*. This supposedly banal event led him to compose a poem foregrounding a moral lesson on the importance of *carpe diem* in the hectic and stressful modern world. The reader is instructed here to remove his tie in order to be able to breathe properly: "LA CRAVATE / DOU / LOU / REUSE / QUE TU / PORTES / ET QUI T' / ORNE O CI / VILISE / OTE- / LA / SI / TU VEUX / BIEN / RESPI / RER" ("THE / PAIN / FUL / TIE / WHICH YOU / ARE WEARING / AND WHICH / ORNAMENTS YOU O CI / VILIZED MAN / TAKE IT / OFF / IF / YOU WISH / TO / BREAT HE / PROPERLY") (192). Meanwhile, the hours on the watch tick away. In order to mitigate – or undo – the poem's rather grim existential message, Apollinaire invites us to engage in a guessing game as we attempt to decipher the riddles that name each of the separate hours on the face of the watch: "Mon coeur" stands for "one" and "les yeux" stand for "two." (We all have one heart and two eyes, of course.) "L'enfant" stands for three (father, mother, and child) ["Mon Coeur" ("My heart") "les yeux" ("the eyes") "l'enfant" ("the child")]. As this game of riddles continues, the watch fob states "COMME L'ON / S'AMUSE / BI / EN" ("HOW ONE / ENJOYS / ONE / SELF"), while the long hand and the short hand move towards midnight, stating "Il / est / - / 5 / en / fin / Et / tout / se / ra / fi / ni" ("It / is / five / to / at / last / And / all / will / be / o / ver"). Thus, the poem communicates a sombre message through a pleasurable, childlike game. As the poem's title suggests, Apollinaire's literary model here is the *Fables* of La Fontaine, which, like the objects in Apollinaire's poem, offer sobering moral lessons through amusing tales. The talking animals and insects in fables such as "La Cigale et la fourmi" ("The Grasshopper and the Ant") or "Le Corbeau et le renard" ("The Crow and the Fox") express a sense of whimsy and cuteness similar in spirit to many of Apollinaire's poems in *Calligrammes*.

Another representative *calligramme* is "Coeur, couronne et miroir" (Apollinaire *Œuvres poétiques*, 197). The poet here juxtaposes three drawings of objects in which the words of the poem – in block letters, except for Guillaume's own name located in the centre of the mirror – trace out the form of the objects. The heart and the crown are placed beside each other and above the mirror, which is the largest of the three drawn objects. In this poem still life becomes a stand-in for a self-portrait. In canny ways, the poet is playing upon conventions of both genres in order to fashion a metaphorical statement about his own lyricism. The heart, which symbolizes the speaker's emotions and desires in the poem, "resembles an upturned flame" ("PAREILLE A UNE FLAMME RENVERSEE"). The crown tells us that "LES ROIS QUI MeuRent TOUR A TOUR RENAISSENT AU COEUR DES POETES" ("KINGS WHO Die ONE AFTER ANOTHER ARE EVENTUALLY REBORN IN THE HEARTS OF POETS"). Poets, like kings, live on a higher plane and they become immortal through their works (Lockerbie and Hyde Greet note a number of earlier occurrences of the image of kings in Apollinaire's work).[14] Finally, the appearance of Guillaume Apollinaire's name in the mirror effects an enduring transformation of the man (whose actual name was Kostrowitsky, or "Kostro" to his friends).

In two other poems from *Calligrammes*, "Il pleut" ("It's Raining") and "Visée" ("Aiming") Apollinaire arranges series of lines of words moving down or across the page. In "Il pleut," the poem which ends the "Ondes" section, the letters are set in long diagonal lines suggesting rain falling: "Il pleut des voix de femmes comme si elles étaient mortes même dans le souvenir" / "c'est vous aussi qu'il pleut merveilleuses rencontres de ma vie ô gouttelettes" / "et ces nuages cabrés se prennent à hennir tout un univers de villes auriculaires" / "écoute s'il pleut tandis que le regret et le dédain pleurent une ancienne musique" / "écoute tomber les liens qui te retiennent en haut et en bas" ("It is raining women's voices as though they were dead even in memory" / "it is also raining you, wonderful encounters of my life, o droplets" / "and those clouds clearing up begin to whinny out a whole world of auricular cities" / "listen if it rains while regrets and disdain cry with an ancient music" / "listen to the links falling that hold you upward and downward"). The simple lyricism of this poem makes it seem rather naive and sentimental when limited to these conventional lines. However, Apollinaire's placement of these lines on the page so as to evoke falling raindrops adds an entire new dimension to this apparently simple poem. A strong feeling of movement and a dynamic transformation of the page link "Il pleut" to his modernist aesthetics. Similarly, in "Visée," a poem from the "War" section of *Calligrammes*, the individual lines of verse are positioned to suggest the long, snaky trajectories of bullets fired on the battlefield. The recurring presence of these concrete poems at irregular intervals throughout *Calligrammes* makes it a major forerunner of later experiments by twentieth- and twenty-first-century poets with visual poetics.

Max Jacob's *Le Cornet à dés*

Max Jacob (1876–1944) is best known for having written the eccentric and brilliant prose poems of his major collection, *Le Cornet à dés* (*The Dice Cup*) (1917). In the preface to that work, Jacob articulates the main points of his aesthetic theory, which stands as one of the most significant statements of French modernism. His view of the poetic text as, first and foremost, a carefully constructed *object* has proved influential. It also reflects his profound familiarity with the work of the Cubist painters. (Like Apollinaire, he was a close friend of Picasso and he shared that painter's radically innovative aesthetic stance.) Jacob's preface to *Le Cornet à dés* is a crucial document for the study of the evolution of the prose poem as a literary genre.

A careful consideration of Jacob's position on the prose poem as a kind of object will highlight some of the key meanings of the term "poème-objet" in France. In his preface to *Le Cornet à dés,* he is chiefly concerned with distancing himself from existing notions of the prose poem and from the work of the major writers of prose poems from the nineteenth century. "On a beaucoup écrit de poèmes en prose depuis trente ou quarante ans," writes Jacob; "je ne connais guère de poète qui ait compris de quoi il s'agissait et qui ait su sacrifier ses ambitions d'auteur à la constitution formelle du poème en prose" ("Many prose poems have been written over the last thirty or forty years; I know hardly any poets who have understood what a prose poem is and who have managed to sacrifice their personal ambitions as authors to the formal constitution of the prose poem"). Then, in a sentence revealing the cornerstone of his own aesthetic theory, he states that "[l]a dimension n'est rien pour la beauté de l'œuvre, *sa situation et son style y sont tout*" (emphasis added) ("length [la dimension] does not matter for the beauty of the work, *its style and its situatedness are all that matters*"]). The two terms "style" and "situation" occupy a central place in Jacob's articulation of his version of modernism. However, he deploys each of these terms in an idiosyncratic – though lucid – manner. Theo Hermans explains the relation between "style" and "situation" for Jacobs as follows: "'style' bears mainly on the creation of the artistic product and is considered in the first place from the point of view of the author, whereas 'situation' refers to the artistic effect resulting from the perception of 'style' by the reader" (120). Jacob emphasizes that, by using "style," he is not referring to the expression of an author's personality. As Hermans notes, for Jacob "[s]tyle is the consciously artistic use of language, implying a subordination of subjective sensibility to the demands of artistic structuration. Being 'la volonté de s'extérioriser par de moyens choisis' … style is focused primarily on the selection and deployment of particular artistic means, on 'la mise en œuvre des matériaux'" (121). Thus Jacob favours impersonality in art, rejecting Romantic tendencies towards lyrical effusiveness: "L'émotion artistique n'est ni un act sensoriel, ni un acte sentimental" ("Emotion in art is neither an act of the senses nor an emotional act"), he asserts in the preface (15). The internal harmony and order of the poem are, then, the basic components of "style" as he understands it.

Jacob begins his 1916 preface to *Le Cornet à dés* by arguing that "[t]out ce qui existe est situé. Tout ce qui est au-dessus de la matière est situé; la matière elle-même est située" ("[e]verything that exists is situated. Everything that is beyond materiality is situated; materiality itself is situated") (13). He thus confers a privileged status to the sense of situatedness or "situation." Yet his use of this term requires clarification. Hermans finds that "[f]or Jacob, the notion of 'situation' seems to refer primarily to the recipient's awareness of the distinct and individual nature of the work as well as to the conceptual effort needed to penetrate the verbal and imaginative world of the poem. The greater this effort, the more intense the aesthetic pleasure, since 'plus l'activité du sujet sera grande, plus l'émotion donnée par l'objet augmentera'" ("the greater the subject's activity, the stronger the emotion created by the object will be") (124). Indeed, as Jacob once wrote, "[l]'œuvre doit être éloignée du lecteur. Elle doit être située dans un espace lointain, entourée d'un monde, vivant dans un au-delà tout en reflétant la terre, portée sur une nuée tout en étant claire" ("[t]he work must be at a distance from the reader. It must be situated in a distant space, surrounded by a world, living in a beyond while still reflecting the earth, carried on a cloud while remaining clear [light]") (*Esthétique* 31).

In a famous passage near the end of his preface to *Le Cornet à dés*, the poet presents his view of the prose poem considered as an object. This passage merits close scrutiny:

> Rimbaud a élargi le champ de la sensibilité et tous les littérateurs lui doivent de la reconnaissance, mais les auteurs de poèmes en prose ne peuvent le prendre pour modèle, car le poème en prose pour exister doit se soumettre aux lois de tout art, qui sont le style ou volonté et la situation ou émotion, et Rimbaud ne conduit qu'au désordre et à l'exaspération. Le poème en prose doit aussi éviter les paraboles baudelairiennes et mallarméennes s'il veut se distinguer de la fable. On comprendra que je ne regarde pas comme poèmes en prose les cahiers d'impressions plus ou moins curieuses que publient de temps en temps les confrères qui ont de l'excédent. Une page en prose n'est pas un poème en prose, quand bien même elle encadrerait deux ou trois trouvailles. Je considérerais comme tels les dites trouvailles présentées avec la marge spirituelle nécessaire. A ce propos, je mets en garde les auteurs de poèmes en prose

> contre les pierres précieuses qui tirent l'œil aux dépens de l'ensemble. *Le poème est un objet construit et non la devanture d'un bijoutier. Rimbaud, c'est la devanture du bijoutier, ce n'est pas le bijou: le poème en prose est un bijou.* (17, emphasis added)

> (Rimbaud broadened the field [champ] of sensibility and all writers owe him a debt of gratitude, but writers of prose poems cannot take him as a model, for the prose poem, in order to exist, must submit itself to the laws of all art, which are style or will and situatedness or emotion, and Rimbaud leads only to disorder and exasperation. The prose poem must also avoid Baudelairean and Mallarmean parables if it wishes to distinguish itself from the fable. You will have understood that I do not consider as prose poems the notebooks full of more or less odd impressions which some of my fellow writers publish from time to time. A page of prose is not a prose poem, even if it contains two or three interesting finds. I would consider such so-called finds [trouvailles] as fitting to the prose poem if they carried the necessary amount of wit. In this respect, I will warn authors of prose poems against verbal jewels that attract the eye at the expense of the poem as a whole. *A poem is a constructed object and not the display window of a jeweller's shop. A Rimbaud poem is a jeweller's display window and not a piece of jewelry: a prose poem is a piece of jewelry.*)

Here, Jacob unequivocally rejects all purely ornamental or showy effects in the prose poem, (mis)taking Rimbaud's texts from the *Illuminations* as examples of such decorative writing. The defining quality of a true prose poem, by contrast, is its inner architecture, its constructedness and its autonomous existence, set apart from the emotions of a lyrical subject. Much like the Cubist painters, Jacob eschews the idea of the artwork as a reproduction of a pre-existing reality; he promotes, instead, the importance of the inner organization of the artwork as its *raison d'être*: "Une œuvre d'art vaut par elle-même et non par les confrontations qu'on en peut faire avec la réalité ... On dit devant un objet d'art: 'Quelle harmonie! quelle solidité! quelle tenue! quelle pureté!'" ("A work of art has value in and of itself and not through the connections one can make between it and reality ... One says, looking at an art object: 'What harmony! What solidity! What decorum! What purity!'") (Preface 17).

Let us now turn to an examination of the prose poems from *Le Cornet à dés*, which reflect what is at stake in Jacob's embracing of the idea of the *poème-objet*. Significantly, the title of the collection itself refers to an object: a dice cup. Through the image of the *cornet à dés*, the poet is referencing the repertory of objects commonly selected by still-life painters as well as the idea of poetry as a game of chance played between writer and reader. Michel Leiris clarifies the meanings which this title playfully encodes:

> *Le Cornet à dés*, livre au titre ambigu évoquant, sous la forme bien délimitée d'un objet de nature morte, le hasard sans limites, ce hasard dont le nom provient d'un terme arabe désignant un jeu de dés, de sorte que l'axiome mallarméen – auquel il n'est pas exclu que Jacob ait songé – pourrait se lire: *Un coup de dés jamais n'abolira le jeu de dés*. Cornet, qui n'est pas sans ressembler au gobelet de l'escamoteur. Dés, qui pourraient figurer dans un tableau cubiste de la grande époque et font traditionnellement partie des accessoires de la Passion, puisque c'est aux dés que les soldats romains jouèrent entre eux la tunique du Christ. (9)
>
> (*The Dice Cup* is a book with an ambiguous title, evoking in the well-demarcated form of a still-life objet, unlimited chance [le hazard], that chance whose name comes from an Arabic term designating a game of dice, so that the Mallarmé axiom – which Jacob may well have been thinking of – could be restated as follows: *A throw of the dice will never abolish the dice game.* The dice cup, which bears a certain resemblance to the conjuror's cup. The dice, which could be an element in a painting from the high Cubist period and which are traditionally one of the stock accessories of the Passion of Christ, since the Roman soldiers were playing against each other at dice in order to win Christ's tunic.)

As Leiris suggests, Jacob is deliberately appropriating the title of Mallarmé's masterpiece of experimental writing *Un Coup de dés* (*A Throw of Dice*) (1897) in order to displace and rework its poetics. *Le Cornet à dés* replaces the high seriousness of Mallarmé's work with a ludic, humourous writing based on parody. Jacob consciously foregrounds his use of parody in the titles of some of the individual poems: "Poème dans un goût qui n'est pas le mien, à toi, Rimbaud" ("Poem written in a Style not Mine, to you, Rimbaud") (29); "Poème dans un goût qui n'est pas le mien, à toi, Baudelaire" ("Poem written in a Style not Mine, to you, Baudelaire"). Other poems in *Le Cornet à dés* are named after a particular genre – "Roman feuilleton" ("Serial Novel") (89), "Roman d'aventures" ("Adventure Novel") (128), "Conte de Noël" ("Christmas Tale") (76) – even though (or because!) they dismantle the standard conventions of each of these genres in an oddly comic send-up.

Reading the prose poems of *Le Cornet à dés* requires skill and patience, as would any game of chance. These poems consistently aim to entrap the naive, literal-minded reader looking for a realistic narrative – "Encore le roman feuilleton" ("The Serial Novel Again") – or a paraphrasable meaning. As in a Cubist painting, the "point" of the artwork is not in the subject matter, which serves as no more than a pretext. Rather, the aesthetic techniques by which the poet has organized the subject matter and the resulting internal coherence of the poem are given greatest importance. It is these features, by which the *poème-objet* takes shape, that the reader who has grasped the premise of Jacob's textual game will concentrate on.

In "Kaléidoscope" (404), for example, the poet makes an implicit metapoetic statement through the title of the poem: the poem itself will offer dazzling, shifting views and images, just as a kaleidoscope would. The reader is invited to gaze into this "magic" instrument:

> Tout avait l'air en mosaïque: les animaux
> marchaient les pattes vers le ciel sauf l'âne
> dont le ventre blanc portait des mots écrits et
> qui changeaient. La tour était une jumelle de
> théâtre; il y avait des tapisseries dorées avec
> des vaches noires; et la petite princesse en robe
> noire, on ne savait pas si sa robe avait des soleils
> verts ou si on la voyait par des trous de haillons.
>
> (Everything seemed to be part of a mosaic:
> the animals were walking upside down with
> their paws toward the sky except for the donkey
> whose white belly had words written on it
> and the words kept changing. The tower was
> an opera glass; there were golden tapestries
> with black cows; and the little princess in a
> black dress, you could not tell if the dress had
> green suns on it or if you were looking at it
> through the holes of beggars' rags.)

The poem thematizes – and simultaneously *performs* – radical transformations of one thing into another. The thing seen can itself become a kind of text or page to be read: "l'âne dont le ventre blanc portait des mots écrits et qui changeaient" ("the donkey whose white belly had words that kept changing written on it").

Theatricality and illusion subvert stable representation. The poem clearly parodies the poetics of Rimbaud's texts from *Illuminations*, which also rely on theatricality, illusion, and endless transformations, with no stable self or narrative to "centre" the text. Jacob clues the reader in to his game of parody by suggesting that the illusory image before our eyes may turn out to be thread-bare: "on ne savait pas si sa robe avait des soleils verts ou si on la voyait par des trous de haillons" ("you could not tell if the dress had green suns on it or if you were looking at it through the holes of beggars' rags"). The reader of these poems must confront, and work with, uncertainty and doubt as he or she labours to adapt to Jacob's eccentric compositional techniques. In fact, doubt was a valued aesthetic principle for Jacob, as he wrote in a letter to Jacques Doucet, dated September 1907:

> [S]elon moi, le plaisir est dans le mouvement, il faut *ballotter* le spectateur: l'émotion esthétique c'est le doute. Le doute s'obtiendra par l'accouplement de ce qui est incompatible (et ceci sans amener l'étonnement stable) par l'accord des langages différents, par la complexité des caractères … En poésie, l'intérêt naîtra du doute entre la réalité et l'imagination, la perturbation dans les siècles et les habitudes positives … Le doute voilà l'art!
>
> ([F]or me, aesthetic pleasure comes from movement, you must shake up [ballotter] the viewer: aesthetic emotion involves doubt. You create a sense of doubt by joining together things that are incompatible (and without resorting to a stable sense of surprise) through the harmony of different languages, through the complexity of the characteristics shown … In poetry, the reader's interest springs from the confusion / doubt between reality and the imagination, a mixing of time periods and positive habit … Doubt is fundamental to art!][15]

It is, indeed, the unexpected mixing of different genres and the sudden changes in perspective which confuse, delight and challenge the reader of these prose poems. As Jacob remarked to Robert Guiette, he was consciously accumulating false starts, non sequiturs and shifts in tone in his writing in order to fashion a distinctive textuality:

> Lisez *Le Cornet à dés*! On commençait une histoire qu'on laissait inachevée, on menait le lecteur de glissements en glissements jusqu'au néant: on paraissait ne donner aucun sens aux poèmes, on accumulait des mots sans suite, on débutait gravement pour tourner dans un calembour. On

> simulait de hautes vues sur le Cosmos avec un éclat de rire dans la bouche. L'art de la déception était celui du glissando, de l'abrutissement des autres, de la gratuité, de la légèreté, l'art de laisser l'intelligence en panne, comme m'écrit un jeune homme de seize ans.
>
> (Read *The Dice Cup*! [In it], you began a story which you left unfinished, you led the reader from one skid / slide [glissement] to another into oblivion: you seemed not to give any meaning to the poems, you accumulated words incoherently, you started out in a serious way only to veer off into a pun. You faked great cosmic visions while laughing heartily. The art of deception in that text involved glissandos, the debasement of others, gratuitousness, frivolousness the art of leaving intelligence stranded, as a sixteen-year-old youth writes to me) (130–1).[16]

The prose poem "Vie double" ("Double Life"), also from *Le Cornet à dés*, provides a further illustration of Jacob's subversive, Cubist-influenced aesthetics:

> Le château a deux tours pointues et nous nous allongeons sur le mamelon d'en face. La vieille demoiselle a l'air d'un maître-autel; le perron du château a l'air d'un maître-autel et le voilà qui s'envole vers nous soutenu par des colombes. Or, ce maître-autel laissait tomber des prospectus: *Vente de charité*. Et la demoiselle m'en offrit un sans s'apercevoir que j'avais plus de droit à être le vendu que le vendant, l'acheté que l'acheteur et le bénéficiaire que le bénéficiant. (378)
>
> (The castle has two pointed towers and we lie down on the hillock opposite it. The old miss looks like a high altar; the castle stoop looks like a high altar and now it's flying off towards us held up by doves. So, this high altar was dropping handbills: *Charity Sale*. And the old miss offered me one without noticing that I had more right to be the thing sold than the seller, the thing bought more than the buyer and the recipient more than the thing received.)

A Cubist multiplication of different perspectives on the same scene characterizes this poem, as the focus keeps shifting: one element of the poem is said to look like another, which resembles another again, and so on. An unstable chain of substitutions, inspired by end-rhymes, gives the poem its structure, while confusing the reader, who seeks coherence. Jacob generates this confusion strategically. His goal is not to imitate reality or produce a thematic meaning. Instead, he creates a complex internal structure in his poems through effects of sound resemblances, paronomasia, rhyme. In "Vie double" the rhyme between "demoiselle" and "maître-autel" leads to a dizzying switch in identities, a *doubling* of identities which finally extends to the narrator himself, whose role becomes divided and, thus, defined: "j'avais plus de droit à être le vendu que le vendant, l'acheté que l'acheteur et le bénéficiaire que le bénéficiant."

The creation of a self-sufficient and self-referring work distinguished by its complex internal order is Jacob's aim. His sophisticated *poèmes-objets* use humour to mock the realist aesthetic, to denounce that aesthetic as a dead-end.

The Object in Surrealist Art and Thought

The Surrealist movement was formed in France after the First World War. As a grouping of poets and artists that was to become a dominant force in the arts internationally, Surrealism focuses on the merging of rationality and the irrational, of dream and reality, to produce a higher state of consciousness, or "surreality." In his 1924 *Manifeste du surréalisme*, poet André Breton (1896–1966), the leader and chief spokesman for the group, articulated the defining features of the new Surrealist aesthetic. The Surrealists found a vital source of inspiration in transgressive, erotic art and literature of the past, which they discovered most often in works by writers who had cultivated the fantastic and the irrational as the basis for their visions. Strongly influenced by their reading of Sigmund Freud, the Surrealists privileged dreams as a creative catalyst, inasmuch as the unconscious expressed itself most powerfully through dreams, according to Freud. The Surrealists cultivated various practices of *automatism* – writing or drawing in the absence of any censoring by the rational, conscious self. Freud had also argued that the unconscious finds expression in humour, in his 1905 book *Jokes and Their Relation to the Unconscious*. Accordingly, the Surrealists developed their own idiosyncratic practices of what they called "black humour" (many examples of "black humour" from literature before and during the Surrealist movement are collected in Breton's *Anthologie de l'humour noir* of 1930). The majority of the most famous Surrealist works were created in the 1920s and 1930s, although the movement "officially" ended in 1969, three years after Breton's death.

The object plays a key role in the elaboration of the Surrealist aesthetic. In a lecture he gave in Prague in 1935 entitled "Situation surréaliste de l'objet" ("Surrealist Situation of the Object") Breton speaks of a *"crise fondamentale de l'objet"* (*"fundamental crisis of the object"*):

> C'est ... essentiellement sur *l'objet* que sont demeurés ouverts, ces dernières années, les yeux de plus en plus lucides du surréalisme. C'est l'examen très attentif des nombreuses spéculations récentes auxquelles cet *objet* a publiquement donné lieu (objet onirique, objet à fonctionnement symbolique, objet réel et virtuel, objet mobile et muet, objet fantôme, objet trouvé, etc.) c'est cet examen seul qui peut permettre de saisir dans toute sa portée la tension actuelle du surréalisme. (OC Vol. II, 474)
>
> (It is ... essentially on *the object* that surrealism's most lucid gaze has been focused these past years. It is the very careful examination of numerous recent speculations to which this *object* has publicly given occasion (the dreamlike object, the object with a symbolic function, the real and the virtual object, the moving and the mute object, the phantom object, the found object, etc.); it is this kind of examination alone which can allow us to understand the contemporary tension of surrealism fully.)

Before exploring the significance of the various categories of Surrealist object referred to in this quotation, let us first consider why the object attracted such fascinated attention among Surrealist artists and poets. In his excellent study *Surrealism and the Crisis of the Object*, Haim N. Finkelstein explains that "[t]he Crisis of the object implies a new orientation vis-à-vis the world of things, an overthrow of accepted notions of reality ... Thus, in its immediate form, as one of the things which surround us in daily life, the external object may become an extension of our subjective self and serve as a point of departure for a *connaissance* of reality" (1). By removing objects from their usual environment and recontextualizing them, one could experience a transformed reality, the Surrealists thought. The object could thus become a conduit to the Marvellous – or "le merveilleux quotidien." The process of the transformation of the object could lead to "une sensation très nouvelle, d'une nature exceptionnellement inquiétante et complexe" ("a truly new sensation, of an exceptionally disturbing and complex nature"), Breton wrote. The goal of the process was that of *"dépayser la sensation"* (*"to disorient sensation"*) (OC Vol. II, 481).

One of Breton's earliest discussions of the Surrealist object appears in his 1924 essay "Introduction au discours sur le peu de réalité" ("Introduction to the Discourse on the Dearth of Reality") (OC Vol. II, 265–80). Here he valorizes the idea of "fabriquer, dans la mesure du possible, certains de ces objets qu'on n'approche qu'en rêve et qui paraissent aussi peu défendables sous le rapport de l'utilité que sous celui de l'agrément" ("creating, insofar as possible, some of those sorts of objects which one may approach only in dreams and which appear every bit as indefensible from the point of view of usefulness as from the point of view of pleasure") (277). He then describes one such object, a bizarre book with a gnome as its spine:

> C'est une de ces dernières nuits, dans le sommeil, à un marché en plein air qui se tenait du côté de Saint-Malô, j'avais mis la main sur un livre assez curieux. Le dos de ce livre était constitué par un gnome de bois dont la barbe blanche, taillée à l'assyrienne, descendait jusqu'aux pieds. L'épaisseur de la statuette était normale et n'empêchait en rien, cependant, de tourner les pages du livre, qui étaient de grosse laine noire. Je m'étais empressé de l'acquérir et, en m'éveillant, j'ai regretté de ne pas le trouver près de moi. Il serait relativement facile de le reconstituer. *J'aimerais mettre en circulation quelques objets de cet ordre, dont le sort me paraît éminemment problématique et troublant.* J'en joindrais un exemplaire à chacun de mes livres pour en faire présent à des personnes choisies.
>
> Qui sait, par là je contribuerais peut-être à ruiner ces trophées concrets, si haïssables, à jeter un plus grand discrédit sur ces êtres et ces choses de "raison"? (277, emphasis added)
>
> (It was one night recently, while sleeping, at an open-air market held near Saint-Malô, that I had discovered a rather strange book. The spine of this book consisted of a wooden gnome whose white beard, carved in the Assyrian style, went down as far as his feet. This statuette was of a normal thickness and did not at all, however, prevent me from turning the pages of the book, which were made of thick black wool. I had rushed to acquire it and, in waking up, I was sorry not to find it near me. It would be relatively easy to reconstitute it. *I would like to put into circulation a few objects like this, whose fate appears to me to be highly problematic and disturbing.* I would affix a copy to each of my books in order to give them as a present to some persons I'd chosen.
>
> Who knows, in that way I could perhaps contribute to the ruination of those concrete trophies which are so loathsome, I could throw greater discredit on "rational" beings and things?)

Although this bizarre dream object (like the "Nosferatu tie" Breton describes in *Les Vases communicants*) has constituted a powerful and inspiring Surrealist image, it is interesting to note that Breton, in fact, went on to create only one actual concrete object based on something he had seen in a dream (see OC Vol. II, 558–9). Nonetheless, the project he favours in "Introduction au discours sur le peu de réalité" of the creation of dream objects that can be placed in circulation socially remains a provocative suggestion.

Found objects engage the Surrealist imagination just as decisively as do dream objects. In his 1928 text *Nadja*, Breton evokes his visits to Paris flea markets in search of strange, unsettling and unexpected objects which he calls "l'objet insolite" ("the peculiar object"). He once remarked of his visits to the Saint Ouen flea market: "J'y suis souvent allé en quête de ces objets qu'on ne trouve nulle part ailleurs, démodés, fragmentés, inutilisables, presque incompréhensibles, pervers enfin au sens où je l'aime, comme par exemple cette sorte de demi-cylindre blanc irrégulier, présentant des reliefs et des dépressions sans signification pour moi" ("I have often gone there in search of those objects which one finds nowhere else, out of fashion, in fragments, beyond use, almost incomprehensible, and perverse in the sense that most pleases me, like for example that sort of white irregular half-cylinder, presenting reliefs and digressions that are without meaning for me") (59). Finkelstein accounts for the peculiar attraction of such objects in this way: "In *Nadja*, as elsewhere in Breton's work, the bizarre object will be found in semi-darkness, on a dusty shelf in a small, obscure store or in a forgotten corner of the *marché aux puces* … Lost and unknown, these objects do not quite seem to belong. Those are precisely the qualities Breton is looking for in the object as he experiences 'le mouvement spécial, indéfinissable, que provoque de notre part la vue de très rares objets' ['the special, undefinable movement which the sight of very rare objects provokes in us']" (16).

In many of these characteristically Surrealist objects, (perversely) erotic overtones are evident – for example, in a bronze woman's glove that the narrator discovers in *Nadja* or in a spoon Breton found at the flea market: "a large wooden spoon with a handle supported by a small shoe (which forms part of the handle itself)," as Finkelstein describes it. He comments on the sexual significance of this odd object: "A side-view of the spoon presents the silhouette of a slipper, a transformation which Breton associates in his mind with the magic transformation of the pumpkin-carriage in the Cinderella story. Thus, the desire for an object has been satisfied, but what had created this desire in the first place? This aspect is unravelled slowly as certain associations, which have existed in Breton's mind with regard to the spoon, soon clarify its erotic nature: 'pantoufle=cuiller=pénis=moule parfait de ce pénis' ['slipper=spoon=penis=perfect mould of this penis']. The fitting of the leg to the shoe in the Cinderella story is obviously charged, too, with erotic symbolism. Finally, Cinderella's slipper signifies a *lost object*, symbolizing for Breton the unique unknown woman he has longed for" (26–7).

It was actually Salvador Dalí who proposed the most detailed and influential classification of the Surrealist object. In the December 1931 issue of the journal *Le Surréalisme au service de la révolution* (*Surrealism in the Service of Revolution*), Dalí presented a list of six different types of Surrealist object:

1. Symbolically functioning object (automatic origin);
2. Transubstantiated objects (affective origin);
3. Objects to project (oneiric origin);
4. Wrapped objects (diurnal fantasies);
5. Machine objects (experimental fantasies);
6. Moulded objects (hypnagogic origin).

Between 1930 and 1935 the Swiss artist Alberto Giacometti was closely associated with the Surrealists and his artworks of that period exercised a decisive influence on the group's aesthetic ideas. Giacometti provided the immediate inspiration for Dalí's notion of the "symbolically functioning object" with his piece *Suspended Ball.* Art historian Fiona Bradley describes *Suspended Ball* as follows: "A ball with a slit in it, suspended over a wedge shape, it is a sculpture which calls out for the participation of the viewer. The ball begs to be swung over and along the wedge, trailing ambiguous sexual metaphors as it goes. The sculpture seems to be about desire and the frustration of desire" (43).

One of the most compelling manifestations of the Surrealists' according pride of place to the object was the exhibit of Surrealist objects at the Charles Ratton gallery in Paris in 1936. The exhibit brought together examples of several different categories of objects, all of them emblematic of the Surrealists' cultivation of the bizarre, the irrational, the shocking and the unusual. The exhibit presented "a star-shaped biscuit found by Dora Maar, to which was added an inscription signed by Raymond Roussel declaring it an 'outcome' of a breakfast he had had on a specific date in 1923; ... the 'couverture d'un livre ayant séjourné dans la mer' ('cover of a book which had spent time in the sea') and encrusted with shell-fish, found by Léonor Fini" as well as "[a] tray of *objets trouvés* exhibited by Dali includ[ing] a woman's shoe, a plaster cast of a foot, a pornographic toy, etc.," as Finkelstein reports (53–4). In his own description of this 1936 exhibit, Breton understands the objects displayed as revealing "le premier stade de l'énergie poétique que l'on trouve un peu partout à l'état latent mais qu'il s'agissait une fois de plus de révéler" ("the first stage of a poetic energy which one finds here and there in a latent state but which one had to reveal anew") (OC Vol. II, 1200). The exhibit also featured "Ready Mades" by Marcel Duchamp, Native American and Oceanian masks and fetishes, and odd-looking natural objects: "des 'objets naturels,' minéraux (cristaux contenant de l'eau mille fois millénaire), végétaux (plantes carnivores), animaux (tamanoir, oeuf d'oepyornix), des 'objets naturels interprétés' (un singe en fougères) ou 'incorporés' à des sculptures, des 'objets perturbés' (c'est-à-dire modifiés par les agents naturels, incendies, tempêtes, etc.)" ("'natural objects,' minerals (crystals containing very ancient water), plants (carnivorous plants), animals (the great anteater, an oepyornix egg), 'interpreted natural objects' (a monkey made of ferns) or 'incorporated ' into sculptures, 'disturbed objects' (i.e., objects modified by natural agents, fires, storms, etc.)"), according to Breton's own description (OC Vol. II, 1199). These various types of natural objects, which appear unreal or fantastic, stimulate the imagination by bringing the outer world of nature close to the subjective realm of dreams and fantasies. As Breton remarked of the strange stalagmites and undersea corals in a grotto in the Vaucluse he had visited: "l'inanimé touche … de si près l'animé [in such cases] que l'imagination est libre de se jouer à l'infini sur ces formes d'apparence toute minérale" ("what is inanimate comes so close to being animated [in such cases] that the imagination is free to play infinitely upon those forms, which have an entirely mineral appearance") (Breton, "Langue des pierres" ("The Language of Stones"), *L'Amour fou* (*Mad Love*) 15).

The primacy of the object as catalyst for the creation and experiencing of *le merveilleux* is a recurring idea in Breton's thought, and in the literary works and artworks produced by members of the Surrealist group. Indeed, one should note that the most famous instance of the Surrealist image – Lautréamont's image of the beauty of the encounter between an umbrella and a sewing-machine on a dissecting table – involves the juxtaposition of two unrelated objects in a new context. The radicalization of the role of the object in the texts of Rimbaud and

Lautréamont became a crucial touchstone for the development of the Surrealist aesthetic and for their entire world view.

One of the objects displayed in the 1936 Charles Ratton gallery show has become uniquely famous as the quintessential expression of the Surrealist sensibility: Meret Oppenheim's *Breakfast in Fur.* Oppenheim had left her native Switzerland for Paris in 1932, at age eighteen. She quickly became involved with the Surrealists after arriving in Paris. To create her piece for the *Exposition surréaliste d'objets* (*Surrealist Exhibition of Objects*), she bought a cup, saucer and spoon at a department store, covered them with Chinese gazelle fur and entitled the work *Tasse, soucoupe et cuillère revêtus de fourrure* (*Cup, Saucer and Spoon Covered in Fur*). It was Breton who then renamed the piece *Déjeuner en fourrure* – a provocative title, as Belinda Grace Gardner explains: "The title that Breton concocts for the object, *Déjeuner en fourrure,* which evokes Édouard Manet's scandalous painting *Le déjeuner sur l'herbe* (1863) as well as Leopold von Sacher-Masoch's no less scandalous *Venus in Furs* (1870), still enhances [the object's] erotic aura. The commodity item transformed into an animal state not only brings to a head the Surrealist passion for clashing disparities ... But as a 'veiled' body ... it also serves as a projection surface for manifold speculation. In the eroticizing context of Surrealism the 'fur cup' becomes a fetish, a symbol of female sexuality" (12). An ordinary meal becomes strange, savage, and disturbing as a result of Oppenheim's fusion of animal fur with the typical objects forming a place setting. Thomas McEvilley sees in this piece a disruption of the nature-culture dichotomy – a disruption which resurfaces obsessively in many of Oppenheim's works.[17]

A final major expression of the Surrealist fascination with the object is the invention of a new genre, the "poème-objet," by Breton. He defines this hybrid genre in this way: "Le poème-objet est une composition qui tend à combiner les ressources de la poésie et de l'art plastique et à spéculer sur leur pouvoir d'exaltation réciproque" ("The poem-object is a composition which tends to combine the resources of poetry and visual art and to speculate on their potential reciprocal exaltation") (Breton SP 284). He adds that "[l]e premier poème-objet a été présenté par André Breton en 1929" ("[t]he first poem-object was presented by André Breton in 1929") (SP 284). A representative example of his *poèmes-objets* from 1934 combines a short text and a pocket-knife tied to a small piece of cardboard. This is the text written on the cardboard:

Le torrent automobile de sucre candi
Prend en écharpe un long frisson végétal
Étrillant des débris de style corinthien

(The automobile stream made of candied sugar
Makes a scarf of a long plant shiver
Tearing to pieces Corinthian-style debris)

These lines, in typically Surrealist fashion, offer startling and irrational juxtapositions of unrelated words conjuring up dreamlike images. Through their appearance alongside the pocket-knife, they acquire further connotations of danger, eroticism and potential violence. The verbal and visual elements of the poem complement and also contradict each other, as in some of Apollinaire's more complex calligrams. José Pierre describes the mode of interaction of the words and object in Breton's 1934 *poème-objet* as a crossing of the boundary between subjective and objective realms in a fusion of the ordinary and the otherworldly: "A première vue, il n'y a ici rien de commun entre l'élément lyrique et l'élément objectif ... Il n'en est que plus clair à mon sens que Breton tente ici de faire basculer l'objet – cet humble canif – dans le champ poétique, de l'intégrer comme équivalent d'un fragment d'écriture, de quelques vers, dans le champ subjectif du poème tandis que, réciproquement, le poème écrit tend à prendre la qualité objective du canif ... Ainsi, une œuvre d'apparence aussi modeste n'en ambitionne-t-elle pas moins de se situer en ce 'point' d'où subjectivité et objectivité, lyrisme et banalité, message poétique et objet utilitaire cesseraient de se voir 'perçus contradictoirement'" ("At first glance, there is nothing in common here between the lyrical element and the objective element ... It seems to me very obvious that Breton is attempting here to tip over the object – that humble pocket-knife – into the poetic field, to integrate it into it as the equivalent of a written fragment, a few lines of verse, in the subjective field of the poem whereas, reciprocally, the written poem tends to take on the objective quality of the pocket-knife ... Thus, an apparently modest work nonetheless has the ambition of situating itself at that 'point' from which subjectivity and objectivity, lyricism and banality, poetic message and utilitarian object would stop being 'perceived as opposites'") (136–7). In a later *poème-objet*, from 1936, Breton glued words and sentence fragments which he had cut out of a newspaper or magazine onto a cigarette packet. The short poem attached to the packet reads: "L'Océan glacial / jeune fille aux yeux bleus / dont les cheveux / étaient déjà blancs" ("The icy Ocean / a young girl with blue eyes / whose hair / was already white") (qtd. in José Pierre 137). The pleasures of smoking and of heterosexual eroticism both come into play as the poet's words merge with this everyday object and its possible connotations.[18]

Victor Segalen's *Stèles* (1914)

One of the most remarkable examples of the *poème-objet* in the twentieth century is Victor Segalen's 1914 text *Stèles*. Segalen (1878–1919) was originally trained as a doctor. In this capacity, he had sailed with the French merchant marine to Tahiti in 1904. His first novel, *Les Immémoriaux* (*Those Without Memory*), was inspired by his Tahitian experience. In April 1908, Segalen began studying the Chinese language at the Institut des Langues Orientales in Paris. Then, in 1909, he travelled to China to continue his study of Chinese culture – in particular, Chinese archaeology and statuary. His discovery of Chinese funerary steles at various sites eventually led to his conceiving of a new literary genre, the "stele" – a type of poem that represents a stone stele, bearing an epigraph in Chinese characters, followed by an original poem in French by Segalen. These poems in a sense "imitate" a pre-existing referential object which is emblematic of Chinese culture. They have a solid, rectangular, object-like presence on the page. (In the original 1914 edition – and in a 1982 critical edition by Henri Bouillier – each poem is, further, surrounded by a rectangular line. This heightens the visual impression which the reader has of each poem as a free-standing object, autonomous and solid).

The "stele" is a fascinating and innovative type of poem. It emerged from the interpenetration of two very different cultures: European and Chinese. Segalen has consciously set out to elaborate new literary forms through his experience in China:

> Je cherche délibérément en Chine non pas des idées, non pas des sujets; mais des formes, qui sont peu communes, variées et hautaines. La 'forme stèle' m'a paru susceptible de devenir un genre littéraire nouveau, dont j'ai tenté de fixer quelques exemples. Je veux dire une pièce courte, cernée d'un cadre rectangulaire

> dans la pensée, et se présentant de front au lecteur.[19]
>
> (I am constantly seeking in China, not ideas, not subjects; but forms, which are uncommon, varied and lofty. The 'stele form' seemed to me capable of becoming a new literary genre, of which I have tried to concretize a few examples. What I'm talking about is a short text, circumscribed in thought by a rectangular frame, and presenting itself to the reader head-on.)

Segalen's discovery of the steles in China provided him with a perfect opportunity to formulate his culturally hybrid and unprecedented genre of the *poème-stèle*. The poet expressed his admiration for the steles he had seen, writing that "[i]l est certain qu'elles sont belles, et que leur forme quadrangulaire, surface présentée à l'oeil, solidement verticale, reposant sur la tortue sculpturale ..., il est certain que cette forme est bellement, purement, classiquement chinoise" ("[i]t is certain that they are beautiful, and that their quadrangular shape, a surface presented to the eye, solidly vertical, lying on a tortoise sculpture ..., it is certain that this form is beautifully, purely, classically Chinese") [Segalen, *Briques et tuiles*, 813].

To understand fully the meaning that Segalen would attribute to his *poèmes-stèles*, one must turn to a consideration of his idiosyncratic theory of exoticism, expressed especially in his "Essai sur l'exotisme" ("Essay on Exoticism"). Exoticism, for Segalen, is a catalyst to creativity. It functions not merely as a "theme" or as subject matter; rather, exoticism, as he redefines it, becomes a powerful and effective creative *method*. Segalen rejects the facile and simple-minded uses of exoticism which late-nineteenth-century French writers such as Pierre Loti all too often expressed in their works. Segalen calls for a revitalized, complex notion of literary exoticism, in which the exotic results from, and states, the intense and jarring contrast between the world of the European traveller (or "l'exote," as Segalen calls him) and the foreign culture which he or she encounters. The sense of disorientation and "shaking up" of one's identity that the experience of the exotic, in Segalen's sense, makes possible can, then, function as an indispensable resource to creativity. Following Segalen's notion of the exotic, Philippe Postel characterizes the poet's encounter with China from 1909 to 1913 in this way: "l'exotisme ... consiste à mettre en contact un sujet (Segalen) et un objet (la Chine) définis l'un à l'égard de l'autre par une diversité maximale, de façon à faire naître, du choc ainsi provoqué, une forme nouvelle (le stèle-poème)" ("exoticism ... is the putting in contact of a subject (Segalen) and an object (China) defined by a maximum difference from each other, such that, from the shock provoked by their contact, a new form (the stele-poem) is born") (47).

The poems in *Stèles* have, at times, been misinterpreted by Western readers, and so it is important to develop a clear understanding of Segalen's project in creating these hybrid texts. First, although readers have frequently assumed that the poems were actually translations of traditional Chinese poems, in fact Segalen's poems in French are his own creation. It is true that the epigraphs, written in Chinese characters, which he includes in his poems were adapted by Segalen from traditional Chinese sources, which Quin Haiying identifies in an essay: "les épigraphes proviennent de sources assez diverses: (a) des livres classiques chinois ...; (b) des expressions chinoises toutes faites ...; (c) des stèles chinoises; (d) des phrases forgées par le poète lui-même" ("the epigraphs come from a fairly broad range of sources: (a) classical Chinese books ...; (b) stock Chinese expressions ...; (c) Chinese steles; (d) sentences invented by the poet himself") (114). Although these epigraphs in Chinese do complement the meaning of the poems in French, Segalen, of course, recognized that most of his European readers would not be able to decipher these messages written in Chinese characters. The characters serve, primarily, as an emblem of otherness, as a constant reminder to the reader of the cultural differences separating him or her from the world which the poems evoke. By ceaselessly reiterating the idea of difference or diversity (a cornerstone of Segalen's theory of the exotic), the Chinese epigraphs thus fulfil a fundamental aesthetic and political role.

Although Segalen acquired first-hand experience of twentieth-century China, modern China did not interest him; indeed, he expressed contempt for it. It was really ancient China that fascinated him – that is, the country that he had encountered in his readings and on his 1909 archaeological expedition. The language of the poems of *Stèles* reflects this preference. As Philippe Postel notes, "Segalen écrit dans une langue qui tente d'imiter le chinois classique (*wenyan*), c'est-à-dire la langue traditionnelle de la littérature chinoise" ("Segalen is attempting to imitate classical Chinese (*wenyan*), that is the traditional language of Chinese literature") (55). The French in *Stèles* does not attempt to reproduce specific qualities of the classical Chinese language in any direct manner. However, a few basic features of Segalen's language in the collection are strongly influenced by their Chinese model. The heavy use of monosyllabic French words in *Stèles* is the most notable example of this. Postel explains that "en chinois classique, chaque caractère constitue une entité sémantique autonome" ("in classical Chinese, each character constitutes an autonomous semantic entity") (56), and the poet himself expressed his great enthusiasm for including large numbers of monosyllabic words in his "Chinese" poems, speaking of "mon amour croissant du monosyllable, comme représentant une densité du son supérieure, un état plus avancé du mot" ("my increasing love of the monosyllable, as it represents a higher density of sound, a more advanced state of the word") (VS / HM: 236).

Segalen divides the collection into six sections, five of which correspond to the five directions into which geographical space was separated in classical Chinese thought: north, south, east, west, and the centre. (To these, the poet adds his own category of steles "du bord du chemin" to reinforce the notion of the reading of *Stèles* as a journey along a – symbolic – road or path.) In his study of *Stèles*, Victor P. Bol summarizes the significance of these spatial categories:

> [L]a notion de *l'espace* jouait un rôle de premier plan, au point qu'elle apparaît comme une catégorie particulière de l'esprit chinois. Elle repose sur un schéma de base assez simple. La terre est conçue comme un plateau carré, fini, dont les limites sont celles mêmes de la terre chinoise, bordé par les Quatre-Mers, au-delà duquel il n'y a que chaos et confusion … [Ce carré] est lui-même divisé en cinq parties formées par quatre secteurs déterminés par les diagonales, lesquelles viennent joindre les angles d'un carré médian inscrit, dénommé "espace du Milieu." … ces directions sont chargées d'une valeur symbolique et à chacune sont associées dans l'esprit chinois un certain nombre d'emblèmes – couleurs, animaux légendaires, etc. – qui manifestent leur vertu et, magiquement, la rendent efficace. (16–17)
>
> ([T]he notion of *space* played a major role, to such a degree that it appears to be a special category in the Chinese mind. It is based on a fairly simple basic schema. The earth is conceived as a square, well-defined plateau whose limits are those of China itself, bordered by the Four-Seas, beyond which there is only chaos and confusion … [This square] is itself divided into five parts formed by four sectors determined by diagonals, which

join together the angles of a median inscribed square, called "Middle space." … [T]hese directions are loaded with a symbolic value and each one is associated in the Chinese mind with several emblems – colours, legendary animals, etc. – which manifest their virtue and, magically, make it effective.)

Bol also indicates that each of the four directions is associated with traditional symbolic values for the Chinese: the south "est le lieu du pouvoir et de l'énergie" ("is the place of power and energy"); the east "est le domaine '*de la sociabilité, de la bonté*'" ("is the domain 'of sociability, of goodness'"); the north, "de couleur noire, est le lieu de la vertu" ("black in colour, is the place of virtue"); and the west "préside aux actes guerriers et à la magie car il est tourné vers le domaine des Barbares, qui échappent à la civilisation" ("presides over heroic acts and magic for it is turned towards the domain of the Barbarians, who are outside civilization") (17–18). Segalen draws extensively on this symbolism of spatial categories, extracting from it the overall theme for each section of *Stèles*.

The original steles which Segalen saw in China were flat, rectangular stones bearing inscriptions of commemoration and praise. They were often funerary steles. Consequently, the poet repeatedly focuses on ideas of mortality, of time passing, and of eternity in these poems. His words, as if written on stones, convey timeless truths, messages to be passed on from generation to generation. "Le recueil de *Stèles* s'apparente aux recueils d'inscriptions sur bronze et sur pierre apparus en Chine au douzième siècle" ("The collection of *Steles* is related to the collections of inscriptions carved in bronze and stone which appeared in China in the twelfth century"), as Philippe Postel observes (60).

It is essential to realise that Segalen's goal is not to imitate or merely reproduce objects from Chinese culture. In reading *Stèles* one becomes constantly aware of a tension between the effort at recreation of the objects that provided the pre-text for the poems before us and an act of idiosyncratic appropriation of those objects.

Rilke's *New Poems*

Rainer Maria Rilke (1875–1926) is one of the great modernist poets. His early breakthrough as a poet came with the *Neue Gedichte* (*New Poems*) (1907, 1908). Although Rilke was born in Prague and led a peripatetic life throughout several European countries, and wrote in German,

I include a discussion of his *New Poems* in this chapter because these poems were shaped by the years he spent in Paris between 1903 and 1908, where he was the secretary of the sculptor Auguste Rodin from September 1905 to May 1906. Rodin's practice as a sculptor and his specific view of the art object had a decisive influence on Rilke.

New Poems, first published in two separate parts, contains 189 poems, many on mythological and Biblical themes, many evoking places and things. It is the *Dinggedichte* or "thing poems" which are the best-known feature of the collection. The term "Dinggedicht" did not originate with Rilke himself. In a 1926 essay, the critic Kurt Oppert proposed a division between subjective lyric poems and what he called "Dinggedichte," which focus on an object rather than on subjective emotion. Besides two well-known nineteenth-century German poems by Mörike and Meyer, most of the examples of *Dinggedichte* Oppert cites come from Rilke's *New Poems*. Yet, perhaps surprisingly, relatively few of the poems in *New Poems* present a description of an individual object. I count about twenty such poems in the collection. However, it is important to realize that Rilke used the term thing ("das Ding") in a fairly capacious, extended sense. So, poems describing places (such as a town square or a landscape) or buildings (such as a cathedral) or even people ("Spanish Dancer") do constitute *Dinggedichte* for him. Lawrence Ryan defines "*Dinggedicht*" in Rilke's work as follows: "The term has been taken to refer to the exact depiction of a real 'object,' involving a reduction of the 'subjective' element that is generally regarded as constitutive of the lyric genre. The relation is more complex: on the one hand, the 'subjective' element is transformed into an 'objective' embodiment … and it in turn reshapes the 'subjective' perspective. The 'new' in such poems is the transformation of self-projecting perspectivism by its incorporation into the 'real' self-sufficiency of a 'Ding' (such as the Sphinx or the medieval cathedral) or … into the 'imaginary' self-sufficiency of poetic metaphor."[20] As Ryan's definition indicates, Rilke is less concerned than the American modernist poets like Williams and Oppen with subtracting subjectivity from the poem. Rather, a mutually constitutive interplay of subjectivity and objectivity is evident in his poems.

In *New Poems*, Rilke mostly uses the sonnet as a vehicle for his artistic vision. This choice of the sonnet makes sense. Because of its concentrated, fourteen-line form divided into four stanzas (two quatrains followed by two tercets), the sonnet has a solid, thing-like appearance on the page, reflecting the notion of the poem as object. At the same time, given the emphasis on motion and multiple perspectives that characterizes Rilke's art of description in *New Poems,* he is able to change the sonnet into a dynamic entity, creating a tension between its fixed appearance and the valorization of movement in the descriptions that the poems present. Thus, Rilke's descriptions of these things are not at all static. As William Waters argues, "the poems strikingly refrain from suggesting that there *is* a locatable essence behind or apart from this interaction of facets and reflections; where the titles might seem to speak of entities, the poems show 'things' to be compositions of motion and abstraction."[21]

Several of the most famous poems in the collection focus on an object poised between movement and stasis: a caged panther in the Jardin des Plantes; a blue hydrangea whose petals signify both fading and blossoming; a Roman fountain with constantly moving waters; a rubber ball in someone's hands, about to be thrown or bounced.

"Die Rosenschale" ("The Bowl of Roses") (NP J. Cardona, trans. 196–201) discloses the complications inherent in Rilke's art of description. Curiously, before beginning his description of a bowl of roses, the speaker first evokes the image of two boys fighting, "zu einer Etwas sich zusammenballen, / das Hass war und sich auf der Erde waltzte / wie ein von Bienen überfallnes Tier" ("balled up together into a single thing / named Hatred, struggling in the dirt / like an animal crazed and beset by bees"). Then, in the second stanza, he addresses the same "you" who has seen the boys fighting but "now you know how you have forgotten, / for before you lies the brimming bowl of roses" ("Nun aber weisst du, wie sich das vergisst: / denn vor dir steht die volle Rosenschale"). The contrast between the angry fight and the calm, silent bowl of roses reinforces the idea of beauty and contemplative gazing which the poet will now explore. However, strangely, this opening contrast between the two images – boys fighting and bowl of roses – also threatens to disrupt the act of contemplation to which the poem invites the "you" addressed, and also, implicitly, invites the reader, who is a second "you" here. Rilke has positioned this poem last in the first half of *New Poems*. Like the poems on Apollo which open both the first and the second halves of the collection, "The Bowl of Roses" assumes particular importance. For this reason, I would like to pay close attention to Rilke's descriptive strategies for evoking this object.

Rilke's description of the roses seamlessly blends literalness with metaphor: Looking at the roses, the beholder sees "Soundless existence, endlessly opening, / … as if recessed / to sheer inwardness, a strange tenderness and self-illumination to its outer rim: / … // that one opens up like a lid, / and there beneath it lie only eyelids, / closed, as if they were asleep ten times over, / as if they had to absorb some inner vision" ("Lautloses Leben, Aufgehn ohne Ende, / ... wie Ausgespartes / und lauter Inneres, viel seltsam Zartes / und Sich-bescheinendes – bis an den Rand: ... // dass eins sich aufschlagt wie ein Lid, / und drunter liegen lauter Augenlider, / geschlossene, als ob sie, zehnfach schlafend, / zu dampfen hätten eines Innern Sehkraft"). As the contemplation of the roses continues to suggest metaphors and images to the beholders – the I and the you – in successive stanzas, Rilke keeps moving farther away from direct description even as his gaze remains intensely fixed on the object being described.

So, in this poem there is a fundamental tension between the thing to be captured in words and the linguistic processes aimed at (re)constituting it. This tension affects reading. As Carsten Strathausen argues, in *New Poems* "[t]he gaze must oscillate between (reading the) word and (seeing the) thing without ever coming to rest at either one of the poles. A successful reading of Rilke's poems is one that switches back and forth at such high speed that the two realms seem to become one. World and word are thus being fused together as they appear to become superimposed one upon the other. The look of things, in other words, is nothing but an optical illusion in the eye of the reader" (202). Although the aesthetics of *New Poems* is firmly rooted in the bringing together of language and things, Rilke's actual enactment of this aesthetic suggests the incommensurability and separateness of the two, of language and things, even as his rhetoric induces the reader to sense their merging – via the "optical illusion" Strathausen identifies in *New Poems.*

2 Cubism and the Poetry of the Object: Pierre Reverdy's Aesthetics of Impersonality

"J'ai horreur de parler de moi."

– Reverdy, Letter to Pierre Albert-Birot (1918)

("I can't bear talking about myself.")

"De tous les poètes, en effet, Reverdy est le plus objectif, c'est-à-dire le mieux capable de poser sur Soi, comme sur un objet, un regard extérieur."

– Georges Poulet, *Études sur le temps humain III* (206)

("Of all poets, to be sure, Reverdy is the most objective, that is to say the best able to fix on himself, as though on an object, an exterior gaze.")

"For to grasp objects and remove them from the world, is to attack the world's integrity. Hence, not only letting go, but grasping too, may produce a sense of *loss of contact* ... The very act of grasping objects, of seeking contact with the exterior, implies a threat both to the outside world and the inner self."

– Graham Dunstan Martin, "Jules Supervielle: A Poetry of Diffidence" (in Roger Cardinal, 107–9)

Pierre Reverdy (1889–1960) is one of the twentieth-century French poets who has most often been described as a "poète de l'objet." This term implies both a foregrounding of the description of observed realities in his work and a bracketing or effacement of subjective emotion. In a 1957 essay on his poetry, Albert Béguin presents what was to become a critical commonplace concerning Reverdy's work. "On dirait à tout instant," Béguin writes, "que sous la pression du regard le poète espère contraindre les objets et les êtres à se rendre à sa merci. A force de les contempler et de les dire, ne va-t-il pas les faire exister d'une existence nouvelle, plus pleinement réelle, plus conforme à leur secrète essence, qui échappe à nos regards distraits? *De là, dans l'œuvre de Reverdy, tous ces poèmes qui semblent devancer ce que tel de ses cadets, Francis Ponge ou Jean Tardieu, appelle la poésie de l'objet*" ("One could say that at each moment, through the pressure imposed by his gaze the poet hopes to force objects and beings to yield to him. By means of contemplating them and describing them in words, will he not give them a new existence, more fully real, better suited to their secret essence, which slips away from our distracted gaze? *Hence, in Reverdy's œuvre, all those poems which seem to anticipate what some of his younger peers, Francis Ponge or Jean Tardieu, call the poetry of objects*") (264, emphasis added). To elucidate what is implied in his use of the term "la poésie de l'objet," Béguin explains that "[a]pparemment, le poète renonce à s'exprimer lui-même, il se condamne à l'absence, pour s'employer uniquement à décrire ce qu'il perçoit ... mais à le décrire de telle sorte que cette réalité cesse d'être inerte et s'approfondisse de signification savoureuse" ("[a]pparently, the poet has given up on expressing his own subjectivity, he condemns himself to absence, in order to limit himself only to describing what he perceives ... but to describe it so as to make that reality no longer inert and to deepen its delectable meaning") (265).

Similarly, Jean-Pierre Attal, in a 1962 article on Reverdy's poetry, emphasizes the strong impression of impersonality that the poet succeeds in creating:

> Or la poésie de Pierre Reverdy ne raconte rien, ne décrit rien, ne chante ni ne grince; les mots qui la constituent ne sont pas liés ensemble, mais seulement placés côte à côte. Ils ne servent qu'à nommer, et ce qu'ils nomment se réduit à ce que les sens du poète perçoivent. (307)
>
> (Pierre Reverdy's poetry tells no story, describes nothing, neither sings nor moans; the words that constitute it are not joined to one another, they are only placed side by side. Their only function is to name, and what they name is reduced to what the poet's senses perceive.)

When one first encounters Reverdy's poems, one is, indeed, struck by a curious impression of impersonality. The poem "Écran" ("Screen") for example, from his 1918 collection *Les Ardoises du toit* (*Roof Slates*), is representative of his (early) poetics:

Écran

Une ombre coule sur ta main
La lampe a changé ta figure
La pendule bat
    Le temps dure
Et comme il ne se passe rien
Celui qui regardait s'en va
  Le monde se retourne et rit
Pour regarder tout ce qui vit
    On marche
Un tournant au bout de la route
      Une forêt
Un pont sans arches
    Et la maison où je vivrais
Il faut partir coûte que coûte
Et l'ombre qui passait
    Celui qui regardait
Le monde qui riait
      S'évanouissent
Au fond contre le mur
    Des silhouettes glissent (OC Tome I 228)

(Screen

A shadow flows over your hand
The lamp has made your face change
The clock strikes
      Time lasts
And since there is nothing happening
The man who was watching departs
  People turn around and laugh
To look at all that exists
    You walk
A turning at the end of the road
      A forest
A bridge without arches
    And the house where I would live
One must leave at all costs
And the shadow that was passing

The man who was looking
People who were laughing
Disappear
At the far end against the wall
Silhouettes slip away)

The reader is confronted in this poem with an apparently random series of events. Because of the lack of punctuation and the use of parataxis, the connections between what is occurring in one line and the preceding or following line are unclear. Despite the appearance of the first-person pronoun "je" in line thirteen, no stable observing consciousness can be inferred in this scene. Objects ("la lampe," "la pendule," "une forêt," "un pont," "la maison") dominate the scene. Any possible human actors have been replaced by substitutes such as detached body parts ("ta main") or shadows or silhouettes ("une ombre," "l'ombre qui passait," "Des silhouettes glissent"). Otherwise, the impersonal pronoun "on" ("On marche") and the demonstrative pronoun "celui" ("Celui qui regardait") introduce indefinite, anonymous actors into the enigmatic world of this poem. Moreover, the lack of a stable left margin and the predominance of blank spaces surrounding and isolating individual lines of the poem accentuate and reinforce the impression of disorientation and indefiniteness. As verb tenses move unpredictably between the present, the *passé composé* and the imperfect, the scene cannot be anchored clearly in time.

Throughout his collections of poetry, running from *Poèmes en prose* (*Prose Poems*) of 1915 to the posthumous *Sable mouvant* (*Quicksand*) (1960), Reverdy focuses again and again on the same fairly limited range of objects, which he presents in varying combinations and patterns from one poem to another. These objects, generally designated by the definite article ("the door," "the lamp," "the window") refer back to material reality while taking on a nascent – though uncertain – symbolic function, as in the poem "Coin obscur" from the 1921 collection *Coeur de chêne* (*Oaken Heart*):

Coin Obscur
On ferme la porte
Le courant
La croix
Le panneau blanc s'écaille
Les armes sur la main

Aucun appel dans l'air
Ou sur le fil
Le même silence qu'hier
Dans la bâtisse aux angles bleus de froid
Autour de la pelouse fraîche
Des éclats de tambours
Un battement de larmes
Un grand nombre de jours
Des bêtes galopent au sens du tourbillon
De la boule emportée
Des traits de feu
Sur les pistes plus sombres
Enfin quelques visages familiers
Sortent de l'ombre. (OC Tome I 324)

(Dark Corner
Someone closes the door
The draft
The cross
The white billboard's paint flaking
Weapons in hands
No call in the air
Or on the wire
The same silence as yesterday
In the building with angles blue from cold
Around the dewy lawn
Drum rolls
A beating of tears
A great many days
Animals gallop in the direction of the whirlwind
From the ball-lightning carried away
Flashes of fire
On the darker trails
Finally a few familiar faces
Emerge from the shadows.)

One notes in this poem a tendency to position phrases used as individual lines, without a verb. This practice heightens the sense of alienation and absence that defines the atmosphere of Reverdy's early poems. Concrete nouns alternate with abstract nouns as the poem moves forward, giving us the impression that, although the scene presented here is anchored in reality, it also gestures towards a half-perceived, half-intuited spiritual significance. The title "Coin obscur" plays upon a thematics of darkness and light, day and night or nightfall which recurs throughout Reverdy's work, combining literal and figural levels of meaning.

As is evident in "Ecran" and "Coin obscur," objects perform multiple functions within Reverdy's poetry. They off-set and counterbalance the grammatical and structural vagueness and indefiniteness of the poems by constantly reminding the reader of everyday material reality; through metonymy, they link the poems to lived reality. At the same time, the continual emphasis on the presence of objects, even as any possible observing consciousness in the poems remains shadowy and marginal, creates a disturbing but fascinating feeling of estrangement. Reverdy's development of this innovative textuality is, in large measure, a result of his decisive encounter with Cubism after 1910.

Reverdy's Encounter with Cubism: The Aesthetics of Impersonality

Born in Narbonne in the south of France in 1889, Reverdy moved to Paris in 1910. Between 1910 and 1926, he became closely associated with the Cubist painters Pablo Picasso, Georges Braque, and, in particular, Juan Gris. Reverdy was both a close friend of these painters and a very lucid commentator on their work. The achievement of the Cubists shaped his theories of the work of art as well as determined the textuality of his early poetry. Indeed, Reverdy is generally acknowledged as the French poet whose work can most relevantly be described as "Cubist."[1] The incisiveness and intelligence of his analyses of Cubist art make Reverdy, along with Yves Bonnefoy and Jacques Dupin, one of the most gifted of the many French poets writing art criticism in the twentieth century.

The basis for Reverdy's aesthetics is his rejection of mimesis. As he writes in his landmark 1917 essay "Sur le cubisme" ("On Cubism"), "[l]e cubisme est un art éminemment plastique; mais un art de création et non de reproduction ou d'interprétation" ("[C]ubism is a highly visual art; but an art based on creation and not on reproduction or interpretation") (OC Tome I 459). He considered the work of art (for which Cubist paintings stand, in his thought, as a guiding example) to be fundamentally autonomous and autotelic. He argued that art should not be seen as reproducing a pre-existing reality; rather, an artwork was constituted by the artist's selection and reordering of a small number of elements of reality. These elements, rearranged into unprecedented combinations according to a precise logic, formed the painting or the text. This selection of elements, configured into a new arrangement, constitutes "un art de création et non de reproduction." For Reverdy, art must be purged of the anecdotal, as any lapse into story-telling would lead to a facile, unsatisfying "realism" which true art needed to transcend:

> Nous sommes à une époque de création artistique où l'on ne raconte plus des histoires plus ou moins agréablement mais où l'on crée des œuvres qui, en se détachant de la vie, y rentrent parce qu'elles ont une existence propre, en dehors de l'évocation ou de la reproduction des choses de la vie. Par là, l'Art d'aujourd'hui est un art de grande réalité. Mais il faut entendre réalité artistique et non réalisme; c'est le genre qui nous est le plus opposé. (OC Tome I 460)

> (We are living in a time of artistic creation when artists no longer tell stories more or less pleasantly but when they create works which, while detaching themselves from life, also return to it because they live their own kind of life, outside of the evocation or reproduction of the things of everyday life. In this sense, today's Art is an art of great reality. But one must understand that it is an artistic reality and not realism which is the genre most opposed to our aims.)

According to this view, all the contingent, superficial aspects of reality were to be disregarded. The artist was to choose only the most basic features of things in order to rework them into a new visual or verbal order. In this regard, Reverdy praised Picasso for having developed "un art *réellement plastique* soucieux de la réalité des objets jusqu'à leur matière, en dehors de tous les charmes, de toutes les illusions et apparences trompeuses de l'atmosphère" ("an art which is *truly visual* (*réellement plastique*) concerned with the reality of objects in their very materiality, and eschewing any interest in charm, illusion and the deceptive appearance of atmosphere") (OC Tome I 586). Consequently, "Picasso reste toujours plastique et *matérialise*; il écarte le pittoresque et n'*idéalise* jamais" ("Picasso remains constantly visual [plastique] and concrete; he sets aside picturesque effects and never *idealizes*") (OC Tome I 588). For Reverdy, creating a work of art required one to "ramener à une unité, sur le papier ou sur la toile, des éléments que le mouvement de la vie disperse dans la réalité, et ... les unir" ["bring together into a unifed whole, on paper or on canvas, elements which the movement of life disperses in everyday reality, and ... to unify them"] (NEP 119). So, for example, a painter looking at a glass should ignore the surface details of its physical appearance, abstracting from it only the round shape of its base:

> De l'objet, Picasso prétendit ne dégager par conséquent que ce qui en est permanent et substantiel, ne prendre que la matière nette et écarter le sentiment qui la dénature et l'enveloppe. La forme du verre l'arrête et non pas le reflet changeant et lumineux qui joue dans le cristal.
>
> (From the object, Picasso claimed thus to take only what was permanent and substantial, to take only pure materiality and to avoid feelings, which distort and cover up. The shape of a glass interests him and not the changing, luminous reflection at play in the crystal.) (NEP 201–2).

As Julia Husson notes, the Cubists felt the need to create "a more solid architecture which would be its own justification and not just a support for a subject or 'story'" (22). In other words, as Reverdy's mentor Max Jacob declared in his preface to *Le Cornet à dés*, "[l]e poème est un objet construit et non la devanture d'un bijoutier" ("[t]he poem is a constructed object and not a jewelry shop display window").

In practice, Reverdy's aesthetic position required, first, a breaking down of everyday reality into its constituent elements. Following this process of dismantling the real, the artist's or poet's task was to recombine these fundamental elements of the everyday world into a different kind of order. The internal connections between the various parts of the finished work, once they were apprehended by the viewer or the reader, would lead to an appreciation of the work's significance and value.

Within Reverdy's aesthetic theory, the term "l'esprit" (the mind) plays a primary role. The mind of the artist or poet discerns the relations between elements of the real to be reordered; the mind of the reader or viewer, in turn, perceives the logical links between these elements as presented in the completed artwork. So, the creation and the understanding of the work depend on the rational and intuitive faculties of the mind.

The aspect of his aesthetic theories for which Reverdy remains best known is his notion of the image. He defines the image as the result of a bringing together of two distant, though not *opposed*, realities. In a

1918 essay, published in *Nord-Sud* (*North-South*) (a journal of art and literature which he edited), Reverdy proposes this distinctive definition:

> L'Image est une création pure de l'esprit.
> Elle ne peut naître d'une comparaison mais du rapprochement de deux réalités plus ou moins éloignées.
> Plus les rapports des deux réalités rapprochées seront lointains et justes, plus l'image sera forte – plus elle aura de puissance émotive et de réalité poétique. (OC Tome I 495)
>
> (The image is purely a creation of the mind.
> It comes into being not through a comparison (or simile) but through the bringing together of two more or less distant realities.
> The more the relationship between the two realities brought together is distant and appropriate [juste], the stronger the image will be – the greater its emotional power and poetic reality will be.)

Reverdy cautions that there must be some compelling connection between the two realities being used if the image is to be vital and valid: "Deux réalités qui n'ont aucun rapport ne peuvent se rapprocher utilement. Il n'y a pas de création d'image. Deux réalités contraires ne se rapprochent pas. Elles s'opposent" ("Two realities which have no relationship at all to each other cannot usefully be brought together. No image can be created in that way. Two opposite realities do not complement each other. They oppose each other") (OC Tome I 495). He adds that an image, if it is to have genuine poetic value, must not be gratuitous or grotesque: "Une image n'est pas forte parce qu'elle est *brutale* ou *fantastique*, mais parce que l'association des idées est lointaine et juste" ("An image is not powerful because it is *brutal* or *fantastic*, but because the association of ideas in it is distant and correct") (OC Tome I 495). Accordingly, various misuses of the image are to be rejected:

> L'image montée en épingle est détestable.
> L'image pour l'image est détestable.
> L'image de parti pris est détestable. (OC Tome II 556)
>
> (The image on display is loathsome.
> The image given for its own sake is loathsome.
> The biased image is loathsome.)

Cubism constituted a radical break with the conventions of Western art that preceded it. Since the Renaissance, one-point perspective had been central to Western painting, providing a basis through which to make sense of spatial relationships in the scenes depicted by painters. Rejecting perspective, the Cubists presented a flattened surface on which multiple different moments in time were telescoped together. In this way, they refused to reproduce a referential reality; rather, as Reverdy stated in "Sur le cubisme," they aimed to produce an aesthetic object characterized by its own internal order.

Cubism and Still Life: *Au Soleil du plafond*

The Cubist painters – like Reverdy, in his early Cubist poems – chose to limit the subject matter of their works to a few neutral elements. Very often, their paintings focused on objects from the studio or from a café (bottles, glasses, newspapers, playing cards, dice, musical instruments) and the still life became a favourite Cubist genre. In the earlier period of "Analytic" cubism (before 1912), their paintings featured a restricted, neutral range of colours: grey, brown, white. Thus, their art could appear unduly austere. In defence of this aesthetic austerity, Reverdy spoke of the hidden richness inherent in these artworks:

> Pourtant on s'étonnait que ces mêmes constituants [des tableaux cubistes] fussent un peu pauvres d'abord; comme certains s'inquiètent à présent même quelquefois qu'ils le soient trop longtemps demeurés – un peu trop de violons, de pipes, de paquets de tabac, de guitares. Mais on s'aperçoit cependant aujourd'hui que les éléments de ce langage sobre et dénudé, quoique avec une grande prudence et beaucoup de discrétion, se renouvellent. (NEP 80)
>
> (Still it was surprising that these same constituents [of Cubist painting] were rather austere [pauvres] at first glance; as some people worry even now at times that they remained minimal [pauvres] for too long – a few too many violins, pipes, packets of tobacco, guitars. But one notices nonetheless today that the elements of this sober and spare visual language are being renewed, although with much caution and discretion.)

By limiting the repertory of objects to be taken as subject matter, these artists were able to deemphasize the subject matter. They thus encouraged the viewer to pay attention mainly to the techniques by which the objects could be arranged into surprising new visual configurations. Reverdy adapted this lesson from Cubist painting into his own poetry: each detail of the poem becomes significant primarily through its structural role within the text.

As art critic Robert Rosenblum argues, time in Cubist works is irreducibly ambiguous, "for one senses neither duration nor instantaneity, but rather a composite time of fragmentary moments without permanence or sequential continuity" (40). Rosenblum shows how Cubism reflects the radical intellectual and aesthetic shifts that marked the rise of the avant-garde in Europe in the early twentieth century:

> For a century that questioned the very concept of absolute truth or value, Cubism created an artistic language of intentional ambiguity. In front of the Cubist work of art, the spectator was to realize that no single interpretation of the fluctuating shapes, textures, spaces, and objects could be complete in itself. And, in expressing this awareness of the paradoxical nature of reality and the need for describing it in multiple and even contradictory ways, Cubism offered a visual equivalent of a fundamental aspect of twentieth-century experience. (9)

Such examples as "Ecran" or "Coin obscur," discussed above, indicate to what extent the reader of Reverdy's early poetry encounters precisely the sort of Cubist textuality that Rosenblum describes. The poems offer patternings of signs, events, and objects which systematically resist all attempts to decipher them or to derive some sort of "story" from the fragments that they present. An ambiguous tone characterizes each poem.

The Cubist still life assumes central importance as a model for the textuality of the poems of Reverdy's earlier collections, as Andrew Rothwell has shown.[2] One of the poet's most thoughtful and revealing discussions of the role of the object in his poetics appears in his piece on the still life genre, "La Nature aux abois" ("Nature at Bay") (1940) (NEP 29–35). Reverdy indicates in his essay that he considers the still life to be a uniquely important art historical genre. He asserts that "[l]a nature morte, dans l'histoire de l'art, est une révolution matérialiste sourde et à très longue portée" ("[t]he still life, in the history of art, represents a muted materialist revolution which is far-reaching") (NEP 34). The genre constitutes a seamless fusion of human subjectivity and the object world, he finds: "Ce sont les objets dont un peintre se sert

– ou le poète les mots qui les désignent – qui deviennent les moyens d'expression les plus prêts, les seuls propres à rendre ses sentiments et ses idées sensibles et intelligibles" ("It is the objects which a painter uses – or a poet using the words which designate these objects – which become the most apt means of expression, the only ones able to make his feelings and ideas felt and intelligible") (NEP 32). Reverdy's valorization of the still life (which has generally been treated as a minor genre by art historians) reflects his commitment to an aesthetics of impersonality: "Notre plus grande intimité, nous ne pouvons l'exprimer qu'avec des matériaux qui nous sont extérieurs et étrangers" ("We can only express our most intimate emotions by using materials which are exterior and foreign to us") (NEP 32). (This last sentence expresses a general trend within the work of the *poètes de l'objet*.)

Reverdy, thus, values the still life as an antidote to the excesses of unfettered lyricism. A neo-classical restraint informs the genre, although its apparent simplicity is deceptive:

> Immobile et impassible, la nature morte est le noyau de l'art statique. Comme la poésie la plus dense et la plus isolée, elle émerge très peu au-dessus des efforts sans nom de la mer démontée. Mais c'est de ce côté qu'on s'abrite du courant perfide du ressac qui entraîne au lyrisme enfantin de dessin animé.
>
> Dans la nature morte, la matière et l'esprit s'affrontent en un combat réglé entre des limites restreintes et régi par le maximum exigible de loyauté. (NEP 34)

> (Motionless and impassible, the still life is the core of a static art. Like the densest and most isolated poetry, it emerges only a little above the nameless efforts of the upset [démontée] sea. But it is here [de ce côté] that one protects oneself from the perfidious current of the undertow which leads to a cartoonish and childish lyricism.
>
> In the still life, matter and mind confront each other in a kind of ordered combat happening within strict limits and regulated by the most absolute loyalty.)

Despite the air of reticence and emotionlessness that is the hallmark of the still life genre, Reverdy nevertheless perceives a struggle in still life between the creative mind constructing the artwork and the objects from the referential world that form the subject matter. His statement "Dans la nature morte, la matière et l'esprit s'affrontent en un combat réglé entre des limites restreintes" ("In the still life, matter and mind confront each other in a kind of ordered combat within strict limits") is an apt description of the functioning of still life in the object poems of Ponge, Apollinaire, Rossi, and other poets fascinated by the genre. Conflict and harmony may both play equally determining roles in the construction of the still life poem or painting. This is why Reverdy's interpretation of still life in this seminal essay focuses on the genre as expressing a static equilibrium ("Immobile et impassible, la nature morte est le noyau de l'art statique") but also an unresolved tension ("la matière et l'esprit s'affrontent en un combat").

The complexity of Reverdy's engagement with the still life emerges again in the short collection of prose poems *Au Soleil du plafond* (*At the Ceiling's Sun*) (1955), which reads like a gallery of verbal descriptions of everyday objects. Although the things evoked in these short texts may be ordinary, even banal, the aesthetic processes through which Reverdy transforms them in order to write his own Cubist-influenced poems are highly sophisticated and challenging.

Au Soleil du plafond was originally to have been a collaborative effort, featuring still lifes by the major Cubist artist Juan Gris accompanying prose poems by Reverdy. The project would have consisted of twenty lithographs by Gris combined with twenty prose poems by Reverdy. However, following a quarrel between the artist and the poet in 1920, only eleven of the lithographs by Gris were completed.[3] Reverdy and Gris had begun working on the project in 1916–17, and their original title was "Entre les quatre murs et sur la table" ("Between the four walls and on the table"). (This title implies a metaesthetic reflection on the spaces characteristically associated with Cubist art, so that the poems and lithographs here refer primarily to the page or the canvas itself rather than to a referent outside the page or canvas.) After Gris's death in 1927, the publication of *Au Soleil du plafond* was postponed until 1955.

Of the three great Cubist painters – Picasso, Braque, and Gris – Reverdy met Gris first. He maintained close personal ties with him during his years in Paris. The two men were very similar in temperament and they shared comparable views concerning the nature of the artwork. As Christopher Green demonstrates in his critical study *Juan Gris*, Reverdy's poetry (and his ideas on poetry) and Gris's paintings (and ideas on painting) share a number of significant features. Gris's work was equated by critics with an emphasis on logic and clarity, as well as modesty (Green 13–15). Such qualities also characterize Reverdy's approach to (creating) art. In his study of Gris, Green frequently points out the similarities between Gris's creativity and Reverdy's, noting how profoundly the two men influenced each other. Noting that Gris, in contrast to Picasso, was seen as a "methodical" artist (Green 20), Green further indicates that "[i]t is Reverdy who most succinctly connects the notion of compositional structure with the notion of logical order. He does so in his little book *Self Defence* which was published in 1919 with a dedication to Gris. 'The logic of a work of art,' he writes, 'is in its structure. The moment the ensemble holds together and is balanced, it is logical'" (Green 32).

As we shall observe in studying still-life poems from *Au Soleil du plafond*, Reverdy plays upon verbal ambiguity – a practice surely connected to the techniques of visual ambiguity for which Gris in his still-life paintings is well known. Gris often composed a painting around what could be called "pictorial rhymes," in which the visual similarities between two unrelated things were manipulated as the basis for a single image. (Such a creation of "pictorial rhymes" reminds one of Reverdy's notion of the image as a fusion of two distant, but strangely connected, realities.) Green discusses several examples of this pictorial rhyming in Gris's art: "Gris's rhymes operate cohesively in his paintings of 1918–22 as an underpinning of compositional geometry, much as they do with rhythm in Reverdy's and Huidobro's poetry of the time. They amplify structural relations as they bring 'distant realities' together. Thus, in *Harlequin at a Table* … the rhyming ellipses of the knotted cord, the glass-top, the eyes and the mouth draw the gaze to different points on the canvas to tie a simple network of connections. And the rhyming of leg and table-leg makes metaphor and structure signify together: the figure, the object on the table and the pictorial architecture all 'stand' upon a rhyme" (Green 64). Maurice Raynal also remarks on the innovativeness of these pictorial rhymes, stating that "such a metaphorical representation gives the qualities of one thing to another, and *vice-versa*. The pears have fruit dish curves, the fruit dish has the soft swelling body of pears. In this case, the objects fused to construct a new metaphorical object are directly related by contiguity. Fruit dishes are designed to hold fruit, including pears. From 1918 on, Gris's metaphors, like the image-making of the poets of the Reverdy circle, often fused objects whose relatedness was not a given in this way" (Raynal qtd. in Green, 154).

If we turn now to some prose poems from *Au Soleil du plafond*, the links between Reverdy's Cubist poetics and the paintings of Gris will be clear. Let us look, first, at the poem "Soupière":

Soupière

Le monde de la faim, la fin du monde.
La soupière est comme un globe terrestre sur
la table. Et du globe fendu couvercle soulevé,
l'odeur monte et une tête et des bras blancs
dans un nuage.
Et la tête riait – la tête riait et flottait
d'un bout à l'autre de la table.
Du parfum à la faim, par un chemin
plus long, ramenant les ardeurs du fond d'un
autre songe. (OC Tome II 1372)

(Soup Tureen

The world of hunger, the end of the world.
The soup tureen is like a globe on the table. And
from the split-open globe lifted lid, the aroma rises and a
head and white arms in a cloud.
And the head was laughing – the head was laughing
and floating from one end of the table to the other.
From scent to hunger, by a longer route, bringing back
ardor from deep within another dream.)

Through its unusual images, the poem constitutes a visual impression of the likeness of unlike things (as in Juan Gris's pictorial rhymes): the soup tureen resembles a globe; the steam rising from the soup creates a shape like that of a laughing head. Reverdy subtly echoes these visual resemblances by means of sonorous resemblances created by paronomasia: "le monde *de la faim, la fin* du monde"; "Du *parfum à la faim.*" Our reading of the poems requires negotiating exactly the sort of struggle between perceiving mind and perceived objects which the poet deemed fundamental to the aesthetics of still life in "La Nature aux abois." That struggle is controlled and underscored here by the rigid limits of the page / canvas as it fixes images in words.

A Cubist blurring of distinctions between figure and ground, between subject matter and support, occurs in "Soupière" in a deliberately ambiguous fusion of the still-life object and the optical illusion generated by it: "Et du globe fendu couvercle soulevé, l'odeur monte et une tête et des bras blancs dans un nuage." The raised lid of the soup tureen and the split globe it resembles are presented in apposition, as though there were no distinction between them. The reader's eye hesitates now between two distinct realities and is lost in their intermingling. This combining of two separate realities perfectly corresponds to Reverdy's theory of the image, once again.

By the middle of the poem, the dense cloud of steam rising from the soup has *become* a head ("Et la tête riait – la tête riait et flottait d'un bout à l'autre de la table"). If art is to create a new reality, rather than mimetically reproduce a referential object or scene, then this bold sort of transformation becomes indispensable.

In the final short paragraph of the prose poem no verb tense is evident. The present participle "ramenant" ('bringing back") effectively abolishes temporal distinctions. Again, the poet is following standard Cubist conventions by fusing distinct temporal units together. His skilful use of assonance and rhyme suggests a hidden order concealed within the scene, as though a whole world of experience, memory and dream were contained in an otherwise banal arrangement of objects on a table.

The other still-life objects selected by Reverdy as the basis for his poems in *Au Soleil du plafond* refer to and evoke the characteristic objects of Gris's still-life paintings: a coffee mill, a pipe, a book, a guitar, a violin, a fan, a lamp, a checkerboard, a bottle, a flower vase, and so on. Each of these poems combines a sense of muted, indirect evocation (reminiscent also of Mallarmé's poetry) with typically Cubist distortionary techniques.

"Violin" presents a particularly interesting case of the mutual influence of different arts. Reverdy's poem gestures simultaneously towards music here and towards painting. (Christopher Green reports that "[e]specially in 1913, the guitar and violin are a ubiquitous feature of Gris's still-lives" [Green 151]). The violin acts as a visual anchor to the poem and a source of emotionally resonant sound:

> **Violon**
> Le tiroir repoussé, la porte refermée, les mains s'attardaient seules dans l'espace – les yeux toujours ouverts, un écho tremblant encore à nos oreilles. Déjà le violon s'était tu quand les pieds, que l'on ne voyait pas, continuaient à battre la mesure sous la table. Frontières dépassées, notes perdues dans l'air, tous les fils dénoués au-delà des saisons reprennent leur tout et leur ton sur le fond sombre du silence. (OC Tome II 1368)

(Violin

With the drawer pushed back, the door closed, the hands were lingering alone in space – the eyes still open, an echo still trembling in our ears. Already the violin had fallen silent as the feet, which could not be seen, kept continuing to beat the rhythm under the table. With the borders crossed, the notes lost in the air, all the threads unknotted beyond seasons take up their all and their tone against the dark backdrop of silence.)

The poem works primarily as a metaesthetic meditation, conveying at the same time traces of melancholy and loss. Somewhat ironically, the musical instrument named in the title is associated with silence and absence: "Déjà le violon s'était tu …" "notes perdues dans l'air." The beautiful sounds which it had created persist only as "un écho tremblant encore à nos oreilles." Yet sound, rhythm, and structure yield an austere aesthetic beauty in this poem which almost doubles – or replaces – the "lost" notes whose insistent force is echoed by the repeated use of past participles: "repoussé," "refermée," "ouverts," "dépassées," "dénoués."

It is in "Damier" (OC Tome II 1371) that Reverdy makes his debt to, and dialogue with, Cubist painting most explicit:

Damier

Sur l'ordre du regard au pli trop net de la moulure les carrés blancs et noirs où se posent les doigts, le bout des ongles. C'est un chemin tracé entre ce cadre étroit et moi qui perds la tête. Un buisson où se cache l'endroit où passent les murmures. Dans la salle d'été avec un feu éteint le plafond ramasse et deux grosses figures les yeux baissés.

(Checkerboard

Following the order of the ornamental moulding's gaze with its too strict fold, the white and black squares where one's fingers are placed, one's fingertips. A path is traced within this narrow frame and as for me I'm going mad. In a bush is hidden the place where murmurs are passing. In the summer room with a fire that's out the ceiling gathers together and two big faces with their eyes lowered.)

The poet is here reminding us of the Cubist painters' fondness for including chessboards and checkerboards in their works and, more obliquely, of the Cubists' reliance on the grid as the basis for the visual patternings central to their paintings. Thus, the object inspiring the writing of the poem is repeated – or superseded – by the distortionary technique through which it comes to be conceptualized and reordered. As in the poems I quoted from *Plupart du temps* (*Most of the Time*), the human body is fragmented here, evoked exclusively as disembodied individual parts: "les doigts" ("the fingers"), "le bout des ongles" ("the fingertips"), "deux grosses figures les yeux baissés" ("two large faces with their eyes lowered"). The poet jokingly acknowledges this through the phrase "moi qui perds la tête" ("I who am losing my head"), which now reliteralizes a figure of speech. By this segmentation and erasure of the human figure, Reverdy reasserts his rejection of the portrait in art. He also makes us think of the many Cubist "portraits" in which the human figure is so absorbed into abstract patterns of lines and planes that it becomes so obscured as to be barely recognizable.

As the object poems of *Au Soleil du plafond* so powerfully demonstrate, for Reverdy, the text itself functions as a kind of object. Like Ponge (as we shall see in chapter 3), he achieves a unique fusion of text and thing. In her article "Pierre Reverdy and the 'Poème-Objet'," Julia Husson asserts that the poet's emphasis on the materiality of language and on typographical innovation in his early poetry allows him to convey to the reader a sense of the overriding importance of the poem's concrete, visual aspects:

> The first step towards giving each poem an individual character, an identity as an object, was the new typography. Reverdy set out his poem on the blank page as a painter might a picture, with a feeling for the masses of words almost as concrete elements. The poem is no longer a dense mass of lines of similar lengths divided or not into equal stanzas. Each poem has its own particular "shape." The lines often start halfway in from the margin, or sometimes a simple word may be isolated in the middle of the page or on the right-hand side. The poems [in *Les Ardoises du toit*], all except one, are never long enough to take up more than one page and thus the whole poem may be seen at one glance in its entirety, from beginning to end, with its own characteristic form. (Husson 26)

As his idiosyncratic use of typography highlights the poem's "architecture," it compels the reader to pay close attention to the structural relationships between words and syntagms.

In Reverdy's poetry, even individual words can acquire the status of objects. Husson finds that "[e]ach word [in the poems] has the figurative appearance of a concrete thing" (Husson 26). She even argues that "his words are not symbols – they are themselves, concrete objects that we all know" (Husson 28). Jean-Pierre Attal makes a similar point, stating that "il faut préciser que Reverdy perçoit les mots également comme des choses; il voudrait presque nommer les mots ... Les mots ont donc, pour cette conscience attentive, la faculté de se séparer des choses qu'ils nomment, de devenir à leur tour des choses qui volent dans l'air, sorte d'araignées ou d'oiseaux" ("one must note that Reverdy perceives words like things; he would almost want to make all words into nouns ... Words thus have, for his alert consciousness, the faculty of separating themselves from the things which fly through the air like spiders or birds") (307).

Of course, the decisive influence of Saussurian linguistics, of structuralism and post-structuralism on Literary Studies in recent decades has taught us to be suspicious of – indeed, dismissive of – any claims regarding a necessary or motivated or symmetrical relationship between words and things, between texts and the objects which they describe. The reader of *la poésie de l'objet* will find, however, that a persistent fantasy of the consubstantiality of the text and the object, as well as the presentation of the text *as* object, informs many of the works in this tradition (which, as I am arguing here, constitutes a central tradition within twentieth-century French poetry). Hence, we must avoid dismissing these critical claims assimilating text to object, even as we pay careful attention to the way in which the object may (only) serve as a pre-text or convenient occasion for writing.[4]

It should be clear by now that Reverdy's fascination with, and use of, objects stem from a number of separate motivations. There are, accordingly, ambiguities evident in his poetics of the objects which we will need to explore further. Jean-Luc Steinmetz emphasizes the paradoxical place of the object in Reverdy's poetics.

> Placé sur le parcours de ces mouvements [that is, the unstable shiftings of tense and direction in Reverdy's poems], l'objet acquiert une consistence inattendue. Il nous intéresse d'ailleurs moins par l'utilisation quasi picturale qui en est faite que par sa spéciale teneur, une franchise, une sincère

pauvreté ... *Cependant, loin d'être un gage de réunification, l'objet trahit plutôt une dispersion et l'on serait bien en peine d'en fabriquer un univers assuré.* (66)

(Placed on the pathways of these movements [that is, the unstable shiftings of tense and direction in Reverdy's poems], the object acquires an unexpected solidity. It interests us less, moreover, by the quasi-pictural use which the poet makes of it than by its special content, an honesty, a sincere humility ... *Nevertheless, far from being a token of reunification* [*gage de réunification*], *the object betrays rather a dispersal and one would have considerable difficulty creating a stable universe from it.*)

Despite the object's standing for concreteness and materiality, Steinmetz observes that in Reverdy's work "[c]haque objet pose une question" ["[e]ach object asks a question"] (Steinmetz 71). The Reverdian object (and his word-objects, in Husson's and Attal's readings) is never simple or inconsequential. It is always poised between referring to concrete reality and acting as a possible symbol for a deeper meaning to be sought. (E.g., the many doors and windows recurring in his poems evoke the image of a room or house while suggesting the possibility – or impossibility – of escape and passage.) One must, further, examine very closely the modes of interaction and dependency between subject and object which the Reverdy text always implies, however marginal the subject may seem in most of his poems. I would like, next, to explore the evolution of the place of the subject in his later poetry in order to recontextualize the development of his poetics of the object.

"J'ai horreur de parler de moi": Subjectivity in Reverdy's Poetry

"Je voudrais être loin de moi
Je suis trop près."

– Reverdy, "Enfin" ("Finally") (OC Tome II 333)

("I wish I were far from myself
I am too near.")

As our examination of Reverdy's poetry published from 1915 to 1930 has revealed, his work from this period foregrounds details from interior scenes, landscapes of still-life *tableaux*, and the Cubist-influenced poetic techniques by which this material can be taken apart and rearranged to yield a new "reality" (Reverdy's term). His critics have generally privileged the notion of impersonality in approaching his *œuvre*. Marie-Josèphe Rustan observes, for example, "[s]a poésie est très impersonnelle même et surtout quand elle dit *je* ... Elle est bâtie, construite sur la destruction de ce moi" ("[h]is poetry is very impersonal even and especially when it uses *I*. ... It is constructed upon the destruction of this self") (469). Likewise, Patricia Terry emphasizes the qualities of reticence and depersonalization that appear to be at the heart of his poetics: "Where Apollinaire, even at his most unorthodox, still used his own emotions as the materials of his poems, Reverdy allows himself to be apparent, if at all, only as an abstract presence, the mind that both orders and inhabits the still life or the landscape. Very much in the manner of the Cubist painters ... Reverdy exists in his works as a diffuse intensity by his very refusal of a perspective that would dictate the way in which the elements of the poem or the painting are to be perceived" (xvi).

Although these critics' views are entirely relevant and accurate with respect to Reverdy's poetry up to 1930 (collected mainly in *Plupart du temps*), a radical shift occurs in the collections of poetry he published beginning in 1937, with *Ferraille* (*Scrap Iron*) and later collected in the omnibus volume *Main d'œuvre* (*Manpower*). These poems reflect a change that had actually taken place much earlier – indeed, as early as 1921, the year of the poet's conversion to Catholicism. In Reverdy's later poetry, the first-person subject becomes dominant. His later pronouncements concerning poetry and poetics show this new orientation: "[l]a poésie n'est pas dans l'objet, elle est dans le sujet" ("[p]oetry is not in the object, it is in the subject") (CEP 129). He declared that "le poète est un four à brûler le réel" and that "la poésie vient des poètes" ["the poet is an oven for burning reality"; "poetry comes from poets"].

As Andrew Rothwell demonstrates in his excellent study *Textual Spaces*, "[i]n striking contrast to the rather impersonal aesthetic attitude of his cubist period, [Reverdy] continued to insist, from this point [June 1924] right up to the end of his career, that poetry was essentially a matter of self-expression, in the interests of both self-knowledge (of the sort a moralist might seek) and existential self-definition" (Rothwell 222). He adds that, in the later poetry, "gone is any suggestion of the ideal equilibrium between internal and external worlds on which his cubist approach was based. Now, any phenomenon at all can acquire a mental 'overlay,' becoming a 'sign' for the *je* to read of his presence in the world; the result is a huge expansion of the emotional content of reality, leading in turn to a very different type of figurality" (Rothwell 252). In these later poems Reverdy's statement "[l]a nature c'est moi" ("[n]ature is myself") (OC Tome II 783) defines the poetic subject's relationship to the landscape and its characteristic objects, which become a reflecting surface for the projection of his inner states. The first poem of *Ferraille* displays signs of the emergence of this new aesthetic:

Le Cœur tournant
Il ne faut pas aller plus loin
Les bijoux sont pris dans la lyre
Les papillons noirs du délire
Remuent sans y penser la cendre du couchant

A peine revenu des voyages amers
Autour des cœurs jetés au fond des devantures
Sur l'avant-scène des prairies et des pâtures
Comme des coquillages nus devant la mer

A peine remué par l'amour de la vie
Des regards qui se nouent aux miens
Des visages sans nom des souvenirs anciens
Diamants de l'amour qui flottent sur la lie

Pour aller chercher au fond dans la vase
Le secret émouvant du sang de mon malheur
Il faut plonger la main aux racines du cœur
Et mes doigts maladroits brisent les bords du vase

Le sang qui jette sur tes yeux ce lourd rideau
L'émotion inconnue qui fait trembler ta lèvre
Et ce froid trop cruel qui emporte ta fièvre
Froisse dans tous les coins le linon de ta peau

Je t'aime sans jamais t'avoir vue que dans l'ombre
Dans la nuit de mon rêve où seul je peux y voir
Je t'aime et tu n'es pas encore sortie du nombre
Forme mystérieuse qui bouge dans le soir

Car ce que j'aime au fond c'est ce qui passe
Une fois seulement sur ce miroir sans tain
Qui déchire mon cœur et meurt à la surface
Du ciel fermé devant mon désir qui s'éteint (OC Tome II 275–6)

(The Turning Heart
You must not go any farther
The jewels are caught in the lyre
The black butterflies of delirium
Unthinkingly stir the ashes of sunset

Scarcely returned from bitter travels
Around the hearts thrown to the back of the display windows
In the foreground of fields and pastures
Like naked seashells before the sea

Scarcely moved by the love of life
Glances linking with my own
Nameless faces from old memories
Diamonds of love which float on the dregs

To go looking at the bottom in the mud for
The poignant secret of my unhappy blood
You must plunge your hand right to the heart's roots
And my clumsy fingers break the edges of the vase

The blood which throws this heavy curtain on your eyes
The unknown emotion which makes your lip tremble
And this too cruel coldness which carries off your fever
Crumples in all its corners the lawn of your skin

I love you without ever having seen you but in shadow
In the night of my dream where only I can see
I love you and you've not yet left the number
A mysterious shape that moves through the evening

For what I love is really what passes
Only once on this defective mirror
Which tears my heart and dies on the surface
Of the sky shut tight before my perishing desire)

By contrast with the depersonalized, fragmented scenes of such earlier collections as *Les Ardoises du toit* (*Roof Slates*), this poem reads like a direct personal confession. The emotional experience of a first-person subject clearly motivates its images and thematics. At the same time, Reverdy's use of a stable left margin and regular four-line stanzas here instead of the style "en créneaux" of his early collections, in which blank space constantly suggested effacement and absence, reflects his abandonment of Cubist aesthetics in the 1920s and after.

The images in "Le Coeur tournant" are exceptionally striking. The poet continues to adhere to the view of the image articulated in his 1918 *Nord-Sud* essay, as a fusion of two distant but strangely related things. Now, though, the image remains openly in the service of the expression of the emotions of a lyrical subject: his being in love, the frustration of that love, the extinguishing of his desire at the end of the poem. In this poem, as in those of the late collections *Plein verre* (*Full Glass*) (1940), *Le Chant des mers* (*The Song of the Seas*) (1944–8), or *Bois vert* (*Green Wood*) (1946–9), "reality ends up simply confirming the aspects of the *je*'s existential condition (contingency, mortality, aging) about which he was looking to the external landscape for reassurance," as Andrew Rothwell comments, adding that "mind and world are bound together in an ambiguous metaphorical continuum" in these late poems (Rothwell 262). Such a figural fusion of perceiving subject and object world does not settle the problem of subjectivity, however: "It seems then that the world of Reverdy's late poetry consistently refuses, or proves unable, to yield up the self-image for which the *je* asks" (Rothwell 265).

One might wonder, at this point, why subjectivity proves to be such an intractable problem for Reverdy. Although his earlier poems are thoroughly grounded in an aesthetic of impersonality, it is, paradoxically, a dilemma of subjectivity which may be the ultimate focal point in the development of his *œuvre*. It has been suggested that both his embracing of Cubism and the Cubist still life, and then his religious conversion of 1921 and the move from Paris to the small Normandy village of Solesmes in 1926 to a house near the abbey there, can be interpreted as (unsuccessful) attempts to overcome the problem of subjectivity. For Reverdy, subjectivity is a closed structure, a kind of trap. It imposes limits that are stifling, unendurable. "C'est moi," he once wrote, "C'est toujours moi et je ne peux davantage savoir ce que je suis aujourd'hui, que je ne savais ce que j'étais et valais à vingt ans. Parce que c'est moi" ("It is I," he once wrote, "It is always I and I can no more know what I am today than I knew what I was and amounted to when I was twenty. Because it is I").[5] Elsewhere, in the poem "Santé de fer" ("Iron Constitution") (OC Tome II 363) he wrote: "Je ne suis que moi-même dans les jeux du miroir" ("I am only myself in the mirror's reflections"). These statements reflect his sense of subjectivity as a burden and help to explain his need to move beyond it.

In spite of – or perhaps, because of – these anxieties of subjectivity, Reverdy was always extremely reluctant to write about his own life, or to provide details of his biography to others. When Jean Rousselot requested that he provide biographical material for the critical study on his poetry that Rousselot was then preparing for the Seghers "Poètes d'aujourd'hui" (Poets of Today) series (a very well-known and respected series), Reverdy responded by writing to Rousselot, "Mais je crois qu'il est inutile de parler de ces choses-là avec trop de précision. Vous n'atteindrez jamais le personnage réel, alors inventez-le. D'après ce que je vous dis" ("But I think it is useless to speak of such things in too much detail. You will never reach my true character, so invent it. Using what I am telling you").[6] He also stated: "Je n'ai jamais trouvé ma propre histoire intéressante pour moi-même. Imaginez que je ne peux pas penser qu'elle puisse l'être davantage pour d'autres" ("I have never found my own story interesting. You can imagine that I can't think it might be of any greater interest for others").[7] These remarks are somewhat surprising, coming from a poet who also believed that "[l]e poète n'a qu'un seul personage – lui-même – foyer de l'univers" ("[t]he poet has only one character – himself – the heart of the universe").[8]

Recent scholarship exploring Reverdy's childhood and adolescence in Narbonne before his 1910 move to Paris helps to illuminate the reasons for this difficult struggle with subjectivity that so marks his œuvre. Robert Kenny has proposed an interpretation of the biographical in Reverdy's work that reorients the significance of this issue. In his article "Le Nom effacé," Kenny argues that "[f]or Reverdy, poetic activity was nothing less than a constant *re-invention* of self in the fullest etymological sense, an unending quest to discover or find again a lost self" (5).

Despite the evident impersonality overlaying so much of Reverdy's poetry, Kenny finds that certain figures or masks for the self recur in these texts. The child is one double for the poet. This figure of the child "has its roots in, and derives its resonance from, that very biographical past which Reverdy was often at such pains to disguise or deny," he comments (6). Along with this child figure, metaphorical and real images of the father play an important role in his texts, Kenny states. In his letters to Rousselot, the poets speaks of his father with extravagant praise: "Je devais beaucoup à mon père. C'était un être remarquable dont je ne suis que l'ombre" ("I owed a great deal to my father. He was a remarkable person. I am but his shadow") (Reverdy, *Lettres à Jean Rousselot* 50–1). During his Paris years, Max Jacob acted as an important mentor to Reverdy as well; yet the young poet became strongly ambivalent towards Jacob, satirizing him as "le Mage Abel" ("Abel the Magus") in his Cubist "novel" *Le Voleur de Talan* (*The Thief of Talan*) (1917). In addition to his actual father and Jacob (in the role of poetic father / mentor), God the Father dominated Reverdy's life from 1921 (the year of his conversion to Catholicism) to 1927 (when he lost his religious faith).

One might argue that defining himself through – and against – these significant father figures enables the act of writing for Reverdy. Along with this persistence of a reference to the father, a curious silence concerning the mother characterizes his work. In her fascinating article "Présences du blanc, figures du moins," Eliane Formentelli identifies a "blessure illocalisable et désoriginée" ("unlocatable wound without origin") at the heart of Reverdy's work, a wound connected to a "triple impasse sur le corps, l'histoire et le sujet" ("triple blockage concerning the body, personal history, and the subject") that recurs throughout the poet's writings. The aesthetic of impersonality for which Reverdy is celebrated becomes for Formentelli an "absence du sujet." She asserts that this "absence du sujet … par ses éclats et ses marques blanches dans la structure, la grammaire, elle serait sans doute à mettre en rapport avec l'élision, presque totale, blanche elle aussi, et si rare chez un poète, de la figure maternelle" ("absence of subjectivity … by its flashes and its blank traces in the structure and grammar [of Reverdy's writings] should doubtless be seen in relationship to the almost total elision of the figure of the mother, also a blank space [in the text], and so rare in a poet's work") (282).

In his major critical study of Reverdy's poetry, *Horizon de Reverdy* (*Reverdy's Horizon*), Michel Collot also emphasizes the primary significance of parental figures in the unconscious elaboration of the poet's texts. Collot discovers an Oedipal thematics at work in Reverdy's obsessive return to the image of the setting sun: "Si ce spectacle revêt pour le poète une telle importance, c'est qu'il y voit la projection de ses propres fantasmes … Reverdy voit dans le coucher du soleil une *blessure* … Cette hémorragie, en effet, est rapportée le plus souvent par Reverdy à une origine bien déterminée: la plaie d'une victime singulière" ("If this spectacle (image) carries such great importance for the poet, it is because he sees in it the projection of his own unconscious phantasies … Reverdy sees a *wound* in the image of sunset … This hemorrhaging is, indeed, most often related for Reverdy to a very specific origin: the wound of a singular victim") (Collot 15). He finds that the poet "assimile symboliquement la victime cosmique – lumière, soleil ou ciel – à un personnage de son monde intérieur" ("symbolically assimilates the cosmic victim – light, sun or sky – to a character from his own inner world") (16). Collot then demonstrates that a specific "personnage" is being evoked in these images of the sunset as a bloody wound against the sky. "A travers l'astre [i.e., the setting sun], c'est une instance inconsciemment haïe qui semble visée, et tout tend à prouver qu'il s'agit du Père" ("By means of this star [i.e., the setting sun], an unconsciously hated figure [instance] seems to be targeted, and everything [in Reverdy's œuvre] tends to prove that this figure is the Father") (21). He concludes that "[l]e père est celui qui, bien qu'absent, est toujours présent à l'esprit du poète, et c'est pourquoi il n'a pas besoin d'être désigné nommément" ("[t]he father, although he is absent [Reverdy's father died in 1911], is always present in the poet's mind, and that is why he does not need to be explicitly named") (115). At the same time, Collot argues that "[t]andis que le spectacle diurne était dominé par la figure du père … la nuit est envahie par la présence de la mère et par les puissances de la confusion. L'espace nocturne apparaît comme le négatif de l'espace diurne" ("[w]hereas the diurnal spectacle [which the poems present] was dominated by the figure of the father … the night is invaded by the presence of the mother and her power to create confusion. The poems' nocturnal space appears as the negative equivalent to their diurnal space") (119). This negativity, associated with the night as a figure for the maternal, has an ultimately Oedipal significance: "'Douceur' de la féminité, mais aussi horreur de la Mère 'terrible': le plaisir que procure la venue de la nuit est mêlé d'une angoisse affreuse. Tout se passe en effet comme si elle correspondait à cette abolition mythique du tabou de l'inceste qui est l'une des situations caractéristiques de la phase oedipienne" ("'Sweetness' of women, but also a feeling of horror before the 'terrible' Mother: the pleasure which the coming of the night gives is mixed with a horrific anguish. Indeed, it is as though such sweetness corresponded to the mythic abolition of the incest taboo, which is one of the characteristic situations of the Oedipal phase") (122).

Collot's detailed analysis of this overarching Oedipal fantasy underlying Reverdy's texts implies a reworking of the poet's relationship to internalized figures of the father and the mother. By taking possession of, and reconfiguring, these relationships through writing, Reverdy, in his poems, encodes the child subject's fantasy of the "family romance" of which Freud has written. Through fantasy, the child gains access to (illusions of) controlling the processes of birth and creation of genealogies over which, in reality, she or he has no control.[9]

The notion proposed by Collot that Oedipal anxieties form a (or the) basis for Reverdy's writings becomes all the more convincing if one considers the impact of biographical factors unearthed by Kenny, which he discusses in "Le Nom effacé" ("The Name Erased"). Kenny discovered tangled and difficult problems of legitimacy and identity that marked Reverdy's early life. His summary of his findings deserves to be quoted at length:

> Reverdy's mother, Jeanne Rose Esclopié, was born in Narbonne on 23 May 1861. In September 1884, at the age of 23, she married Victor Léopold Turcan, a cook from Perpignan and in May 1886 she gave birth to a daughter who was registered as Henriette Léontine Marie Turcan. Three years later, on 11 September 1889, at 3, Boulevard du Collège, a male child was born at eleven in the morning. On the 16 September a midwife presented this child for registration at the Mairie. She would give neither the name of the father nor that of the mother and so the child was registered as born 'de père et de mère inconnus' [of unknown father and mother] and was given only the names Henri Pierre. Jeanne Rose Turcan (née Esclopié), known as Georgette, moved to Toulouse where Henriette and Henri Pierre went to school. In June 1895 Georgette and Victor Turcan were divorced and it was only in December of the same year that Henri Reverdy added his name to his son's birth certificate by an act of 'reconnaissance de paternité' [recognition of paternity]. Two years later, in August 1897, Henri Reverdy and Georgette Esclopié were married at Toulouse where Georgette was still living at 3, Allée Lafayette. In 1889 [*sic*] Pierre began his studies at the Collège Victor Hugo in Narbonne. In November 1901, after barely four years of marriage, Henri Reverdy and Georgette Esclopié were divorced at Narbonne. Henriette went to live with her mother in another part of Narbonne while Pierre remained with his father at the house of Victor Reverdy, Pierre's grandfather. In 1909 Reverdy was exempted from military service on the grounds of a 'maladie de coeur' [heart ailment] and in October 1910 he left for Paris. One month later, Henri Reverdy ('quoique ruiné' [albeit ruined] as Pierre put it) married Marie-Thérèse Matignon, a woman thirty years his junior whom he had met in Béziers and by whom he already had two young daughters, born in 1909 and 1910. But Pierre Reverdy's birth certificate still described him as 'fils de Henri Reverdy et de mère inconnue' [son of Henri Reverdy and of unknown mother].

> It was not until May 1911 that Georgette Esclopié by an 'acte de reconnaissance' [act of recognition] legally acknowledged herself to be Pierre's mother. Four months later Henri Reverdy was dead and Pierre returned to Narbonne where he mourned the loss of his 'modèle' in the company of his mother, his sister, a newly-widowed Mme Reverdy only two years his senior and her two babies-in-arms. (Kenny 23)

I include this information not because I regard it as providing a key to "unlock" the secrets lying behind Reverdy's texts, but rather because it indicates how urgent and complex the issue of identity was for Reverdy very early in his life. Identity is, no doubt, a question that all poets struggle with, in various ways. In Reverdy's case, the anxieties and incoherences attending upon this question of identity and subjectivity posed a particularly unwieldy problem. Writing, for him, was not only a means of transforming or (re)creating reality but a means of reaching (towards) the self. In his letters to Rousselot, the poet made clear how urgent a matter writing was for him, saying that "[é]crire m'a sauvé – j'ai sauvé mon âme … J'ai écrit comme on s'accroche à une bouée" ("[w]riting saved me – I saved my soul … I wrote the way one grabs onto a buoy").[10]

If subjectivity for Reverdy is undermined by gaps, silences, incoherences, and loss, then one can more readily understand why he was so attracted to still life and to the poetry of objects, and to the idea of the poem itself as an "objet de remplacement" ("replacement object"). Reverdy famously stated that "[l]a poésie est le bouche-abîme du reel désire qui manque" ("poetry is the stop-gap [bouche-abîme] for the desired real which is missing / lacking"). In this view, the poem constitutes an object that may counteract the sense of emptiness and absence that haunts collections of poetry such as *Les Ardoises du toit*: "La poésie est dans la formation d'un objet de remplacement susceptible du combler au coeur de l'homme le vide qu'y produit l'absence d'un objet réel désiré, de tout le réel désiré" ("Poetry consists of the shaping of a replacement object which is capable of filling the emptiness in the heart of man, the emptiness produced by the absence of the desired real object, of all of desired reality") (OC Tome II 1252).

3 The Text as Object: Francis Ponge's Verbal Still Lifes

"Le poète ne doit jamais proposer une pensée mais un objet, c'est-à-dire que même à la pensée il doit faire prendre une pose d'objet."

– Ponge, "Natura Piscem Doces," *Œuvres complètes* Vol. I, 178

("The poet must never propose a thought but, instead, an object, that is to say that he must make even thought take the pose of an object.")

> Pourquoi la nature morte?
>
> Le point est celui-ci:
>
> Un homme vraiment sensible éprouve à propos du spectacle le plus ordinaire, le plus prochain (familier, quotidien, banal), est capable en tout cas d'éprouver
>
> Le sentiment de la merveille et du drame, de l'épaisseur et de la variété de la nature, de l'intransigeance de la nature, du sacré, de l'ordre, du vertige, du mystère, du fatal. L'enthousiasme et la terreur sacrée dans le même temps le saisissent.
>
> La beauté, le drame, le tragique de chaque chose et de chaque arrangement de choses lui sont immédiatement sensibles. (OC Vol. II 756)
>
> (Why the still life?
>
> The point is this: A truly sensitive man feels that the most ordinary, close-at-hand things seen (things familiar, everyday, banal), he is capable in any case of feeling
>
> A sense of drama and of the marvelous, of the solidity and the variety of nature, of nature's intransigence, a sense of the sacred, of order, of dizziness, mystery, fatality. Enthusiasm and sacred terror seize hold of him at the same time.

The beauty, drama, tragedy of each thing and of each arrangement of things are immediately felt by him.")

More than any other poet of the twentieth century Francis Ponge (1899–1998) has been called the poet of objects. The complexity and authority of Ponge's verbal descriptions of everyday objects, collected in his first major book *Le Parti pris des choses* (*Taking the Side of Things*) (1942) and in later volumes such as *Pièces* (*Pieces*) (1961), *La Rage de l'expression* (*The Passion for Expression*) (1954), and *Le Savon* (*Soap*) (1965), have attracted considerable attention from critics. Jean-Paul Sartre's incisive 1944 study "L'Homme et les choses" ("Man and Things") is the outstanding early essay on Ponge's work; in the decades following that piece, many of the influential critics in French Studies have also devoted articles to Ponge's poetry, from Jean-Pierre Richard to Jacques Derrida, from Michael Riffaterre to Gérard Genette.[1]

Ponge's first published work was a series of short, quirky satirical poems entitled *Douze petits écrits* (*Twelve Little Writings*) (1926). Between 1919 and 1944, he began writing short prose poems exploring objects. He turns to this exploration of the object world, initially, out of a sense of disgust with the hypocrisy and the shabby, materialistic values of bourgeois society. In bourgeois culture, he felt, language became cliché-ridden and degraded, as social inequalities led to stultifying and mechanical lives. By concentrating on finding the *raison d'être* of individual objects, and making this discovery the focus of his idiosyncratic prose poems, he could reach a sense of integrity and simplicity absent from the human culture around him. By "taking the side of things" (as he proclaims he is doing in the title *Le Parti pris des choses*), by examining the peculiarities of natural and man-made objects, Ponge found a means to renew language while altering one's awareness of the world. He felt that the things that surround us require that we give them a voice through writing. As he states in his long text "Le Carnet du bois de pins" (1952): "Bois de pins, sortez de la mort, de la non-remarque, de la non-conscience! … Surgissez, bois de pins, surgissez dans la parole" ("Pine woods, emerge from death, from obscurity, from unconsciousness! … Come forward, pine woods, come forward into speech") (Ponge OC Vol. I, 384–5).

Ponge's work reveals an apparent paradox in its approach to things. On one level, his texts deemphasize the importance of human subjectivity, as he discards Romanticism's anthropocentric perspective and Romantic poets' appropriation of objects as mere reflectors of human subjectivity. At the same time, though, the goal of his project is a new kind of humanism. Despite his predilection for spotlighting things above all, rather than people, the poet still declares that "il y a toujours du rapport à l'homme ... Ce ne sont pas les choses qui parlent entre elles mais les hommes entre eux qui parlent des choses et l'on ne peut aucunement sortir de l'homme" ["poetry is always related to man ... It is not things which speak among themselves but men among themselves who speak of things and it is not possible to leave man behind [sortir de l'homme]") ("Raisons de vivre heureux" ("Reasons to Live Happily") *OC* Vol. I, 198). He aims at a reciprocal relationship in which things benefit from humans' attention while the human describer respects the integrity and otherness of things: "Il n'y a que l'esprit pour rafraîchir les choses. Notons d'ailleurs que ces raisons [d'écrire] sont justes ou valables seulement si l'esprit retourne aux choses d'une manière acceptable par les choses: *quand elles ne sont pas lésées, et pour ainsi dire qu'elles sont décrites de leur propre point de vue*" ("Only the mind can refresh things. Let us note, besides, that these reasons [to write] are correct or valid only if the mind returns to things in a manner which is acceptable to things: *when their pride is not injured and when they are, so to speak, described from their own point of view*") ("Raisons de vivre heureux" *OC* Vol. I, 198, emphasis added).

At first glance, Ponge's goal of exploring and praising things in poetry for the mutual benefit of things and humanity seems a straightforward project and many of his critics have taken his stated intentions grounding his work at face value. Richard Stamelman describes Ponge's poetics as follows: "The word gives breath to the object, causing it to vibrate and its sounds to reverberate." Using language to bring objects to life, the poet thus (ostensibly) bestows a new vitality on what he names: "Out of muteness comes speech and out of passivity and petrification comes an actively moving object. The act of speech, which the object-in-the-world acquires, heralds its projection into being" (688).

To reinforce this view of his poetics as a life-giving force for the "dead" object world, Ponge has christened the result of his joyous and playful transformations of objects into worlds "l'objeu" and "l'objoie" – terms which have subsequently been adopted by Ponge scholars. The object, as it becomes a text, functions as an "objeu" for him and then, in a further stage of development, an "objoie." The term "objeu" – a hybrid combining "objet" and "jeu de mots" – emphasizes the ludic and light-hearted impulses behind the poet's working with language and things. "Objoie," by extension, implies a spirited and quasi-erotic production of a verbal equivalent of a thing. (The verb "jouir" also means "to come" in a sexual sense in French.)

Ponge's own definition of "l'objeu" is offered to the reader in the long prose text describing the sun, "Le Soleil placé en abîme" ("The Sun Placed in an Abyss") (Ponge *OC* Vol. I, 776–94). This definition has become an often-quoted touchstone in criticism on his work:

> ... nous l'avons baptisé l'*Objeu*. C'est celui où l'objet de notre émotion placé d'abord en abîme, l'épaisseur vertigineuse et l'absurdité du langage, considérées seules, sont manipulées de telle façon que, par la multiplication intérieure des rapports, les liaisons formées au niveau des racines et les significations bouclées à double tour, soit créé ce fonctionnement qui seul peut rendre compte de la profondeur substantielle, de la variété et de la rigoureuse harmonie du monde. (Ponge. *OC* Vol. I, 778)
>
> (I have baptized it the *Objeu*. In it, the object of my emotion is first placed *en abîme*. The vertiginous thickness and absurdity of language, considered in themselves, are manipulated in such a way that, through the inner multiplication of relationships, through links formed at the level of roots and double meanings, there emerges the kind of textuality (fonctionnement) which alone can render the depth, variety, and rigorous harmony of the world.)

The tendency to use this passage as a basis for understanding the relationship between language and things in Ponge has often led readers to conclude that a happily symbiotic relationship exists between these two key elements of his poetry and poetics. As I will show in the following discussion of his work, such an optimistic view of the poet's textual techniques for securing the transformation of things into poems may be naive – or, at least, one-sided. It is possible to detect a fundamental ambivalence at the heart of Ponge's textualization of objects. The import of this ambivalence may best be grasped by reading Ponge's poetry through the tradition of still-life painting.

Ponge and the Still-Life Tradition

Following the example of the painters of the still-life tradition, much of Ponge's poetry finds its subject matter in commonplace, supposedly unremarkable and insignificant objects placed in everyday settings. Deliberately limited in its scope and subject matter, the still life is primarily concerned with (to quote the title of Norman Bryson's brilliant study of the genre) "looking at the overlooked." In still-life paintings, as in so many Ponge prose poems, human beings are conspicuously absent, relegated to the role of implied observer of the objects displayed in the picture. Rejecting the portrait-painter's exploration of the complexities of human psychology and the history painter's study of great events, the still-life painter quietly celebrates the sensuous appeal, the visual and tactile beauty of the things of this world. A modest and understated genre, the still life requires a contemplative attitude of its audience. Like Ponge's work, this genre is devoted to "taking the side of things."

Yet these very qualities which represent the strengths of the still life have led to its marginalization. Since its emergence as an independent genre during the sixteenth and seventeenth centuries, it has all too often been undervalued by art connoisseurs, if not dismissed outright as a minor, trivial art form. It has been regarded as merely decorative or, in the case of seventeenth-century Dutch still lifes, as a reflection of the bourgeoisie's taste for ostentatious display and material acquisitiveness. Bryson traces the history of this misapprehension concerning the genre:

> [Still life] has always been the least theorized of genres, and when the academics that launched the first theoretical accounts of painting came to mention it at all, they did so disparagingly: still life was always at the bottom of the hierarchy, unworthy of the kind of superior attention reserved for history painting or the *grande manière*. (8)

Bryson notes, further, that this neglect and misreading of the genre continues today:

> Though the twentieth century has seen a tremendous proliferation of exhibitions of still life, and of catalogues and monographs dealing with matters of chronology, provenance and connoisseurship, *interpretation* of still life has generally languished on all sides. (8)

Because the sorts of images presented in the still life – that is, most often the table and the pleasures it offers to the eye and mouth – so readily evoke a sense of ordinariness and familiarity, these images can be mistakenly read as trivial. (The objects of Ponge's poetry, like "Le Pain" ("The Bread"), "L'Orange" ("The Orange"), "La Pomme de terre"

("The Potato"), or "La Cruche" ("The Jug") obviously share this fate.) However, as anyone who has gazed carefully at a still life will realize, the impression of familiarity which these paintings rely upon forms only one aspect of their meaning. In fact, these pictures succeed in estranging what was apparently ordinary, in order to make us apprehend as mysterious, even bizarre, what we had initially assumed was commonplace. As Bryson asserts, the still-life painter brings us closer to everyday reality, only to create, and exacerbate, a feeling of radical separateness from the objects of our perception:

> In the routine spaces still life normally explores, habit makes one see through a glass, darkly; but when the object is revealed face to face, the departure from the habitual blurs and entropies of vision can be so drastic that the objects seem *unreal, unfamiliar,* un-creatural.

In his desire to re-make the things he observes, Ponge arrives at a comparable practice of the defamiliarization of the commonplace. The uncanny effect which the traditional still life (and Ponge's texts) produce often derives from an emphasis on *trompe-l'oeil* realism, an effect generated by the painter's or poet's meticulous rendering of the textures and surfaces of objects. The beholder gazing at a still life feels charmed by an impression of sensuous immediacy as he or she looks at succulent dishes or lovely flowers; at the same time, he or she is reminded that the enticing scene being viewed is no more than an illusion fashioned by a paintbrush on a two-dimensional surface. So, by denying the beholder access to the world of sensuous immediacy that it represents, the still life cautions the beholder that pleasure is fleeting, that the world of appearances may be grounded in uncertainty. The still life genre is actually rooted in ambivalence, as E.H. Gombrich argues:

> [E]very painted still life has the *vanitas* motif "built in" as it were, for those who want to look for it. The pleasures it stimulates are not real, they are mere illusion. Try and grasp the luscious fruit or the tempting beaker and you will hit against a hard, cold panel. The more cunning the illusion, the more impressive, in a way, is this sermon on semblance and reality. Any painted still life is *ipso facto* also a *vanitas*. (178)

Characteristically, the still life's strong appeal to the senses is openly contradicted in many of these paintings by signs that foreground the *vanitas* motif. Some painters may juxtapose human skulls or timepieces with images of tempting food or drink. Certain Ponge texts, such as "La Bougie" and "La Cigarette," ironically echo the *vanitas* theme, as the reader watches the objects being slowly consumed by the flame that nourishes them.

Besides its incitement to hedonistic pleasure coupled with a *memento mori* warning of life's transience, the genre has provided painters with a means of exploring processes of perception and representation, as Dennis Adrian notes:

> [A] consistently viable tradition in French art [is] that of the treatment of still-life as a poetic vehicle allied to perceptual exactitude. This is of course a notion first coming to flower in the early eighteenth century, when French art began to grant this kind of subject the metaphysical gravity formerly reserved for figurative subjects. Even in Chardin we recognize still-life not only as a vehicle for philosophical reflection but as the perfect genre for the examination of artistic processes themselves, since its focus is necessarily upon the relational aspects of perception. (30)

Still lifes, like all paintings, play upon vision and its transformation through art. They demonstrate new, more sensitive ways of seeing. In like fashion, Ponge, through his preoccupation with revitalizing the human subject's relationship to the object world, relies upon the transformation of words to achieve his goal. His numerous techniques for taking words apart, for experimenting with their appearance and sounds by reactivating forgotten etymologies and juggling with signifiers, may approximate a painter's experiments with visual perception. (In chapter 2, likewise, we saw how Reverdy's use of paronomasia and other forms of language play are comparable to Juan Gris's use of pictorial rhyming in his paintings.) Ponge asks us to examine language more carefully and zestfully, even as he expands on our ways of paying attention to things in their complex presence.

His short descriptive piece "Plat de poissons frits" ("A Plate of Fried Fish") (*OC* Vol. I, 768) reveals his masterly appropriation of still-life motifs. The choice of subject matter here suggests that a conscious dialogue with painting inspired the writing of the text, since a platter or frying pan of fish has been used as subject matter in Cubist still lifes by Picasso and Braque. (Like Reverdy, Ponge was a close friend of both these artists and he responds to their aesthetics in his own work.) In these paintings the flatness of the platter on which the fish are displayed doubles the flat plane of the canvas itself in a sort of painterly *mise en abyme.*

"Plat de poissons frits" begins with an exclamation of sensual delight: "Goût, vue, ouïe, odorat … c'est instantané" ("Taste, sight, sound, smell … it's instantaneous"). The poem appeals to all of the reader's senses at once, blending gastronomic and aesthetic enjoyment in the manner of a classic still life. Following this invitation to savour the sensory pleasure which the plate of fish provides, Ponge attempts to recapitulate the stages of the transformation of the fish as it is cooked:

> Lorsque le poisson de mer cuit à l'huile s'entrouvre, un jour de soleil sur la nappe, et que les grandes épées qu'il comporte sont prêtes à joncher le sol, que la peau se détache comme la pellicule impressionnable parfois de la plaque exagérément révélée (mais tout ici est beaucoup plus savoureux) ou (comment pourrions-nous dire encore?) … Non, c'est trop bon! Ça fait comme une boulette élastique, un caramel de peau de poisson bien grillée au fond de la poêle … (OC Vol. I, 768)

> (When the fish from the sea cooked in oil opens up, one sunny day on a tablecloth, and when the big swords inside it are ready to drop off, when the skin comes loose like the impressionable film sometimes does from the exaggeratedly revealed plate, (but everything here is much more delectable) or (how can I describe it further?) … No, it's too good! It becomes like a little elastic ball, a caramel made of fish skin well grilled at the bottom of the skillet …)

Parentheses and ellipses here perform a crucial rhetorical function. They indicate how decisively description must falter in the presence of this delectable dish: "(mais tout ici est beaucoup plus savoureux)," "(comment pourrions-nous dire encore?)." Poet and reader surrender to a visual, olfactory and gustatory seduction, suggested by auditory effects such as assonance and paronomasia: "Goût, vue, ouïes, odaurades: cet instant safrané …" ("Taste, sight, sound, smell / sea bream: this saffroned instant …"). The three sets of ellipses in the poem enact a detouring of the descriptive process, which must yield to the intense attractions of the things it is attempting to record "objectively."

Ponge ends the text with a nautical fantasy that discloses the propensity of the platter of fried fish to inspire the imagination:

> C'est alors, au moment qu'on s'apprête à
> déguster les filets encore vierges, oui! C'est

> alors que la haute fenêtre s'ouvre, que la voilure claque et que le pont du petit navire penche vertigineusement sur les flots
> Tandis qu'un petit phare de vin doré – qui se tient bien vertical sur la nappe – luit à notre portée.
>
> (Then, at the moment when one prepares to taste the still virgin fillets, yes! It is then that the high window opens, that the sails snap and that the bridge (deck) of the little boat leans forward vertiginously upon the waves,
> While a little lighthouse of golden wine – standing upright on the tablecloth – shines within reach of us.)

Using metaphor and metonymy to change a simple meal of seafood and wine into a voyage on the high seas, the poet shows us how 1) delicious food and drink, 2) a skilful still-life painting, and 3) figural language, can create potent pleasures and fantasies. The text, like the (painted) object it evokes, brings a whole world of sensory enjoyment and adventure onto the table before us, "à notre portée" ("within reach"). As an homage to still-life paintings and an example of Ponge's virtuoso descriptive talents, "Plat de poissons frits" underscores the affinities between his poetry and the paintings of objects which he so admired.

It should be stressed, however, that Ponge is not copying the still-life tradition in an unreflective or simple-minded manner. Rather, he has developed his own personal, difficult poetics of still life. This poetics can be fully appreciated only if one remains constantly attentive to the poet's feeling for language, which constitutes the basis of his art. His obsession with words, and his unique sense of the relationship between words and things, shapes the writing of his texts above all.

Ponge and Language: The Art of Description or Words as Things

In "My Creative Method" (1947–8), one of the most explicit of his statements of his own *art poétique*, Ponge defines the interdependent relation of words to things in his work through the formula "PARTI PRIS DES CHOSES EGALE COMPTE TENU DES MOTS" ("TAKING THE SIDE OF THINGS EQUALS TAKING WORDS INTO ACCOUNT"):

En somme voici le point important:
PPC égale CTM.
Certains textes auront plus de PPC
à l'alliage, d'autres plus de CTM ... Peu
importe. Il faut qu'il y ait en tout cas de
l'un *et* de l'autre. Sinon, rien de fait. (OC Vol. I, 522)

(In short this is the important point:
PPC equals CTM [Taking the side of
things equals Taking Words into Account].
Some texts will have more PPC and others
more CTM ... No matter. There must in
any case be the one *and* the other.
Otherwise, nothing accomplished.)

This formulation, "PPC égale CTM" (meaning "Parti pris des choses égale Compte tenu des mots") suggests a symmetrical, exact equivalence between the role of things and the role of words in Ponge's poetics. This idea of a symmetry between words and things has subsequently been generally taken as an entry point to understanding his texts properly. The texts do, indeed, rely on language as their subject matter as much as they rely on things. (So, for example, the poem "L'Huître" ("The Oyster") focuses as much on the particularities of the French word "huître" as on the particular qualities of an oyster). However, the presumably unproblematic equation of "parti pris des choses" and "compte tenu des mots" indicated by the "equals" sign linking these two expressions is somewhat misleading. In fact, the notion of a perfect balance which the poet achieves in crafting language to produce a verbal equivalent of an object does not necessarily correspond to the actual results of his practice. A divided allegiance or split set of priorities motivating Ponge's poetics becomes apparent in another excerpt from "My Creative Method," in which he favours the object as the focus of writing in one sentence while favouring language as the focus of his writing in the next:

De Deux mécanismes personnels
Le premier consiste à placer l'objet choisi (dire comment dûment choisi) au centre du monde; c'est-à-dire au centre de mes "préoccupations"; à ouvrir une certaine trappe dans mon esprit, à y penser naïve-

ment et avec ferveur (amour)
Dire que *ce n'est pas tellement l'objet (il ne doit pas nécessairement être présent)* que l'idée de l'objet, y compris le mot qui le désigne. Il s'agit de l'objet comme notion. *Il s'agit de l'objet dans la langue française,* dans l'esprit français (vraiment article de dictionnaire français).
(OC Vol. I, 531, emphasis added)

(On Two Personal Mechanisms
The first consists of placing the object (while saying how it was duly chosen) at the center of my "concern"; to open a particular trapdoor in my mind, to think about it naively and fervently (lovingly)
To say that *it is not so much the object (it does not necessarily have to be present)* as the idea of the object, including the word which designates it. What matters is the object as a notion. *What matters is the object in the French language,* in the French mind (truly a French dictionary entry).)

Following the logic of this passage, it becomes possible – even essential – to read Ponge's texts as presenting a struggle between language and things in which language serves a defensive function, allowing the poet to master the object of his contemplation. In a key passage of "My Creative Method" Ponge indeed confesses to harbouring certain anxieties regarding the object *in its singularity:*

La variété des choses est en réalité ce qui me construit … Mais par rapport à l'une d'elles seulement … *si je n'en considère qu'une,* je disparais: elle m'annihile. (OC Vol. I, 517)

(*The variety of things is really what constructs me* … But in relation to a single one of them … *if I only consider one,* I disappear: it [elle] annihilates me).

To avoid this "annihilation" by the object whose uncanny individuality he fears, he resorts, then, to using language as a means of "taming" the object, as it were:

Et, si [la chose] n'est que mon prétexte,
ma raison d'être, s'il faut donc que j'existe,
à partir d'elle, ce ne sera, ce ne pourra être
que par une certaine création de ma part à
son propos.
Quelle création? *Le texte.* (OC Vol. I, 517)

(And if [the thing] is only my pretext,
my reason for being, if I must exist, taking
it as my point of departure, it can only be
through a particular creation of mine
concerning the thing.
What kind of creation? *The text.*)

As Jean-Pierre Richard has argued, writing descriptions of objects permits Ponge to drown the objects in words (or, to return to the poet's own term, to "annihilate" them).[2] His verbal "definition-description" (as Ponge also calls his own texts), having thus replaced the object that inspired it, provides the poet with an opportunity to possess the object on his own terms. In a sense the object sacrifices itself to language in order to be recreated as a text. This process of doing away with the actual object in its difference and strangeness, which constitute both its attraction for Ponge *and* a source of acute anxiety, seems to me to account for a crucial – and under-explored – aspect of his poetics. The process also links his art, once again, to the still-life tradition, in which signs of sensuous pleasures and abundance (sumptuous feasts, beautiful objects) commingle with signs of mortality (skulls, timepieces, wilted flowers, dead animals) in a single, ambiguous image. Criticism on Ponge's work has not yet sufficiently emphasized the powerful connections in his poetry between his appropriation of things in language and a recurring preoccupation with mortality. On the contrary, his texts are generally read through metaphors of birth and growth.[3]

Almost as if he were performing an exorcism of the inescapable fascination that things have on his imagination, the poet has structured a number of short texts, particularly in *Le Parti pris des choses* and *Pièces*, around the violation and sacrifice of the object described. In "L'Orange," the orange is squeezed so hard that it yields its juice as "ses cellules ont éclaté, ses tissus se sont déchirés" ("its cells have burst, its tissues have been torn") (OC Vol. I, 20). Following this brutal squeezing, the describer emphasizes the orange's "façon particulière de parfumer l'air et de *réjouir son bourreau*" ("particular way [façon particulière] of perfuming the air and *giving pleasure to its torturer/executioner*") (OC Vol. I, 20, emphasis added). The oyster of "L'Huître" meets a similar fate, as it is forced open by means of a "couteau ébréché et peu franc" ("chipped and not very honest [peu franc] knife") (OC Vol. I, 21) to become a martyr to its cruel fate: "Les coups qu'on lui porte [à l'huître] marquent son enveloppe de ronds blancs, d'une sorte de halos" ("The blows which it [the oyster] receives mark its container with circles, with a sort of halo") (OC Vol. I, 21). The violent actions performed in these poems may be interpreted as analogous to the writer's own destruction of objects in order to abstract from them their essential qualities, or their "qualité différentielle," as Ponge would put it. In order for these object poems to be created, the muteness and autonomy of the object standing apart from the human world must yield to a loquacious rendering of the object in – and *as* – words. In this way, the object has sacrificed itself to "feed" literature and to satisfy the reader's imagination.

"Le Feu" ("The Fire") (OC Vol. I, 23) may be read as an allegory of the descriptive process which I have just outlined. At first glance, this short text consists merely of a brief visual evocation of the progress of a fire moving from its early stages to its conclusion:

> Le feu fait un classement: d'abord toutes
> les flammes se dirigent en quelque sens ...
>
> (Fire classifies: first all the flames move
> in a particular direction [sens] ...)

In the second paragraph, Ponge shifts from (pseudo-)objective description to try to seize the essence of fire through figural language:

> L'on ne peut comparer la marche du feu qu'à
> celle des animaux: il faut qu'il quitte un endroit
> pour en occuper un autre; il marche à la fois comme
> une amibe et comme une girafe, bondit du col, rampe
> du pied ...
>
> (The way fire moves / walks can only be
> compared to the gait of animals: it has to leave
> one spot in order to occupy another; it walks both

> like an amoeba and like a giraffe, jumps with its
> neck, crawls with its foot ...)

The final paragraph combines the literal and figural approaches that characterized the first two passages:

> Puis, tandis que les masses contaminés avec
> méthode s'écroulent, les gaz qui s'échappent sont
> transformés à mesure en une seule rampe de papillons.
>
> (Then, whereas the masses which have been
> methodically contaminated collapse, the gases
> which escape are gradually transformed into a
> single flight / rise of butterflies.)

It should be evident now that this elliptical piece is more than a straightforward description of fire. As always in Ponge, the thing being described is constantly altered – or distorted – by the language that envelops it. "Le Feu" can even be interpreted as a metapoetic reflection on the power and the voraciousness of literary language, which nourishes itself, much like the fire Ponge evokes, by assimilating reality into itself. In the first paragraph, the poet attributes intelligence to fire, as it moves in a calculating, decisive fashion: "Le feu fait un classement." Then, through a double simile, he transforms the fire in motion into a monster so odd that it conforms to no known bestiary: a creature half giraffe, half amoeba. A final metaphor reveals the magical ability of fire to produce optical illusions: "les gaz qui s'en échappent sont transformés à mesure en une seule rampe de papillons." Two complementary processes are at work, here, each assimilable to the other: in watching the movements of the fire, the reader is in reality watching the movements – that is, the turnings away from the literal towards figuration – of the poem's language. The poet indicates his awareness of the analogy between the metamorphic powers of figuration and those of fire through the ostensibly descriptive terms "L'on ne peut comparer ...," "*comme* une amibe et *comme* une girafe" (emphasis added), "sont transformés ... en."

In the end the fire generates beautiful images (like literary language) – the butterflies rising from the text before us. However, this lovely image cannot make us forget that fire acts primarily as a destructive force in the poem. It first "contaminates," then consumes whatever it touches. It acts cold-bloodedly, "avec méthode" ("with method"), like a Cartesian intellect.[4]

Because the poet so consciously associates the destructive power of the fire with the workings of the imagination, as it operates through figuration, one senses in "Le Feu" an ambivalent admission of the more harmful effects of literature upon reality. Like the fire, which can exist only by consuming substances it can burn, the human imagination can create literary works only by feeding upon reality. Like Ponge's fire, literature generates images of great beauty. Its continuous ingestion and metamorphosis of reality may nonetheless be viewed as monstrous (hence the figure of the amoeba-giraffe, a creature from a B-grade horror film!). Ponge again and again reminds us in his work that a real thing must be "sacrificed" – to the imagination, to language – in order for his poems to exist. The interdependency of creation and destruction remains an obsessive leitmotif of *Le Parti pris des choses*, *Pièces*, and *Le Savon*, among other Ponge texts. Reading these descriptions of things, one wonders whether it is possible for literature to represent reality without destroying (our sense of) reality. The still-life tradition, featuring pictures of half-consumed meals or flowers that will soon wilt and die, offers a striking parallel to Ponge's poetics of the object here, once more.

The above readings of "Le Feu" and other poems indicates a general drive in his texts towards a destruction of the object – a drive that counterbalances the optimism, joy, and humanist impulses and commitments that the poet himself has declared to be the *raison d'être* of his work. It is, thus, important to acknowledge the existence of a more sombre Ponge than the one that many of his readers have discovered.

This staging of the sacrifice of the object in a number of representative Ponge texts has other, equally disturbing consequences. Feminist critics such as Shirley Jordan and Yvette Bozon-Scalzotti have noted a powerful and persistent strain of misogyny in the poet's remarks on the feminine and in his tendency to associate (many) objects with the feminine as he describes them. Challenging the widely accepted view of Ponge as a humanist writer renewing language and perception, Jordan argues that "for the female reader at least, much of his work is anything but a site of renewal. Inscribed within his texts or objects are a number of underlying assumptions about gender attributes which are so solidly rooted in a straight-forward patriarchal framework as to render it somewhat surprising that this aspect of his writing has escaped comment" (Jordan 35). Jordan reminds us that Ponge, in his essay on the sculpture of Germaine Richier, identifies nature with woman and the feminine (OC Vol. II, 601–5) and that, in his practice, "to capture nature in writing is always a sexual conquest and a battle of wills" (Jordan 36). She adds that "[t]his struggle relies on one of patriarchy's staple assumptions: the female / *chose* must be controlled and tamed. She has a fascinating otherness that Ponge wishes to penetrate and lay bare, but which can also spell danger" from a masculist perspective (36). Ponge's frequent characterizations of writing as an erotic, (hetero)sexual activity make this violent domestication of the female / *chose* most troubling.

Bozon-Scalzotti echoes Jordan's concerns about Ponge's treatment of the feminine / things. "Les références à la femme qui accompagnent la description de la chose reprennent volontiers les clichés péjoratifs habituellement associés au 'féminin.' L'eau, par exemple, est 'folle' et 'hystérique'; elle est aussi 'une véritable esclave' qui 'ne tend qu'à s'humilier'" ("The references to women which accompany the description of things enthusiastically recycle the pejorative clichés generally associated with 'the feminine.' Water, for example, is 'mad'[folle] and 'hysterical'; it [elle] is also 'a veritable slave' who 'is inclined only to humiliate itself'") (231). After showing that "[l]es choses grammaticalement féminines – ce sont aussi les plus nombreuses – sont décidément plus malmenées que les masculines," Bozon-Scalzotti finds that "plutôt qu'à faire jubiler la chose, comme il le prétend, Ponge s'applique au contraire à la faire souffrir" ("[t]hings which are grammatically feminine – these are the most numerous [in French] – are decidedly more manhandled [in Ponge's poems] than masculine nouns," Bozon-Scalzotti finds that "rather than giving pleasure to things, as he claims to do, Ponge concentrates, on the contrary, on making them suffer") (232). As I indicated earlier, a significant number of Ponge prose poems end with the sacrifice and death of an object: "La Cigarette" ("The Cigarette"), "La Bougie" ("The Candle"), "L'Orange" ("The Orange"), "Le Cageot" ("The Crate") and many others. Although these textual "deaths" may be interpreted as elaborate poetic conceits, the cautionary remarks of Jordan and Bozon-Scalzotti may make one reinterpret these poems as (in part) expressions of a latent misogyny. Bozon-Scalzotti urges us to look more seriously at the implications of Ponge's gendered subjugation and killing off of objects: "Non seulement la souffrance, mais la mort de la chose est aussi nécessaire à Ponge que celle de l'héroïne au romancier" ("Not only the suffering, but the death of the thing is as necessary to Ponge as that of the heroine for the (male) novelist") (232).

It may not be farfetched, then, to think of "L'Orange" or "L'Huître" as Ponge's Emma Bovary or Anna Karenina, headstrong but vulnerable heroines killed off by the writer at the end of their respective stories. In my comparison, further on, of Ponge's poetry and Claes Oldenburg's sculptures of objects, I will return to this problem of misogyny and of the feminization of objects.

The Text as Object

A recurring idea in Ponge's work is the notion of the text itself as a kind of object, the ultimate consequence of his embracing the aesthetic position of "PARTI PRIS DES CHOSES EGALE COMPTE TENU DES MOTS," which is, precisely, the view of the text as being itself an object. The Ponge text acquires its own specific order, solidity, and individuality, following the example of the things about which the poet writes:

> De quoi, s'agit-il? Eh bien, si l'on m'a
> compris, de créer des objets littéraires
> qui aient le plus de chances je ne dis pas
> de vivre, mais de s'opposer (*s'objecter,*
> se poser objectivement) avec constance
> à l'esprit des générations, qui les intéressent
> toujours (comme les intéressent toujours les
> objets extérieurs eux-mêmes), restent à leur
> disposition, à la disposition de leur désir et
> goût du concret; de l'évidence (muette)
> opposable, ou de représentatif (ou présentatif). (OC Vol. I, 520)

> (What is my goal as a writer? Well, if I
> have been properly understood, it is to create
> literary objects which have the greatest chance,
> not so much to live, but to oppose themselves
> (*objectify themselves,* present themselves
> objectively) enduringly to the mind of generations
> of readers, who will continue to find them
> interesting (just as external objects themselves
> interest them), remaining at their disposal, at the
> disposal of their desire and their taste for
> concreteness; for silent facts, or for what is
> representative (or presentative).)

He proposes that these man-made, written "objects" would even serve as an improvement over natural objects:

> Il s'agit d'objets d'origine humaine, faits et
> posés spécialement pour l'homme (et par l'homme),
> mais qui atteignent à l'extériorité et à la complexité,
> en même temps qu'à la présence et à l'évidence des
> objets naturels. *Mais qui soient plus touchants, si*
> *possible, que les objets naturels, parce qu'humains;*
> plus décisifs, plus capables d'emporter l'approbation
> (OC Vol. I, 520, emphasis added)

> (These are manmade objects, created and set
> up specially for man (and by man) but which reach
> exteriority and complexity, and at the same time the
> presence and naturalness of the objects of nature.
> *But which are more touching, if possible, than natural*
> *objects, because they are human; more decisive, more*
> *capable of earning approval*)

The poet expresses here a preference for written "objects" over natural objects, as though written objects could assimilate all of the attributes of natural objects, even supplanting them with a deeper perfection ("plus décisifs, plus capables d'emporter l'approbation").

Ponge's conception of the text as a sort of object is not mere fancy. He has stated that he wishes to express the concrete presence, the "épaisseur" of physical objects through "l'épaisseur sémantique des mots" ("the semantic thickness of words") (OC Vol. I, 203). The materiality of language, rendered as writing, does give it a visible and physical presence (as sentences, pages, books) which can be likened to that of things, as Maurice Blanchot has stated:

> … la matérialité du langage … fait que les mots
> aussi sont des choses, une nature, ce qui m'est
> donné et me donne plus que j'en comprends …
> [Dans le langage] … tout ce qui est physique
> joue le premier rôle: le rythme, le poids, la masse,
> la figure, et puis le papier sur lequel on écrit, la
> trace de l'encre, le livre. Oui, par bonheur, le langage
> est une chose: c'est la chose écrite, un morceau

> d'écorce, un fragment d'argile où subsiste la réalité de la terre. Le mot agit, non pas comme une force idéale, mais comme une puissance obscure, comme une incantation qui contraint les choses, les rend *réellement* présentes hors d'elles-mêmes.
>
> (... the materiality of language ... is such that words are also things, a part of nature, that which is given to me and gives me more than I can even understand. [In language] ... everything that is physical is foregrounded: rhythm, weight, mass, appearance, and also the paper on which one writes, the trace of the ink, the book. Yes, happily, language is a thing: it is the thing written, a bit of bark, a clay fragment on which the reality of the earth subsists. The word acts, not like an ideal force, but like an obscure power, like an incantation which constrains things, makes them *really* present outside themselves.)

The physical features of the literary text that Blanchot mentions here provide written language with a unique concreteness and presence. The book stands before the reader as a tangible object, separate and other. At once abstract and materially present, language, in the form of books, can fulfill his desire for a man-made substitute for the natural object.

A fundamental aspect of this process or fantasy of transforming objects into language and of creating verbal objects through writing is the act of naming. Ponge's readers have frequently observed that nomination occupies a primary place in his poetics. For him, "[n]ommer, c'est créer" ("[t]o name is to create") as Bernard Valette states. (27) Denis Hollier explains exactly what is at stake in this poetics of nomination:

> Le premier acte d'Adam fut d'imaginer un nom aux êtres de la création, par quoi, dit Hegel, "il les anéantit dans leur existence"; c'est-à-dire qu'ouvrant ce qui est à plus que ce qui est, à l'excès de la parole, il introduit dans le monde la disparition et la mort comme ses possibilités les plus propres ... Le pouvoir de nommer ne viendrait à l'homme que par l'anticipation d'un anéantissement

> total consécutif mais dont paradoxalement il lui offre les moyens de surmonter les effets. (90)
>
> (Adam's first act was to imagine a name for the beings of creation, an act by which, says Hegel, "he destroyed their existence"; that is to say, in opening up what exists to more than what exists, to the excess in speech, he introduced disappearance and death into the world as their most characteristic possibilities ... The power of naming would then come to man only through the anticipation (foreshadowing) of a total destruction to follow but, paradoxically, this power also offers him the means to surmount its effects.)

The fantasies of naming that subtend Ponge's œuvre combine an annihilation of the material world (or the fear of such an annihilation) with its recreation in words, as the names of things. "Chaque chose ainsi enracinée dans son nom et son absence aura sa place dans l'œuvre complète à venir de Ponge, Paradis d'après le déluge" ("Each thing thus anchored in its name and its absence will have its place in Ponge's complete work to come, as in a Paradise after the flood"), Hollier writes.

This quasi-magical belief in the creative power of naming links Ponge's thought to a long tradition in Western poetics whose source is generally identified as Plato's *Cratylus*. Indeed, Ponge's wish to uncover the "qualité différentielle" of each thing he contemplates in order to formulate a rhetorical *equivalent* (his term) to the thing recalls the debate in the *Cratylus* concerning the relationship between words and things. The relationships between the two may be viewed as arbitrary (the position which was taken by Ferdinand de Saussure to elaborate his structural linguistics at the end of the nineteenth century) or else as a necessary relation, motivated by a profound and hidden connection linking words to the things they represent. Ponge's thought typically oscillates between these two positions, though he very often comes close to endorsing the latter view; he seems to believe that a secret and necessary connection binds each individual thing to the word that stands for it. Claudine Giordan observes that "[l']accent mis sur le travail lexical, 'l'épaisseur des mots,' fait présager que la conception pongienne de la langue est présaussurienne. Sa sémantique ... est avant tout lexicologique" ("[t]he underscoring [by Ponge] of lexical effects, 'the thickness of words' leads one to anticipate that Ponge's conception of language is pre-Saussurian. His semantics … is above all lexicological") (489). Giordan argues that Ponge's notion of language is quite specific and selective:

> Mots et noms sont constamment placés en synonymes dans cette écriture … La plupart des titres de ces textes sont des noms (précédés d'un article défini) ou des syntagmes nominaux. L'écrivain cherche des étymologies qui soient des noms. (Giordan 490)
>
> (Words and names / nouns are constantly presented as synonyms in his writings … Most of the titles of his texts are nouns (preceded by the definite article) or nominal syntagms. The writer looks for etymologies which are nouns / names.)

In many cases, an entire Ponge poem is derived from a playful meditation upon the name of a given thing. The poems "Les Mûres" ("The Blackberries"), "La Cruche" ("The Jug") and "Les Olives" ("The Olives") (OC Vol. I, 17–18, 751–2, 753–4) provide particularly apt examples of this art of naming. "Les Mûres" ends with the statement: "Sans beaucoup d'autres qualités – *mûres*, parfaitement elles sont mûres – comme aussi ce poème est fait" ("Without many other qualities – *ripe* (*blackberries*), absolutely they are ripe (blackberries) – as this poem also is complete"). In this case the poet's fascination with names as the essences of things leads him to attempt a humorous conflation of naming and describing in the phrase "*mûres*, parfaitement elles sont mûres," which (especially if it is heard rather than read) can be translated "*blackberries*, they are perfectly blackberries" or "*ripe*, they are perfectly ripe." Doubly tautological, the phrase suggests that the name "mûres" expresses the "truth" of the thing.

"La Cruche" can be considered one of Ponge's most complex and fully explored assimilations of a thing to the word that names it. To describe the pitcher, he begins with a surprising reversal, focusing on the word "cruche" instead of the thing:

Pas d'autre mot qui sonne comme cruche. Grâce à cet U qui s'ouvre en son milieu, cruche est plus creux que creux et l'est à sa façon.

(No other word resounds like jug [cruche]. Thanks to that U which opens up in its center, jug [cruche] is more hollow than hollow and is hollow in its own way.)

Without any transition, he then speaks of the thing itself as though he were still discussing the word naming it: "C'est un creux entouré d'une terre fragile: rugueuse et fêlable à merci" ("It is a hollow surrounded by fragile earth: rough and crackable"). Then, in the next paragraph of the poem, the fusion of the word and thing is completely taken for granted, so that the reader can no longer distinguish which of the two "cruches" is being discussed.

Cruche d'abord est vide et le plus tôt possible vide encore.
Cruche vide et sonore.
Cruche d'abord est vide et s'emplit en chantant.

(Jug is first empty and as soon as possible empty again.
Empty and sonorous jug.
Jug is first empty and it fills while singing.)

The written text, in its tantalizing physical immediacy and solidity, seems to offer the poet – and the reader – a replacement for the (absent) object which it would represent. Jean-Luc Lemichez sees Ponge's repetition and impassioned excavation of the names of things as a project, impossible but compelling, for closing the gap between desire and its fulfilment:

Tenter de faire apparaître l'objet par la répétition obsessionnelle du mot en sa racine: *l'obsession, forme intensive de la présence* est, dans le texte de Ponge, la forme compensatoire de ce manque d'être insistant de l'objet, de cet *intensif de l'absence* qu'est l'hallucination. (429)

(To attempt to make the object appear by the obsessive repetition of the root of the word: *obsession, the intensive form of presence*, is, in Ponge's text, the compensatory form of that insistent lack of being in the object, of that *intensifier of absence*, hallucination.)

Ultimately, this privileging of naming has potentially disruptive consequences. Claudine Giordan finds that this fetishization of the noun / name reintroduces into Ponge's work an idealism which he had claimed to have rejected in favour of a commitment to materialism:

> Si la trandescendance est explicitement barrée des textes pongiens au nom du matérialisme antique, c'est dans cet imaginaire de l'écriture – nomination, métaphore de l'amour – unité, qu'elle resurgit et se masque. (Giordan 491)
>
> (If transcendence is explicitly banished [barrée] from Ponge's texts in the name of a sense of materialism dating back to Antiquity, it is in that imaginary of writing – naming [nomination], that metaphor of love – that it reappears and conceals itself.)

Ponge's Later Work: Towards an Open-Ended Textuality

Most of Ponge's earlier prose poems focusing on objects are brief and self-contained, only about one or two pages long. He gradually moved away from writing these short, dense texts (which critics have referred to as "textes bouclés" or "textes clos"), gravitating towards writing extended, repetitious series of "notes" around a given object. In 1947–8, five years after the publication of *Le Parti pris des choses*, the poet wrote *Le Carnet du bois de pins* (*The Pine Wood Notebook*). It is the first of his many published notebooks or dossiers for a projected "finished" text yet to come (which the notebook, in the end, replaces). Like the diary recording the stages of a work-in-progress or like a series of preparatory sketches for a painting, *Le Carnet du bois de pins* – and *Le Savon* (1967), *La Fabrique du pré* (*The Making of the Meadow*) (1973), *Comment une figue de paroles et pourquoi* (*How A Fig Made of Words and Why*) (1977), or *La Table* (*The Table*) (1991), in particular – proceed by means of rewriting, corrections, repetition, and changes. The poet thus constantly redefines the parameters and focus of his creativity; the finished product now matters less to him than the exploration of the process of its coming into being. Through this replacement of a completed work by the notes that precede its creation, "the work" is then, in a sense, taken apart, broken down into various separate stages of its slow maturation.

In my view, this departure from Ponge's earlier practice in the later texts does not constitute a repudiation of the still-life aspects of his work, which are most dominant in the picture gallery collections like *Le parti pris des choses* and *Pièces*, featuring short verbal descriptions of things. Rather, in his later open-ended, process-oriented writings, Ponge succeeds in radicalizing the still life by recasting its traditional aesthetics. The radicalization of still life by Picasso and Braque (about whom Ponge wrote several critical essays)[5] may well have been an inspiration for his own re-workings of the genre.[6]

Le Savon takes shape as a concatenation of fragments. The text is highly discontinuous, as each of its short segments is quickly interrupted and replaced by another fragment, written in an entirely different style. *Le Savon* is written as a number of separate genres housed within a single text, including a page-long parody of the textuality of Mallarmé's *Un Coup de dés* (*OC* Vol. II, 392) and a short mock-playlet on soap featuring actors, dialogue, stage directions, and so on (*OC* Vol. II, 373–8). *Le Savon* ends with three different essays and five appendices in which Ponge repeatedly changes the angle from which he is observing the object. Once again, Ponge's own text is imitating the object it describes. Because a bar of soap is slippery and difficult to grasp when it is wet, *Le Savon* also keeps slipping from the reader's grasp, thwarting all efforts to reduce it to a set form or message (although, in this case, Ponge does foreground the political context of the work to an unusual degree, as he had begun working on *Le Savon* during the Second World War and eventually completed his text for a broadcast on German radio in 1967).[7]

In *Le Savon*, the soap, and the text, become objects for the poet to play with. Along with him, we enjoy this text-object; we are also "cleaned" and renewed by our contact with it. Referring to the bar of soap as a "[p]ierre magique!" ("magic stone!") (*OC* Vol. II, 362), he praises its qualities of "bubbly" effervescence and exuberance. We encounter the bar of soap "parmi une ivresse lucide et chatoyante, ou plutôt une effervescence, une ebullescence à froid d'où nous sortons d'ailleurs, et voilà la grande leçon – les mains plus propres, plus pures qu'avant le commencement de cet exercice" ("within a lucid and shimmering drunkenness, or rather an effervescence, a bubbliness in the cold state [à froid] from which we emerge – and here is the great lesson – with cleaner, purer hands than we had before the beginning of this exercise") (364–5). The soap's excessive "volubility" is then likened to speech: "Pour un savon, les principales vertus sont l'enthousiasme et la volubilité. Au moins la facilité d'élocution" ("For a bar of soap, its principal virtues are enthusiasm and volubility. Or at least an ease of elocution") (365). Following the object's example or "lesson," the style of Ponge's text, too, grows "savonneux, moussant, écumeux – comme la bave aux naseaux du cheval qui galope" ("soapy, foaming, lathery – like the snot from the nostrils of galloping horses") (366). Consequently, *Le Savon* perfectly actualizes the basic features of Ponge's "objeu" and "objoie." At the same time, it reminds us of the importance of the still life tradition for the poet. Like the objects typical of that tradition's iconography, the bar of soap is transient, doomed to disappear after any prolonged contact with water (water being almost always an ambivalent force in Ponge).[8] The balance between sensuous pleasure and the *memento mori* theme that characterizes still life is constantly foregrounded in *Le Savon.* Nevertheless, unlike the objects in a conventional still life, the bar of soap here keeps jumping out of its frame or frames. The boundaries of representation which might have contained and tamed the object fail to restrain its subversive playfulness and ambiguity. By breaking the frame in this way, Ponge complicates our dialogue with the object, for we cannot presume to have understood something which will not adhere to a fixed definition or description. The bar of soap persists in resisting our efforts to make it ours (and *resistance* becomes a politically loaded term in this text, written in large part during the dark days of the Occupation in France). Through its ungraspability and resistance to being appropriated in words – a resistance which Ponge translates into textual processes of discontinuity and disruption – the object leads us to a moral lesson. Like the still lifes of Braque or Chardin or the fables of La Fontaine, *le savon* – and *Le Savon* – teach us to relinquish our aspirations towards mastery of the (object) world around us.

Comment une figue de paroles et pourquoi adopts an even more radical approach to the representation of the object. In this text, Ponge offers a dizzying array of separate possible versions of the same short description of a fig, each version slightly different from all the others. The text had originated as the three-page prose poem "La figue(sèche)," included in *Pièces* (*OC* Vol. I, 803–5). The poet explains his project of multiple rewritings of the same object poem in the "Avant-propos" to *Comment une figue de paroles et pourquoi*:

> Plusieurs expériences m'ayant convaincu, en revanche, de l'intérêt manifesté par certains aux *livraisons* (à proprement parler) de cette sorte, j'ai résolu d'exposer, une bonne fois, à longueur de pages, et, cette fois, sans le

> moindre retenu, tout le grand nombre de feuillets qu'il m'avait fallu gâter pour mener à son achèvement (je veux dire à son efficacité), quoi donc? Quelle espèce d'ouvrage?
>
> –Eh bien, un texte édicté, "ordonné" de pleine puissance et autorité personnelle sans autre cause ni raison que mon Bon Plaisir, et capable pourtant de gagner quelques suffrages: comme il en advint, justement, à cette FIGUE SECHE. (CFPP 56)
>
> (Since several experiments had convinced me of some people's interest in these sorts of *deliveries* (in the literal sense), I decided to show, once and for all, over many pages, and, this time, with no holding back, the great many sheets I had had to spoil in order to take to its conclusion (I mean its effectiveness) what then? What sort of work?
>
> –Well, a text dictated, "ordered" with full personal power and authority for no other reason than my own Good Pleasure, and nonetheless able to win a few votes: thus it led to this DRIED FIG.]

This time Ponge is actually reversing the usual priorities by which a literary work is evaluated. He is exposing to the reader's gaze the writerly labour which is normally kept hidden from view; he is showing us "tout le grand nombre de feuillets qu'il m'a fallu gâter pour mener [le texte] à son achèvement." The work he thus produces remains difficult to categorize ("quoi donc? Quelle espèce d'ouvrage?") because it challenges the boundaries that are supposed to distinguish a "finished" work from the process of its production. The editor for the original edition of *Comment une figue de paroles et pourquoi*, Jean Ristat, has used typographical variations to make visible to the reader the successive stages of the work's unfolding: "La première écriture est imprimée en caractères gras," he writes, "les corrections (ajouts, râtures, variantes) en caractères maigres" ("The first version is printed in heavy type, the corrections (additions, crossings out, variants) in thin type") (CFPP 7). Ristat indicates that he attempted "de *décrire* le manuscrit, chaque fois que la typographie ne permettait pas de *faire voir* la complexité du travail de la 'création': mots entourés, ou rayés, phrases supprimées que j'ai essayé de déchiffrer, parfois sans succès" ("to *describe* the manuscript, each time that the typography did not allow me to *show* the complexity of Ponge's work of 'creation': words circled, or crossed out, suppressed sentences which I tried to decipher, sometimes with no success") (CFPP 7). These problems that Ristat faced in trying to make every stage of the writing of *Comment une figue de paroles et pourquoi* legible reveal the repressed contingencies and multiplicities of invention that are usually suppressed in the critical privileging of the "final" version of a text.

Here is one of the numerous version of "La Figue" compiled by Ristat:

La Figue
La Figue qui n'est qu'une pauvre petite massue,
qui n'est aussi qu'une pauvre gourde, est molle
et rare. C'est une pauvre gourde, à l'intérieur de
laquelle, comme dans une église de campagne (le
portail ouvert), luit un autel scintillant.
C'est une grosse tétine dont on peut s'emplir
la bouche, comportant une sorte de pâte comme
une confiture trop cuite, trop sucrée, réduite, remplissant
la bouche et sablée de pépins, de pépites, craquant
sous la dent.
Une petite poire de caoutchouc baroque, très
espagnole, rouge et or. Un pauvre petit argument-massue. (CFPP 204)

(The Fig
The fig which is but a poor little club, which is also but
a poor calabash / dimwit, is soft and rare. It's a poor calabash / dimwit, inside of which, as in a country church (with
its principal door open), a sparkling altar gleams.
It's a large nipple with which one can fill one's mouth,
containing a sort of paste like an overcooked jam, too
sugary, reduced, filling one's mouth and flecked with pips
and seeds, that crack under one's tooth.
A little Baroque rubber pear, very Spanish, red and
gold. A poor little argument-bludgeon.)

At the bottom of the page where this passage appears, Ristat adds in a note that "[c]ette page, entièrement manuscrite, comportant ajouts, étonnante à cette place dans le dossier, ne porte aucune date. Elle est quadrillée à la manière des pages de cahiers d'écolier" ("[t]his page, entirely handwritten, and including additions, a surprising thing to find in this spot in the dossier, has no date. It is lined like the pages of a schoolboy's notebook") (CFPP 204).

In reading this endless series of variations on what was originally a short, self-contained prose poem, the reader must confront the many false starts and revisions normally concealed by the (illusory) "finished" version of a work. These multiple variants on the same topic also convince us of the unlikeliness, even the impossibility, of capturing a thing in words, if even a simple piece of fruit, a fig, can generate a potentially infinite series of descriptions of itself. None of the individual descriptions is an adequate representation of a fig since in any single description, some essential detail may be omitted. One may be reminded, too, of the Cubist painters' practice of refracting an object into multiple different angles or views, all telescoped together as a single-but-plural image which resists being coopted by the beholder's gaze.

The reader might wonder why this specific object, the fig, so fascinated Ponge that he was prompted to keep rewriting it over and over. Here, his eroticization of objects that are figured as female in his prose poems (in "Le Huître" or "De l'eau" ("About Water"), for example) reaches a new level, as the erotic attributes of the fig, which resembles the female genitals, are overtly acknowledged in his verbal sketches of it: "La figue est molle et rare, écrivais-je ... Une pauvre gourde, une pauvre bourse d'avare. Une pauvre couille (ou glande)" ("The fig is soft and rare, I wrote ... A poor calabash / dimwit, a poor miser's purse. A poor testical (or gland)") (OC Vol. II, 766). The fig is compared not only to the female genitals here, but also to a breast: "épaisse et cédant, se retirant sous la dent, comme une tétine" ("thick and yielding, withdrawing under the tooth, like a nipple") (767). Ponge's taking this feminized object and making it submit to a very lengthy series of (eroticized) rewritings directed by his excited gaze reminds us of the troubling relationship between his poetics of the object and misogynist literary traditions. Although he describes the writing of *Comment une figue de paroles et pourquoi* as "un acte d'amour ... au langage" (788), we must wonder whether we are, in fact, dealing with "an act of love" or an example of highly stylized pornography. This sexual – or sexist – sub-text to his brilliant description of the fig underscores, yet again, the darker and more unsettling sides concealed behind the joyously playful practices of "l'objeu" and "l'objoie."

La Table, another one of his open-ended or seemingly "unfinished" texts, was Ponge's last published work. Significantly, the object being taken apart and reassembled in this case is the very thing (or place) where the poet did his writing. The writing of *La Table* allowed him to explore the table – an object equally important to literary and visual arts traditions. Writers have needed the flat surface of a table or desk to do their work. Still-life painters have generally included the surface of the tabletop in their paintings, and their studios, because it provides them with a flat surface for arranging and displaying the objects to be painted. The choice of subject matter in *La Table* reemphasizes the ongoing dialogue with painting which guides Ponge's creativity in crucial respects.

In certain earlier prose poems, Ponge had highlighted the human observer's sense of the object as distant, even unapproachable. A single object – an object studied in its singularity – could "annihilate" him, he wrote. In *La Table*, by contrast, a strong feeling of intimacy links subject and object in a harmonious relation. Nostalgia frames the poet's perspective:

> Je me souviendrai de toi, ma table,
> table qui fut ma table, table n'importe laquelle,
> table quelle qu'elle soit.
> La table, quant à moi, est où je
> m'appuie pour écrire ou peut-être plutôt
> pour attendre d'avoir à écrire. (OC Vol. II, 914)

> (I will remember you, my table,
> the table which was my table, any old
> table, any table at all.
> The table, for me, is the place
> I rely on / lean on to write or perhaps rather
> to wait to need to write.)

As always, he begins with a "scientific" or (pseudo)zoological look at the materiality of the object: "{La table {généralement quadrupède (plus rétive qu'un âne) / doit être trainée ou portée: elle ne se déplace pas toute seule (c'est ce qui est sympathique en elle). { {Fidèle mais il faut y aller. La table est une amie fidèle mais il faut y aller } } / est un plateau de bois carré ou rectangulaire} où placer les choses qui adviennent ou qui vont être utiles et s'asseoir auprès ou devant les pieds dessous ou dessus" ("{The table {generally a quadruped (more stubborn than a mule) / must be dragged or carried: it cannot move on its own (that is what is likeable about it). { {Faithful but it must get on (il faut y aller) / The table is a faithful friend but it must get on } } / is a square or rectangular stage of wood upon which to place whatever things come along or which are going to be useful and before or near which to sit down with your feet on or under it"] (*OC* Vol. I, 921). Then in a typical

Pongian gesture, he leaps from a consideration of the referent (the piece of furniture) to an exuberant verbal act of juggling with "table" as signifier and suffix:

> Pour avoir une véritable table {il suffit
> d' / mais il faut} enlever sa vérité à véritable. A
> supportable cet insupportable suppor, à portable
> ce por, à épouvantable son épouvante, à démontable
> son démon (il suffit de le démonter), à redoutable
> sa redoute. En un mot, de ne garder que le suffixe
> hors de toute signification.
> Table n'est qu'un support, à peine plus
> qu'un suffixe, un suffixe avec sa consonne ou
> je dirai mieux: sa colonne d'appui, appuyé le dos
> contre sa colonne d'appui. (OC Vol. I, 935)

> (To have a veritable table {it's enough
> to / but you must} remove verity from veritable.
> Remove that unbearable bear from bearable,
> remove the demon from demontable [= collapsible]
> (it's enough to collapse it), remove formi from
> formidable. In a word, to keep only the suffix
> apart from any signification.
> A table is only a support, hardly more than
> a suffix, a suffix with its consonant or, better still:
> its spinal column, with its back against its spinal
> column.)

Here, as in *La Fabrique du pré* or *Comment une figue de paroles et pourquoi*, by a long series of repetitions, digressions, revisions, and addenda, the poet attempts to textualize the object. This urge to continue offering new definitions-descriptions of the thing, none of which is complete or satisfying on its own, suggests that Ponge is *failing* to produce a verbal equivalent of the thing, as much as he is succeeding in reaching his goal. If there is a "truth" of the object that literature can discover and make known to the reader, then that "truth" may emerge only from an unarrested movement, or slippage, between an extensive number of different versions of the (written) object. Such a slippage or unstable movement is central to the sort of representation which Ponge practises in his later texts. Deconstructive philosopher Jacques Derrida, whose reading of Ponge I will be discussing at the end of this chapter, would term such a productive slippage difference ("la différance").

Ponge and Claes Oldenburg: Radicalizing the Still Life

Scholarly discussions of Ponge's relationship to the visual arts have generally focused on the poet's own writings on art and on comparisons between his works and those of the artists about whose works he has most often written: Braque, Chardin, Giacometti, and Fautrier, in particular.[9] However, as I will now argue, perhaps the most relevant and fruitful parallel to the texts of Ponge in the visual arts are the object sculptures of Swedish-American artist Claes Oldenburg (b. 1929).

Although no direct influence between Ponge and Oldenburg exists, they share a remarkable number of affinities in their uses of the object. Like Ponge, Oldenburg is well-known for his complex, eccentric, and surprising recreations of familiar, banal objects. He has created large sculptures of a banana, a light switch, a baked potato, a shrimp, a drum set, a saw, a typewriter, an ice bag, a fan, and many other familiar everyday objects. Both Ponge and Oldenburg often choose to pay attention to objects that are consumed and discarded in daily life, so that their works comment indirectly on the wastefulness of consumer society. Both men remake objects into (e)strange(d) versions that puzzle, trouble, and please the reader or beholder. Oldenburg alters objects, especially, through changes in scale and texture. He has created a giant hamburger, a giant lipstick, a giant Good Humour Bar, and a giant clothespin, among other sculptures. He frequently chooses a hard object as a source for a work in order to refashion it into a soft, sagging version; his soft drum set, soft bathtub, or soft fan are famous examples. Just as Ponge challenges the "I"-centred lyricism of the Romantics, Oldenburg rejects the focus on human subjectivity that has characterized Western art since the Renaissance.

As we have seen, Ponge uses writing on objects in order to explore language. The words that name the things he describes thus become the real focus of his texts. Similarly, Oldenburg's chosen objects serve to some extent as pretexts for his exploration of materials and aesthetic processes. As Barbara Haskell notes, "[t]he function, reference, and history of these original objects are relatively unimportant to Oldenburg. In his Giant Ice Bag, for example, he is not attempting to say anything about an ice bag, but is concerned more with forms and states of matter than the emotions attached to a particular piece" (9). Oldenburg works with a few simple geometric forms, in combination with one another, to fashion his sculptures. "It is the variation of these forms (basically the circle and the rectangle) that produces the subject," as Haskell explains. "The Ice Bag, for example, is [quoting Oldenburg] 'a low cone surmounted by a disk,' the hamburger is four circles or 'three of my old bottle caps defining the space by layered disks,' the Giant Shirt with Brown Tie is a 'large rectangle with a "tail" and Fagends are elongated cylinders'" (9). Oldenburg generates comical, almost magical effects for the viewer as these basic shapes are transmuted into new forms, familiar but strange.

Like Ponge, Oldenburg is fascinated by "change, movement, and metamorphosis" (9). Haskell explains that "[h]is soft works are constantly changing configuration and position, constantly being rearranged. They participate in life processes through the force of gravity, [Oldenburg's] 'favorite form-creator,' the common denominator among phenomena." The hard works, too, are affected by, and stand for, change: "Many of the hard works are composed of several parts whose positions are constantly being altered and rearranged" (9).

An emphasis on humour and a concealed but obsessive eroticism further connect Ponge's texts to the artworks of Oldenburg. Barbara Rose asserts that "eroticism is the dominant theme throughout [Oldenburg's] work" (10). She shows that many of his objects function in part as disguised sexual metaphors:

> Basically, he classifies objects as male, female, or ambisexual. To the first category belong all the phallic objects – ray guns, the baseball bats and so forth. Hamburgers, tires, telephones, and such an object as *Giant Soft Swedish Light Switches* are female. Dormeyer mixers, the peeled banana, the fans, and the soft drainpipes are ambisexual, according to Oldenburg. (Rose 170)

Thus, the juxtaposition of the rounded forms of the ("female") hamburger sitting on the floor and the phallic shape of the ("male") ice cream cone suspended in the air above and beside the hamburger suggests a comically coital scene taking place. Oldenburg has explicitly likened the "dripping" ice cream to sperm, in this case. Ponge's verbal exploration of the "eroticized" female shapes of the oyster in "L'Huître" or the orange in "L'Orange" are equally exuberant – but, as I have argued, quite unsettling, if considered from the perspective of the female viewer or reader.

This erotic exuberance reflects Oldenburg's commitment to making art that "seems constantly alive," that is "full to the point of overflowing as life itself," as Barbara Rose puts it (9). At the same time, in keeping with the still-life tradition to which his work is responding, Oldenburg's objects convey reminders of mortality and impermanence. For example, when he creates a mock-monument by placing a giant lipstick on tank wheels, the object is referencing war, death, and destruction as much as it plays on ideas of (feminine) beauty and artifice. Likewise, his giant cigarette butts make us think of the pleasure of smoking *and* of the health risk that cigarette smoking entails. Both Ponge and Oldenburg are playing with the still life in unprecedented ways; nevertheless, both are consciously manipulating the genre's traditional meanings and motifs. Their work ties together tradition and innovation to an unusual degree. "The presence of death defines life," Oldenburg has said, echoing the insight which is most central to the still-life tradition (qtd. in Haskell 10).[10]

Derrida's *Signéponge*: Ponge Désigné

I have so far characterized the still life as a genre in which the painter's own subjectivity – or, better, human subjectivity in general – is all but absent. Yet, it is possible to detect the discreet near-invisible presence of the painter through his or her signature. Indeed, painters often place their own signature concealed in a corner of the picture – a fact of which Ponge is fully aware. A close reading of Ponge's prose poems reveals bits of the poet's name and initials playfully hidden within a number of his texts, as in these examples: "… se servir d'un couteau ébréché et *peu franc*, s'y reprendre à *plusieurs fois*" ("… to use a chipped, *not very honest* knife, to make *several attempts*") (*OC* Vol. I, 21, emphasis added); "Mais où *l'éponge* réussit toujours, l'orange jamais" ("But where *the sponge* always succeeds, the orange never does") (*OC* Vol. I, 20, emphasis added); "… sa *façon particulière* de *parfumer* l'air" ("… *its particular way* of *scenting* the air") (*OC* Vol. I, 20). These gestures of self-consciously fragmenting his name and inserting it into the text are ambiguous, though. On one level, this can be read as the equivalent of a painter's discreetly "signing" a canvas. Otherwise, one could assume that the poet is dispersing – or disseminating – bits of "himself" into his text, to promote the idea of a loss of "subjectivity" resulting from his commitment to taking the side of things. Then again, it is equally possible to see Ponge as taking possession of things, or as asserting his mastery over them, by these acts of "signature."

The ambiguous status of the signature in Ponge's work and the philosophical dilemmas surrounding the relationship of the author's signature / name / identity to the things about which he or she writes and to the texts he or she creates are the focus of Jacques Derrida's magisterial study *Signéponge* (1977) (*Signsponge* [1982]). Like all of Ponge's critics, Derrida acknowledges the poet's fascination with describing things and his proprietary desire to make the things which he describes "his own." Referring to the poet's contrasting the orange to the sponge ("l'éponge" in French) in "L'Orange," Derrida takes the sponge as a metapoetic metaphor for the peculiar acts of writing and naming central to Ponge's work:

> L'éponge – la chose *et* son nom. La chose
> *est* son nom …
> D'une part, l'éponge éponge le nom propre,
> le met hors de soi, l'efface et le perd, le souille aussi
> pour en faire un nom commun … Mais simultanément
> l'éponge peut retenir le nom, l'absorber, l'abriter en soi,
> le garder. (Derrida 65)

> (The sponge – the thing *and* its name. The thing
> *is* its / his name …
> On the one hand, the sponge expunges the proper
> name / noun, places it outside itself, erases it and loses it,
> *dirties* it as well in order to make it into a common
> noun … But simultaneously the sponge can hold onto
> the name, absorb it, shelter it within itself, keep it.)

Thus, "l'éponge" as a metaphor for (Ponge's) writing is able to perform – or cannot *not* perform – two mutually contradictory acts at once. These two acts (asserting identity and possession; obliterating identity and possession) constitute the self-divided but necessary basis for writing in Ponge's case. (Derrida assumes Ponge's writing as both idiosyncratically particular to him *and* as an exemplary case that reflects the status of post-modern European writing in general).

As Derrida reads further and further (into) Ponge's textuality, he demonstrates how the odd permutations of Ponge's name and initials, or "signature," end up "unsigning" ("désigner") the author from "his" text: "Le signe éponge la signature. Le signe éponge" ("The sign absorbs the signature. The sign absorbs") (Derrida 101). So, the more

Ponge's name(s) proliferate(s), the less stable his textualized subjectivity becomes. As Ponge practises it, writing operates, then, as an undoing, a deferral of presence and meaning, a taking apart of selfhood and identity. Ponge's obsession with "le propre" (which means both "what is clean" and "what is one's own" in French) acts as a symptom of anxieties of presence and subjectivity lying behind or within his fascination with things.

Derrida also plays deconstructively with the eroticism of Ponge's texts, with the feminization of things and the sexual metaphors there. He proposes a tongue-in-cheek reading of Francis Ponge's name / signature according to which "Francis" is a male / masculine / virile / active partner to "Ponge," his female / feminine / passive "other half":

> Éponge, diriez-vous, c'est une figure féminine plutôt ... matière passive
> ...
> Francis Ponge se sera donc bien marié. Avec
> lui-même d'abord. Francis et Ponge forment un couple
> hétérosexuel harmonieux. Francis tranche par sa virilité,
> il introduit la décision dans l'indécidable éponge, et Ponge
> la feminité – l'épouse – en prend son parti. Mais réintroduit sans cesse
> l'équivoque ignoble. (Derrida 67)

> (You would say that sponge is a rather feminine
> figure ... passive matter
> ...
> Francis Ponge will then have married himself.
> Francis and Ponge form a harmonious heterosexual
> couple. Francis cuts / is decisive [tranche] by his virility,
> he introduces decisiveness into the undecidable sponge,
> and Ponge, womanliness – the wife – makes the best of
> the situation [en prend son parti]. But constantly
> reintroduces ignoble uncertainty [l'équivoque].)

The signature (signifier for self) and the things to which it attaches itself are fused in an unstable mix, then. An act of signing whose meaning is ambiguous goes on and on. "Sa signature ... déborde. Se déborde" ("His signature ... overflows. Overflows itself"), Derrida writes (121). By tracing the continuous "débordement de la signature" ("overflowing of the signature") (81) central to Ponge's œuvre, Derrida makes clear that the standard tendency among Ponge's critics to unify the relationship between the describer / subject and the described / object into a stable relation performs a serious misreading of the ways in which the poet (un)writes the relation *between* subjectivity and objects.

Could one apply Derrida's insights on the "débordement de la signature" ("signature's overflowing") to a reconsideration of the place of subjectivity in the still-life tradition as a whole? If so, then his insights would force us to rethink the notion that, through writing or painting, the subject takes possession of, or asserts mastery over, the represented objects. One could no longer assume that human agency, located "outside" or "beyond" the frame, was nevertheless the absent centre supplying the coherence or meaning of the work. One would need to become attentive to the multiple ways in which human subjectivity (figured as name, signature, gaze or perspective) is, in fact, dispersed, problematized and transformed through its investment in the object world and its passage into the space of verbal or visual representation. Description, then, would be seen as a fundamentally ambivalent process of de-scription, linked as much to the displacement and dismantling of identities of subject and object as to reconstituting the referential world as words and images. Let us keep this approach in mind as we consider further examples of object poetry in the chapters to come.

4 Description as Transfiguration: Jean Follain's (Meta)Poetics of the Object

"Il ne s'agit pas de panégyrique, ô poète,
mais de voir les choses telles qu'elles sont."

– Follain, *Usage du temps*, 84

("The point is not to write a panegyric, o poet,
but to see things just as they are.")

"Sous le soleil tout apparaît
symbole de rien."

– Follain, *Espaces d'instants*, 19

("Under the sun everything appears
a symbol of nothing.")

"Durant un certain instant privilégié cet objet peut nous paraître en soi si précis qu'il en devient transfiguré, et un élément du mystère du monde, un motif irremplaçable d'appréhension de ce mystère. Ainsi tel objet, fût-il pratiquement médiocre ou inutilisable, en devient poétiquement nécessaire, affirmatif de la nécessité de la poésie même."

– Follain, qtd. in *Lire Follain* 26

("During a certain privileged instant an object can appear to us to be in and of itself so precise that it becomes transfigured, and an element of the world's mystery, an irreplaceable motif for fathoming this mystery. Thus, a particular object, even if it be practically mediocre or useless, becomes poetically necessary, affirming *the necessity of poetry itself.*")

"Ce sont d'ailleurs les vocables les plus usés, les plus détériorés, ceux qu'on appelle couramment les plus simples qui se transfigurent de la façon la mieux visible, la plus réelle. Ceux-ci ont été chargés à travers le temps abondamment d'émotion, de pensée, de vérité et d'hypocrisie."

– Follain, "Le Langage de la poésie," 16

("It is the most worn-out words, the most deteriorated ones, those generally called the simplest, which are transfigured in the most obvious and realest fashion. Those words have become abundantly weighted down over time with emotion, thought, truth and hypocrisy.")

Jean Follain (1903–71) is, along with Ponge, the twentieth-century French poet whom critics have most often called a "poète de l'objet."[1] In his collections of poetry, from *La Main chaude* (*A Run of Luck*) (1933) to posthumous volumes such as *Ordre terrestre* (*Earthly Order*) (1986), he organizes nearly every poem around two or more scenes from everyday life, set within a more or less distant past. The silent presence of objects in these poems provides a focus for the observed scene. Follain's use of these objects to centre his texts also emerges in his autobiographical prose works, such as *Canisy* (1942) or *L'Epicerie d'enfance* (*The Childhood Grocery Store*) (1938), which feature domestic scenes and sketches proceeding by description, rather than action. (These texts read somewhat like a novel minus its plot.) Follain's fascination with objects and his commitment to developing a poetics out of this fascination create a potent link between his work and that of the great still-life painters.

Perhaps the best starting-point for approaching this body of work is the series of prose reflections on objects presented in the first of the three segments of Follain's 1947 book of prose poems, *Tout instant.* In these brief meditations on things, the poet valorizes, in particular, the uniqueness of individual objects, as well as their ability to act as containers or signifiers for the passage of time, as in the following prose poem:

> *Un chant s'élève de chaque objet.* L'artisan y a enfermé
> un peu de son corps qui avait bien connu l'amour, puis avait
> porté longtemps une maladie, à moins qu'il ne se fût
> simplement éteint de vieillesse. Chant du bois, de l'acier, du
> cuivre. On entend à travers les siècles ricaner les bourreaux,
> les filles rire d'une voix sauvage, les folles bêler, l'enfant

gazouiller. *L'objet ne s'évanouit pas*. On trouve de si multiples choses dans les poches des voyageurs: des canifs, de petits carnets, une minuscule vis oubliée lors d'un démontage, un bout de ficelle entortillé, quelques graines de carottes ou de panais, de ces mêmes graines que l'homme, alors sédentaire et courbé vers la terre, lançait dans le petit sillon qu'il avait creusé dans la plate-bande de l'enclos. Devant les yeux du promeneur, l'horizon se dilue. Lui, porte en tête maint secret, des restes d'amour, des désirs un moment consistants, mais qui s'évaporent *tandis que l'objet, même s'il l'a oublié, reste en poche comme un talisman*. Fouillant un jour les vieux vêtements *dans lesquels notre corps alourdi et guetté, fût-ce de très loin par la mort*, n'entre plus, on retrouve le rouage d'une frêle machine dont on doit faire effort pour retrouver l'usage. On le retourne longtemps entre ses doigts alors qu'au loin se couche un soleil d'histoire. (TI 11–12, emphasis added)

(*A song rises from each object.* The artisan who made it enclosed within it a little of his body, which had known love well, then had been ill for a long time, unless it had simply been extinguished by old age. A song of wood, of steel, of copper. Across the centuries you can hear executioners snickering, girls laughing in a savage voice, mad women wailing, a child babbling. *The object does not swoon.* Such a variety of things can be found in travellers' pockets: pocketknives, little notepads, a tiny screw forgotten during a dismantling of something, a bit of knotted string, a few carrot or parsnip seeds, the same type of seed which the man, who was then squatting and bent towards earth used to throw into the little furrow that he had dug in the flowerbed of the paddock. Before the eyes of the person strolling, the horizon blurs. *He* carries many a secret in his mind, leftover love, desires which had briefly had consistency, but which evaporate *whereas the object, even if he has forgotten it, stays in his pocket like a talisman.* One day as we are going through our old clothes into which our body, made heavy and awaited, very distantly, by death, no longer fits, we find the cog of a frail machine whose use we must make an effort to remember. We keep turning it over for a long time between our fingers while in the distance a historical sun sets.)

In this passage, as in Follain's poems, (almost) nothing "happens." The speaker simply notes that, as if by magic, ordinary objects such as a pen-knife, a tiny screw or a bit of tangled string found by chance in a coat pocket can become catalysts for an intense and sudden reliving of moments from the past (one's own past or a more general, shared past of humanity). One is reminded of Proust's narrator's unexpected discovery / recovery of "lost time" via the madeleine in *Combray*, except that, here (as is characteristic of Follain's world view) the objects evoked are humbler and devoid of symbolism. Where Proust's Madeleine can be read as a metaphor for spiritual meanings (its shell-like shape recalls the shells displayed on Christian pilgrims' clothing and the madeleine functions, metaphorically, like a communion water), Follain's objects resist being read as anything other than themselves. Where metaphor is central to the significance of Proust's great novel, Follain, as he himself and his critics agree, completely eschews metaphorization. The poet has, indeed, declared that "[l]a comparaison – la métaphore c'est la comparaison – m'horripile un peu. Je l'aime beaucoup chez les autres … Mais moi je ne veux pas l'employer parce que j'ai trop le sentiment que les choses sont incomparables" ("[c]omparisons – metaphor is a comparison – exasperate me a bit. I like them in other people's work … But I myself do not want to use them because I am too aware that things cannot be compared to one another.")[2]

Although the short text from *Tout instant* quoted above is designated as a "prose poem" by its author, it appears curiously lacking in any overt poetic effects or techniques. The lyricism here, as elsewhere in Follain, is modest, muted. The banality of the objects named in this text belies their assimilation by the speaker to lyrical effusiveness ("Chant du bois, de l'acier, du cuivre"). Much as a still-life painter invites us to find profound and dazzling beauty and meaningfulness in humble, everyday things, Jean Follain seeks to discover a sense of transcendence through the contemplation of seemingly banal objects. He then renders this sense of transcendence in words. Elsewhere in *Tout instant*, Follain writes that "[l]a finesse des choses donne sa noblesse à l'univers. Derrière chacune un mot de passe reste caché" ("[t]he refinement of things gives nobility to the universe. Behind each one a password remains hidden") (TI 13). Similarly, in one of the passages I quoted as the epigraph to this chapter, he writes: "Durant un instant privilégié cet objet peut nous paraître en soi si précis qu'il en devient transfiguré, et un élément du mystère du monde, un motif irremplaçable d'appréhension de ce mystère" ("For one privileged instant this particular object can appear to us so precise in and of itself that it becomes transfigured, and an element of earth's mystery, an irreplaceable reason for fathoming this mystery"). While a lyrical self seems absent from the text, the objects described and juxtaposed on the page by the poet become a conduit for emotion. An act of substitution grounds Follain's poetics of the object as memories and images surface in the poem by means of the objects: "On entend à travers les siècles ricaner les bourreaux, les filles rire d'une voix sauvage, les folles bêler, l'enfant gazouiller" ("Across the centuries one can hear executioners snickering, girls laughing a savage laugh, madwomen wailing, a child babbling.") The solid, tangible presence of the objects constitutes an unwavering centre for the text and an indispensable resource for the poet's creativity.

Time and mortality are a constant preoccupation in Follain's work, as the ending of the above poem suggests: "Fouillant un jour les vieux vêtements dans lesquels notre corps alourdi et guetté, fût-ce de très loin par la mort" ("One day, going through old clothes which our body, gone heavy, which death awaits from far away"). In a characteristic gesture which is, once again, evocative of the traditional thematics of the still-life tradition, he unearths reminders of death and mortality in supposedly uneventful or neutral scenes. Time has a polyvalent function in Follain's work. The poet is equally preoccupied with the notion of the instant – that is, the moment of time when a change or disruption of routine and of harmony suddenly occurs – and the idea of duration. Duration is present in his poems by means of the evocation of long periods of time whose vestiges remain detectable in a particular scene occurring decades, or even centuries, later. This foregrounding of the representation of temporality once again recalls Proust's work.

To place these thematic considerations in context, let us turn now to a reading of a Follain poem, "Choses et êtres," which appears in the collection *D'après tout* (*As Everything Goes*) (1967):

Choses et êtres
Dans les faubourgs on entend
gémir des presses
tirer le vin
et même en temps de guerre.
Tout près les âcres herbes
le renard malheureux
une joueuse nue à demi
une corbeille vide

la route monotone
une question qu'on pose. (*D'après tout* 10)

(Things and Beings
In the outlying districts one hears
presses sighing
as they draw wine
even in wartime.
Very near by the bitter grasses
the unhappy fox
a half-naked woman playing
an empty basket
the monotonous road
a question someone asks.)

At first glance, the poem is unremarkable. Terse and unemphatic, it first presents one ordinary event, the working of a wine-press in a suburban setting. It then shifts to a rather banal landscape, where elements are noted in a sort of list: "le renard malheureux / une joueuse nue à demi / une corbeille vide / la route monotone / une question qu'on pose." Why should we pay attention to this scene, one might ask?

In answer, I would like, first, to appeal to remarks made by the poet Eugène Guillevic in his tribute to Follain, "Un poète majeur" ("A Major Poet"), published in 1981, ten years after Follain's death. Guillevic, who knew him well and who ranks among Follain's most insightful readers, acknowledges that Follain has often been misread: "Follain a été tout de suite admis comme poète, admis et loué. Mais, à mon avis, souvent à faux. On ne l'a pas compris et encore maintenant beaucoup ne le comprennent pas. On l'a considéré comme un petit maître et ses poèmes comme des tableautins" ("Follain was immediately acknowledged as an important poet, admired and praised. But, in my view, often mistakenly. People did not understand him and still today many people do not understand him. He was considered a minor poet and his poems, little pictures") (17). Contradicting this conventional view of Follain as a minor figure, Guillevic declares: "Pour moi, Follain est un grand poète," adding that "ce n'était pas la grande histoire qui le passionnait, plutôt les petites choses où se révélaient les grandes, et les rapports humains dans l'histoire. Aussi l'a-t-on pris pour un miniaturiste, on n'apercevait pas la profondeur, disons, métaphysique, de l'histoire" ("For me, Follain is a great poet," adding that "what excited him was not History but little things in which big events revealed themselves, and human relationships in history. Thus, he was taken for a miniaturist, people did not notice the, shall we say, metaphysical depth of history [in his poems]") (17). Like Guillevic, many of the most celebrated poets of Follain's own generation and later generations have identified him as a key figure in twentieth-century French poetry. Philippe Jaccottet, André Frenaud, Jean Tardieu, Jean Tortel, and Jacques Réda have written critical essays and poems in praise of Follain's artistry.[3] If our cursory initial reading of "Choses et êtres" has concluded that the poem shows us nothing of interest, perhaps, then, we need to reconsider our reading of this poem before proceeding further.

In reassessing the poem, we might begin by speculating about the reasons for the poet's bringing together of "things" and "beings" in, and as, the title. What sort of relationship between animate and inanimate elements of this poem – or of the extratextual world towards which it gestures – does he intend us to perceive? The title the poet has chosen hides a question, then. Our discovery of a question hidden behind the title of the poem is all the more appropriate, given that the poem ends, literally, with "une question qu'on pose." So, although one may have (mis)taken "Choses et êtres" for a bland listing of a few randomly chosen bits of a scene from everyday life, it should already be apparent that an implicit questioning of what "reality" is and how one perceives it provides the impetus for the writing of this text.

The statement made in the first four lines is straightforward. However, two unusual details stand out in these lines: the wine-presses *moan* ("on entend / gémir des presses") and the action of the presses continues "même en temps de guerre." The possibility of war as a backdrop disturbs the otherwise tranquil scene, even as the assigning of a human attribute (moaning) to an inanimate thing disrupts the stable binary opposition positing "things" and "beings" as separate and clearly differentiated from one another.

As we pursue our rereading of "Choses et êtres," Follain's careful artistry is further evident. The second half of the poem lists six elements: three things ("choses"), two beings ("êtres") and one abstract noun. This abstract noun ("une question qu'on pose"), like the verb "gémir" and the reference to war earlier in the poem, introduces a disruption. The binary pair named in the title ("Things and Beings") must now accommodate a third category – if we accept that a question is not a concrete thing like grass, a basket or a road, the other things named in the poem's last lines. Follain's poems gravitate towards *order* and *harmony* (his critics and the poet himself frequently use these particular terms to define his textual world and one of his main collections carries the title *Ordre terrestre*). However, because of this tendency, readers have often overemphasized the sense of order in his texts. In "Choses et êtres," and in other Follain poems we will study, what threatens to disrupt "order" may, in fact, be the dominant feature of the poem – that is, the feature upon which the meaning of the poem ultimately depends.

In the listing of noun phrases presented in the second half of "Choses et êtres," the poet juxtaposes elements among which there appears to be no common denominator: "les âcres herbes / le renard malheureux / une joueuse nue à demi / une corbeille vide / la route monotone / une question qu'on pose." The choice of nouns used to compose the list may look random, but the adjectives which Follain has chosen as qualifiers for these nouns discloses a nascent thematic development in these final six lines: the grasses are "âcres" (bitter); the fox is "malheureux" (unhappy); the girl playing is "nue à demi" (half-naked); the road is "monotone" (monotonous), and the question has no accompanying answer. Each adjective suggests negativity or absence. Precisely, by suggestion, the poet leads the reader towards a deepened awareness of the complexities of the real – and of the literary representation of the real.

If I have lingered over explicating "Choses et êtres" at length, this critical gesture is strategic. As Guillevic noted in his remarks in "Un Poète majeur" quoted earlier, Jean Follain's work has often been misread. His body of work, therefore, needs to be (re)placed in its full context, if we are to reach a better understanding of Follain's contribution to French poetry. In particular, I would argue that his work has not yet been appreciated as an important response to the development of modernism in France. If read superficially, his texts give the impression of reproducing a lost world of the past, specifically Canisy or Saint-Lô, the site of the author's childhood in Normandy in the years before the First World War. Many readers have seen, and dismissed, Follain as a poet of facile nostalgia, interested only in reviving traces of an earlier historical period. Distracted by the apparently conservative content and spirit of his verse and prose, these readers have missed the more innovative and challenging aspects of his work.

To measure Follain's contribution to French poetry, one must realize that he had strong personal and aesthetic connections to several of the key proponents of modernism. His links with Max Jacob, Ponge, and Reverdy were especially decisive. Max Jacob acted as Follain's poetic mentor during the early years of the young poet's career. Follain's own ideas on poetry and poetics were very much shaped by Jacob's views and example. Indeed, in Follain's essays and talks on poetry, he frequently quotes Jacob, acknowledging him as a major influence. He writes, for instance, that "Max Jacob accorde la chance la plus grande de vivre à certaines œuvres qui ayant eu l'apparence du superficiel ont pourtant passé par le gouffre du sérieux" ("Max Jacob grants the greatest chance of survival to certain works that, although they may have seemed superficial, nevertheless were able to cross the gulf of seriousness").[4] Follain's own poetry would be a perfect illustration of the type of work described by Jacob in this quotation. (One discovers, indeed, that each time he quotes Jacob, the older poet's ideas are echoed in Follain's poetic practice).

It was Pierre Reverdy who arguably provided the most powerfully influential model for the constitution of Follain's poetics. Whereas Jacob served as the source for many of Follain's basic ideas about poetic representation, Reverdy's example permeates Follain's work at every level. Like Jacob, Reverdy shaped Follain's thinking about language, form, and representation. Quotations from Reverdy's essays and aphorisms from *Le gant de crin* (*The Horsehair Glove*), *Le Livre de mon bord* (*The Book From My Viewpoint*), *Cette émotion appelée poésie* (*This Emotion Called Poetry*), and other books appear in nearly all of Follain's writings on poetics. However, I would contend that Reverdy's influence on Follain is more unconscious than conscious. The formal and thematic concerns of Reverdy's textual world haunt the younger man's poems. This ghostly presence / absence of Reverdy accounts, in part, for the uncanny feeling which so many of Follain's poems can induce in the reader.

A comparison between a representative poem by Reverdy and one by Follain will underscore the interrelatedness of their achievements. The poem "Tard dans la nuit" from *Les Ardoises du toit* (*Roof Slates*) reveals many of the characteristic features of Reverdy's poetry, which we encountered in chapter 2:

Tard dans la nuit ...
La couleur que décompose la nuit
La table où ils se sont assis
Le verre en cheminée
La lampe est un cœur qui se vide

C'est une autre année
    Une nouvelle ride
Y aviez-vous déjà pensé
    La fenêtre déverse un carré bleu
La porte est plus intime
  Une séparation
    Le remords et le crime
Adieu je tombe
  Et c'est un coin
Des bras qui me reçoivent
Du coin de l'œil je vois tous ceux qui boivent
  Je n'ose pas bouger
Ils sont assis
    La table est ronde
Et ma mémoire aussi
Je me souviens de tout le monde
Même de ceux qui sont partis. (1918)

    (Late in the night ...
The colour which night decomposes
The table where they are sitting
The chimney glass
    The lamp is a heart being emptied
It's another year
    A new wrinkle
Had you already thought of that
    The window spills out a blue square
The door is more intimate
  A separation
    Remorse and crime
Farewell I'm falling
  And it's a corner
Arms opening to receive me
From the corner of my eye I see them all drinking
I dare not move
They are seated
    The table is round
And so is my memory
I remember everyone
    Even the ones who have left.)

This short, cryptic poem presents an impersonal scene with no fixed viewpoint. Each line of the poem stands out as a solitary fragment related (or unrelated?) to the others. The first-person subject is in a marginal position with respect to the scene described. Objects assume a primary importance: the table, the lamp, the window, the door. Abstract nouns (separation, remorse, crime) become almost tangible and similar in function to the concrete nouns. Significantly, the poem ends with a statement concerning memory and forgetting – a frequent and ambivalent theme in Reverdy's poetry.

Now let us turn to another poem from Follain's 1967 collection *D'après tout*:

Force des choses
Croyant entendre frapper
on prend la lampe on ouvre la porte
pour ne trouver que le vent
ce n'est pas le vieil infirme
ni la bête effarée
qui frôlante et tremblante
jouit pourtant d'exister
toutes les fenêtres sont bien fermées.
Beaucoup
refusent le souvenir
mais l'oubli n'est complet jamais. (Jean Follain. *D'après tout* 37)

(The Force of Things
Thinking you hear a knock
you take the lamp you open the door
and find there only the wind
it is neither the sickly old man
nor the terrified animal
who, barely touching and trembling,
nonetheless delights in existing
all the windows are tightly closed.
Many people
refuse to remember
but nothing is completely forgotten.]

It should be clear that Follain's choice of objects here is directly influenced by Reverdy, whose poems obsessively return to a naming of *"the* door," "*the* window," "*the* lamp" – all of which are present in "Force des choses." Follain's use of impersonal third-person pronouns in this case ("on prend la lampe," "Beaucoup / refusent") also reiterates a standard feature of the older poet's work. Like most of Reverdy's poems, "Force des choses" is only one page long. Its coherence depends upon an organizing of discrete fragments into a more or less unified scene. The thematics presented in Follain's poem echo those of Reverdy's texts too; waiting, absence, and confinement generate a mood of disquiet in "Force des choses," much as they do in the poems of *Plupart du temps* (*Most of the Time*). Most tellingly, Follain's poem concludes with a general, perhaps metaphysical statement about memory and forgetting, proving how thoroughly he is a disciple of Reverdy. I do not mean to imply that Follain has "copied" Reverdy's work or that his poetry lacks originality. Rather, I am suggesting that one's assessment of the significance of Follain's achievement is incomplete without an understanding of the profound struggle with the major figures of French poetic modernism that shaped his poetry. At this point, the theories of poetic influence formulated by Harold Bloom in *The Anxiety of Influence: A Theory of Poetry* (1973) will help clarify the ways in which Follain is responding to Reverdy's poetry and the consequences of this response.

Bloom's theory posits that literary history is constituted by each writer's struggle to overcome the influence of his or her precursors in order to assert and impose his or her own voice. This struggle with the great works of the past takes place at a largely unconscious level and plays itself out in a highly charged, violent manner. Bloom appeals to Sigmund Freud's theory of the Oedipus complex, transforming Freud's model for the psychosexual development of the human subject into a metaphorical battle in which the younger poet (or "ephebe") labours to defeat (the influence of) the great poets who preceded him (the "strong poets," in Bloom's terminology). Just as Freud's Oedipal (male) subject unconsciously wishes to kill the Father and sleep with the Mother, Bloom's ephebe wishes to beget his progeny (i.e., his texts) by consorting with the Muse, having overcome the influence of his literary "Fathers," whose work he felt had overshadowed his own. Bloom describes several distinct phases through which the younger poet must pass in his coming to terms with his precursors' influence in order to avoid merely repeating what the precursors had already written. The first of these phases is called "clinamen," referring to a swerving away from the precursor's work, from the themes or tropes most characteristic of the precursor's style.

If we re-examine Follain's "Force des choses," we can, I think, see the effects of clinamen in several lines. Although "Force des choses" does repeat many notable features of Reverdy's verse, it also reorients and deflects the precursor's thematics in important ways. A mood of anxiety and uncertainty surfaces in most of Reverdy's texts. Follain, here, evokes a sense of fear and uneasiness but, in line seven, contradicts and challenges this feeling of fear, stating that the terrified beast / animal "jouit pourtant d'exister." (This line is all the more pregnant with meaning, given that the title of one of Follain's best-known collections of poetry is *Exister*.) The ending of "Force des choses" extends this rewriting and changing of Reverdy's poetry further: "Beaucoup / refusent le souvenir / mais / l'oubli n'est complet jamais." In Reverdy, the danger of forgetting and loss is always present. For him, writing can seem a futile struggle to retrieve and preserve what cannot, ultimately, be preserved. Follain, on the contrary, swerves away from this world view (to use Bloom's term, this constitutes an instance of "clinamen"). Unconsciously, he is responding to the powerful but oppressive example of Reverdy's poetry by altering the direction and force of his precursor's work. Although Follain does not attempt the daring and radical experiments with typography and representation that typify Reverdy's work during his Cubist period, the uses of fragmentation and the shifts in perspective in Follain's verse nonetheless pay tribute to the influence of modernist (Reverdian) poetics. Thus, his work is deeply indebted to modernism on a number of levels. As already stated, Max Jacob's ideas about poetics are of decisive importance for him. In particular, Follain's absorption of Jacob's idea of the poem as an object – articulated most famously in the preface to *Le Cornet à dés* (*The Dice Cup*), as we saw in chapter 1 – links his work to the sort of self-conscious and aesthetically sophisticated metapoetics that is central to the modernist poets' achievement.

At the simplest level, the assimilation of the poem to the status of an object is a consequence of Follain's sense of the writing of poetry as an artisanal act: "Si insolite que paraisse son contour, quelle que soit sa dimension," he writes, "un poème doit être façonné, artisanalement façonné" (However odd its shape may seem, whatever its size, a poem must be crafted, crafted as though by an artisan).[5] Moreover, he repeatedly refers to Jacob's view of the poem as an "objet construit" (a constructed object):

> Pour rester dans le mot objet, Max Jacob
> ne pensait-il pas comme, au fond, tous les

poètes que le poème lui-même devait être
un objet soumis à sa propre densité, comme
suspendu dans l'espace et s'y trouvant entouré
comme d'une zone de silence? Il disait alors
que le poème se trouvait "situé." Il y fallait mots
et syntaxe appropriés.

(To continue with the word object, didn't Max
Jacob think that, basically, like all poets, the
poem itself must be an object submitting to its own
density, as if suspended in space and finding itself
surrounded by a zone of silence? He said that then
the poem was "situated." The appropriate words and syntax were
necessary [if this was to be achieved].)[6]

Follain's own poems are generally ten to fourteen lines long, with each line containing six to ten syllables. The poems sits like a dense block of words on the white page. A Follain poem acquires an air of solidity and concreteness; in a sense, it resembles an object.

Follain's critics have noted the overarching importance that this symbiotic relationship between the text and the object has in the formulation of his poetics. Henri Thomas remarks that a Follain poem "est lui-même objet, à la fois ouvert et secret" ("is itself an object, both open and secretive") (12). Jacques Réda carries the analogy even further, in describing one of the short poems from *Territoires* as follows: "la pièce ainsi obtenue, d'une extrême densité, d'un grain extrêmement serré, devient elle-même un objet brut dont les arêtes sont soulignées par chaque retour à la ligne, dont chaque facette est mise en valeur sans nuire pourtant à l'unité organique de l'ensemble" ("the poem thus produced, which is extremely dense, and has a very tight texture [d'un grain extrêmement serré], becomes itself a rough object whose stops are underscored by each line break, and whose every facet is emphasized without diminishing at all the organic unity of the poem as a whole") (126). Elsewhere, Alain Lévêque offers a more fanciful transformation of poem into thing: "Le poème follainien, quand il est réussi … quand il prend, comme monte une pâte, acquiert alors la consistance, la gravité, la finesse d'un objet, d'une chose faite de main d'homme et tenue avec la tendresse, le respect qu'elle mérite" "A Follain poem, when it is successful … when it comes together [quand il prend], as dough rises, acquires the consistency, the gravity / seriousness, and the fineness of an object, a manmade thing held with the tenderness and respect which it deserves") (117). Accordingly, a completed Follain poem "gagne la présence, le poids, l'évidence d'un fruit posé sur une table de cuisine que dore le couchant. Il se tient là – c'est tout – pour notre jouissance, à portée immédiate de notre mémoire et de nos sens, à portée surtout de notre langage, comme un objet familier que l'on voit enfin véritablement" ("achieves the presence, the weight, and the factualness [évidence] of a fruit placed on a kitchen table lit by the light of sunset. It lies there – that's all – within immediate reach of our memory and our senses, above all within reach of our language, like a familiar object which one at last truly sees") (117).

Follain himself would certainly share these notions of the consubstantiality and equivalency of word and thing, of text and object. When discussing his views on language, he tends to assign words much the same status he gives to things. Just as his poems and prose texts focus generally on objects that have existed for long periods of time and that bear traces of their multilayered history, the poet also prefers to valorize words which show the effects of their long existence: "Ce sont d'ailleurs les vocables les plus usés, les plus détériorés, ceux qu'on appelle couramment les plus simples qui se transfigurent de la façon la mieux visible, la plus réelle" ("It is, besides, the most worn-out words, the most deteriorated ones, those commonly considered the simplest which most visibly and authentically become transfigured"), he writes.[7] Follain's faith in words and his conviction that the relationship between words and things is not purely arbitrary has far-reaching consequences for the interpretation of his work. His short prose text "L'H de l'attelage et le sang du dragon" (EE 75–6) will help to highlight the direction of his thinking on this complex issue. In "L'H de l'attelage et le sang du dragon," the narrator tells an anecdote centering on a child's discovery of a metal letter "H" on the ground as he is walking one day in the country:

> Il se promenait dans les allées et, sous un ciel
> où passaient les cumulus, contemplait les plates-
> bandes du potager: graines serrées, tiges vieilles,
> feuilles silencieuses pleines de canaux, étaient là
> rassemblées … Devant le plus grand carré …
> il aperçut une lueur dans une motte durcie … Il
> s'arrêta, prit au sol remué la motte hérissée et

> *dégagea la chose luisante, une lettre de métal, un H classique, strictement construit avec sa barre reliant le milieu de chaque jambe parallèle, avec deux empattements à chaque jambe; c'était une lettre solide et point grêle.* (emphasis added)
>
> (He was walking in the paths / lanes and, beneath a sky where cumulus clouds were passing, he contemplated the beds of the vegetable garden: seeds planted closely together, old stalks, silent leaves full of veins (canaux), were gathered there. … Before the biggest one … he noticed something gleaming in a hardened clod of earth … He stopped, took the rough clod from the disturbed ground and *pulled the shining thing, which was a letter made of metal, a classic H, carefully made with its horizontal line linking the middle of each parallel vertical leg; with two joinings* [*empattements*] *on each leg; it was a solid, not at all slender letter.*)

In this anecdote the letter "H" is understood fully as a *thing*. It becomes a piece of language hidden in nature, waiting to be found by a wandering child who is daydreaming. This childlike fantasy in which letters are transformed into a part of the natural world reflects Follain's faith in language, his wish-fulfilling assimilation of letters and words to the things they represent.

As the anecdote concerning "L'H de l'attelage" continues, the child asks his grandmother (whose surname begins with "H") what the significance of the mysterious letter might be:

> Alors la vieille dame prit *l'objet*, le considéra, le retourna sans apparente émotion, ses yeux épiant l'arête vive et le contour, et déclara: "Ça vient de l'attelage."
>
> C'était le vieil H d'une des cocardes de l'attelage des beaux jours fructifiants, attelage dispersé depuis cinquante ans. (emphasis added)

(Then the old lady took *the object*,
considered it, turned it over with no
apparent emotion, as her eyes focused
on the sharp edge and the contour,
and she declared: "This comes from
the carriage."
It was the old H from one of the
carriage crests from the glorious old days, a
carriage dismantled and scattered for fifty
years.)

Like the other objects that grace Follain's texts, this letter "H" carries with it an aura of past time that imparts a sense of mystery and strangeness to the scene described. The ending to this brief anecdote further reinforces the associations between the objects of the natural world and writing which form the basis for a fantasy which subtends Follain's entire œuvre. Having discovered the hidden letter "H," the boy now comes across a plant with unusual properties, "une plante dont le nom lui revenait mal à la mémoire": "Comme il l'interrogeait de nouveau, la grand-mère dit: 'C'est du sang de dragon, tu t'en servais, petit, pour faire de l'encre rouge" ("a plant whose name he had difficulty remembering": "As he began to ask her more questions, the grandmother said: 'It's dragon's blood, you used it when you were a little boy to make red ink'"). The small boy has learned, then, that letters of the alphabet can become things, and that natural objects like plants can produce the ink necessary for the writing of texts. By its double assimilation of language to nature and nature to language, "L'H de l'attelage et le sang du dragon" allows the reader to enter into one of the most essential, but most problematic, fantasies that underpin Follain's literary creativity, one could argue. If Follain is so convinced that there is an adequation between language and things, should we then dismiss him as a reactionary or a naive writer? Does he share the perspective of a Romantic poet like Victor Hugo, who dreamed of the consubstantiality of language and nature? How do Follain's perhaps childlike views about the closeness between language and nature relate to the influence of modernist aesthetics on his work?

To explore these issues – these apparent contradictions – in more depth, I would like to turn now to a discussion of some other ways in which Follain approaches objects in order to derive a poetics from their presence. The connections between his texts and the two areas of painting; cataloguing and collecting will elucidate critical issues at the core of his profound but odd engagement with the realm of objects.

Follain and Chardin: Still Life and the Feminine

"J'aime que mon texte se place dans un format déterminé, comme quand on est devant une toile. Et après avoir écrit une page de prose, il m'arrive de dire qu'il me manque un rouge ou qu'il me manque un gris. Ce rouge ne sera pas donné par un toit rouge, non il sera donné par un 'que,' par une conjonction ou par un mot qui articulera la phrase. Ce sera rouge pour moi."

– Follain, RSH 169

("I like my texts to be placed in a well-defined format, as when one stands before a painting. And after writing a page of prose, I sometimes say that I need some red or I need some gray. This kind of red will never be given to me by a red roof, no it will be given by a 'that' [que], by a conjunction or by a word which will articulate the meaning of the sentence. That will be a red for me."]

"Chaque chose pourtant veillait et travaillait pour sauver son éternité."
– Follain, "Natures mortes" ("Still Lifes") ET 63

("Each thing nonetheless was watching and kept working to save its eternity.")

Almost all of Follain's critics state that his poems resemble pictures. Jean Rousselot, for instance, writes of Follain's œuvre that "[e]n ce Canisy intérieur qui est devenu le nôtre, tout se déroule avec lenteur et gravité dans une lumière dorée, les choses sont dans un ordre parfait ... les êtres plongés dans une sorte d'attente méditative qui suspend l'écroulement fatal des chairs, l'écoulement implacable du temps. *Il y a là du Vermeer, du Chardin et du still life*" ("[i]n that inner Canisy which has become our own, everything occurs slowly and gravely in a golden light, things are in perfect order ... and all beings are plunged into a sort of meditative waiting which suspends the fatal collapse of the flesh, and the implacable flowing away of time. [*In Follain's texts*] *there is an element of Vermeer, of Chardin, and of still life*") (15). In like fashion, André Frénaud equates a Follain poem with a painting: "Au point de perfection où il a porté son art, ce sont les couleurs et la tendre chaleur humaine des objets qui progressent jusque vers nous et nous éclairent comme dans ce tableau de Renoir la petite fille qui lit, c'est son livre qui l'illumine" ("At the point of perfection to which he has carried his art, it is the colours and the tender human warmth of the objects that move toward us and enlighten us, as in that Renoir painting of the little girl reading, it is her book which illuminates her").[8]

One of the most insightful readers of Follain with respect to the links to painting in his poetry was Francis Ponge. Follain reports in his *Agendas* that on one occasion, Ponge expressed admiration for his work by comparing his poems to the paintings of Chardin: Ponge "compare le poème de son ami à un Chardin ou à une 'pomme mouillée' (A 178)" ("compares his friend's poem to a Chardin painting or to a 'moist apple'"] (Rouffiat 209). The comparison to the art of Chardin is especially apt, as the eighteenth-century French artist's career and words closely parallel those of Follain. Like Follain, Chardin was dismissed as a minor figure by many of his contemporaries. As still life (in which Chardin excelled) was considered a minor, "low" genre within the hierarchy of the genres prevailing in the eighteenth century (as we have seen herein previously), Chardin was relegated to a secondary status within French art until the mid-nineteenth century.[9] Chardin's own personal modesty and his commitment to still life and domestic genre paintings favouring a realistic focus surely contributed to the critical misevaluation of his work; in this, his fortunes as an artist recall those of Follain as a poet. In a short article entitled "Un Peintre subversif qui s'ignore" ("An Unconsciously Subversive Painter"), Pierre Rosenberg explains that Chardin's paintings are misleading in their surface simplicity and banality:

> Rien de plus simple, en apparence, que l'art de Chardin. Au premier coup d'œil et sans aucune hésitation, on comprend les sujets de ses tableaux. Rien de plus banal que ces lièvres et ces lapins morts, ces ustensiles de cuisine ou ces portraits au pastel, ces femmes faisant la lessive ou ces garçonnets construisant des châteaux de cartes ... Simplicité trompeuse qui a laissé dans l'embarras les historiens d'art et jusqu'aux écrivains forcés d'admettre qu'ils "n'entend[aient] rien à cette magie." (27)

(Nothing is simpler, apparently, than Chardin's art. At first glance and without hesitation, one understands the subjects of his pictures. Nothing is more banal than those dead hares and rabbits, those kitchen utensils or those pastel portraits, those women doing laundry or those small boys building castles of cards ... A deceptive simplicity which has left art historians perplexed and which has even forced writers to admit that they "understand nothing of this magic.")

However, as Rosenberg goes on to demonstrate, once one moves beyond a superficial response to his work, Chardin's genius becomes evident. In a century that admired history painting – that is, the representation of grand historical or Biblical scenes – above all, Chardin remained steadfastly committed to the representation of what he saw before him. Like Follain, he reinvented realism for his century. Again like Follain, he focused in his paintings on single moments of time in which a revelation or transformation seems about to unfold (perhaps). These silent, ambiguous moments fascinate and frustrate the beholder, who wonders what the figure in the painting (most often, a woman or a child), is thinking: a servant girl who has returned home from the market (*La Pourvoyeuse* [*The (Female) Provider*]), or a servant drawing water from a cistern, or a child blowing soap-bubbles or a child playing with a spinning top.

At the same time, the domestic subject matter in these paintings (as in Follain's poems) accounts for only part of their interest. The artist and the poet are actually exploring complex aesthetic issues through their representation of scenes of everyday life. As Philip Conisbee points out, "Chardin creates an extraordinarily strong sense of physical presence – but it is the physical presence of paint that we really experience, in the cunning guise of still-life objects" (90). Critics of Follain's poetry and of Chardin's art very frequently single out the impression of "unity" and "harmony" that both men's works produce (e.g., Conisbee writes of Chardin (19): "For him, the act of representation was a discovery of unity"). This sense of unity and harmony perfectly expresses the dual focus of the poet's and the artist's works: an exploration of aesthetic techniques for recreating a scene taken from reality combined with an abiding concern with capturing and rendering the salient features of that extra-aesthetic reality.

Follain's and Chardin's fundamental aesthetic and thematic concerns are thus closely related. One particular area of convergence between the two men's artistic concerns that is very notable is the representation of women and the connections between the feminine and domestic space as the source of inspiration and subject matter. As Philip Conisbee notes, "Chardin's pictorial world is inhabited almost entirely by women and children ... His women range up the social scale from scullery-maids, to governesses, to bourgeois mothers, and as far up as one or two rather grander bourgeois ladies. It is a quiet domestic world of attention to everyday routines, interrupted only by absorption in other thoughts which momentarily distract from the task in hand" (178). The inclusion of so many women in these paintings is not, per se, grounds for critical attention, necessarily. However, the kinds of values implicitly linked to women and the feminine in Chardin's art are far from neutral. Conisbee continues: "In his depiction of women ... Chardin extols *'les vertus simples et paisibles'* (*the simple and peaceful virtues*) moderation, modesty and good order, which were, for example, those advocated by Mme de Lambert in her widely read educational manual *Avis d'une mère à son fils et à sa fille* (*Advice of a Mother to Her Son and Daughter*), first published in 1728 ... Similar ideals of womanhood are expressed in the great compendium of enlightened thought, the *Encyclopédie*, edited from 1751 by Diderot" (178). Consequently, Conisbee concludes, "Chardin almost invariably preferred to present an image of womanhood closer to the ideal advocated by the *Encyclopédie* and other treatises where her role in modern society is discussed: this woman is devout, domesticated and withdrawn from the bustle and temptations of the larger world" (179).

For his part, Follain evinces a comparable fascination with representing women and a comparable narrowness of focus. Women in his texts are most often either engaged in household tasks or pictured in domestic settings. Some of these women – usually, the young women – are gently eroticized. They remain silent, almost always. Writing the poems allows the male subject access to women, and women's bodies, posed in intimate, private settings where they are unaware of being observed. The poems feel intimate, though never quite voyeuristic.

This mutual fascination with women and the feminine in both the artist and the poet calls for further elucidation. How should we understand the cultural bias or necessity that motivated this choice of subject matter and this particular treatment of that subject matter? In the fourth chapter of *Looking at the Overlooked*, entitled "Still Life and 'Feminine' Space," Norman Bryson asserts that "to understand still life of the table one needs to take into account the asymmetry of the sexes with regard to the domestic space of which the table is the centre" (160). The work of Chardin is of particular interest to Bryson as he develops his analysis of the operations of gender politics in the constitution of the space of the still-life painting. Initially, he emphasizes Chardin's sensitivity to his own intrusion, as a male painter, into the "other" space of the domestic sphere: "the work of Chardin is acutely sensitive to the dangers of disruption that emerge when painting and domestic space collide ... But Chardin works hard to record the domestic scene *in such a way that the presence of painting does not disrupt the harmonies it values there*" (166, emphasis added). Bryson regards Chardin's characteristic aesthetic choices as determined by the unique relationship to (female) domestic space that his paintings cultivate: "The goal of [Chardin's] lazy, peripheral focus is non-invasive participation in the spaces of the household. Informal composition and peripheral haze in Chardin are the means of overcoming the barrier created by the household division of labour, and the tension it creates" (167).

Nevertheless, in spite of his evident sensitivity to, and sympathy towards, the women featured in his paintings, the artist may be viewed as limiting or confining these women within a strictly delimited role. "Chardin's women," Bryson remarks, "are far more locked into domestic chores than, for example, the women in the households of Vermeer or Metsu. They are given no dramas or confidantes; and physically they are presented as creatures of labour, always absorbed in the task in hand. Chardin's insistence on his own powers of painterly technique consequently has the effect of polarising this unskilled manual labour of the women in this house, and his own supremely skilled dexterity. At the same time that his technique works to overcome his position as outsider in the household, its virtuoso aspect widens the gulf" (168).

This sort of critique could also be addressed to Jean Follain's use of domestic space in a number of his poems. He, too, could be charged with imposing a limited view of women's work and women's subjectivity. In Follain's poems, women's bodies do submit themselves to the male gaze silently, without talking back to the male observer.

Cataloguing, Collecting, and *L'Épicerie d'enfance*

"Things lead lives like people do, and they prosper, like people, on the strength of their character."

– Thatcher Freund, *Objects of Desire: The Lives of Antiques and Those Who Pursue Them* (22)

As I noted in the Introduction, the poetry of the object in France can usefully be linked to the tradition of the *leçon de choses* (*lesson from things*) given in Third Republic French schools. Childhood and the child's openness to new experiences and sensations is at the heart of the *leçon de choses*. The poetry of things draws upon a similar faculty in the reader. The teacher, like the poet, helps awaken the child's curiosity about the world in order to bring him / her into a deeper awareness of the life of things. In her 1988 essay "Poésie: leçon de choses, mythologie" ("Poetry: Lesson from Things, Mythology") poet Marie-Claire Bancquart explores the importance of the *leçon de choses* for French schoolchildren as analogous to poetry's ability to heighten the reader's responsiveness to the object world:

> Il existait en France, dans les écoles primaires de la Troisième République, des cours et des livres de "leçons de choses." On y apprenait à toucher les objets, à évaluer leurs propriétés, et leurs qualités par rapport à nous. Le bâton de craie colle à la langue. D'une feuille de bégonia coupée en morceaux, et maintenue sur la terre, on peut faire naître plusieurs bégonias.
>
> Ainsi apprenait-on peut-être moins, quand on était un enfant sensible, un usage des choses ou une intimité avec elles, que l'étrangeté du rapport qui existe entre elles et nous: un étonnement devant leur présence indéniable, insistante et leur autonomie dans le fond inexplicable. (139)

> (There existed in France, in the primary schools of the Third Republic, courses and books on "lessons from things." In these courses one learned how to touch objects, how to evaluate their properties, and their distinguishing qualities, in relationship to us. A piece of chalk sticks to your tongue. From one begonia leaf cut into bits, and left on the ground, one can create several begonias.
>
> Thus a sensitive child could learn, perhaps, less the uses of things or an intimacy with them, than the strange quality of their relationship to us: a sense of surprise before their undeniable, insistent presence and their fundamentally unexplainable autonomy.)

In this essay, as in her own poetry, Bancquart foregrounds the mysterious, even uncanny, side of things and of the natural world. During the *leçon de choses* the schoolchild is struck by the strangeness of the apparently banal, unremarkable things being studied. Like the reader of object poetry, the child thus learns from these lessons, as Bancquart puts it, "cet étonnement préservé devant la distance et à la fois la proximité des choses" ("that sense of astonishment before the simultaneous distance and closeness of things to us"). The relationship between the child and the object is also the focus of Jean Follain's prose text *L'Épicerie d'enfance*, which opens with evocations of a small child's creation of his personal "épicerie" composed of empty tin cans which he has found outdoors and gradually assembled into a new, idiosyncratic order within one room of the house. The building up of this collection of cans into an imaginary "épicerie" prefigures the work of the adult / poet who the child will one day become. At the same time, *L'Epicerie d'enfance* sheds light on what is at stake in writing about objects and collecting individual poems into book-length volumes. Follain's entire enterprise as a "poète de l'objet" is mirrored in a kind of *mise en abyme* through this "épicerie d'enfance."

Before entering into a discussion of the poet's description of his creation of "l'épicerie," let us explore the idea of collecting things. Why do (some) people collect things? How could one interpret collecting as a cultural practice?[10] Maurice Rheims's *La Vie étrange des objets: histoire de la curiosité* (*The Strange Life of Things: A History of Curiosity*) (1959) provides a useful starting point for a discussion of collecting. Rheims begins by establishing a basic distinction between the "collectionneur" and the "amateur":

> L'amateur est bien différent du collectionneur. Il cherche la perfection de l'harmonie et la beauté. Il aime les objets non en fonction de leur suite dans une série, mais plutôt pour leur diversité qui l'enchante et correspond à ses multiples états d'âme. (4)
>
> (The enthusiast [l'amateur] is quite different from the collector. He seeks the perfection of harmony and beauty. He loves objects not according to how they fit into a series, but rather for their diversity, which delights him and corresponds to his multiple states of mind / moods [états d'âme].)

Rheims declares that small children show a particular fascination with collecting objects, as Follain's text will also reveal. "Dès son plus jeune âge," writes Rheims, "l'enfant a des gestes réflexes de collectionneur. Il s'attache à des morceaux d'étoffes, à des poupées ou à des soldats de plomb; les objets servent de pièces de jeu, de remparts à sa sécurité et matérialisent son univers" ("From his youngest age, the child has a collector's reflexes. He gets attached to bits of fabric, dolls or lead soldiers; the objects act as game pieces, provide security and materialize his personal world") (25). Rheims notes a close connection between the constitution of the child's own subjectivity and his or her attachment to objects: "L'enfant s'identifie à l'objet qu'il possède, joue avec lui comme avec un double qui supporte sans dommage les mauvais coups, sert à la fois de bouc émissaire et de gri-gri protecteur. Son existence confirme celle de son propriétaire, sa plasticité permet de transposer toutes les situations où il y a conflit" ("The child identifies with the object he possesses, plays with it as though with a double who can put up with blows and remain undamaged, acting both as a scapegoat and a protective amulet. Its existence confirms that of its owner, its plasticity enables a transposition of any situation where there is conflict") (26). Thus the child's relationship to the objects which he or she collects is multifaceted and intensely symbolic. The subject's existence depends upon the physical presence of objects and his or her marshalling of them into an order in which he or she discovers a different sense of self.[11]

Follain's *L'Epicerie d'enfance* opens with his presentation of his childhood home, focusing especially on its hidden corners and the things stored there: "L'habitation d'enfance était grande et froide avec néanmoins beaucoup de coins où régnait la chaleur. Dans cette maison, des caves aux greniers, on aurait pu trouver maints échantillons en poids de pierre, de fer ou de cuivre … en planches pour la charpente, en bouteilles" ("The childhood home was large and cold but it nonetheless had many warm nooks. In that house, from the cellar to the attic, could be found many samples in stone, iron or copper … in planks of wood to be used for carpentry, in bottles") (EE 9). He is especially attracted to the memory of the "[s]ecrète symphonie d'odeurs" ("[s]ecret symphony of odors") that defined the atmosphere unique to the house.

In the third paragraph of this opening passage, Follain describes the creation of the "épicerie d'enfance" in detail. I wish to quote this passage at length in order to underscore its relevance to Follain's formulation of his poetics of the objects:

> Par un besoin d'encyclopédie, pour pouvoir étiqueter, classer, conserver, l'enfant de la maison avait voulu créer ce grave amusement d'une grande

épicerie avec toute la gamme des produits, et, dans chacun de ces produits, toute la gamme des catégories: sardines à l'huile bien sûr, mais aussi à l'estragon, aux achards, à la tomate, aux truffes, et aussi sans arêtes et en boîtes de tous formats.

Cet enfant aimait que dans leur vie les hommes retors, horticulteurs minutieux de la création, aient créé tant d'espèces et de catégories. (EE 10)

(From an encyclopedic urge, in order to be able to label, to classify and to conserve, the child of the house had attempted to create that serious amusement: a large grocery store with a whole range of products, and, in each of those products, the full range of categories: sardines in oil of course, but also with tarragon, with relish, with tomatoes, with truffles, and also deboned and in cans of all sizes.

That child loved the fact that crafty men, those minute horticulturists of creation, had created so many types and categories.)

He adds that the child "eût voulu détenir un grand et à la fois très précis catalogue armorié de la terre, mais qu'en même temps tout fût confondu dans l'exquise minute" ("would have wanted to possess a great and also very precise emblazoned catalogue of the earth, but that at the same time everything be melted together [confondu] in an exquisite moment of time") (EE 10). So, the outcome of the child's serious playing ["ce grave amusement"] is the creation of a vast catalogue of things within an idealized moment of harmony ["que tout fût confondu dans l'exquise minute"]. Follain's own poems, with their constant assembling of diverse objects into a moment of felt unity, can be read as an extension of this original scene evoked in *L'Epicerie d'enfance*. Curiously, the powerful sense of plenitude created in this passage is quickly offset by an awareness of emptiness, of a literal "vide":

... il devait revenir aux songes qu'apportaient
ces boîtes de conserves, ces fioles, ces bidons,
ces paquets, ces fins sachets couverts de figurines,
de sentences, de reproduction des médailles de con-
cours, et *qui n'enfermaient plus que du vide*: tous
ces "saumons des présidents," ces "phosphatines
fallières," ces "chocolats Lombard." (EE 10–11, emphasis added)

... he had to return to the dreams brought
to him by those cans of preserves, those flasks,

> those drums, those packages, those fine small bags covered in figurines, aphorisms [sentences], reproductions of models from contests and *which now held only emptiness*: all those "presidents' salmon," those "phosphatines fallières," those "Lombard chocolates.")

Finally, the child sets up his personal "épicerie":

> Il ramassait toutes les boîtes ou enveloppes de produits alimentaires partout où il pouvait les dénicher, sur les routes du matin et du crépuscule, et parfois jusque dans la fange silencieuse et triste des fosses. Censées emplies, ces boîtes et ces enveloppes, elles retrouvaient vie dans ses mains quand il les rangeait sur les étagères de l'épicerie. Cette chose était peu avouable près des grandes personnes qui avaient sa garde, et qui ne pouvaient approuver ces insolites cueillettes de vieille ferraille et de vieux papiers sous une campagne toute rayonnante d'autres offrandes. Il rentrait, traversant la grande salle, tout son butin, par pudeur caché sous son sarrau noir, sous sa chemise, ou à même sa peau. Son épicerie était située dans une pièce pourvue d'une grande armoire, et qu'on lui avait abandonnée: une petite pièce au sol battu, aux murs d'argile où pénétraient de temps en temps les lourdes vapeurs de la buanderie voisine.
>
> Cette idée d'épicerie avait été donnée à l'enfant par de plus petits qui venaient parfois jouer à la maison. Ils arrachaient d'abord de l'argile au mur des communs et, de leurs mains inexpertes, ils s'essayaient à la pétrir pour confectionner de menus objets: un cœur, un cheval. (EE 11)
>
> (He gathered all the tins or envelopes of food products wherever he could dig them up, on roads in the morning or at dusk, and sometimes even in the silent and sad mud of ditches. Since he imagined them to be filled, those tins and packets came back to life in his hands when he arranged them on the shelves of the grocery store. This situation was somewhat embarrassing for the adults taking care of him, as they could not approve of those odd gleanings of old scrap metal and old papers in a countryside that shone with other offerings. He would come home, crossing the big room, with his loot discreetly hidden under his overalls / smock, under his shirt or even pressed against his skin. His grocery store was located in a room equipped with a large cupboard, which had been left to him: a little room with an earthen floor and clay walls where from time to time the heavy steam from the neighbouring laundry would enter.

> This idea for a grocery store had been given to the child by some younger children who sometimes came to the house to play. They would first tear some clay from the walls of the outbuildings and, with their inexperienced hands, would attempt to knead it in order to create little objects: a heart, a horse.)

This passage can serve as a figural origin for the act of writing for Follain, inasmuch as the poet's verbal inventory of types of canned goods (like his lists of things in his poems more generally) doubles and replays the child's game of placing objects in series. The cornucopian plenitude of the child's grocery store re-emerges in, and as, words. As a result of this process, "ces boîtes et ces envelopes ... retrouvaient vie dans ses mains"; a quasi-magical transformation (or, to use Follain's preferred term, transfiguration) takes place. An exchange occurs between subjects and objects whereby the child (poet) restores life and presence to the discarded objects by collecting them, just as the objects bestow a sense of joy and identity on their collector.

In his study *La Quête de l'objet: pour une psychologie du chercheur de trésor* (*The Search for the Object: Towards a Psychology of the Treasure-seeker*), Hubert Van Gijseghem explains how the collector of objects becomes transformed by what he or she collects: "[l'homme] est le seul dans l'univers des vivants à conserver l'objet, à l'investir au-delà de sa pure fonctionnalité" ("[man] is the only creature alive who conserves objects, valuing them beyond their mere usefulness") (15). As in the opening passage from *L'Epicerie d'enfance* quoted above, the object, when appropriated by a human collector, may assume a quasi-magical status:

> Une mystérieuse alliance se tisse entre l'homme
> et sa chose. Tout laisse croire que l'objet affectionné
> détient une sorte de puissance magique. On attache
> au cou, au poignet, à la cheville ou on glisse dans sa
> poche: porte-bonheur, talisman, charmes, médaille,
> crucifix, relique, fétiche. (17)
>
> (A mysterious pact is formed between a man and
> his thing. It would seem that the beloved object
> holds a sort of magical power. People attach it to
> their neck, their wrist, their ankle or they slip it into
> their pocket: a good-luck charm, a talisman, a medal,
> a crucifix, a relic, a fetish.)

Such objects can afford their possessor an indispensable sense of security, pleasure, and identity. "A proximité du corps, à portée de la main; ils s'offrent à la caresse, à la manipulation, on 'joue avec'!" ("Close to the body, within reach; they invite being caressed and manipulated, we 'play with them'!"), as Van Gijseghem puts it.

If one reads the opening passage from *L'Epicerie d'enfance* as an origin for the writing of a poetry of objects, then the tin can – "la boîte" – acquires an exemplary status; it acts as the Follain object *par excellence*. This is precisely how Françoise Rouffiat has interpreted the role of "la boîte." In a brilliant passage from her book on Follain, Rouffiat demonstrates how the tin cans of *L'Epicerie d'enfance* can be interpreted as an "archétype de l'objet chez Follain" (Rouffiat 51). The tin can is a humble, ordinary object, generally overlooked and taken for granted. It serves as a container for foodstuffs and is thus associated with nourishment and the feminine still-life world that Follain's poetry evokes, much like Chardin's art. Most importantly, the tin cans collected by the child in Follain's text are *empty*. Although the colourful labels on the tins promise that the tins hold delicious foods ("saumons des présidents," "chocolats Lombard"), they in fact hold nothing; they may, therefore, become the perfect vehicle for the child poet's imagination to fill with significance. Moreover, the child has gathered together an abundance of tins to be assembled into orderly rows on the shelves of his personal "grocery store." This arrangement of beautifully labelled cans prefigures the poet's arrangement of poems into sequences in the collections of his adulthood. "Cette épicerie est tout un poème," writes Rouffiat, "une véritable œuvre d'art où la valeur de signe des objets, porteurs de marques recueillis dans un catalogue, l'emporte sur leur valeur d'usage et même d'échange" ("This grocery store is like a poem, a veritable art work in which the sign value of objects, the carriers of brands collected in a catalogue, trumps their use value and even their exchange value") (48).

The child's creation of his "épicerie" is one of the more idealized moments in Follain's œuvre. Yet even here, a certain ambiguity intrudes. One notes that the child seems curiously embarrassed or guilty about his playtime activities, as Follain writes that the child's treasure-hunt search for discarded tin cans "était peu avouable près des grandes personnes qui avaient sa garde, et qui ne pouvaient approuver ces insolites cueillettes de vieille ferraille et de vieux papiers sous une campagne toute rayonnante d'autres offrandes" ("was somewhat embarrassing for the adults taking care of him, who could not approve of those odd gleanings of old scrap metal and old papers in a countryside full of other offerings") (EE 11). Hence, the small boy feels the need to sneak his beloved cans into the house: "tout son butin, par pudeur caché sous son sarrau noir, sous sa chemise, ou à même sa peau" ["his whole hoard of loot, discreetly hidden under his black overalls / smock, under his shirt or even held against his skin"] (EE 11).

The child's sense that he is doing something dirty or embarrassing ("peu avouable") here is striking, and surprising. What could account for his apparent psychological discomfort? Perhaps the sense of partial guilt or embarrassment associated with collecting in Follain's text can be traced to the possible ambiguities of the act of collecting itself, as some theorists have understood it. Jean Baudrillard, for example, in his 1968 sociological study *Le Système des objets* (*The System of Objects*), regards the impulse to collect objects as a childish, even psychosexually regressive trend:

> La phase active de collectionnement semble
> se situer entre sept et douze ans, dans la
> période de latence entre le prépuberté et la puberté.
> Le goût de la collection semble à s'effacer avec
> l'éclosion pubertaire, pour ressurgir parfois aussitôt
> après. Plus tard, ce sont les hommes de
> plus de quarante ans qui se prennent le plus
> souvent de cette passion. (123)
>
> (The active phase of collecting seems to occur
> between seven and twelve years of age, in the
> period of latency between prepuberty and puberty.
> The taste for collecting seems to disappear with
> the onset of puberty, sometimes resurfacing
> immediately after. Later on, it is men
> over forty who most often get caught
> up in this passion.)

In this regard, collecting can be interpreted as a compensatory activity, "une régression vers le stade anal, qui se traduit par des conduits d'accumulation, d'ordre, de rétention agressive, etc." ("a regression to the anal phase, which translates into acts of accumulation, order, anal retentiveness, etc.") (123).

Whether one accepts this view as a general truth about collecting and collectors or not, Baudrillard's assertion about possible links between collecting and anality may help to account for the somewhat incongruous feeling of guilt attending the child's search for tin cans in Follain's text, particularly because the narrator declares that the child originally conceived the idea for his project by watching smaller children making objects (a heart or a horse, for example) out of mud. (The connections between mud and anality here are obvious.)

In any case, the impulse to collect things remains intimately tied to the writing of poems and the gathering of series of poems into collections, for Follain. In another study of collectors and collecting, Werner Muensterberger argues that a passion for collecting may function, at an unconscious level, as "a device to screen off and master deeper doubts and ambiguities" (7). Muensterberger finds that "by searching for objects and, with any luck, discovering and obtaining them, the passionate collector combines his own re-created past consoling experiences with the fantasied past of his objects in an almost mystical union" (14). Jean Follain's œuvre, organized as it is around the objects' dependence upon the poet for their own "salvation," constitutes a perfect illustration of Muensterberger's ideas about collecting, one could say. The poet's repeated designation of the salvation of the objects as the goal of his writing and his search for privileged objects to retrieve from the past correspond closely to the profile of the true collector, as formulated by Muensterberger and other theorists.

5 The Object as (M)Other: Guillevic's Poetry and Object-Relations Theory

In his magisterial study of twentieth-century French poetry, *Onze études sur la poésie moderne* (*Eleven Studies of Modern Poetry*) (1964), Jean-Pierre Richard situates Eugène Guillevic (1907–97) in the company of Reverdy and Ponge, as a *poète de l'objet*. Like them, Guillevic returns again and again to the object as a catalyst for the writing of poetry; yet his relationship to the object is ambivalent, inasmuch as the object remains remote and ungraspable in his poems, even as the poet strives to approach it and render it in words. For Guillevic, Richard writes, "toujours se reproduit … le même drame: en un seul geste l'objet s'impose et se dérobe … Nous avons beau aimer les choses, nous avons beau projeter vers elles toute la richesse pénétrante de notre désir, toute l'inclusivité de notre conscience, les choses se ferment, ou s'écartent, échappent à la prise. A notre élan elles répondent par une non-réponse; à nos avances elles opposent une fin de non-recevoir" ("the same drama always repeats itself: with a single gesture the object imposes itself and slips away … However much we love things, however much we project onto them the penetrating richness of our desire, the entirety of our consciousness, things close up, or move aside, escape our grasp. They respond to our enthusiasm by a non-response; they oppose a goal of non-receiving to our advancing toward them") (183). Paradoxically, though, this very obstinate remoteness of the things which the poet sees becomes an incitation and a stimulant to writing. As we shall see, the development of Guillevic's œuvre from 1938, when he published *Requiem,* to the late 1990s is determined by his complex and varying strategies for overcoming the barrier of silence and otherness separating the perceiving subject from the object world before him.

In 1942 Guillevic published his first collection of poems, *Terraqué* (*Of Earth and Water*). This text was almost immediately acknowledged as a major work. *Terraqué* is subdivided into several sections, each containing roughly twenty short poems. The first of these eleven subdivisions, entitled "Choses" ("Things"), features some of Guillevic's best-known poems. Many of them recall the types of thematics of the object we have noted in collections by Follain (who was a close friend of Guillevic's and a great admirer of his work). Guillevic's presentation of objects is more terse, strange and understated than Follain's, however, as is evident in this representative poem from *Terraqué*:

Deux bouteilles vides
Au grenier dans un coin.
Le vent secoue les tuiles
Et la charpente.

Deux bouteilles vertes
Qu'attire le centre de la terre
Et que retient la lumière. (T 22)

(Two empty bottles
In a corner of the attic.
The wind shakes the tiles
And the roof frame.

Two green bottles
Which the centre of the earth attracts
And the light keeps hold of.)

Here, the two bottles are presented twice. At first, their silent presence in the attic is simply noted. They appear self-sufficient, separate from the speaker and the natural world; the violent action of the wind does not affect them. In the second stanza of the poem, however, the bottles have somehow been transformed: no longer "vides" (empty), they are "vertes" (green). They have become part of the elemental world beyond the poem, figured as "le centre de la terre" (the earth's centre) and "la lumière" (light). The poem moves from a bare, laconic presentation of objects, as in a conventional still life, to the sense, in the final two lines, of a mysterious force beyond the surfaces of everyday reality.

In fact, a generalized atmosphere of uneasiness – even dread – characterizes the poems of *Terraqué*. The opening poem of the collection, which provides entry into Guillevic's imagined world, offers a startling example of the aura of anxiety associated with objects in this early collection:

L'armoire était de chêne
Et n'était pas ouverte.

Peut-être il en serait tombé des morts,
Peut-être il en serait tombé du pain.

Beaucoup de morts.
Beaucoup de pain. (T 17)

(The cupboard was made of oak
And was not open.

Perhaps dead men would fall out of it,
Perhaps bread would fall out of it.

A lot of dead men
A lot of bread.)

The cupboard in the poem is solid ("de chêne"), closed, forbidding. It is described in the imperfect tense – the tense of unfinished action in the past in French. It lingers in the speaker's memory. The cupboard seems mysterious, inaccessible, even though it stands directly in front of the speaker. The use of the conditional in the second stanza ("il en serait tombé") underscores the fundamental uncertainties that this object confronts us with. Although this is an ordinary item of household furniture, it holds itself at a distance and conceals its contents. The speaker can only guess at what it might contain. The hidden interior of the cupboard invites the speaker to speculate – to dream about – what it could contain: either corpses or bread would fall out of the cupboard, if we dared to open it. Yet opening the cupboard remains an unrealized, perhaps unrealizable, fantasy. In the elliptical, repetitive ending of the poem ("Beaucoup de morts / Beaucoup de pain"), the doubled use of "beaucoup," suggesting a huge storage space hidden within the cupboard, makes it even more uncanny and threatening.

To Guillevic's critics, no less than to the poem's speaker, this closed cupboard and the poem framing it have posed a tantalizing interpretive problem. This poem has elicited more critical commentary than almost any other French poem of the twentieth century. Guy Allix, for instance, finds in it "cette ambivalence initiale du 'secret' de la chose qui traduirait, dans l'esprit du poète, tout à la fois le désir et la crainte. Cependant que le poète reste sur le seuil, *séparé*. L'armoire reste infranchissable, impénétrable; elle garde son secret, sa solitude" ("that initial ambivalence of the 'secret' in the thing which would translate, in the poet's mind, into both desire and fear. While nevertheless the poet stays on the threshold, *separate*. The cupboard remains unreachable, impenetrable; it keeps its secret, its solitude") (219).

The cupboard presents an unyielding resistance to the speaker's curiosity and to the language that he would use to unlock the object's secrets. The cupboard takes on a larger, metaphorical significance in *Terraqué* – and in Guillevic's œuvre in general – because of its provocative placement here, at the entry-point to the œuvre. The malaise which the speaker feels in response to the object's heavy silence is a feature that will recur in most of his early poems. Anxiety pervades *Terraqué*. As Michael Brophy observes, an acute ambivalence marks the human subject's engagement with objects in the collection. The oaken cupboard thus reads as a figure for an ambivalence that objects contain or induce:

> En fait, le poète saisit la présence de l'armoire à la fois comme menace (elle abriterait "des morts") et comme promesse (elle abriterait "du pain"), comme seuil d'un monde spectral et hallucinant, et comme support apaisant du quotidien. Aucune solution, aucune jonction ne s'offre dans le texte entre ces deux possibilités; il n'y a qu'une parfaite égalité des contraires dont la tension intermédiaire, aiguisée par l'identité de la structure syntaxique, reste encore à creuser et à comprendre. (10–11)
>
> (Actually, the poet understands the presence of the cupboard both as a threat (it could contain "dead men") and as a promise (it could contain "bread"), as the threshold of a spectral and hallucinatory world, and as the soothing basis of everyday existence. No solution and no joining together is offered between these two possibilities in the text; there is only a perfect equality of opposites whose intermediary tension, sharpened by an identical syntactical structure, still remains to be examined thoroughly and understood.)

So, despite its solidity and its size, the oak cupboard comes to seem fantastical and unreal, as its presence induces the speaker to imagine its frightening or consoling contents. Significantly, Guillevic himself has designated this text describing the oak cupboard as his most representative poem: "mon poème réclame" ("my signature poem") or "[m]on panneau" ("[m]y billboard") (VP 102).

The oaken cupboard is only one of several objects presented in "Choses" to be enveloped in an atmosphere of possible violence or dread. In "Fait-divers" ("Human Interest Story") (T 19), the speaker begins by asking, "Fallait-il faire tant de bruit / Autour d'une chaise? // – Elle n'est pas du crime" ("Was it necessary to make such a fuss / About a chair? // – It is not part of the crime"). The strangeness of the chair is then heightened, as it becomes both personified and radically separate from the speaker: "Elle ne veut plus rien, / Elle ne doit plus rien, / Elle a son propre tourbillon, / Elle se suffit" ("It wants nothing more, / It owes nothing more / It has its own vortex, / It is self-sufficient"). Elsewhere, images of violence are overtly presented or obscurely evoked. The sight of a slaughtered ox in "Boeuf écorché" – "C'est de la viande où passait le sang" ("This is meat through which blood used to flow") (T 25) – causes one to feel fear, while awakening a need in the poem's speaker to make contact with this once living, now dead creature. A sense of primitive blood sacrifice vies with a movement towards tenderness in the poem.

The landscape in *Terraqué* often seems menacing and harsh. The subject fears the presence of monsters in the night ("Des milliers d'yeux jaunes luisent dans la forêt, / Me réclament le sang" ("Thousands of yellow eyes shine in the forest, / demanding my blood") (T 37). The stark elemental seascapes of Brittany, where Guillevic was born, and to which his poetry constantly returns, are dominated by rocks, water, earth. The megaliths ("menhirs") so common in Brittany become animated, threatening: "Les menhirs la nuit vont et viennent / Et se grignotent" ("The megaliths wander back and forth at night / And gnaw on one another) (T 57). A black giant who sleeps among the fossils at the bottom of the sea rises and stares, so that

Les astres au creux du ciel ont froid
Et viennent se chauffer coude à coude.

Les yeux morts de cent mille morts
Tombent dans les rivières
Et flottent. (T 56)

(The stars in the hollow of the sky are cold
And come to warm themselves side by side.

The dead eyes of one hundred thousand dead men
Fall into the rivers
And float there.)

The sense of dread and anxiety so recurrent in Guillevic's first collection is overdetermined. Critics have proposed various interpretations to account for this disquieting textual atmosphere. Stella Harvey, in *Myth and the Sacred in the Poetry of Guillevic* (1997), argues that the rituals, superstitions, and legends of Brittany have had a decisive influence on Guillevic's notion of landscape as reflecting the presence of the sacred, in an often primitive sense. Harvey writes that "[t]he landmarks of Carnac [Guillevic's birthplace] – the menhirs, the fountain, the cemetery, the sea – are 'magnified' to archetypal proportion. Permeated with ancestral presence, Guillevic's Brittany is a point of juncture of *le temps vécu* and mythical atemporality" (3). Harvey's insight is extremely relevant for interpreting this poetry, especially since Guillevic frequently referred to himself as "un homme de la préhistoire." One should also remember that *Terraqué* was published in 1942, during the Second World War. The strong presence of historical violence certainly influenced his writing.[1]

Although I acknowledge the importance of these critical approaches to *Terraqué*, I shall suggest a different interpretive strategy for coming to terms with the aura of darkness, violence and ambivalence grounding the poems of this collection. Before turning to a more theoretical discussion of these poems, I would first like to consider remarks made by Guillevic in conversation with Alain Vircondelet and Lucie Albertini. During a book-length series of interviews with Albertini and Vircondelet, the poet recounts his first childhood memory:

Pour moi, *c'était l'âge de la maternelle.*
Mon premier souvenir date de ce temps-là.
J'avais trois ans. Mes parents avaient acquis
une cuisinière neuve où un couvercle avec
une assez longue poignée mickelée fermait
le trou à feu.

Une fin d'après-midi, j'étais seul dans la
cuisine – *ma mère n'était pas sur mon dos* –

j'ai soulevé ce couvercle, il est tombé, il s'est
cassé. *Alors, tremblant, j'ai attendu ma mère…*
… Mais pour moi, l'événement précis, c'est ce
couvercle cassé, ce cercle solide et si parfaitement
rond que j'ai brisé. *Mon premier souvenir est donc*
un souvenir de culpabilité, dans une gendarmerie,
sous une mère tyrannique. (VP 13–14, emphasis added)

(For me, *it was when I was in kindergarten.*
My first memory dates from that time. I was
three years old. My parents had bought a new
stove with a lid that had a fairly long nickel
handle that covered the stove opening.
At the end of the afternoon one day, I
was alone in the kitchen – *I was not saddled*
with my mother…
… But for me, the exact
event was that broken lid, that solid and
perfectly round circle that I broke. *My first*
memory is thus a memory of guilt, in a police
station, under a tyrannical mother.)

In this memory fragment, an indelible association is established between a broken object, the fear of an anticipated maternal severity, and an overwhelming sense of guilt. This particular configuration of images, fears, and experience becomes closely connected for Guillevic with early childhood: "l'âge de la maternelle" ("kindergarten age"). This remembered scene reads almost like a confession of (original) sin. Given the importance that the poet attributes to this scene, it can be taken as a point of origin for his imaginative life and for his work, which are the focus of the discussions with Albertini and Vircondelet in *Vivre en poésie.* In *Terraqué,* as we have seen, a close connection is created linking everyday objects such as the oak cupboard or the chair to a powerful sense of fear. In this first collection, and in many later collections of poetry by Guillevic, traces of a troubling, even malevolent, presence associated with a maternal figure (a trope rather than a person) persist.

In the retelling of the poet's childhood memory in the above quoted passage, a surprisingly strong anxiety accompanies each evocation of the mother: "Alors, tremblant, j'ai attendu ma mère"; "Mon premier souvenir est donc un souvenir de culpabilité … sous une mère tyrannique." In fact, Guillevic's mother is mentioned quite frequently in *Vivre en poésie*. The poet speaks of her unwarranted harshness. Her presence seems to overshadow and determine Guillevic's sense of self:

> Sage? Vis-à-vis de ma mère, je mentais
> forcément, ma mère m'a inculqué la
> culpabilité. Tout ce que je faisais était mauvais.
> Je rentrais, je me lavais les mains, je me
> baissais: j'étais coupable. En elle, dans son
> œil bleu glacial et son nez pointu perpétuellement
> soupçonneux, perçais toujours une arrière-pensée. (VP 71)

> (Well-behaved? In dealing with my mother,
> I necessarily lied, my mother taught me to
> feel guilty. Everything I did was bad. I came
> home, I washed my hands, I bent down: I was
> guilty. Within her, in her icy blue eye and her
> always suspicious pointy nose, an
> ulterior motive always came through.)

In this description the mother is transformed almost into a sort of wicked witch from fairy tales: "son oeil bleu glacial," "son nez pointu perpétuellement soupçonneux." Guillevic adds that "[m]a mère m'ayant toujours dit que je ne serais bon à rien, que je mourrais sur l'échafaud, que jamais une femme voudrait de moi … *j'avais un désir de revanche sur ces bénédictions, mais il n'était pas primordial*" ("[m]y mother always told me that I would be good for nothing, that I would die on the gallows, that no woman would want me … *I desired revenge for those blessings of hers, but this desire of mine was not absolute*"] (VP 72, emphasis added). The poet's avowed desire for revenge here is telling. The consequences of this preoccupation with "revenge" need to be explored.

Curiously, although most of the poet's memories of his mother in *Vivre en poésie* are very vivid, in some cases he experiences difficulty in answering his interviewers' questions about her:

> Q. – Un tout petit enfant, on l'imagine dans une relation de tendresse avec ses proches. As-tu été élevé au sein?
> G. – Oui, et alors? Je n'en garde aucun souvenir …

Q. – Ta mère ne t'a jamais tenu par la main?
G. – Sûrement si, ce n'est pas possible autrement, mais je n'en garde aucun souvenir. Ni agréable ni pas. Sa main sur mes fesses ou sur ma joue, ça je la connais. (VP 16–17)

(Q – One imagines that a very small child would be treated with tenderness by those close to him. Were you breast-fed?
G. – Yes, what of it? I have no memory of it …
Q – Did your mother never take you by the hand?
G. – She most likely did, but I have no memory of it. Either pleasant or not. I *do* remember her hand on my buttocks or on my cheek.)

Guillevic's lack of memory in this passage is somewhat surprising. Nevertheless, as psychoanalytic theory attests, what one cannot remember may be as crucial in the formation of one's subjectivity as what one does remember clearly.

Guillevic's enduring preoccupation with the textualized, imagined figure of the mother does have important consequences for the development of his œuvre, as most of his critics agree. In *Terraqué*, the sense of fear in several poems has explicit connections to the maternal. In one poem the speaker imagines that perhaps "la tourbe est montée des marais, / Pour venir lanciner, suinter dans le silence / Et nous suivre partout / Comme une mère incestueuse" ("the peat has risen from the swamps, / To come throbbing, oozing in the silence / And to follow us everywhere / Like an incestuous mother") (T 46). In another poem, "Naissance," the speaker addresses the mother directly:

Mère aux larmes brûlantes, l'homme fut chassé de vous –
De vos tendres ténèbres,
De votre chambre de muqueuses.

(Mother crying burning tears, [the] man was driven from you –
From your tender darkness,
From your mucous chamber.) (T 52)

Thus, a multifaceted engagement with the maternal is central to the evolution of Guillevic's poetry – and to the role of the object within that poetry. At this point, I wish to turn to the theories of British psychoanalyst Melanie Klein, as a possible approach to elucidating the critical function of these maternal figures in Guillevic's work, since they affect the relationship between the subject and the object world in fundamental ways.[2]

Object Relations in Guillevic's Early Poetry: A Kleinian Perspective

"... from birth onwards, a relation to objects, primarily the mother (her breast) is present"

– Melanie Klein, "The Origins of Transference" *Envy and Gratitude* (51)

"The idea of the internal object is one of Klein's most important discoveries, yet one of the most mysterious. The experience that the subject has of an object inside himself gives him a sense of existence and identity. Our relations with objects comprise what we are."

– R.D. Hinshelwood, *A Dictionary of Kleinian Thought* (68)

The theories of Viennese-born British psychoanalyst Melanie Klein (1881–1960) constitute a rich avenue of speculation for arriving at a closer understanding of the role of objects and the maternal in Guillevic's poetry. Klein formulated a complex and controversial view of the psychosexual life of infants and very young children. The catalyst for her development of her theories, which depart substantially from Sigmund Freud's, was her observation of small children playing with toys and drawing pictures while in a clinical setting, observed by an analyst. She interpreted their play as the equivalent of free association (i.e., uncensored talking) by adults in analysis. Klein was struck by the aggressiveness, even the sadism, involved in much of this playing. She attributed the violence which she observed in children to the operations of intense intrapsychic conflict that had originated in earliest infancy. This led her to revise Freudian theory by relocating the onset of the Oedipus complex and the constitution of the superego to a much earlier point in psychic life than that postulated by Freud. For both Freud and Klein, the Oedipus complex, characterized by extremes of love and hate, aggression and desire, guilt and envy, was the crucial, determining crisis in the human subject's psychosexual evolution. Klein, nonetheless, argued that the Oedipus complex must occur during the first few months of life, in early infancy.

In her theories, from the beginning, Klein accorded primary importance to the role of the mother in the child's psychosexual development, especially to the mother's breast. She postulated that the mother's breast was the first "object" around which the infant's sense of self would evolve. Whereas Freud had privileged the father as law-giver and phallic rival to the male child, Klein focused on the mother and the objects associated with her as the basis for her new view of psychic life.

Klein's use of the term "object" requires contextualization. She regarded the subject's adult consciousness as formed in response to his or her relationship to an early internalized representation of an "object" (meaning, roughly, a representation of a body part related to a person). In *A Dictionary of Kleinian Thought*, R.D. Hinshelwood defines the term "object" as follows:

> A somatic sensation tugs along with it a mental experience that is interpreted as a relationship with an object that wishes to cause that sensation, and is loved or hated by the subject according to whether the object is well-meaning or has evil intentions (i.e., a pleasant or unpleasant sensation). (34)

Consequently, the child's bodily sensations of pain or well-being feel as though they were caused by an (internalized) object to which he or she attributes benevolent or malevolent intentions. This is, then, the basis for the infant's earliest relationship to his or her "objects." As Hinshelwood indicates, the infant subject's sense of his or her relationship to objects later evolves into different modes of interaction:

> Later, fantasy comes to be less connected with bodily sensations as, with the depressive position [occurring at four to six months], the internal world comes to be populated more with symbolic, rather than concretely actual, objects ... However, remnants of the primitive concrete objects survive and are occasionally experienced as somatizations and psychosomatic conditions (36)

In other words, psychic traces of the powerful, often volatile sensations that the infant subject had experienced in relation to the internalized objects persist later in life. These traces of affect can be revived, in new configurations. They can unconsciously influence adult psychic states.

In the passage quoted above, Hinshelwood refers to a distinction basic to Kleinian thought: the separation between "the paranoid-schizoid position," which dominates the first few months of life, and "the depressive position," which begins halfway through the first year of life. Klein describes the infant's psyche during the paranoid-schizoid position as constituted by introjected parts of bodies (especially the mother's breast) in pieces. These fragments (or "part objects") are experienced by the infant as malicious and threatening ("the bad breast") or as nurturing and benevolent ("the good breast"). Through various intrapsychic mechanisms, such as projection, the infant attempts to effect the course of his or her relationship to his world of internal "part objects" by expelling those objects felt to be harmful while retaining beneficial ones. As the infant subject enters "the depressive position," he or she must come to terms with the breast and other objects as *whole* objects containing both beneficial and dangerous aspects. At this point, the breast is no longer imagined as split into two separate, oppositely-valenced "part objects." A strong sense of loss occurs with the onset of the depressive position; yet there is also a vital maturation.

Klein stated that the central preoccupation in her theories was a concern to discover the root causes for the harsh, potent sense of anxiety that she had observed in so many of her child patients. She eventually asserted that this overwhelming feeling of anxiety was the result of the small child's sense of fear and guilt stemming from the often sadistic fantasies of aggression against the mother's body that prevail during the paranoid-schizoid position. The main thrust of her clinical interventions with her patients became an effort to alleviate this pervasive feeling of anxiety.

The world of Guillevic's early poems in *Terraqué* displays close affinities with the inner world of the infant, as theorized by Melanie Klein. We have already noted the atmosphere of violence, aggression, and darkness in these poems. Marcel Arland has commented that the poems reflect "la peur que donne à un enfant le mystérieux pays qui l'entoure; c'est pour dominer cette crainte et apprivoiser ce pays, qu'il en nomme et affronte les menaces" ("the fear which the mysterious country surrounding him gives to a child; in order to overcome that fear and to tame that country, he names its threats and confronts them") (17). Similarly, Jean Pierrot finds that the most striking feature of *Terraqué* is "la présence d'une atmosphère profondément angoissée" ("the presence of a profoundly anguished atmosphere") (10). Most readers have noted the strong associations between the words "terraqué" and "traqué" ("hunted") or "terreur" ("terror"), and, indeed, the object world surrounding the speaker in these poems can at any moment become menacing or malevolent. As Jean-Pierre Richard remarks, "[m]er, étang, caillou, tout devient monstre [in *Terraqué*]. Le rêve de l'objet s'achève en tératologie" ("[the s]ea, the pond, the pebble, everything becomes a monster [in *Terraqué*]. The dream of the object ends in a teratology") (235).

In Guillevic's early poems – as in the world of intrapsychic fantasies experienced by the infant subject of Melanie Klein's theories – reality is unstable, even terrifying. In *Terraqué,* as Marcel Olscamp states, "l'auteur est aux prises avec une réalité louvoyante, insaisissable, qui échappe totalement à son contrôle et qui menace constamment de l'engloutir" ("the author is struggling with a reality which is wavering, ungraspable, which completely escapes his control and which constantly threatens to swallow him up") (99). In this text, even the simple image of a commonplace thing can lead to frightening fantasies:

Cette pomme sur la table,
Laisse-la jusqu'à ce soir.

Va! Les morts n'y mordront pas
Qui ne mangent pas le pain,
Qui ne lèchent pas le lait. (T 27)

(This apple on the table,
Leave it alone until this evening.

Go on! The dead will not bite into it
They do not eat bread
They do not lick milk.)

Like the image of the oak cupboard with which *Terraqué* begins, this ordinary apple summons forth fantasies of death and destruction. The apple is associated here with images of a potential eating, biting, chewing, and sucking: precisely the cluster of phantasized actions which Klein evokes in describing the infant subject's absorption of the mother's breast as a "part object" during the paranoid-schizoid position. Moreover, the opening image of the cupboard, which could contain "[b]eaucoup de morts" or "[b]eaucoup de pain," is highly reminiscent of Klein's notion of early intrapsychic life as obsessed with the "good" breast and the "bad" breast as alternating possible part objects for absorption or attempted expulsion. Guillevic's images of a predataory, feared "mère incestueuse" ("incestuous mother") (T 46) heighten the possibility of a correlation between the imaginary scenes evoked in *Terraqué* and the phantasies analysed by Klein.

The presence of the maternal – always linked to anxiety – emerges again and again in passages like these ones, where the breast is explicitly mentioned:

Mais ton sein pointe dru
Contre le jour qui traîne.

(But your breast sticks straight up
Against the sluggish day.) (T 23)

*

J'étais bien dans les grottes
Aux montagnes du père
Dans le sein de la fleur. (T 54)

(I felt good in the caves
In the father's mountains
In the flower's breast.)

*

Bouillie de provinces, de lits,
Plus oreiller que tous les seins – La source.

(Pap of provinces, of beds,
More of a pillow than any breast – The spring.) (T 50)

Most often in these examples, the breast is idealized; however, it can also be devalorized:

Car la source n'est plus la source
Crachait des pierres, et dans la bouche
Un bout de sein vieux. (T 50)

(For the spring is no longer the spring
It was spitting stones, and had in its mouth
A scrap of old breast.)

These lines from the poem "Naissance" ("Birth") clearly point to an unresolved struggle with a figure of the mother and her phantasized malevolence, which the writing of the poems repeats and deflects. In a relevant parallel to the aims of such writing, the infant as described by Klein feels himself – or herself – to be deeply vulnerable, yet far from powerless. In phantasies, the infant acts, imagining that he or she is attacking the "bad" breast by biting it or sucking it dry (as "les morts" do in the poem about the apple quoted above). "Bad" objects can also be expelled in phantasy from the infant's body.

To defend himself against this terrifying world of threatening objects, the Guillevician subject uses language. The writing of poems performs a sort of taming of a dangerous reality. Through language, the poet labours to control anxiety. Unconscious phantasies of violence are countered by conscious artistry. As Jean Tortel asserts, Guillevic's early poetry acts as "un manuel d'apprentissage des rites d'exorcismes qui soulèvent et apaisent d'obscures puissances telluriques" ("a learner's manual of rites of exorcism which excite and soothe dark telluric powers") (14). By establishing a new connection based on closeness and intimacy with the things he describes, the subject lessens their potential menace, even as he acknowledges the intensity of unrealized violence that the objects may conceal. Writing becomes a form of appropriation of things and, simultaneously, a means of counteracting destructive phantasies. Like the forms of play used by Klein to stimulate a working through of violent phantasies in her patients, writing performs an exorcizing function in *Terraqué*, as Tortel and others have suggested.

As we move now to a discussion of *Carnac*, *Ville* (*City*), *Paroi* (*Wall*), *Du Domaine* (*Of the Estate*), and other later collections of poetry, it will be important to keep in mind how the poet has framed the role of objects in *Terraqué* and which strategies he has employed to transform the scary presence of objects into something familiar, if not fully knowable or understandable.

Reconciliation with *La Mer(e)*: *Carnac*, *Ville*, *Paroi*, and *Du Domaine*

After publishing the major collections *Terraqué* and *Exécutoire* (1947), Guillevic experienced a lengthy period of creative stagnation in the 1950s. At that time an ardent Communist, he was urged to write formulaic poetry in order to promote Communist values. His main work from that period, *Trente-et-un sonnets* (*Thirty-one Sonnets*), was regarded by critics (and, finally, by Guillevic himself) as trite, uninspired, and aesthetically uninteresting. Following the publication of *Trente-et-un sonnets*, Guillevic was silent for seven years, but he returned to his creative sources with the publication of *Carnac* in 1961. Between the writing of *Carnac* in 1960 and the year of his death (1997), he went on to produce most of his best work.

Carnac is a crucial transitional text that marks the beginning of Guillevic's maturity as a poet. The writing of this collection led him back to the stark and beautiful landscape of Brittany dominated by huge expanses of sea and sky. As noted previously, one of the most famous features of the Brittany landscape are the stone megaliths, or *menhirs*, that gesture back to a prehistoric past. To Guillevic, the stones carry a strong symbolic meaning; they connect the modern world to a vanished world of the sacred. Aubrey Burl has traced the history of these stone megaliths:

> The very first megaliths may have been no more than solitary menhirs, single standing pillars put up as territorial markers or as ancestor-stones near the settlements of [Brittany's] first farmers. There are still hundreds of isolate stones in Brittany and they are almost impossible to date. It is known, however, that some were decorated with carvings of early Neolithic stone axes or shepherd's crooks ... showing how ancient the stone itself must be. (12)

As the *menhir* becomes a synecdoche for Brittany in Guillevic's poems, it places the poems in a framework of a primitive closeness to nature and a sense of awe before nature's power.

Guillevic himself has underscored the importance of the writing of *Carnac* for him: "*Carnac* a été une grande joie pour moi, une délivrance. Je me retrouvais vraiment, je retrouvais mon pays, la terre, la mer, je me revivais tel que j'avais été" (VP 158).

In *Carnac* the sea acts as the focus for the speaker's engagement with the landscape, as the text begins with these words:

> Mer au bord du néant,
> Qui se mêle au néant,
>
> Pour mieux savoir le ciel,
> Les plages, les rochers,
> Pour mieux les recevoir. (C 143)
>
> (Sea at the edge of nothingness,
> Which mingles with nothingness,

To know the sky better,
The beaches, the rocks,
The better to receive them.)

These opening lines set the stage for a long (143–209) contemplation, description, and questioning of the sea. The speaker examines the sea and the landscape from a multiplicity of different angles. Each new angle of approach adds to the complexity of his understanding of the sea's meanings, while also frustrating his desire to make it mean any one thing. The more he attempts to understand what the sea is, the more it resists encapsulation in language.

The poet's metaphors expand our understanding of the sea, yet take it further and further beyond itself. For example, he addresses the sea as "Femme vêtue de peau / Qui façonnes nos mains, // Sans la mer dans tes yeux, / Sans ce goût de la mer que nous prenons en toi, // Tu n'excéderais pas / Le volume des chambres" ("Woman dressed in skin / Who fashions our hands, // Without the sea in your eyes, / Without this taste of the sea that we find in you, // You would not exceed / The volume of the rooms") (C 143). Here, he personifies the sea. Elsewhere, he endows it with (super)human qualities:

Mer sans vieillesse,
sans plaie à refermer,
sans ventre apparemment. (C 149)

(Sea that is ageless,
With no wound to heal / close up
With no belly it seems.)

The speaker's descriptions of the sea are often paradoxical and cryptic: "La mer comme un néant / Qui se voudrait la mer" ("The sea like a void / Which would wish to be the sea") (C 144). If the sea is a "néant" (a nothingness or abyss), then it cannot be described or encompassed; yet, if it has a will ("[q]ui se voudrait"), that would make it similar to a sentient, intelligent being.

The sea keeps changing from one page to the next in *Carnac*, constantly eluding definition. It refuses to yield its secrets, thus maintaining a tantalizing dialogue with the speaker. In its maddening presence / absence, the sea resists all attempts to be transformed into a verbal image:

On dirait que ça te répugne
de mouiller ce que tu touches.

Comme si c'était
te donner trop. (C 182)

(It would seem that it is repulsive to you
to moisten what you touch

As though it were
giving too much of yourself.)

Constantly shifting, the sea can assume any form, or discard it: "Infatigable, fatigué – / Mais quelle est l'épithète / Qui ne te conviendrait?" ("Tireless, tired – / But what adjective / Would not suit you?") (C 186).

In making a dialogue with the sea central to the poetics of *Carnac*, Guillevic is also continuing – and revising – the preoccupation with the maternal whose ubiquitousness we observed in *Terraqué*. The speaker in *Carnac* tells the sea that "[i]l y a des hommes / Qui ne voient en toi que la nourricière" ("[t]here are men / Who see in you only the wet-nurse"] (C 194), transforming it into a kind of womb that can nurture a multitude of creatures within itself: "Ils n'ont pas l'air de te comprendre, / Ceux qui vivent dans toi, / Ceux qui sont faits de toi, / Ces poissons, ces crevettes" ("They do not seem to understand you, / Those who live in you, / Those who are made of you, / Those fish, those shrimp") (C 170). This body (of water) holds and cradles a variety of different creatures and the language of Guillevic's poem imitates the rocking rhythm of the waves: "Ruminant, toi, / Rabâchant, rabâchant" ("You ruminate / Endlessly repeating the same thing [Rabâchant, rabâchant]") (C 180).

As any French-speaking person knows, there is a close homophony in French linking sea ("mer") and mother ("mère"). Guillevic in *Carnac* consciously (or unconsciously in part?) plays upon this homophony, as the speaker addresses the sea, acknowledges its fundamental otherness, yet tries to encompass its fascinating mutability in words. Insofar as *Carnac* involves a literal and figurative return to origins for the poet, it constitutes an effort to rework the atmosphere of violence and anxiety associated with the maternal in *Terraqué* into a different kind of relation. Stella Harvey draws our attention to

Guillevic's fusion of personal and cosmic histories in his representations of Carnac:

> In 'L'épopée du réel' of *Carnac* the touch of the poet-artisan recreates the sacred space-time of the origin … in *Carnac* the drama of cosmic genesis, the creation of form from chaos, is correlated with the emergence of the individual subject and the concomitant crisis of separation from the mother, and how both these dramas are re-enacted in the process of poetic creativity: 'la transformation que l'écriture s'impose au moi' ('the transformation which writing imposes on the self'). (70)

She adds that "[i]n *Carnac* recourse to the cosmogonic myth signals an attempt to restore harmony to the anguished world of *Terraqué*. It involves an effort to repair the subject's relationship with the mother in an archaic drama of mourning" (73). The emphasis on mourning and separation which Harvey finds in *Carnac* takes us back, once again, to the theories of Melanie Klein.[3] As the subject (theorized by Klein) moves from the early paranoid-schizoid position – which was dominated by part-objects, aggression, and violence – to the depressive position, the subject experiences a sense of mourning and loss as he or she recognizes the mother and her breast as "whole" objects containing both "good" and "bad" elements. The subject's development and sense of self depend on her or his ability to negotiate the experience of mourning that the depressive position necessitates.

As Gavin Bowd notes, in *Carnac* "[t]he 'essence' of the sea is its negativity: its being is necessarily to *not* be" (104). In this way, Guillevic's text follows the speaker's ultimately frustrated attempts to overcome the barriers separating him from the sea in order to absorb it into his text:

> On peut plonger en toi.
>
> Tu l'acceptes très bien,
> Même tu le demandes.
>
> Mais ce n'est que toucher
> Un passé légendaire
> Qui s'oublie dans ta masse
>
> Dont tu parais absente. (C 169)

(One can dive into you

You accept it gladly,
You even ask for it.

But it is only touching
A legendary past
Which forgets itself in your massiveness [masse]

From which you seem absent.)

He comes to accept the sea's otherness and difference in the end:

Sois ici remerciée
De n'être pas pareille à nous

Dont le rêve est toujours
D'être réconciliés

Quand pourtant
Ce n'est pas possible. (C 197)

(Let me here thank you
For not being like us

Whose dream is always
To be reconciled

When nevertheless
That is not possible.)

If a full reconciliation with, or understanding of, the sea remains out of reach for the speaker, his acceptance of the limitations of linguistic representation and the process of having engaged "la mèr(e)" in an extended dialogue do, finally, lead him to a deeper awareness, similar to the process of mourning, as he addresses the sea one last time as the poem concludes:

Toi, ce creux
Et définitif.

Moi qui rêvais
De faire équilibre. (C 209)

(You, this hollow space [creux]
That is definitive.

I who dreamed
Of creating balance.)

With this final affirmation of the sea / mother, accepted now in its very negativity and incommensurability, a new phase in Guillevic's representation of the object has begun. In later collections of poetry from the 1960s and 1970s, such as *Ville* (1969), *Paroi* (1970), or *Du Domaine* (1977), he will adopt a large object / space as a focus for description and dialogue, devoting an entire book-length poem to each of these "things." At times, they can evoke the same sense of danger and anxiety that characterized the objects of *Terraqué*. They also often generate a feeling of strangeness and radical otherness, such as that which defined the presence of the sea in *Carnac*. However, these new object / spaces generally lead the poet to a different stage of imaginative participation in the "being" of objects, through which he continues to formulate and revise his poetics.

In both *Ville* and *Paroi*, the speaker approaches an object that is fascinating and fearful. In a long series of brief poems he aims to lessen the distance separating him from the object before him. As in *Carnac*, he again and again endeavours to define the object, to transform it into words. Although *Ville* constitutes a description of Paris, the city itself is never named. About the composition of this long work, Guillevic has commented that "si je n'avais pas écrit *Ville*, je ne pourrais plus vivre à Paris. Ce livre, je l'ai écrit parce que je ne supportais plus la ville … Après avoir écrit et publié ce livre … je me suis senti beaucoup mieux à Paris. Je m'y supporte et je supporte cette ville" ("had I not written *Ville*, I could no longer live in Paris. I wrote that book because I could no longer stand the city … After having written and published that book, … I felt much better living in Paris. I can handle myself and I can handle the city") (VP 176). As the text opens, the speaker first attempts to describe the city through its outward characteristics. He discusses the noises particular to the city (V 15) and the facades of the buildings (V 19). He tries to capture it using adjectives:

Pas autre chose encore, la ville,
Guère autre chose qu'une lueur
Où sont brodés des adjectifs:

Tourbillonnante, gigantesque, tentaculaire, –
Des adjectifs

Qui, comme d'habitude,
Ont l'air d'accueillir
Et qui vous diluent. (V 10)

(The city is not anything else
Hardly anything else but a glimmer
On which some adjectives are stitched:

Swirling, gigantic, tentacular, –
Adjectives

Which, as usual,
Seem to welcome you
And which dilute you.)

Like the sea in *Carnac*, the city resists transformation into words, so much so that the speaker conceded that "[l]a ville est comme un mot / Que je ne connais pas" ("[t]he city is like a word / That I don't know") (V 33). As the text unfolds, the speaker introduces various metaphors as he attempts to chart the constant metamorphosis through which the city realizes itself. He calls it "Taupinière" ("Molehill") (V 43) or "Spirale" ("Spiral) (V 47). The spiral figure aptly represents the process by which the city moves towards itself but away from itself, over and over, in this long poem:

Spirale, cependant, puisque la ville cherche
A se réunir, à se rassembler,
A n'être plus qu'un point
Où trouver sa puissance.

Et qu'il lui faut aussi
Faire le mouvement

Exactement inverse,
En même temps. (V 47)

(A spiral, nonetheless, since the city strives
To meet (with) itself, to gather itself together
To be no more than a point
In which to find its strength.

And because it also needs
To make the exact
Opposite movement
At the same time.)

Here, again, the speaker would "possess" the city (V 60), yet it remains elusive. Nevertheless, he is able to define himself in relation to the city and thus achieves a kind of victory: "Je vis dans le moi-même / Tangentiel à la ville" ("I live in myself / Tangential to the city") (V 93). Even though the city's paradoxical nature, its labyrinthine complexities and strange logic, lead the speaker to question – even to undo – the statements he wishes to make about it, the speaker it still able to arrive at a new type of dialogical relationship with it. Through a sensitive and finely honed linguistic performance, the poet allows his text to be shaped by the difficult, challenging object that he faces. His own subjectivity is subtly altered by his patient and persistent efforts to come to terms with what the city represents.

In *Paroi*, Guillevic continues his quest to encounter and to transform an object that challenges him, fascinates him, and inspires fear in him. The *paroi* – a wall – is emblematic of the Guillevician object, for it is irreducibly ambivalent. It may protect and shield the poem's speaker, but it also frustrates his desire to penetrate beyond its outer surface in order to discover the secrets hidden behind that surface. Indeed, Guillevic refers to the *paroi* as "une question sans réponse" (P 22). At 223 pages, *Paroi* is substantially longer than *Ville* (146 pages). This difference in length suggests that the wall, both as concrete presence and as metaphor, has a singular importance for Guillevic's poetic imagination.

Even as he is drawn to try to describe the wall, the speaker fears it may conceal a trap into which he could unwittingly fall:

Mais l'imaginer,
Se la représenter,
Hypothétiquement,

C'est aussi bien
Peut-être un piège.

Car l'image nous habitue,
Nous déprend de notre méfiance. (P 121)

(But to imagine it,
To represent it to oneself,
Hypothetically,

It may just as well
Perhaps be a trap.

For the image makes us accustomed,
Relieves us of our mistrust.)

If language is fundamentally separate from reality, it is surely an error to assume that language could fully reproduce an object or be able to assimilate it. In this case, the *paroi* is a particularly slippery and unmanageable object for the poet. It intimidates him and escapes his grasp: "Parfois certaines choses / Faisaient office de paroi" he writes, "Car s'il y a paroi / Il y a masse derrière, / Et qu'est-ce que c'est?" "Mais toujours le soupçon venait / Que la paroi, la vraie paroi, / Etait ailleurs" ("Sometimes certain things / Acted as a wall // For if there is a wall / There is a mass behind it. / And what is it?" "But always the suspicion came / That the wall, the true wall, / Was elsewhere") (P 33). It seems that this object absolutely cannot be defined:

La paroi n'aurait donc
Rien de spatial.

Ce serait ce sur quoi
Butent fatalement
Mes possibilités, mes capacités.

En somme ce serait
La manifestation de mes limites.

Mais je te sens, paroi,
Tout à fait autre chose. (P 51)

(The wall would thus not be
Spatial.

That would be what
My possibilities, my capacities

Necessarily come up against.
In short that would be
The indication of my limitations.

But I can feel you, wall,
That you are something entirely different.)

If figural language remains one of the most effective tools by which poetry can assimilate the real, here figural language seems to be of little usefulness: "A la paroi, j'y crois / Par force. // Ce n'est pas allégorie, / Ce n'est pas métaphore, / C'est réalité" ("I believe in the wall / By force. // It is not an allegory, / It is not a metaphor, / It is reality") (P 118).

By its stubborn resistance to the interrogative gaze of the speaker, the wall comes to stand for "tyranny" (P 190). Moreover, as a signifier of tyranny, it is transformed into yet another figure of the maternal for Guillevic: "Elle serait un peu mère, / La paroi. // Mère ou marâtre, / N'insistons pas" ("It could be considered a bit like a mother, / The wall. // Mother or stepmother / Let's not insist") (P 123). At this point, the wall represents a negative, implacable authority that thwarts all attempts to overcome its defences. It is an absolute obstacle. However, the poet pursues his perhaps Quixotic task of fashioning a verbal object to equal the hypnotic power of the *paroi*: "De toute façon, / Il faut inscrire. // Il faut noter, graver, / Insérer ce qu'on grave" ("In any case, / One must write things down. // One must note things, inscribe them, / Insert what one records") (P 197). He actually makes fun of his own anxiety concerning it:

C'aurait été plus drôle
Si derrière la paroi
Il y avait eu
...
Des démons, des gnomes,
Des fantômes, des dragons, des vampires, (P 140)

(It would have been odder / funnier
If behind the wall
There had been
...
Demons, gnomes,
Ghosts, dragons, vampires,)

In the end, the speaker does reach a provisional truce or state of understanding with the *paroi*:

Etre paroi.

Se confondre
Avec la paroi.

L'intégrer.
S'intégrer.

Rêver le temps.
Devenu corps. (P 223)

(To be a wall
To merge [se confondre]
With the wall.

To take it in.
To integrate oneself with it.

To dream time.
Become body.)

Guillevic's often playful language in *Paroi* permits him to counteract anguish by modifying the meaning of the wall / *marâtre*: "Pourquoi ne pas jouer / Ou tenter de jouer, / Même avec la paroi, // Quand jouer c'est guérir, / Aussi peu que ce soit" ("Why not play / Or try to play, / Even with the wall, // When to play is to heal, / Even just a little") (P 188). By writing graffiti on the wall (P 199–201) the speaker can move beyond the impression of total separateness and difference with which his reflections on, and against, the wall began. The desire for dialogue engenders a new sense of communion with the object, despite its intransigence. In this way, *Paroi* follows a pattern very similar to that evident in *Ville* and *Carnac*.

The gradual evolution in Guillevic's representation of the object which one can trace from *Terraqué* to *Carnac*, through *Ville* and *Paroi*, reaches a high point of development in the late 1970s, with the writing of *Du Domaine*. Many of his critics agree that this text marks the poet's attainment of his mature style and the furthest evolution of his thematics. Jean-Marie Gleize calls *Du Domaine* "l'expression la plus aboutie de l'œuvre de Guillevic" ("the most accomplished work in Guillevic's œuvre") (199).

In this text the first-person speaker declares himself to be the owner of his *domaine*, an enclosed area of parkland that contains a multiplicity of flora and fauna, which the speaker evokes and addresses in the poem. He undertakes the establishment of an inventory of its distinctive features. The *domaine* inititally appears to be an actual place, which Jean Pierrot describes as follows:

> Ce domaine nous ferait plutôt songer à un jardin, et même un jardin d'agrément, une sorte de mélange de parc à l'anglaise et de paysage de bocage breton. Le poète mentionne des allées, des arbres, des buissons, des haies, une source ou des fontaines. Végétaux et fleurs sont souvent évoqués: fougères, jonquilles, roses, etc. Ce jardin est habité ou traversé par quelques animaux, lièvres ou chevreuils. Il est surtout envahi d'oiseaux: rossignol, colibri, hirondelle, épervier, geai ou chat-huant. Mais les espèces les plus répandues sont, apparemment, le ramier et la tourterelle. Il est, semble-t-il, entouré et protégé par un mur. Surtout, il est très souvent question d'un étang. (186)
>
> (This estate would make us think of a garden, and even a pleasure garden, a sort of blend of an English-style garden and a woodland landscape in Brittany. The poet mentions paths, trees, bushes, hedges, a spring and fountains. Plants and flowers are often evoked: ferns, jonquils, roses, etc. This garden is inhabited or walked through by a few types of animals, hares or roe deer. It is above all invaded by birds: hummingbirds, nightingales, swallows, the sparrow-hawk, blue jays, or the brown owl. But the species that recur most often are, apparently, the wood pigeon and the turtle-dove. It seems to be surrounded and protected by a wall. A pond is mentioned particularly often.)

At the outset, the speaker asserts his control over this space: "Dans le domaine que je régis, / On ne parle pas du vent" ("In the estate which I manage / control [régis], / No one talks of the wind") (DD 9).

His ownership of the estate ("que je régis") is certain. However, the text will move slowly away from this opening statement of mastery; the speaker will gradually relinquish this egocentric position towards nature, adopting instead an attitude of openness and dialogue. In this way, the independent, sovereign self that twentieth-century poets have inherited from Romantic poetry yields to a different sort of lyric subjectivity. A participatory, receptive stance now defines the interactions between the poetic subject and the object world:

Dans le domaine,
Chacun

Est à la recherche
De ses coordonnées. (DD 68)

(On the estate,
Everyone

Is looking for
His / Its coordinates / exact location.)

Indeed, towards the end of the text, the speaker reverses his initial assertion of mastery, replacing it with an unanswered question: "Régir le domaine?" ("Control the estate?") (DD 116). In place of an arrogant imposition of human control over nature, the poet opts for a quiet contemplation of individual natural objects, expressed in minimalist, haiku-like fragments:

La grenouille
Se souvient
Qu'elle doit chanter. (DD 144)

(The frog
Remembers
That it must sing.)

*

Des roses
Qui ne pensent pas
A être des roses. (DD 15)

(Roses
That do not think
About being roses.)

*

La branche –
Infatigable. (DD 30)

(The branch –
Indefatigable.)

*

L'ombellifère
Accepte. (DD 100)

(The umbelliferae
accepts.)

*

Le glaïeuil
N'a besoin de personne. (DD 142)

(The sword lily
Needs no one.)

In each of these brief fragments, the self-sufficiency, integrity, and strangeness of the natural world is valorized. Unlike the fearful objects of *Terraqué*, these flora and fauna coexist in harmony with the human subject. Dialogue and exchange guide the interaction between them. If one pays close attention to things, Guillevic shows us, they can teach us indispensable lessons:

Jamais vu l'épervier
Jouer à l'épervier. (DD 113)

(Never saw a sparrowhawk
Playing at being a sparrowhawk.)

*

Est-ce qu'un ramier
S'admire dans son vol? (DD 114)

(Does a wood pigeon
Admire itself in flight?)

The poet has termed "quanta" the 406 lyric fragments that compose *Du Domaine*. He uses this scientific term to indicate that the fragments represent bits of pulsating energy infused with the dynamism of the natural world itself.

A key aspect of the new sense of reconciliation with the object world in *Du Domaine* is achieved through Guillevic's reorienting of the place of the maternal, a process already begun in *Carnac, Ville*, and *Paroi*, as we have seen. *Carnac* was organized around an extended encounter with the sea (*la mer/la mère*) characterized by ambivalence. In *Du Domaine* the poet places a pond ("l'étang") – that is, a much smaller and enclosed body of water – at the centre of his estate. Strong associations with the maternal surface in his evocations of the pond. "L'eau de l'étang, // Veuve / De l'océan" ("The pond's water, // Widow / Of the ocean") (DD 63); "L'eau, // Matrice du cri" ("Water, // matrix / womb of the cry") (DD 83). Here, the maternal object is integrated into a natural space in which it is repositioned. Its significance has altered the water of the pond and is still, unlike the turbulent and always changing waters of the sea. The pond maintains a silent, remote presence:

L'eau de l'étang

Jamais surprise
En flagrant délit. (DD 53)

(The pond's water

Never surprised
Red-handed.)

*

L'étang

Fait lui-même
Sa mythologie. (DD 25)

(The pond

Makes
Its own mythology.)

*

Un silence
Couleur de l'étang. (DD 54)

(A silence
The colour of the pond.)

*

L'eau de l'étang,

Veuve
De l'océan. (DD 63)

(The pond's water,

Widow
Of the ocean.)

*

L'eau,
Matrice du cri. (DD 83)

(Water,
Womb of the cry.)

The *domaine* itself, as an idealized place of refuge, acts as a maternal trope. Jean Pierrot considers it "une projection extérieure de l'univers intérieur du poète, une objectivation de ce refuge idéal auquel … il lui arrive encore … de se complaire. Car ce domaine est aussi un lieu manifestement protégé" ("a projection outward of the poet's inner world, an objectification of that ideal refuge in which … he delights. For this estate is also a place that is clearly protected") (187–8). The textual *domaine* becomes a place to retreat to, but also – more importantly – a transformed maternal space, no longer the dark, terrifying nighttime zone that Guillevic had represented so powerfully in *Terraqué*. *Du Domaine* presents a tamed, harmonious space of exchange and reciprocity in which the object, though still mysterious and other, is not threatening.

By using his creativity to resolve the anxiety of the (maternal) object that had so infused his early poetry, and his early life, Guillevic accomplishes through poetic language what Melanie Klein would term "reparations." The notion of making reparations is essential to her understanding of the function of art. As Simon Harel explains in his Kleinian study of autobiographical texts by French writers Michel Leiris, Antonin Artaud, and René Crevel, from a Kleinian perspective, "l'acte de création permet simultanément d'intégrer et de mettre à distance l'angoisse archaïque de dissociation suscitée par la position schizo-paranoïde" ("the act of creation allows one simultaneously to integrate and to place at a distance the archaic anxiety of dissociation prompted by the paranoid-schizoid position") (21). We have already observed how negativity and destructiveness characterize the infant's world of internalized part-objects in Klein's paranoid-schizoid position. Against the psychosexual violence that prevails in this early position, literary creativity can perform a restorative, "reparative" function. "Chez Klein," Harel writes, "la valeur instauratrice de l'ordre réparateur prétend juguler la destructivité primaire de l'inconscient" ("In Klein's work, the founding value of reparations claims to suppress the primary destructiveness of the unconscious") (83). To Harel, a fundamental relation to the mother – or rather, to a "dédicataire maternel" ("maternal dedicatee") (34) – grounds literary creativity: "La notion de réparation ne représente donc pas seulement l'affirmation d'un colmatage des forces destructrices de la psyché. Elle suppose … l'expression d'un don" ("The notion of reparations thus does not represent only an assertion of the clogging of the destructive forces of the psyche. It implies … the expression of a gift") (88). The goal of this textual labour of reparation is the writing subject's self-renewal or symbolic rebirth: "l'auteur par le travail scriptural recréerait littéralement l'objet afin de mieux s'y projeter. Détruisant et recomposant l'objet élu – source de l'activité créatrice – l'auteur simulerait par l'identification projective son propre deuil et sa (re)naissance" ("through the work of writing the author would literally recreate the object in order to better project him / herself into it. Destroying and recomposing the chosen object – the source of creative activity – the author would simulate his / her own mourning and (re)birth through projective identification") (90). Thus, through creative activity, the matricidal desire that operates "au coeur du modèle kleinien" ("at the heart of the Kleinian model") (110) can be reoriented and transformed. In a sense, this process constitutes Klein's reworking of the Freudian view of art as a "sublimation" of erotic instincts. Yet, lest this theoretical model of psychic redemption through art seem too neat, Harel cautions that the work of reparation that literary texts perform remains necessarily partial and incomplete. Following Klein, he asserts that "la réparation, comme 'compensation mentale,' est une exigence insatisfaite" ("reparation, as a 'mental compensation,' is an unsatisfied demand"] (18).

It is tempting to interpret a later Guillevic text such as *Du Domaine* as a sign of the poet's having overcome anxiety (the catalyst for his earliest poetry) to achieve "la sérénité gagnée" ("serenity attained") (to quote the title of Jean Pierrot's important study of Guillevic's work). Certainly, one notes a definite working towards a poetics of harmonious exchange with the object world throughout his later collections of poetry. Whether this movement towards reciprocity, equilibrium, and peace vis-à-vis the world of things is ever finally completed is not certain, however.

Insofar as a full reconciliation with the object world *is* achieved in Guillevic's poetry, then the results of that reconciliation are most clearly readable in the poetry collections *Euclidiennes* (*Euclidian Poems*) and *Motifs* (*Themes*), which close this chapter.

Animating the Object: *Euclidiennes* and *Motifs*

The collections *Euclidiennes* (1967) and *Motifs* (1987) stand out in Guillevic's œuvre because of the unique form of interaction between subject and object staged in these two texts. In both cases, the objects under scrutiny describe *themselves*, in the first person. The poet becomes a ventriloquist, animating the objects of his curiosity and of his desire. A gentle humour characterizes the approach to naming and describing the object here. Thus, *Euclidiennes* and *Motifs* mark the strongest departure within Guillevic's œuvre from the pervasive feelings of anxiety, even terror, evident in his early collections. In *Motifs*, as we shall see, a final engagement with the textualized figure of the mother also occurs, representing a further stage of development in the poet's working through of ambivalence towards an imagined maternal presence, an ambivalence which the object-relations theory of Melanie Klein has helped us to contextualize and interpret.

At first glance, *Euclidiennes* seems to be a purely playful text that focuses on objects in a simple, light-hearted manner. The poet presumably aims to amuse his readers here, above all. Each poem in *Euclidiennes* reads like a sort of riddle in which a drawing of a geometrical figure in the upper half of each page provides a key to make sense of the verbal description underneath each geometrical figure. Upon closer examination, the poems of *Euclidiennes* demonstrate that Guillevic has combined a comical approach to the representation of objects with a more serious purpose. Just as Jean de La Fontaine in seventeenth-century France had used fables written (ostensibly) about animals to formulate elegant and thoughtful moral lessons concerning human behaviour (particularly concerning humanity's flaws and foibles), Guillevic's talking geometrical figures offer understated and insightful lessons as well. For example, the "sinusoïde" describes itself in this way:

Sinusoïde
C'est fatigant dans les montées,
C'est effrayant dans les descentes

Et les sommets ne donnent,
Aussi bien que les creux,

Que l'idée de l'arrêt
La notion du repos. (E 169)

(Sine Curve
It's tiring going up,
It's terrifying going down

And the highs give only,
As do the lows,

The idea of stopping
The notion of rest.)

As the "sinusoïde" shows us, going from one extreme to another is either "exhausting" or "terrifying." Through its experience of ceaseless up-and-down movement, this figure can teach us the importance of repose as a goal in life. (In this sense, the poem complements the underscoring of the value of harmony and tranquillity which *Du Domaine* also performs.)

Elsewhere in *Euclidiennes*, an Isosceles triangle offers another lesson:

Triangle isocèle
J'ai réussi à mettre
Un peu d'ordre en moi-même.
J'ai tendance à me plaire. (E 174)

(Isoceles Triangle
I've managed to make
A bit of order in myself.
I tend to be pleased with myself.)

The visual impression of "order" and symmetry which the object displays for us becomes an example of the optimal way to live one's life. The lesson offered by this isosceles triangle contrasts sharply with that presented by the equilateral triangle, who declares that "[j]e suis allé trop loin / Avec mon souci d'ordre" ("I went too far / With my concern for order") (E 175). Like a classical French seventeenth-century moralist, Guillevic believes in moderation above all!

The sphere may be the geometrical figure which matters most to the poet, given that he dedicated an entire collection, *Sphère* (1963), to that object. In *Euclidiennes*, he addresses the sphere in one poem, telling it that, by being able to inhabit it, he gains a sense of self:

Je t'aime d'être habituelle,
Espace pour mes jours,
Pour mon regard les yeux fermés.

En toi j'ai place,
En toi je suis,
Je me bâtis. (E 176)

(I like you for being customary,
A space for my days,
For my closed-eyed gaze.

In you I have a place,
In you I am,
I build myself.)

The sphere carries the traditional symbolism of the circle: perfection, enclosure. It acts as an ideal space for the poet's imagination, a place to think, write, and imagine away from the noise and conflict of the world. Whereas the wall represented in *Paroi* concretized the notion of the obstacle blocking the poet's imagination and limiting his freedom, the sphere allows him to exist fully: "En toi, silence, / En toi le temps / Que je recueille, je résume" ("In you, silence, / In you time / Which I gather, I resume") (E 176). From a Kleinian perspective, the sphere could be read as an abstract, appropriated womb, remade into a nurturing refuge for the poet's imagination. By praising the sphere and basing individual poems – as well as the entire collection – on its functioning, he bridges the gap between the formerly terrible maternal image and his own subjectivity. A further step towards psychic integration is achieved.

Euclidiennes is, by Guillevic's own admission, a joyous text. (Indeed, he confesses that is was the only one of his collections that he wrote while in a state of euphoria.) (VP 179) In the end, the words he attributes to the pyramid in his text sum up the deeper significance of these geometrical figures for his readers: "Nous, figures, nous n'avons / Après tout qu'un vrai mérite, // C'est de simplifier le monde, / D'être un rêve qu'il se donne" ("We, who are figures, we have / After all only one real value, // Simplifying the world, / Being a dream which it gives to itself") (E 187). This simplified and harmonious image of existence represents a hard-won, invaluable freedom of the imagination and a new function for the object in Guillevic's work. Again, from a Kleinian perspective, the collection constitutes a rewriting of Guillevic's earliest childhood memory, with which this chapter began. In that anecdote, an agonizing guilt and apprehension of anticipated maternal rage followed the small child's breaking of a round object, a piece of the stove (an object associated with the mother). As if in response to that anecdote, in *Euclidiennes*, Guillevic plays with and celebrates whole, unbroken, abstract objects. By his affirmation of the wisdom "spoken" by these objects, he also enacts what Klein had called reparations. The poet holds these "good" objects he has created within the text. Publishing the book gives the objects a permanent presence. They remain and continue to offer valuable advice, along with amusement.

Motifs, published twenty years after *Euclidiennes* and ten years before the poet's death, employs a similar strategy of giving things a "voice" so as to let them describe themselves. As Michael Brophy remarks, "[d] ans *Motifs*, le poète parle pour les choses, avec les choses, par les choses. Il laisse parler les choses en lui" ("[i]n *Motifs*, the poet speaks for things, with things, through things. He lets things speak in him") (734–5). As the things transform themselves into verbal descriptions, Brophy argues that they perform a "cheminement vers soi par le biais de l'autre" ("progressive movement towards oneself by means of the other") that leads to an enhanced self-knowledge for the poems' speaker (121).

Serge Gaubert notes that in designating these objects as "motifs," Guillevic is assigning them a polyvalent role. Gaubert interprets "motifs" as meaning "qui met en mouvement" ("that which sets in motion") as well as "[s]ujet pour un peintre" ("[s]ubject for a painter") and "[p]hrase musicale" ("[m]usical phrase) (217–18). So, by his choice of "motifs" as a title for this collection, the poet rejects the notion of objects as stationary or static. Just as Ponge moved from writing fixed textual *objets* to creating *objeux* and *objoies*, in *Motifs* Guillevic replaces the closed, immobile oaken cupboard that stands as an entrance-point to his œuvre with objects in movement, in the process of becoming. The aesthetics of openness and process that shape *Motifs* is representative of his later work from the 1970s, 1980s, and 1990s.

The longest section of *Motifs* is entitled "La Mer" (135–213). Twenty-seven years after writing *Carnac*, the poet here resumes his pursuit of a dialogue with *la mer/la mère*. With this long poem Guillevic is returning to *Carnac* in order to rewrite it, in a sense. Now, towards the end of his life, he is reviving the scene of his rediscovery, in 1960, of his strength and focus as a poet, following the dry spell in the 1950s when he devoted himself to writing sonnets under the aegis of Communist Party ideology. Beyond *Carnac*, "La Mer" also provides the poet with a further opportunity to rework the material from his earliest collections, especially *Terraqué*: work that was dominated by the obsessive presence of a menacing maternal figure. In Kleinian terms, that early poetry registered anxious phantasies of vulnerability to attack from "objects" associated with the mother, while enacting imagined attacks on her body. The violent, dark imagery of *Terraqué* was recast by Guillevic in *Carnac* into a poetics of dialogue, openness and a movement towards a deepened inter-subjectivity linking the poem's first-person speaker and the sea, with its ever-ambiguous textual identity of "la mer / la mère."

Now, in this poem ending *Motifs*, Guillevic takes the process of (in Kleinian parlance) reparations enacted towards the phantasy figure of the mother one step further. Here, in "La Mer," the sea itself speaks in the first person, telling of its daily experiences, reflecting on what is particular about its being in order to build a link to the poet, and to the reader. In an act of supreme empathy, Guillevic now provides the sea, originally a hostile presence in his work, with a voice. By humanizing the initially alien object, he re-imagines it in fundamental ways.

The sea first defines itself through stock images, clichés of itself: "Ce besoin / De se répéter / Vague après vague" ("This need / To repeat itself / Wave after wave") (139); "Le soleil / est un oeil / Sur moi, // Et moi je n'ai / Que ma surface // Et mes essais / De mouvement" ("The sun / is an eye / Upon me, // And I have / Only my surface // And my attempts / At movement") (136). However, it also challenges and dispels certain misconceptions through which it had been seen: "Bien sûr / Que je ne suis pas indifférente / A l'égard de mes baleines, // Pas plus à mes algues, / A mon plancton, / A mes palourdes. // *Nous tenons ensemble*" ("Of course / I am not indifferent / To my whales, // Nor to my algae, / To my plankton, / To my pullet shells. // *We hold together*") (141, emphasis added). The sea's feeling of tenderness towards the creatures who live within it is expressed here by the phrase "Nous tenons ensemble," which articulates an idea of crucial importance to Guillevic: the sense of unity and belonging linking the subject to the things around it.

As in *Carnac*, the sea of "La Mer" is profoundly paradoxical: "Pourquoi / N'entendrais-je pas / En dissidence / Avec moi-même?" ("Why / Would I not hear / In dissidence / With myself?") (146). It often asks questions, suggesting the mysteries of being: "Où suis-je / Le plus moi-même, // Dans ma partie / Profonde et noire // Ou dans ma partie / Plus ou moins mobile / Et plus ou moins claire?" ("Where am I / Most myself, // In the part of me that's / Deep and black // Or in the part that's / More or less in motion / And more or less light?") (147). "Moi-même, tout moi-même, / Je me sens la vague / De je ne sais quel océan" ("Myself, all of myself, / I feel I'm the wave / Of some ocean or other") (171). While evoking its literal features, the sea also acknowledges its existence as a literary motif: "Un poète a parlé / D'*uraltes Wehen vom Meer,* // Du souffle de la mer / Plus vieux que le temps" ("A poet spoke / of the *uraltes Wehen vom Meer,* // Of the sea's breathing / Older than time") (156). Nonetheless, it also challenges previous, familiar images by which poets have attempted to make sense of it or control it: "Je suis une page blanche // Sur quoi rien ne s'écrit / Que ma présence" ("I am a blank page // On which nothing is written / But my presence") (155). Guillevic thus succeeds in transforming it into a presence both familiar and unfamiliar.

One of the most significant changes in his re-imagining of the sea in this poem is his insistence on its tender and gently maternal qualities. The sea frequently refers to its rocking, cradling motions, calling itself "Mère du mouvement" ("Mother of Movement") (172). It is explicitly associated with birth: "Je suis toujours // En train de m'accoucher" ("I am constantly // Giving birth to myself") (157).

At the end of the poem, Guillevic returns to the figure of the monster – one of the key images constitutive of the uneasiness characterizing *Terraqué*. In the final pages of "La Mer," the sea speaks of itself as a kind of monster:

Monstre que tu es,
Me crie-t-on parfois.

Je manque d'éléments
Pour en juger,

Mais volontiers
Je le crois:

Je suis un monstre.
Je suis un monstre. (209)

(You are such a monster,
They sometimes shout.

I lack the elements
To judge that,

But gladly
I'll believe it.

I am a monster.
I am a monster.)

Yet, immediately, the notions of fearfulness and violence that had been associated with monsters in his early poetry are questioned:

Mais qu'est-ce
Qui n'est pas un monstre

De tout cela
Que je vois ou devine?

Un monstre, cet azur,
Un monstre, ce clocher.
*

Qu'est-ce qui n'est pas un monstre
Quand on l'attaque,

Quand on réveille
Ses profondeurs?
...
En toute chose
Le monstre est plus ou moins visible. (210)

(But what
Is not monstrous

In everything that
I see or guess at?

This azure is monstrous,
This clocktower is monstrous.
*

What is not monstrous
When it's attacked,

When its depths
Are awakened?
...
In any thing
The monster is more or less visible.)

By now, the poet has come full circle, as "La Mer" reaches its ending. What was most monstrous, threatening, and potentially violent has become familiar and tender, if not fully domesticated by the poet's empathetic imagination. The object is still other, yet that otherness is now a companion to the poem's speaker. At the same time, from a Kleinian perspective, writing has permitted the subject to effect reparations, thus changing a dangerously threatening maternal figure composed of menacing part objects into a benign, if still strange and other, textual presence.

6 Jean Tortel's Poetics of the Desiring Gaze

Jean Tortel (1904–93) is a pivotal, transitional figure within the French tradition of the poetry and poetics of the object. His work bears deep affinities to that of earlier poets of the object, especially to Ponge and Guillevic. At the same time, during the 1970s and 1980s Tortel became a key mentor to younger poets at work elaborating a new avant-garde textuality: Anne-Marie Albiach, Claude Royet-Journoud, Emmanuel Hocquard, Alain Veinstein, and Liliane Giraudon, among others. Tortel's work as a poet and critic responds to, and extends, the tradition of the object poetry studied earlier in this book.

Born in 1904, Tortel was active in the development of poetry and poetics in France for several decades. A first decisive influence on his life as a poet was his meeting Jean Royère, a close relative of Tortel's wife, Jeannette. Royère directed an important poetry journal, *La Phalange* (*The Phalanx*). He championed an aesthetics inspired by Mallarmé at a time when Mallarmé was not seen as the major precursor that he is today. Royère's thinking on a series of fundamental issues, such as the poetic line (*le vers*) shaped Tortel's ideas with lasting force. In 1938, Tortel was named a *fonctionnaire* (*civil servant*) and sent to Marseille, where he became closely involved with the journal *Cahiers du Sud* (*Notebooks of the South*), an association that would continue until 1966, when it ceased publication. In 1941, he published his first book of poetry, *De mon vivant*. Later, in 1952, he edited a special issue of *Cahiers du Sud* on "le préclassicisme français" (French preclassicism) which included articles by Ponge and Jean Tardieu and a generous sampling of poems from the first half of the seventeenth century. Like Ponge's book-length homage to Malherbe, *Pour un Malherbe* (*For a Malherbe*) (an excerpt of which appeared in this issue of *Cahiers du Sud*), Tortel's enthusiastic and insightful critical commentary on this group of French poets has a manifesto-like force. In praising the example of these preclassical poets, he was – quite explicitly – also distancing himself from the example of the Romantics and the Surrealists, with their aesthetics of subjectivity, dream, and inspiration. In a long essay on the French preclassical poets, Tortel asserts that these poets discovered and presented in their poems "un lyrisme fondé sur le réel et qui tend à 'élargir' celui-ci, au-delà des limites ordinaires … Le réalisme foncier de la poésie préclassique doit être souligné" ["a lyricism grounded in reality which tends / strives to 'broaden' it beyond ordinary limits … The fundamental realism of preclassical poetry must be underscored") (138). He adds that "[l]eur modestie touchant le but et l'essence de la poésie est étonnante, quasi choquante pour des esprits habitués aux ambitions romantiques et surréalistes" ("[t]heir modesty concerning the goal and essential nature of poetry is surprising, almost shocking for a mind used to the ambitions of the romantics and surrealists") (147). A major turning point in Tortel's life took place in 1964, when he and his wife moved to a house near Avignon, *Chemin des jardins neufs* (*New Gardens Road*); the name of this place coincidentally reflects the new orientation that would mark Tortel's later poetry. Between 1964, when *Les Villes ouvertes* (*Open Cities*) was published, and 1993, the year of his death, Tortel produced a brilliant and singular body of texts, which most of his critics consider to be his finest work. In this distinctive corpus of garden poetry, he pursues a complex poetics of the desiring gaze. The natural world, through the metonymy of the garden which the speaker sees outside his window, becomes a source of raw material for him and an incitement to writing.

As indicated earlier, strong connections to the poetry of Ponge and Guillevic are evident in Tortel's work. Moreover, he has written important critical studies of both these poets. Like them, he rejects the aesthetic stance and writing practices of the Romantics and the Surrealists. As Catherine Soulier states, Tortel "se méfie du lyrisme, du Romantisme et de son avatar surréaliste; il refuse l'écriture visionnaire, oraculaire, et toutes les poétiques de l'inspiration; il émet à l'égard de la métaphore de vives réticences" ("mistrusts lyricism, [that of] the Romantics or of their surrealist descendants; he rejects the idea of oracular or visionary writing and all poetics based on inspiration; he expresses strong reservations concerning metaphor") (11). Tortel shares Guillevic's predilection for recording the elements of the natural world using very few words (nouns, mainly) which he places against the whiteness of the blank page. Both poets attempt to "transcribe" objects from the natural world without distorting them or twisting them into metaphors.[1]

In his 1971 monograph on Guillevic, Tortel often discloses the fundamental features of his own aesthetics in commenting on Guillevic's practice. He writes, for example, that "Guillevic est un poète de la constatation pure, soit un de ceux pour qui le monde extérieur est ce qui existe. Ainsi, on l'isole aussitôt de la tradition romantique … On le dégage … d'une notion métaphysique de la poésie sur laquelle plusieurs générations ont vécu" ("Guillevic is a poet of mere statement, that is, one for whom the outer world is all that exists. Thus, he can immediately be separated from the Romantic tradition … One can dissociate him from the metaphysical view of poetry which several generations have held") (90). Especially in his later work, from *Carnac* (1960) onward, Guillevic's poetry has a minimalist simplicity, as the speaker of the poems often catalogues the elements of the world around him in almost notational form: it is enough to state that this thing, or that thing, exists. As Tortel observes, "les propositions essentielles de Guillevic sont de l'ordre de la présence, comme le sont 'Il fait beau' ou 'Je t'aime'" ("Guillevic's essential ideas focus on presence, statements such as 'The weather is nice" or 'I love you'") (90). He notes that Guillevic "s'oblige à toujours plus de concision, de fermeté, de clarté" ("forces himself towards ever greater conciseness, firmness, clarity") (14) – which is equally true of Tortel's own poetry.

In 1984, Tortel published *Francis Ponge cinq fois* (*Francis Ponge Five Times*), a volume collecting five essays on Ponge which Tortel had originally published in 1944, 1949, 1953, 1962, and 1975. (The very fact of his returning to Ponge's œuvre so often to comment on it suggests a powerful connection between the two poets' ethical and aesthetic commitments.) Many of his comments in these Ponge essays help to clarify Tortel's view of language and representation. For example, in discussing *Le Verre d'eau* (*The Glass of Water*) Tortel writes that "ce verre d'eau est plus qu'un titre: il est l'image symbolique d'une œuvre qui fait du bien, parce qu'elle lave et désaltère l'esprit; et qui, s'opposant à toute écriture à prétentions excessives, à tout orgueil métaphysique ou idéologique, bref à tout 'magma' même et surtout 'poétique,' c'est-à-dire une grande partie de la littérature de notre temps, rétablit un certain équilibre" ("that glass of water is more than a title: it is the symbolic image of a work which does one good, because it cleanses and quenches the mind; and which is opposed to any writing with excessive pretentions, and to all metaphysical or ideological pride, in short to all types of verbal 'magma' – even and especially the 'poetic' kind, that is to say, to a large part of today's literature. [For this reason, his work] re-establishes a certain balance") (28). He also explains that, in Ponge, "[l]'expression a pour but de fixer ce que l'objet a de spécifique" ("the goal of [w]riting [l'expression] is to set down what is specific to the object") (29). Like Tortel himself, "Ponge est systématiquement modeste" ("Ponge is systematically modest") (30). "Expressing" the object requires a struggle with language: "L'opération ne se résout donc pas en une lutte contre l'objet, mais contre un langage qu'il faut forcer" ("The operation [of writing] does not resolve itself then into a struggle against the object, but against language, which must be tamed") (33). Ponge is focused, through his efforts to manipulate language, on working with the perceiving subject's relationship to the things before him: "Il faut donc, dit Ponge, 'm'occuper de ma relation aux choses', faire jouer jusqu'à la tension extrême le mécanisme de ces rapports" ("I must then, says Ponge, 'be concerned with my relationship to things, make the mechanism controlling that relationship play itself out to an extreme tension'") (75). In Tortel's own poetics, the terms "relations" and "tension" will acquire substantial metapoetic force as well.

The conclusion to Tortel's article "Ponge qui n'a de cesse" ("Ponge Who Will Not Rest / Stop"), presented at the 1975 Colloque de Cerisy, is of particular interest as a reflection on Ponge's poetics and a reflection of Tortel's own practice:

> On peut croire que … le « monde
> muet » de Ponge acquiesce à l'affirmation
> de La Fontaine.
> Car tout parle dans l'Univers,
> Il n'est rien qui n'ait son langage.
> De sorte qu'en fin de compte, le texte propose
> la figure d'un mouvement perpétuel. (87)

> (One can believe that … Ponge's "silent
> world" acquiesces to La Fontaine's affirmation.
> For everything speaks in the Universe.
> There is nothing that does not have its own
> language.
> So that in the end, the text proposes the figure of (an)
> eternal movement.)

His affinities with the work of Guillevic and Ponge are profound. Yet, Tortel has also fashioned a poetics whose particular concerns are rather different from those of his peers. His metapoetic use of terms such as "image," "figure," "body," and "gaze" define a distinct approach to the object and its fascinating otherness. Before looking at any specific poems of Tortel, one must pay careful attention to his discourse concerning the relation of subject / gaze to object(s) / bodies which his poems repeatedly retrace.

Image / Figure / Limits: Tortel's Poetics of the Gaze

A distinction basic to Tortel's understanding of the poetic process is that between "image" and "figure." In an interview with Gil Jouanard, the poet explains how the contrast between "image" and "figure" operates in the writing of poetry, for him: "Je pense que les images que nous recevons, et nous ne recevons que cela puisque les corps sont impénétrables et que nous n'en recevons que les images, elles nous assaillent et menacent sans cesse de nous submerger. Mais nous avons le pouvoir d'en interrompre quelques-unes et de les renverser sur la page en objets de langage. C'est peut-être ça, la nécessité de l'écriture" ("I think the images that we receive, and we receive only that since bodies are impenetrable and we only receive images of them, these images assail us and constantly threaten to submerge us. But we have the power to interrupt a few of them and to reverse them onto the page into objects made of language. That is perhaps the necessity of writing") (214). In the same interview, the "figure" is characterized by Tortel as "l'image renversée, c'est l'image détruite. L'image est un événement psycho-physique et la figure est un événement de langage. Elles se situent dans deux espaces différents ... La figure *relate*, ou constate sur la page *les relations* qui s'établissent continuellement entre l'objet, le langage et celui qui ..." ("the image reversed, the image destroyed. The image is a psycho-physical event and the figure is an event in language. They are located in two different spaces ... The figure *relates*, or states on the page the *relations* that are continuously created between the object, language and the person who ...") (214–15). Tortel also indicates that images do not become "figures" in a straightforward, effortless manner. Various obstacles – which will acquire a powerful thematic and metapoetic significance in his texts – complicate, or even undermine, the functioning of the transferral of the image into the figure which the poem requires.

The notion of "limits" plays a central role in the evolution of Tortel's metapoetics. Indeed, the titles of two of his best-known collections of poems include the term "limites": *Limites du regard* (*Limits of the Gaze*) (1971) and *Limites du corps* (*Limits of the Body*) (1993). These titles, and the occurrences of "limite" or "limites" within many of his individual poems, underscore Tortel's continual awareness of those limits which condition the possibility of creating an exact textual analogue of the visible world. Several different types of "limits" emerge in his poetry: the garden hedge (*la haie*) which stops the gaze and encloses the garden; the frame of the window through which the perceiving subject looks at the natural world; the rectangular page itself, as it supports and constrains writing. Above all, language itself imposes and constitutes a kind of limit. This last point needs special emphasis, inasmuch as one of the crucial links between Tortel and poets of a younger generation in France (Albiach, Royet-Journoud and Hocquard, in particular) is their consciousness of the flaws, gaps and aporias that inescapably limit the ability of language to transcribe the referential world. Discussing Tortel's garden poetry, Suzanne Nash emphasizes precisely this point: "The force of [Tortel's] most recent poetry springs from the sense one has of a pure intentionality, struggling to bring word and image together, so as not to lose the material density of either. But poetry is not linguistic theory, and Tortel has always known that his work is generated out of the fundamental incompatibility of experience and its expression … Modern poets, especially, write despite what they know about language; their figurations constitute systems of value proffered against meaninglessness" (29).

Along with the idea of "limits," the storm (*l'orage*) often resurfaces in these poems. Not (or not primarily) a metaphor, the storm literally shows us what threatens order, stability, and the ordered space of the garden. The danger of a storm, a situation over which one has no control, can radically disrupt the harmony and beauty which the garden represents. The 1968 collection of poems *Relations* (*Relationships*) includes a sequence of twenty poems entitled "Phrases pour un orage" ("Sentences for a Storm") (27–48). The sequence follows the approach and eventual dispersal of a summer storm in the garden. In the third poem of the sequence, the blue sky is described as containing the dark shadow of a potential storm: "L'azur enfante l'ombre / (Le fruit sa pourriture)" (31); "C'est midi, de la lumière / Que vient l'obscur" ("The blue [azure] gives birth to the shadow / (The fruit to its rotting" (31);

"It's noon, light / From which the dark comes") (32). The storm appears from nowhere; it cannot be fully understood or explained:

On ne sait pas
Ce qui s'avance
Et d'où ça vient.

Cette chose
N'est pas d'ici.

Elle est calme et lente,
Inabordable, chaude. (36)

(One does not know
What comes forward
And where it comes from.

This thing
Is not from here.

It is calm and slow,
Unapproachable, warm.)

Then, abruptly: "Une fureur / A remplacé le jour. // Une menace, un craquement" ("A furor / Has replaced the day. // A threat, a loud crack") (39).

When asked if the words "garden" and "storm" are allegorical of what is happening in the writing of his poems, Tortel answered that "[s]i ce côté allégorique existe, je n'y peux rien, mais à coup sûr je ne le cherche pas" ("[i]f that allegorical side exists, I can't help it, but certainly I don't seek it") (94). In his answer, the poet again reiterates his commitment to an aesthetic of literalness, of turning away from image and metaphor.

A further recurring instance of limits or limitations here is the ocular blind spot blocking part of one eye. The blind spot makes viewing (and, therefore, writing) difficult, at risk. In his 1979 collection *Des Corps attaqués* (*On Bodies Attacked*) Tortel explores the problem of seeing and writing through the blind spot in a long sequence of twenty-seven poems entitled "L'oeil taché" ("A Stained Eye") (43–71). The flaw in vision now becomes fully integrated into his poetics:

Oscillante légèrement
Bleutée si je ferme l'oeil droit.

Une épaisseur s'auréole
Évidente arrachée
A l'acte de voir.

Je porte un soleil noir
Mais dérisoire

Inévitable si (je ferme l'œil droit).
Interdit l'écriture. (49)

(Oscillating slightly
Gone blue [Bleutée] if I close my right eye.

An opacity becomes haloed [s'auréole]
Obvious torn

From the act of seeing.
I carry a black but
Derisory sun

Inevitable if (I close my right eye).
Forbids writing.)

At the end of the final poem in the series: "Le regard perverti doubla / Les angles droits et des opaques arbitraires" ("The perverse gaze doubled / The right angles and some arbitrary opacities") (71). Thus, the poems bear witness to the factors that compromise the possibility of the transferral of seen reality into language.

Although Tortel aims to avoid the image, by transforming it into a "figure," he does acknowledge that a certain type of image – "l'image intérieure" ("the interior image") – can surface. He is particularly mistrustful of this type of image, as it belongs to an aesthetic which is contrary to the one he is pursuing. The "interior image" appears when one's eyes are closed; it emerges from dreams, fantasies. In her discussion of Tortel's 1990 collection *Précarités du jour* (*Precariousnesses of the Day*), Catherine Soulier characterizes his sense of "l'image intérieure" in this way: "L'image intérieure, 'obéissant au désir', s'enlève sur fond de vide" ("The interior image, 'obeying desire,' is carried off against a background of emptiness") (65). This "interior image" scorned by the poet is amorphous, insubstantial: "du fait de son caractère amorphe, conséquence de sa permanente mobilité, l'image intérieure s'apparente à de l'eau; une eau épaisse, équivalent substantiel de la nuit" ("because of its amorphous character, a consequence of its constant mobility, the interior image is akin to water; a thick water, the substantial / solid equivalent of the night") (66). Like the storm, Soulier argues, the interior image "n'est plus d'ici; détachée de son objet – de tout objet peut-être – elle est mise au jour d'une profondeur obscure, d'un archaïsme" ("is no longer from here; detached from its object – perhaps from any object – it is the apparition of an obscure depth, of an archaic world") (67).

Writing, for Tortel, takes place via the line of verse – *le vers* – as it imposes a rhythm and form on the act of description. Writing poetry necessarily entails a process of reflection upon *le vers*, in his view. Through a characteristic assimilation of writing to working in the garden, he regards the line of verse crossing the page as similar to a furrow cut into the earth: *un sillon*. Thus he returns to the etymological meaning of the line of verse. As Jean-Michel Maulpoix states, "[i]l en revient au vers pour tracer un sillon plus sûr dans la masse du langage et l'opacité des choses" ("[i]t is the task of the line of verse to trace out a surer furrow in the mass of language and the opacity of things") (17). Tortel acknowledges that he has always devoted considerable attention to his reflections on the line of verse: "La mise en forme découle de là: de se demander ce qu'est un vers. Je le fais, je crois, depuis mes premiers poèmes. Je crois qu'il faut passer par l'histoire du vers, qui comprend le vers classique, s'intégrer à la grande courbe verbale, faites de ruptures et de continuités, de nécessités et de libertés" ("The putting into form comes from that: asking oneself what is a line of verse. I have been doing that, I think, since my first poems. I think it's necessary to review [passer par] the history of the line, which includes the classical line, to integrate oneself into the great verbal curve, made up of breaks and continuities, of requirements and freedoms").[2]

From *Relations* to *Arbitraires Espaces*: Towards a Post-Modern Poetics

To explore Tortel's evolving textual strategies for representing the relationship between language and the natural world, let us turn now to two of his major collections of poems: *Relations* and *Arbitraires espaces*

(*Arbitrary Spaces*). *Relations* was published in 1968, just a few years after he and his wife moved to *Chemin des jardins neufs* near Avignon. It is, perhaps, the best of his poetry collections of the 1960s and 1970s. *Abritraires espaces*, by contrast, belongs to a later period in his poetics. It is his most "post-modern" and most boldly experimental work. Published in 1986, seven years before his death, it carries his practice of, and reflections on, the line of verse further than any of his own (or most of his contemporaries') texts.

In the three short poems that make up the "Liminaire" ("Liminal") section which opens *Relations*, Tortel reveals himself to be highly conscious of the tenuousness, even the impossibility, of the task of achieving an exact representation of reality. The "Liminaire" poems begin in aporia: "Si je commence avec – / Mais lesquels" ("If I begin with – / But which ones") (9). A thematics of silence versus speech highlights the poet's awareness of the limits of language here. The evocation of a storm ("Quand l'orage éclate" 10) brings the notion of the storm as danger and antagonist into play. Yet "Liminaires" ends with a tentative affirmation of the powers of language:

Mais s'arrêtant soudain
Parce qu'on les commande
...
Réclamés et niés
Par ce que je regarde.
...
Les mots qui fêleront
Par trop de méfiance
L'espace et le jardin
Que j'offre à leur courroux
Relatent – c'est leur droit –
Ce qu'ils sont parmi nous. (11)

(But stopping suddenly
Because they are ordered
...
Demanded and denied
By what I look at.
...
The words which will crack

Space and the garden
Through too much distrust
That I offer to their rage
They relate – it's their right –
What they are among us.)

The verb "relatent" in the penultimate line of this opening poem echoes the title *Relations*, making explicit what the focus of the text will be: the manifold relationships among things, the poet's gaze and language. These often unacknowledged relationships will be brought into focus in the poems.

The sequence of poems "Critique d'un jardin" ("Critique of a Garden") (49–66) provides a vivid illustration of what is at stake in Tortel's project. Significantly, the sequence is not simply entitled "Le jardin" ("The Garden") or "Mon jardin" ("My Garden"). His insistence on a critical, reflective perspective on the garden reminds us that he rejects a naive view of language and representation. A metapoetics of description informing his stance towards the garden is immediately evident in the first poem of the sequence:

Irrégulier, humide et transformé
Par les saisons,
Feuille et feuille, les mouvements
Sont verts des futures ombelles.

Instable et mou, jardin découragé.

Après la récolte la planche
Se durcit (mais d'un autre vert
Que celui de l'été).

Le jardin est marron
Quand l'hiver s'épaissit
En maintes herbes non séchées.

Un rectangle est choisi pour être remué.
Le tranchant de la bêche brise
Les mottes d'où le ver sort en spirale,
Lent et mouillé. (51)

(Irregular, humid and transformed
By the seasons,
Leaves and leaves, the movements
Are green with umbels to come.

Unstable and soft, a discouraged garden.

After the harvest the flower bed
Becomes hard (but with a different green
From that of summer).

The garden is brown
When winter thickens
In many grasses not dried out.

A rectangle is chosen to be stirred up.
The keen edge of the trowel breaks
The clods from which the worm emerges in a spiral,
Slow and moist.)

At first glance, this poem appears to present no more than a literal description of a garden scene. However, as readers of poetry well know, even a poem that *seems* to offer only a literal description cannot ever be entirely free of figural language or self-referentiality. Most of the adjectives describing the garden are realistic and banal: "green," "brown," "humid," "not dried." Nevertheless, in the one-line second stanza, the garden is "découragé" – a personification that signals that the speaker is, in fact, adding something to the observed scene. These hints of literary transformation of the real are intensified in the final stanza (translated above):

Un rectangle est choisi pour être remué.
Le tranchant de la bêche brise
Les mottes d'où le ver sort en spirale,
Lent et mouillé.

Here, the rectangular space of the garden where clods of earth are upturned by a trowel mirrors the poet's working with words on the (also) rectangular space of the page. The trowel becomes an analogue for the writer's pen. The poem ends on a humorous note, with the line

"Les mottes d'où le ver sort en spirale," as "le ver" ("the worm") brings to mind its homonym "le vers" ("the line of verse"). The spiral shape corresponds both to the literal movement the worm makes and to the figural "motion" of the poet's imaginative act.

"Critique d'un jardin" is the section of *Relations* most characteristic of Tortel's poetry of the 1960s and 1970s, as evidenced by such collections as *Instants qualifiés* (*Qualified Instants*), *Des Corps attaqués*, and *Limites du regard*. Yet in *Relations* he also moves beyond this descriptive poetry set in, and focused on, the garden. In two sequences of poems from *Relations* – "Explications de textes" ("Explanatory Commentary on Texts") (67–84) and "Gestes de la marquise" ("The Marchioness's Gestures") (85–102) – he embarks on a poetics of appropriation and parodic rewriting which prefigures the work of many contemporary post-modern poets now doing such work. The non-naturalistic view of language evident in these two sequences also prepares one for the late Tortel text *Arbitraires espaces*, in which his approach to the poem is most experimental.

The poems of *Abritraires espaces* present a distinctive aesthetic of *le vers*. At the same time, they enact a more uncertain, even anxious, stance towards the very possibility of reproducing the elements of the natural world in words.

Chose pour dire.
L'informulable.
L'objet pénétré.
Obscur hors de la vue.
Même si c'est très clair si le désir.
S'apaise en lui. (10)

(A thing to be said.
Informulable.
The object penetrated.
Obscure out of view.
Even if it is very clear if the desire
Is satisfied in it.)

Arbitraires espaces begins with a quotation from the writer, critic, and director of the *Nouvelle Revue Française* Jean Paulhan. In post-modern fashion, Tortel will now write poems that echo, while diverging from, the material given in the liminal quotation from Paulhan. He is working with – and / but away from – a pre-textual quotation. The notion of *space* and the images given in the Paulhan quotation remain something to be questioned in Tortel's text, rather than serve as the illustration of a truth guiding his own practice.

The visual poetics of *Arbitraires espaces* are surely the text's most notable feature. As the opening poem quoted above shows, Tortel is foregrounding two particular, and eccentric, aspects of punctuation and layout in each poem: the period at the end of each line and the blank space separating each line from the one preceding it and the one following it. The period at the end of each line continually interrupts our reading of these poems, imposing a distance between the reader and the text, which is intensified by the recurring blank spaces between the lines. The blank spaces isolate each line from those around it. They make us uneasily conscious of the silence from which the words on the page emerge. These two peculiar formal devices – the use of a period at the end of each line and the blank spaces separating the lines – are not gratuitous or decorative. On the contrary, they register Tortel's deepened awareness of the distance between the text and nature in this late collection.

As Jean-Marie Gleize asserts, the title of this collection also suggests a self-referential focus in which the writing is concerned primarily with the line of verse as an aesthetic unit or construct: "L'espace arbitraire, puisque c'est le titre du livre, c'est d'abord le vers, en tant qu'il est (qu'il a telle longueur) par décision arbitraire, arbitraire souligné encore par le fait que le vers ne coïncide pas (nécessairement) avec une unité de sens complète, qu'il laisse donc ainsi le sens en suspens" ("The arbitrary space, since that is the book's title, is first of all that of the line of verse, in as much as it is (it has such and such a length) by an arbitrary decision, an arbitrariness underscored again by the fact that the line of verse does not (necessarily) coincide with a complete unit of meaning, that it thus leaves meaning suspended") (15–16). The obstacle which each period ending each line creates becomes a means of making us (re)consider what a line of verse is, Gleize argues: "Pour faire phrase ... il faudra franchir le point, et le blanc qui est la ligne suivante. Et ce franchissement ... contribue à lester le mot *vers* de son autre sens: Le vers est ce qui tend vers, ce qui avance et va, pour finir *à travers* (le point, le blanc), vers un autre vers, et cet autre vers vers un autre vers encore, etc." ("In order to make a sentence ... it will be necessary to go beyond the period, and the whole space which is the next line. And this going beyond ... contributes to weighting the word *line* [*vers*] from its other meaning: The line [vers] is that which tends towards [vers], what advances and goes, to end *through* [*à travers*] (the period, the blank space), towards another line [vers], and that other line towards still another line, etc.") (16). The consequences of such a bold approach to the line are far-reaching, Gleize believes: "Il s'agit, pour Jean Tortel, sans aucun doute, de contribuer à une définition, ou redéfinition, du vers, après sa déconstruction, sa disparition, sa restructuration 'libre', etc." ("For Jean Tortel, what matters is definitely to contribute to a definition, or a redefinition, of the line, after its deconstruction, its disappearance, its 'free' restructuring, etc.") (16).

Equally notable in this late collection is the preponderance of statements of doubt, negation, negativity, as is clear in the final poem:

Je ne sais pas.
Si je m'intègre.
C'est là toujours pas seulement.
Ici où des blancs arbitraires.
Dénoncent les oscillations.
Que je ne situe pas.
Quand cela remue je dis.
C'est la branche le tremblement.
D'une lumière la vapeur le bruit.
Un corps n'importe quoi. (124)

(I do not know.
If I am integrating myself [Si je m'intègre],
It is always not only there.
Here where arbitrary blank spaces.
Denounce oscillations.
Which I do not locate.
When that stirs I say.
It's the branch the trembling.
Of a light steam noise.
A body anything at all.)

Given the heavy presence of terms such as "Je ne sais pas" ("I do not know") and "Je ne situe pas" ("I do not locate"), the possibility of representing the things the speaker sees before him is fundamentally questioned in these lines. The world ("là" ["there"]) remains radically separate from the text ("ici" ["here"]): "où des blancs arbitraries. / Dénoncent les oscillations. / Que je ne situe pas" ("where arbitrary blank spaces. / Denounce oscillations. / Which I do not locate"). Responding to signs in nature, the speaker says "C'est la branche le tremblement. / D'une lumière la vapeur le bruit. / Un corps n'importe quoi" ("It's the branch the trembling. / Of a light steam noise. / A body anything at all").

This last term, "n'importe quoi," which ends *Arbitraires espaces*, has an ambiguous role in Tortel's poetry. It suggests, first, a refusal to establish a hierarchy among the things he sees, *any* of which may, therefore, become material for a poem. So, "anything at all" can merit inclusion in a poem. Suzanne Nash discussed Tortel's use of the term "n'importe quoi" in conversation with him: "While visiting Tortel recently, I asked him what these last three words of his most recent work – 'anything at all' – which seem to abandon the effort of naming, signified:

> Jean Tortel: To end by saying "It's anything at all," do you know what that avoids? It avoids anguish. It avoids anxiety, what makes us uneasy; people ask themselves questions all the time, in order to know what it is: "Is it a unity?" "Is it a plurality?" "Is it an order?" "Is it to create?" "Is it to change something?" If I have the courage or the laziness – it boils down to the same thing – to say that it is anything at all, then I avoid all that. What I want is to manage to suppress this sickness which is … anguish. (39)

I find it odd that Tortel would perceive evidence of an absence of anguish in his placing "n'importe quoi" (a negative term) at the end of *Arbitraires espaces* – a text in which he repeatedly emphasizes that the thing seen, the "Chose pour dire," is unrepresentable, "informulable." Here, the speaker remains in a position of uncertainty as he labours to perform the act of transcription of nature – an act which he can, at best, imperfectly realize. Is Tortel misreading his own text here? If so, what other misreadings, blind spots, or unknowns may be influencing his poetics? To answer that question, I will now turn to an issue central to Tortel's work: the role of desire and of the object now conceived of as a "body."

The Object as "Body" and the Desiring Gaze in Tortel's Poetry

One of the most compelling – but perhaps most problematic – aspects of Tortel's poetics is the importance he places on desire and on the transformation of the object into a "body." In addressing the issue of the subject's relationship to objects he has selected for transferral into textual figures, he tends to use the term "corps" ("body") rather than "object": "l'objet, dans le vocabulaire que j'emploie, c'est ce qui est là, dans son ambiguïté comme dans ses limites, et que je le regarde ou non. Cet objet, je l'appelle corps, du moment que je le regarde et que par conséquent je le désire. Ainsi, n'importe quel objet – un jardin par exemple – peut être qualifié corps si mon regard … Enfin ça …" ("the object, in the vocabulary that I use, is what is there, in its ambiguity and in its limits, and whether I look at it and when, consequently, I desire it. Thus, any object at all – a garden for example – can be designated a body if my gaze … Well, as for that …").[3]

Tortel's use of "corps" is similar, then, to his use of "objet" and, in fact, he sometimes places the two terms together as though they named a single phenomenon: "En fait, je suis sans cesse devant l'objet-corps (ou les objets): un là-devant dont je suis le flux perpétuel, c'est-à-dire les images, que mon travail est d'interrompre pour n'être pas sans cesse renversé par elles – c'est-à-dire que je les renverse en les transformant en figures, objets de langage" ("In fact, I am constantly in front of an object-body (or objects): a space before me of which I am the perpetual flux, that is to say images, and it is my task to interrupt them so as not to be constantly knocked over by them – that is to say that I reverse them by transforming them into figures, into objects made of language") (Tortel "Montpellier 24.04.78" 87). Desire comes into play in this process of "retournement" which writing effects for Tortel: "Disons que s'accomplit un travail de retournement, *dont la charge érotique est plus ou moins explicite*" ("Let's say that a work of reversal happens, *whose erotic charge is more or less explicit*") (Tortel "Montpellier 24.04.78" 87, emphasis added).

As the object becomes a "body" in Tortel's metapoetic discourse, a certain violence appears in his engagement with this object-body:

> Je suis de ceux qui pensent que l'univers immédiat à partir du regard, et séjour de la quotidienneté, est inépuisable – et je n'ai jamais cherché à dire autre chose que l'espèce de combat, ou de relations corporelles, qui se poursuit avec ce là-devant à la fois ennemi et support. Composé de choses très simples, par exemple un jardin borné par des haies, une chambre. Très simple apparemment, mais que le regard ne saura jamais contenir tout entier. Aussi bien, le texte le déchiffre mal. Projetées par l'objet, les images inépuisables, envahissantes, sont là-devant. Mais elles ne font que s'avancer dans le vent et l'orage. Et tout cela compose une certaine impénétrabilité que le regard désire – une espèce de nuit plus ou moins chargée

d'érotisme, et finalement une sorte d'ignorance à la fois acceptée et niée. ("Montpellier 24.04.78" 87–8)

(I am one of those people who think that the immediate universe from the starting point of the gaze, which is the abode [séjour] of dailiness, is inexhaustible – and I have never sought to say anything but the sort of combat, or bodily relationships, which go on with this space before me [là-devant], which is both an enemy and a support. Made up of very simple things, for example a garden limited by hedges, a room. Apparently very simple, but the gaze will never be able entirely to contain it. Hence, the text has difficulty deciphering it. Projected by the object, the inexhaustible and invasive images are there in front of you. But they merely advance in the wind and the storm. And all of that creates a certain impenetrability which the gaze desires – a sort of night more or less charged with eroticism, and finally a sort of ignorance both accepted and denied.)

To understand what is motivating this transformation of object into body as the focus of the desiring gaze in this complex process the poet describes here, we need to turn to a key intertext informing Tortel's work: Maurice Scève's book-length poem *Délie* (1544). Tortel has confessed that he finds in *Délie* "la première écriture du regard – dont la tension et l'attention n'ont jamais été dépassées" ("the first writing of the gaze – whose tension and attention have never been surpassed") (qtd. by Leuwers in *L'Accompagnateur* (*The Accompanist*) 41). In an extended meditation on his poetics of the desiring gaze in *Le Discours des yeux* (*The Eyes' Discourse*) (1982) and *Feuilles, tombées d'un discours* (*Leaves, Fallen from a Discourse*) (1984), Tortel explicitly pays homage to Scève, admitting that *Le Discours des yeux* "n'aurait pas été entrepris, ni même soupçonné[,] sans le 282e dizain de *La Délie*:

Plus je poursuis par le discours des yeux
L'art et la main de telle pour traicture. (*Feuilles* 58)

(would never have been undertaken, or even thought of without the 282nd dizain of the *Délie*:
The more I pursue by the discourse of the eyes
The art and the hand of such a portraiture.)

Tortel's debt to Scève is made explicit in these two long essays of the 1980s. As I will argue, *Délie* may, in fact, be read as a broader, more general intertext through which to consider Tortel's poetics of the object-body.

Sceve's *Délie* and the *Blason*

French Renaissance poet Maurice Scève's 1544 text *Délie* ranks as one of the major lyric sequences in French poetry. Composed of 449 *dizains,* with 50 emblems interspersed among the poems at regular intervals, *Délie* presents a first-person male speaker's expressions of desire and frustration, his efforts to grasp, while reflecting upon, the most elusive of objects: a woman he calls "Délie," whom he ardently desires (flames are a frequent metaphor for love in this text) but who remains inaccessible. By the use of the subtitle "Objet de plus haulte vertu" (Object of highest virtue), Scève provides a striking but problematic starting-point for what will become a centuries-long tradition of French poetry fascinated by objects. In the case of Délie, the particular object to which the poet / speaker devotes his attention is an unattainable female beloved. The feminization of the object and its tantalizing absence suggest both the otherness of the object (which so many subsequent French poets will also feel) and its necessary but impossible capture.

The uneasy relationship of the male speaker / subject to the object of his thoughts and desires, Délie, is evident from the beginning of the poem. Although the opening dedication reads "A SA DÉLIE" ("TO HIS DÉLIE") the text will, in fact, continually give proof of the impossibility of possessing Délie. The text remains unresolvedly suspended between the two options "SOUFFRIR NON SOUFFRIR" ("TO SUFFER NOT TO SUFFER") – the words which follow the opening *huitain* that precedes the first poem in the sequence of 449 *dizains* in which the speaker imagines a joyous union with Délie and / but subsides into melancholy and defeat, in an ongoing cycle of emotions and fantasies.

The first *dizain* evokes the traumatizing moment of *innamoramento* which creates the male speaker's subjectivity – a divided and fragile subjectivity which may be strengthened, or merely repeated, through the writing of the *dizains* to follow. Délie's gaze is likened to that of the basilisk, the mythic creature that could kill with its glance:

Mon Basilisque avec sa poigant' veue
Perçant Corps, Cœur, et Raison despourveue,
Vint pénétrer en l'Ame de mon Ame.
Grand fut le coup, qui sans tranchante lame

Fait, que vivant le Corps, l'Esprit desvie,
Piteuse hostie au conspect de toy, Dame,
Constituée Idole de ma vie. (7)

(My Basilisk with its piercing gaze
Piercing Body, Heart, and impoverished Reason
Came and penetrated into the Soul of my Soul.
The blow it gave was hard, made
Without a slicing sword, which the living Body,
the Mind, Pitiful host[4] compared to you, Lady,
Constituted the Idol of my life.)

Although she is adored and idealized by the speaker, Délie remains throughout his text an ambiguous object, of whom we receive only fleeting glimpses, as Elisabeth Guild notes: "The object [in *Délie*] is the other, therefore always absent; but this absence makes possible the presence in the *dizains* of different refractions of the other. For instance, a name: 'comme Lune infuse dans mes veines / Celle tu fus, es & seras DELIE' ['Like a Moon infused into my veins / You were, are & will be she, DELIE'] (D 22, 7–8); an unnamed addressee: 'Te voyant rire auecques si grand grace' ['Seeing you laugh with such great grace'] (D 96, 1); a metonymic fragment of the other – hand, neck, eye, eyes; a metaphor presenting a difference within the other, the other as different to any prior self; or a space of reflection, an other self of the subject: 'Miroir meurdrier de ma vie mourant' ['Murderous mirror of my dying life'] (D 307, 2), often potentially deadly" (60).

Thus, the object in *Délie* is lost and dispersed into multiple images and figures that make it more difficult to grasp even as they render it vivid and fascinating. Consequently, the subject, too, is displaced. His represented consciousness shifts from one *dizain* to the next, ever unstable and lacking wholeness and coherence. In her excellent Lacanian study of *Délie*, Nancy M. Frelick demonstrates how "Délie does not seem to be a fixed, constant object, but an unstable, mutable signifier" (90). Frelick argues that the functioning of language in Scève's *Délie* corresponds closely to Jacques Lacan's view of language as a system of signs in which full meaning is constantly absent, as deferral and incompletion are the operations through which words strive for, but do not (quite) reach, their goal. As Frelick states, "[t]he desire for Délie expressed in the text is clearly a metaphor for the search for Knowledge, Truth, and meaning, and like Délie, these 'objects' cannot be possessed: they are beyond our grasp and beyond signification" (99).[5]

The relationship between the perceiving subject and the described object in Scève's *Délie* interests me particularly because in this early modern text, a pattern already emerges which will mark the relations between subject and object(s) in the work of numerous later poets: the obsessive concern with attempting to capture the object in words; the inaccessibility of the object (especially when it is figures as (the) feminine, as in Ponge's "L'Huître" or "De l'eau," among other examples); the sense that subjectivity is undermined if the object eludes its efforts to reach it; the idea that the object stands for metaphorical values which the subject wishes to appropriate.

The world of Scève's *Délie* would, at first glance, seem to be entirely removed from the concerns of Jean Tortel's garden poetry. Yet, in *Délie*, as in Tortel's poems, the eyes and seeing are given pride of place. They centre the text, while functioning in unanticipated or disturbing ways. In the opening *dizain* of the 449 *dizains* which compose Scève's text, the decisive moment of *innamoramento* (a conventionalized textual moment of falling in love) takes place, as the male subject first encounters "his Délie." (In his dedication to his text, Scève explicitly designates her as "sa Délie.") Eyes and the gaze in this initiatory *dizain* perform a crucial, but lethal, role in setting desire in motion:

L'Oeil trop ardent en mes jeunes erreurs
Girouettait, mal cault, à l'impourvue:
Voicy (ô paour d'agréables terreurs)
Mon Basilisque avec sa poignant' veue
Perçait Corps, Cœur, et Raison despourveue,
Vint penetrer en l'Ame de mon Ame. (7)

(The too ardent Eye in my erring youth
Kept imprudently turning, unpredictably,
And look (o fear of pleasant terrors)

(My Basilisk with its piercing gaze
Piercing Body, Heart, and impoverished Reason
Came and penetrated into the Soul of my Soul.)

Délie's gaze, figured as that of a basilisk here "pierces" and "penetrates" the male speaker's body, heart, reason, and "soul of [his] soul" – each of these four nouns being capitalized to underscore its metaphoric significance. Although the image of eyes that shoot darts or flames is a standard conceit of Renaissance love poetry, the reader is nevertheless struck by the violence of the eyes' effect and of the exchange of glances here.

If we next look at *dizain* 288 of the *Délie* (i.e., the poem specifically named by Tortel as the catalyst for his meditations in *Le Discours des yeux*), it is obvious that *dizain* 288, too, presents disquieting and challenging images:

Plus je poursuis par le discours des yeulx
L'art, et la main de telle pourtraicture,
Et plus j'admire, et adore les Cieulx
Accomplisantz si belle Creature,
Dont le parfaict de sa lineature
M'esmeult le sens, et l'imaginative:
Et la couleur du vif imitative
Me brule, et ard jusques à l'esprit rendre.
  Que deviendroys je en la voyant lors vive?
Certainement je tumberois en cendre. (134)

(The more I pursue by the discourse of my eyes
The art, and the hand of such a portraiture,
And the more I admire, and adore the Heavens
Creating such a beauteous Creature,
The perfection of whose lineature
Moves my reason, and my imagination:
And the imitative colour of living flesh
Burns me, and enflames me until I surrender to spirit.
  What would become of me were I to see her living form?
Certainly I would fall to ashes.)

"Le discours des yeulx," the term that inspired the title of Tortel's long prose meditation which constitutes one key to his poetics, is polyvalent in its meaning. As Deborah Lesko Baker points out in her study *Narcissus and the Lover: Mythic Recovery and Reinvention in Scève's Délie* (1986), this expression, "des yeux," could be read as a possessive term, curiously attributing the power of speech to the eyes. Alternatively, it could refer to a discourse *about* or *concerning* the eyes. Since Délie herself never speaks in Scève's text, even as she is described over and over, a basic asymmetry between speech and gaze, as well as between male subject and female object, structures this work. Lesko Baker adds that "[i]n a more specific sense, 'le discours des yeulx' actually described in D.288 represents a further variation of specular fixation at work in the *Délie*. The 'pourtraicture' visually 'pursued' by the lover recalls the fountain and the looking-glass in that it likewise presents a meditated image – a kind of reflection of the Beloved's physical presence" (59).

The death of the male speaker / lover in the final line of *dizain* 288 ("Certainement je tumberois en cendre") reiterates the lethal force originally assigned to Délie's "basilisk" gaze in the opening *dizain*. Lesko Baker explains that this image of "falling into ashes" has an extremely precise meaning in French Renaissance thought. It does not evoke a *literal* death: "the image of 'cendre' climaxes a Ficinian process of self-disintegration [and] it also reaffirms by earthly denegation the spiritual realm to which the eyes' discourse has already willingly ascended in its continual pursuit of the Beloved's reflected beauty" (59). Like the opening image of the "Basilik" gaze, this later metaphor of "tomber en cendre" does, though, gesture towards a dark, violent view of passion and eroticism. In this sense, the influence of Scève's "discours des yeux" on the development of Tortel's poetics of the gaze may be interpreted as reinforcing the more sombre and troubling aspects of Tortel's view of language, representation, and desire. A more violent and ambivalent process may be at work in his poetics than many of his readers have assumed.

At this point, as we move towards the end of our study of object poetics, it is interesting – and disturbing – to reflect on how often in the course of their engagement with objects, the poets studied in the previous several chapters have shifted their attention from the object to the notion (or fantasy) of Woman. The multiple, changing links between the object and the feminine has been a leitmotiv in the present study, as various and contradictory images of Woman proliferate in patriarchal culture generally, as Simone de Beauvoir pointed out in the passages from *The Second Sex* included in the introduction. The vectors of sexual politics conditioning these poets' uses of the object will be countered, in chapter 7, with an exploration of poems from *Blasons du corps masculin* (*Blasons of the Male Body*), Tita Reut's poems describing tools in *Vis cachées* (*Hidden Screws/Flaws*), and Nathalie Quintane's *Chaussure* (*Shoe*). In these contemporary examples, an entirely different approach to the object and its relationship to gender will surface.

7 *L'Objet après L'Objet*: Contemporary French Poetry

A fascination with objects continues in French poetry today. Unlike their twentieth-century predecessors, French poets now generally use the object as a pretext for the creation of quirky and unconventional post-modern textualities. Jean-Marie Gleize has coined the expression "la poésie après la poésie" ("poetry after poetry no longer exists") to describe the work of contemporary innovative poets who move beyond the confines of traditional lyricism. I propose the term "l'objet après l'objet" to designate the unexpected and challenging ways in which these new poets have reinvented the role of the object as a basis for poetics.

Jacques Roubaud's ∈ *(Signe d'Appartenance)* (1967)

Jacques Roubaud's ∈ is one of the most intriguing *poèmes-objets* to have appeared in recent decades in French literature. Roubaud (b. 1932) is a member of the Oulipo group, which was founded in 1960 by poet Raymond Queneau and mathematician François Le Lionnais. The group's main goal is to "[p]roposer aux écrivains de nouvelles 'structures' de nature mathématique ou bien encore inventer de nouveaux procédés artificiels ou mécaniques, contribuant à l'activité littéraire"[1] ("propose to writers new 'structures' of a mathematical nature or else again to invent new artificial or mechanical devices contributing to literary activity"). In his biography of writer Georges Perec, another major figure who belongs to the Oulipo, David Bellos explains the group's *raison d'être* as follows: "Oulipo was not a sect, or a chapel, or a campaign for an 'ism'; indeed it was not really a writers' group at all. It was a research team that aimed to fashion new tools for writing and to refurbish old and forgotten ones. Its operational model was Bourbaki, the group of anonymous French mathematicians who reinvented their entire discipline by starting afresh from first principles" (349). As we shall see, Bourbaki's theoretical work on mathematics provided Roubaud with the metaphoric symbol from which one dimension of ∈'s significance is derived.

By definition, an Oulipian work is always based on a governing constraint, which the writer must respect absolutely. So, for example, in Perec's lipogrammatic novel *La Disparition* (*The Disappearance*), the letter "e" (by far the most common vowel in French) is never used; Michelle Grangaud's first three books of poetry are composed entirely of anagrams; and so on. Although such a rigid use of constraints might seem, at first glance, to constitute a limitation on the writer's creativity, the members of Oulipo claim that, on the contrary, the constraints act as a source of creative strength through the unique challenge they make to writing a cohesive, interesting work.

In ∈, more than one constraint is present. First, Roubaud limits himself to the sonnet in this book. "Ce livre est un livre de sonnets" ("This book is a book of sonnets"), the author states, in his description of ∈:

> Le choix du sonnet à la base s'explique par deux constatations élémentaires: d'une part, il est à peu près admis qu'il est impossible aujourd'hui d'écrire un sonnet; d'autre part, le sonnet représente, dans la poésie à forme fixe (c'est-à-dire dans la poésie à contraintes, donc, pour moi, dans la poésie tout entière) l'expression la plus nette de la poésie occidentale: il appartient à toutes les grandes périodes, on le retrouve chez Dante, chez Cavalcanti, chez Shakespeare, chez Gongora, chez Mallarmé, chez Rilke, chez Hopkins, etc. Interroger le sonnet, c'était pour moi interroger une certaine possibilité de la poésie aujourd'hui, la recherche d'une voie nouvelle à partir d'une histoire, d'une tradition.
>
> Ce livre peut, dans son ensemble, être considéré comme une "histoire" du sonnet: une définition de la forme, une interrogation sur ses origines et ses avatars. (Roubaud, "J'ai choisi le sonnet" 6)

> (My choice of the sonnet can basically be explained by two fundamental observations: on the one hand, it is more or less generally agreed that it is impossible today to write a sonnet; on the other, the sonnet represents, in fixed-form poetry (that is, in poetry using constraints, which means for me, then, all poetry) the clearest expression of Western poetry: it belongs to all the great periods, one finds it in Dante, in Cavalcanti, in Shakespeare, in Gongora, in Mallarmé, in Rilke, in Hopkins, etc. To look critically at the

sonnet was for me to look at a certain possibility for poetry today, the search for a new path on the basis of a history, a tradition.

This book, as a whole, can be considered as a "history" of the sonnet: a definition of the form, a study of its origins and its avatars.)

Roubaud also notes, though, that he has not attempted to write "canonical" sonnets in ∈; some of his "sonnets" are written as prose "paragraphs," as "j'ai voulu recenser tous les types d'aberrations ou de déviations possibles à partir du modèle classique" ("I wanted to go through all the possible types of aberrations and deviations [in the sonnet form] from the starting point of the classic model") (7).

The sonnet has been a constant focus of interest for Roubaud throughout his career as a writer. In addition to having written sonnets himself, he has produced critical studies on the sonnet and anthologies of sonnets. Because the sonnet is based on formal constraints (fourteen lines organized into two quatrains followed by two tercets, a set rhyme scheme, fairly narrowly defined and consistent subject matter), it is not surprising that Oulipo writers like Roubaud and Michelle Grangaud – in her *Poèmes fondus* (*Poems Melted Down*) – would become interested in it. However, as Jean-Jacques Poucel notes, and as Roubaud himself acknowledges in the above quotation, the sonnets in ∈ are not standard, regular examples of the form: "∈ presents a series of broadly varying texts that most readers would not immediately identify as sonnets … it should be noted that none of the poems in ∈ repeat the strophic pattern of traditional sonnets or of any other poem in the collection; each is unique in form. As a sonnet cycle, ∈ therefore bears little resemblance to its precursors" (95).

The other major constraint through which ∈ was written, and through which – or in spite of which – it must be read, is the Japanese game of Go, which Roubaud adopts as a textual model. This game, dating back to 200 CE and still popular today, is played on a "go-ban" – that is, on "a flat board of wood, metal, or cardboard, on which is marked a grid of 19 x 19 lines," as John Fairbairn explains in his *Invitation to Go* (1). A standard game of Go requires 361 stones: 181 black stones and 180 white ones. In Go, the two players make their moves by plonking white or black stones down on the board. As the game proceeds, both players attempt to occupy as much territory on the board as possible, sometimes also capturing their opponent's stones. According to Fairbairn, "[t]he object [of the game] is to form continuous lines or *walls*, of your own stones, so as to surround vacant areas of the board. Every *vacant* intersection inside such 'territories' counts one point for the owner, if he still controls this territory at the end of the game" (5). The winner will be the player holding the most points in the end. Fairbairn also observes that Go is "not really a war game – it is a game of coexistence" (14) – which may help to account for Roubaud's choice of this particular game as a textual model in ∈. Roubaud's fascination with Japanese culture – present in some of his early works like ∈ and continuing in his most recent texts, such as *Tokyo infraordinaire* (*Infraordinary Tokyo*) – further motivated his interest in Go.

∈ itself functions as a kind of abstract *go-ban*. Each poem in ∈ is preceded by a white or black circle, corresponding to the white and black stones used in the game. The poet also includes, in square brackets next to each sonnet, an indication of which move in an actual Go game the poem is meant to evoke. (At the end of the book, Roubaud reproduces a diagram taken from a 1965 issue of the *Go Review* presenting the results of a competition between Go players Masami Shinohara and Mitsuo Takei. This particular game serves as a model for Roubaud's text.)

Roubaud's reliance on constraints proper to the Western sonnet tradition and, simultaneously, on the rules to be followed in a game of Go, might suggest that his text will seem like no more than a mechanical, if novel and interesting, exercise. In fact, just the opposite is the case. The poems in ∈ are hauntingly lyrical, aesthetically sophisticated texts. They display the poet's profound awareness of poetic technique and themes along with his ability to adapt and alter a tradition that carries with it a long history and considerable literary authority. If Roubaud is in some sense inviting his reader to participate in a textual "game," the act of reading that he expects us to perform is in no way frivolous. He may perhaps have selected Go rather than another board game precisely because Go encourages creativity in unique ways. Fairbairn asserts that Go is easy to learn, but difficult to master (not unlike poetry, one might say). He also states that, for very experienced players in a professional game, "[g]o is no longer just a game. It is a medium for creating things of beauty, even once in a while for creating art" (77). The atmosphere of a professional game of Go becomes highly intense and demanding: "For two days [the players] are locked in combat, ten hours a day. This is the atmosphere that leads to a constant striving for perfection, and it is this in turn that leads eventually to art" (77). By combining a requirement for mental agility with the opportunity to create beauty, Go offers an ideal metaphorical model for an Oulipian writer. As Roubaud is a mathematician as well as a poet, Go suits him especially well as a creative model.

In the "Mode d'emploi" ("User's Manual") to ∈, Roubaud presents the reader with four different possible strategies for entering, and proceeding through, his text. One may read it according to the five subsections into which it is divided. One may, alternatively, read the poems as though they corresponded to the moves in an actual game of Go (the game given in Table 2 at the end of the book). Otherwise, one may simply read each individual poem as a separate unit, not in relation to any grouping of poems or any specific context. As Poucel noted, the poems in ∈ only loosely follow the traditional form of the sonnet. Instead, Roubaud creates a varied and highly inventive textuality in which he departs from a fixed formal and prosodic model. In Section 3 of ∈, for example, the author indicates that the entire section "est un sonnet court de sonnets courts en prose" ("is a short sonnet made up of short sonnets in prose"). Such a blending of the sonnet with the prose poem is surprising and challenging, yet a poet of Roubaud's technical skill is able to achieve this formal fusion. In Section 2, he adopts a very different approach: an entire sub-section here features poems organized around the theme of "Élégies et jardins" ("Elegies and Gardens"), while playing on intertexts from Rilke and *Le Roman de Renart* (*The Romance of the Fox*). Section 5 of ∈ remains unfinished – appropriately so, as the actual game of Go upon which Roubaud modelled his text was an unfinished game.

The significant and intriguing variations in his art of the sonnet quickly become apparent if one compares poems from different sections of ∈, or even two poems within the same section. Here is "Jets d'eau et soir" (GO 41):

Jets d'eau et soir

Un petit peu bleu le jet d'eau un très peu
vert le printemps autour des jets d'eau vert noir
arbres de notre rue mère reverdissent
un peu seulement car voyez vous il pleut
toutes sortes d'années dans un entonnoir
dépouillant les arbres et les jets d'eau disent

Un petit peu bois à la douceur un peu
fils du chènevis et quand bouge un insecte
respire nous sur la terre qui s'humecte
la tête sous l'ombrelle de l'eau les yeux
vers la nuit directe. (70)

(Fountains and Evening

A little bit blue the fountain a little
green the springtime around the fountains green black
trees of our street mother grow green again
a little only for you see it is raining
all sorts of years in a barrel
denuding the trees and the fountains say

A little bit drink in the sweetness a little
strands of hempseed and when an insect moves
breathes we on the earth who moisten
the head under the parasol of the water the eyes
towards the direct night.)

The reader notes, first, that the form of this "sonnet" is highly irregular: it is not divided into two quatrains followed by two tercets. The rhyme scheme is unconventional: a b c a b c // a d d a d. The lines are notational. Roubaud uses few verbs here, relying more on groupings of nouns to evoke the scene of a fountain in a natural setting. The thematics of time and the seasons, though, reflects a traditional sense of lyricism.

The opening poem of the collection, "1.1.1. [GO 115]," follows a somewhat more recognizable sonnet structure. Yet, in this case, too, the poem is something of a departure from the traditional model. The interweaving of the emotional life of a subject with the objects and events in nature is foregrounded by Roubaud in the poem. Nonetheless, it is quite irregular, as the first and last lines are strangely truncated.

Roubaud's homage to the sonnet in this text demonstrates convincingly the possibilities for combining a traditional form with uninhibited innovation. ∈ also constitutes a unique contribution to the ongoing development of the *poème-objet* in France.[2]

Le Blason Contemporain: On Women Poets' Objectifying of the Male Body

During the French Renaissance, the 'blason' became a popular and important poetic genre. The 'Blason du corps femenin,' in which male poets presented witty, playful descriptions written in praise or blame of individual parts of the female body, attracted particular attention. In

1990, nine contemporary French women poets published a collective volume, *Blasons du corps masculin*, which updates and recasts this traditional genre. By turns humorous, tender, and defiant, their poems turn the 'blason' genre upside-down in order to unmask the gender politics implicit within it. In their idiosyncratic and surprising *neo-blasons* these women poets express their fascination for – and feelings of ambivalence towards – the male body while undoing its mythic 'power' and its cultural authority. Their work reminds us that no description or portrait is neutral. It also provides a striking example of the preoccupation with representing the body in unconventional ways that has inspired so much compelling contemporary art and literature.

The Sixteenth-Century *Blason*

The study of the relationship between writing and the body has become a recurring motif in recent work in literature and cultural studies. Increasingly, specialists doing research on this topic acknowledge the decisive influence of literary, filmic, and other culturally determined images of the human body upon our understanding of our own, and other people's, bodies.[3] One of the key areas for research on cultural representations of the body over the past few decades has been the exploration of histories of art-historical, cinematic, and literary images of the female body. Feminist theory has guided much of this new work, demonstrating the political stakes in the decoding of the textual and visual processes by which women's bodies have been represented (and distorted) by the male gaze.

In 1990 the publication of a short collection of ten poems by nine women highlighted the presence of a feminist perspective emerging in the traditionally male preserve of French poetry. The collection presents idiosyncratic descriptions of parts of the male body and features a provocative preface by the editor of the book, Constance Aquaviva. The title of the collection, *Blasons du corps masculin*, indicates that these poets, in composing their individual evocations of the male body, were consciously updating and revising – or recycling – an established genre, the *blason*. Unlike other poetic genres, such as the sonnet or the ode, the *blason* belongs to one specific period in French literary history, the Renaissance. This period has maintained an aura of considerable authority for French poets today because it is known as the pivotal historical period for the constitution and development of French poetry as a cultural institution. Thus, the nine women poets and the editor of *Blasons du corps masculin*, Aquaviva, have undertaken a challenging task in deciding to renew and alter a time-honoured genre associated with an age that produced many of the masterpieces of French poetry.

What attracted these women to the *blason*, in particular? What sets the *blason* apart from other genres? The most obvious answer would be that the politics of gender implicit in the *blason* provided a powerful inspiration to their collective poetry project. Indeed, the best-known *blasons* from the sixteenth century are the various *Blasons du corps femenin*. After Clément Marot's "Le Beau Tétin," written in 1535, drew the admiration of several other male poets in France, who then produced their own *blasons*, a whole series of poems written in praise of individual parts of the female body appeared. In these texts, the female body is taken apart, analysed, and fetishized so that the male poet can demonstrate his verbal prowess, his wit, and his technical expertise. In these poems, man speaks and woman is silent. He 'possesses' her by describing her, as she submits to his objectifying gaze. The politics implicit in the *blason* – which, one could argue, is a genre that creates beautiful verbal objects out of gender inequality – justify a revisionary, feminist response from women poets today.

Before examining the work of these contemporary *blasonneuses* at length, it is important to review the history and evolution of the genre during the Renaissance. In what ways might the *blason* be considered a representative phenomenon of that period? In his book *The Body Emblazoned: Dissection and the Human Body in Renaissance Culture*, Jonathan Sawday argues that a fascination with dissection and human anatomy acted as a central, defining aspect of early-modern European culture. Sawday admits, from the outset, that "[t]o deploy a phrase such as the 'culture of dissection' is to suggest a network of practices, social structures, and rituals surrounding the production of fragmented bodies, which sits uneasily alongside our image (derived from Burckhardt) of the European Renaissance as the age of the construction of individuality – a unified sense of selfhood. But the 'scientific revolution' of the European Renaissance encouraged the seemingly endless partitioning of the world and all that it contained" (2). To explain how this "'fashion' for anatomy" (Sawday 44) functioned, he shows that the "culture of dissection" was devoted to the gathering of information and the dissemination of knowledge of the "mystery" of the human body. As such, its ends were proclaimed as being both "useful" and "noble," but the " 'culture of dissection' also promoted the beginnings of what Michel Foucault has analysed as the 'surveillance' of the body within regimes of judgment and punishment" (4). Sawday believes the *blason* genre to be a significant instance of this Renaissance preoccupation with anatomy and dissection. He cites David Norbrook's observation that "the vogue in the sixteenth century for the *blason,* the detailed enumeration of the parts of the woman's body, can be seen as reflecting the new scientific mentality with its mastering gaze, its passion for mapping the world in order to gain power over it" (qtd. by Sawday 192).

One of the most famous definitions of the *blason* was formulated in 1548 by Thomas Sebillet in his *Art poétique françoys* (*Art of French Poetry*):

> Le Blason est une perpétuelle louange ou continu vitupère de ce qu'on s'est proposé blasonner … Car autant bien se blasonne le laid comme le beau, et le mauvais comme le bon … De quelconque coin soit-il sortie, le plus bref est le meilleur, masque il soit agui en conclusion: et est plus doux en rime plate, et vers de huit syllabes: encore que ceux de dis n'en soient regrettés comme ineptes.
>
> (The blason is a perpetual praising or a continuous insulting of what one has chosen to blason … For what is ugly can be blasoned just as well as what is beautiful, the bad just as well as the good … From whatever corner it has come, the shortest blason is the best, but it must come to a sharp conclusion: it is nicer with a flat rhyme [rime plate], and in octosyllables: decasyllabic lines are regrettable because inept.)[4]

Another celebrated definition of the *blason,* which Constance Aquaviva quotes at the opening of her collection of *Blasons du corps masculin,* was proposed by Albert-Marie Schmidt in 1953:

> Un blason? C'est par essence un poème qui vise, non pas à décrire, mais à évoquer parmi les créatures d'un monde esthétique, dont le poète est l'artisan tyrannique, une chose, une couleur, un contour, une notion. Le blason tend à une objectivité aussi grande que possible grâce aux artifices complexes d'une ombrageuse subjectivité, avide de s'anéantir elle-même. Dédaignant d'user d'une gamme de correspondances et d'analogies, qu'il tient pour arbitraires, il se flatte, pourtant, d'être à la fois perçu par tous les sens du lecteur. Extérieurement, il s'accommode de l'allure d'un charme, d'une litanie, d'une kyrielle, d'une incantation. Harcelant l'objet qu'il veut transposer et manifester dans un univers absolu en lançant contre lui une suite d'apostrophes savamment variées et volontairement monotones, il le captive, il s'en saisit, il l'enserre, il le ligote peu à peu dans les mailles

> d'un filet d'or, aux timbres purs, qui devient son secours métaphysique, sa cage perpétuelle, sa défense contre le temps. (Albert-Marie Schmidt, qtd. in Wilson *Descriptive Poetry* 7–8)
>
> (A blason? It is by its nature a poem which aims, not to describe, but to evoke among the creatures of an aesthetic world, whose creator is the tyrannical poet, a thing, a colour, a contour, a notion. The blason is inclined to produce the greatest possible objectivity thanks to the complex tricks of a flagrant subjectivity, eager to nullify itself. Disdaining the use of a scale of correspondences and analogies, which it considers arbitrary, it prides itself, nonetheless, on being perceived by all the reader's senses at once. From the outside, it is satisfied to appear as a charm, a litany, a kyrielle, an incantation. Harassing the object which it wishes to transpose and present in an absolute space by throwing at it a series of cleverly varied and deliberately monotonous apostrophes, it takes the object, appropriates it, squeezes it and binds it little by little in the meshes of a golden net, with pure sounds, and this becomes its metaphysical rescue, its constant cage, its defence against time.)

The scholarly precision of Schmidt's painstaking definition of the *blason* here is evident. However, his definition also discloses an implicit violence characteristic of the genre. Schmidt states that the *blason* "harasses" the object that it intends to represent, "*en lançant contre lui* une suite d'apostrophes" (emphasis added). Then, "il le captive, il s'en saisit, il l'enserre, il le ligote peu à peu dans les mailles d'un filet d'or." Such a forceful appropriation of the object ostensibly being *praised* by the poet becomes especially disturbing when, as in the *Blason anatomique du corps femenin*, the object under scrutiny is a part of a woman's body.

In fact, a certain violence accompanies this poetic genre from its origins. As Robert E. Pike notes, the term *blason* is derived from the field of heraldry: "The word *blason* meant originally the coat of arms printed on a shield, and soon came to mean not only the coat of arms but the description of those arms. By a natural extension the term then passed into common parlance to mean a description of anything at all, and not only a eulogistic description, but a defamatory one" (223). Furthermore, Alison Saunders points out in her book on the *blason* that "[t]he original purpose of the coat of arms was to serve as an identification on the battlefield" (20). So, a close connection to war and violence is inherent in the origins of the term *blason*.

Scholars observe that before 1530 fewer than a score of *blazons* were written, whereas between 1530 and 1580, more than 250 of them appeared (Pike 229). Of these 250, the 'Blasons anatomiques du corps femenin' were by far the most popular and influential. The originator and great promoter of this category of *blasons* was Clément Marot. During a stay at the court of Renée de Ferrare in 1535, Marot composed his poem "Le Beau Tétin," which subsequently inspired various other French poets of the time to show their prowess at composing a *blason* of their own. Pike relates that "[s]even poets wrote nine *blasons* which were sent to Marot at Ferrara, where the Duchess Renée and her ladies judged the best one to be the *Blason du sourcil* (*Blason of the Eyebrow*) by Maurice Scève. Jean de Vauzelles 'blasonned' the Hair; Antoine Heroët, the Eye; Maurice Scève, the Eyebrow and the Tear; Victor Brodeau, the Mouth; Gabriel Chappuys, the Hand; Le Lieur, the Thigh; and a poet who signed himself Albert le Grand, the Ear and the Heart" (230). The *Blasons anatomiques du corps femenin* had ten editions in the sixteenth century, which provides us with a strong indication of the popularity of these poems during the period. Despite (or rather, because of) their popularity, they also provoked hostile responses from some quarters. Charles de la Huetterie wrote eighteen "contreblasons" in reaction against the *blasonneurs'* glorification of the flesh and of sensuality. Similarly, Gilles Corrozet and another, anonymous poet wrote a *Blason contre les Blasonneurs des Membres* (*Blason Against Writers of Anatomical Blasons*) and a *Blason des Blasonneurs des Membres feminins* (*Blason About the Writers of Blasons on the Female Body*) (Pike 230–1).

The conflict between the work of the *blasonneurs* and their detractors does reveal profoundly diverging views of sexuality and the body in sixteenth-century French culture. Nevertheless, in the texts of both of these groups of poets, the female body is subjugated by a male gaze that makes use of the woman's body either for pleasure or for moralizing condemnation. Female subjectivity is erased and covered up by the words of men in both cases.

In order to develop a clear sense of the characteristic features of the Renaissance *blason*, which the 1990s *blasonneuses* have appropriated as a model, let us consider, first, Marot's "Le Beau Tétin":

Le Beau Tétin
Tétin refait, plus blanc qu'un oeuf,
Tétin de satin blanc tout neuf,
Tétin qui fais honte à la Rose,

Tétin plus beau que nulle chose
Tétin dur, non pas Tétin, voire,
Mais petite boule d'Ivoire,
Au milieu duquel est assise
Une Fraise, ou une Cerise
Que nul ne voit, ne touche aussi,
Mais je gage qu'il est ainsi:
Tétin donc au petit bout rouge,
Tétin qui jamais ne se bouge,
Soit pour venir, soit pour aller,
Soit pour courir, soit pour baller;
Tétin gauche, Tétin mignon,
Toujours loin de son compagnon,
Tétin qui portes témoignage
Du demourant du personnage,
Quant on te voit, il vient à maints
Une envie dedans les mains
De te tâter, de te tenir:
Mais il se faut bien contenir
D'en approcher, bon gré ma vie,
Car il viendrait une autre envie.
Ô Tétin, ne grand, ne petit,
Tétin mur, Tétin d'appétit,
Tétin qui nuit et jour criez
Mariez-moi tôt, mariez!
Tétin qui t'enfles, et repousses
Ton gorgias de deux bons pouces,
A bon droit heureux on dira
Celui qui de lait t'emplira,
Faisant d'un Tétin de pucelle,
Tétin de femme entière et belle.

(Marot, in Schmidt, ed. *Poètes du XVIe siècle* 307)

(The Beautiful Breast
Breast remade, whiter than an egg,
Breast of white satin all new,
Breast which puts the Rose to shame,
Breast more beautiful than any other thing
Breast that's hard, no, not Breast, even,
But little Ivory globe,

In whose centre is seated
A Strawberry, or a Cherry
Which no man sees, nor touches,
Unless I judge it proper:
Breast then with a little red tip,
Breast which never moves,
Either to go, or to come back,
Either to run, or to dangle;
Awkward Breast, Dainty Breast
Always far from its mate,
Breast who bears witness
To the remainder of its owner
When they see you, many feel
A desire within their hands
To touch you, to hold you:
But one must restrain oneself
From approaching you, upon my life,
For another sort of desire would surely arise.
O breast, neither large nor small,
Mature Breast, appetizing Breast,
Breast which cries out night and day
Marry me soon, marry me!
Breast which swells and repulses
Your gorgerin with two good shoves,
Rightly one will deem him happy
Who fills you up with milk
Making a virgin's Breast
The Breast of a woman whole and lovely.)

This poem can be understood as a representative example of the *blason* in several respects. It is brief and focuses in minute detail on one specific object. It evokes the object primarily through repeatedly naming it, making it seem present to the reader by means of anaphoric repetition. At the same time, the writing of this poem acts as a titillating exercise in verbal wit and poetic technique. Each of the comparisons in the series of comparisons that opens the poem accentuates a salient feature of the breast while underscoring its appeal to the senses: sight ("plus blanc qu'un oeuf"), touch ("Tétin dur"), taste ("Au milieu duquel est assise / Une Fraise, ou une Cerise"), and so on. Marot's use of measured parallelism ("Soit pour venir, soit pour aller, / Soit pour courir, soit pour baller") and his manipulation of rhyme and rhythm also make the poem pleasurable to the ear.

One might easily interpret this poem as an instance of poetic ingenuity and verbal gallantry. However, such a reading – which has been the standard critical response to the *blason* until recently – leaves out the obvious political problem created by these elegant descriptions through which men take possession of the female body, dismembering it, caressing it with words or insulting it, while the "femme entière et belle" to whom their poems are ostensibly dedicated remains absent.

Another key example of the Renaissance *blason*, which differs to some extent from Marot's practice of the genre, are the five *blasons* of Maurice Scève. (All five were included in editions of the *Blasons anatomiques* after 1536.) In his study of Scève's poetry, *Maurice Scève: Bucolico e "Blasonneur"* (*Maurice Scève: Bucolic Poet and "Blasonneur"*), Enzo Guidici notes a fundamental contrast between the sensuality of Marot's *blasons* and the Neoplatonic abstraction of Scève's: "L'interesse di Marot è un interesse terreno, mondano, vitalistico; il poeta vuole solo godere ed esprimere la gioia di vivere, libera da preoccupazioni morali. L'ispirazione di Scève è invece un' ispirazione elevata, nobile, seria, cioè sostanziale e morale. Marot esiste per vivere e Scève per pensare; il mondo dell'uno è la *vita*, quello dell'altro l'*idea*" ("What Marot is interested in is earthly, worldly, vitalistic; the poet only wants to enjoy and express his joie de vivre, free from moral concerns. Scève's inspiration is, rather, an elevated, noble, serious inspiration – that is substantial and moral. Marot exists to live and Scève, to think; the world of the one is *life* and that of the other, the *idea*") (48). The distinction Giudici establishes between the work of these two poets is particularly evident if one reads Scève's *blason* "Le Front" ("The Forehead") immediately after Marot's "Le Beau Tétin." Here is "Le Front":

Le Front
Front large et haut, front patent et ouvert,
Plat et uni, des beaux cheveux couvert
Front qui est clair et serein firmament
Du petit monde, et par son mouvement
Est gouverné le demeurant du corps
Et à son vueil sont les membres concors
Lequel je vois être troublé par nues,
Multipliant ses rides très-menues,
Et du côté qui se présente à l'œil

Semble que là se lève le soleil.
Front élevé sur cette sphère ronde,
Où tout engin et tout savoir abonde.
Front révéré, Front qui le corps surmonte
Comme celui qui ne craint rien, fors honte.
Front apparent, afin qu'on pût mieux lire
Les lois qu'amour voulut en lui écrire,
Ô front, tu es une table d'attente
Où ma vie est, et ma mort très patente.

(Scève, in Schmidt, ed. *Poètes du XVIe siècle* 307)

(The Forehead
Forehead broad and high, forehead clear and open,
Flat and uniform, covered in lovely hair
Forehead which is a clear and serene heaven
Of the little world, and by its movement
Is governed the rest of the body
And the arms and legs obey its will.
I see it troubled by clouds,
Multiplying its tiny lines,
And on the side which presents itself to the eye
It seems that then the sun does rise.
Forehead elevated above this round sphere,
Where all technical expertise and all knowledge abounds.
Forehead that is revered, Forehead surmounting the body
Like he who fears nothing, save shame.
Forehead visible, so that one might better read
The laws which love desired to write on it,
O forehead, you are a field
Where my life and my death are very apparent.)

Scève quickly moves from a literal description of the forehead ("large et haut … / Plat et uni") to an idealizing metaphorization of it as a "serene firmament." Carnal desire seems absent from the poet's awed contemplation of this corporeal / heavenly dome ("cette sphère ronde, / où tout engin et tout savoir abonde"). As the poet's destiny – his life and death – become legible in the lines of the forehead, now figured as a "table d'attente," it is clear that his *blason* reflects a vision of the female body that is poles apart from the coy sensuality of Marot's "Le Beau Tétin."

Blasons du Corps Masculin

In her introduction to the 1990 collection *Blasons du corps masculin,* Constance Aquaviva explicitly situates the collection in the context of a contemporary backlash against feminism: "Tout semblait aller bien," she writes, "avancer normalement; Sa vieille domination, Sa vie contre la mienne, Son pouvoir à peine contesté, Sa répression spontanée, involontaire et naturelle; tout ça, ça reculait, ça reculait; on y mettait tout notre poids, toute notre force, toute notre volonté, tout notre bonheur, tout notre amour. Et ça s'équilibrait, mes Chéries, ça allait vers l'équilibre … Et ça a reculé, ça a régressé, et ils y reviennent tout doux à leur vieille domination, à leur répression naturelle … Oui, le machisme continue et le sexisme est encore présent partout ou presque." ("Everything seemed to be going well, to be moving along in a normal way; His old domination, His life against mine, His power barely contested, His repressiveness seen as spontaneous, involuntary and natural; all of that was receding, and receding further; we put all our weight, all our strength, all our willpower, all our happiness, all our love into the struggle. And things were moving towards balance … And things went backward, regressed, and the men are quietly resuming their old domination, the repressiveness that is natural to them … Yes, machismo continues to exist and sexism is still present everywhere or almost everywhere").[5] Aquaviva explains that, although the idea of asking women poets to write *blasons* on the male body began as a light-hearted joke, given the current ongoing erosion of women's rights on several fronts, these 1990s feminist poems have a more serious, political role to play: "Voilà ce qui fait que ce livre qui n'était qu'un gag agréable, un clin d'oeil, devient une grimace et une revendication, une vraie! Avec le sourire, ce coup-ci encore. Il est question, aujourd'hui, de célébrer le corps masculin. Ainsi l'auteur sera l'objet, tandis que nous, femmes, jadis l'objet, serons auteurs" ("That is why this book, which was merely a pleasant joke, becomes a grimace and a demand, a real one! Made with a smile, once again. Today we are here to celebrate the male body. Thus the male author will be the object, whereas we women, who were formerly the object, will be the authors").

Blasons du corps masculin is a startling and brilliant collection of poems for a number of reasons. The male body parts chosen by these women poets lead to an original, estranging perspective on male anatomy, since – with the exceptions of Jacqueline Risset's "Blason de la voix" ("Blason of the Voice") and Marie-Rose Lefèvre's "Blason du genou" ("Blason of the Knee") – none of the body parts that appear in this new collection are the same as the ones that the Renaissance male poets had praised (or blamed) in verse. Indeed, most of the male body parts that are featured in these poems will surprise the reader. "Blason d'une tête postérieure" ("Blason of the Back of the Head"), "Blason de la clavicule" ("Blason of the Clavicle"), and "Blason du chromosome y" ("Blason of the Y Chromosome") all produce a peculiar, off-centre view of the male body.

A discussion of the reinvention of the *blason* in twentieth-century French poetry must begin by acknowledging the seminal importance of André Breton's *blason*-like poem "L'Union libre" ("Free Union"), one of the most famous French love lyrics of the past century. The male speaker of Breton's poem recites a nearly exhaustive list of the body parts of his beloved ("Ma femme" ["My woman / wife"]). Breton follows the model of the Renaissance *blason* in his extravagant praising of individual parts of the female body. However, he also updates the traditional *blason*, brilliantly appropriating it as a vehicle for the Surrealist aesthetic, whose key features Breton himself had defined in his influential book *Manifeste du surréalisme* (*Surrealist Manifesto*) (1924).

"L'Union libre" constitutes an almost complete catalogue of the parts of the female body, described from head to toe. Here is the first half of Breton's poem:

L'Union libre
Ma femme à la chevelure de feu de bois
Aux pensées d'éclairs de chaleur
A la taille de sablier
Ma femme à la taille de loutre entre les dents du tigre
Ma femme à la bouche de cocarde et de bouquet d'étoiles de
Dernière grandeur
Aux dents d'empreintes de souris blanche sur la terre blanche
A la langue d'ambre et de verre frottés
Ma femme à la langue d'hostie poignardée
A la langue de poupée qui ouvre et ferme les yeux
A la langue de pierre incroyable
Ma femme aux cils de bâtons d'écriture d'enfant
Aux sourcils de bord de nid d'hirondelle
Ma femme aux tempes d'ardoise de toit de serre
Et de buée aux vitres
Ma femme aux épaules de champagne
Et de fontaine à têtes de dauphins sous la glace

Ma femme aux doigts de hasard et d'as de cœur
Aux doigts de foin coupé
Ma femme aux aisselles de marbre et de fênes
De nuit de la Saint-Jean
De troène et de nid de scalares
Aux bras d'écume de mer et d'écluse
Et de mélange du blé et du moulin
Ma femme aux jambes de fusée. (Breton, *Œuvres complètes, II* 85–7)

(Free Union
My wife with brush fire hair
With heat lightning thoughts
With an hourglass waist
My wife with an otter waist in the teeth of the tiger
My wife with a mouth and a bouquet of stars of the highest
magnitude
With teeth bearing the prints of white mice on the white earth
With a tongue of amber and polished glass
My wife with a tongue of stabbed communion wafer
With the tongue of a doll opening and closing her eyes
With a tongue of incredible stone
My wife with eyelashes of child's handwriting
With eyebrows of the edge of a swallow's nest
My wife with temples of the slate of greenhouse roofs
And of steam on windowpanes
My wife with champagne shoulders
And shoulders of a fountain with dolphin heads under ice
My wife with wrists of matches
My wife with fingers of chance and the ace of hearts
With fingers of fresh-mown hay
My wife with armpits of martens and beech fruit
And Midsummer Night
Armpits of privet hedges and sea snail nests
With seafoam and lock arms
And of a mixture of the wheat and the mill
My wife with spindle legs.)

Clearly, in "L'Union libre" Breton is not so much describing the female body as transforming it over and over by means of a *tour de force* display of unexpected images. The title "L'Union libre" refers both to a couple's sexual relationship without marriage (or "common law" union) and, at a metatextual level, to the poet's inspired combining of unrelated things to create unprecedented images. The freedom of the unfettered (hetero-)sexual imagination is celebrated in the poem, along with an ecstatic heterosexual love.

However, as the woman's body is assimilated by the poet to various birds, animals, and elements of nature, the woman being described remains passive and silent. She submits to the power of the male gaze as it brings her to life in a new, unfamiliar form. Her passivity is emphasized, for Breton's poem includes almost no verbs, except for past participles used as adjectives. "Ma femme" is thus reduced to a series of static noun phrases, presented in apposition. Even more troubling than this insistence on woman's passivity is the violence of certain images in the poem: "Ma femme à la taille de loutre entre les dents du tigre" or "Ma femme à la langue d'hostie poignardée." Despite his idealizing the magically evocative beauty of the female body, the male poet here is also distorting her body – even doing violence to it.

It would be an oversimplification of the male Surrealist poets' and artists' relation to women (or to Woman) to claim that their work was uniformly or relentlessly misogynistic.[6] Nevertheless, their artistic practice frequently foregrounds the expression of a violent heterosexual eroticism with the female body as its focus. Feminist critic Jennifer Patterson regards "L'Union libre" as an instance of the subjection of Woman to an aesthetic – and political – description that alienates her from herself:

> Breton's poem "L'Union libre" depicts the body of Suzanne Muzard, his wife[,] whose only identity is as the property of the poet, as an unnamed woman, "my woman / wife." The woman is a textual possession of her poetic representation, pornographed by the reification of a male self-pleasuring gaze. She is robbed of space and presence and her body is separated into a list of parts. These parts of the body are images to be used for individual poetic and linguistic associations, objects to be played with. The dislocation of her body parts is mirrored by the disruptive and manipulative violence done to the images imposed on it to demonstrate Surrealist principles of language, images which themselves violently present the representational act. (151)

The cultural authority of Breton's "L'Union libre" makes it an indispensable reference-point for subsequent French love poetry but, for women poets writing after Breton, such as the nine *blasonneuses* in the

Aquaviva collection, his poem may, rather, serve as a lingering reminder of the sexist attitudes towards women which have surfaced in the treatment of the female body by many male French poets from Ronsard to Denis Roche.

Although none of the nine contributors to Aquaviva's collection of *blasons* makes explicit reference to "L'Union libre," nonetheless, they were certainly all aware of the importance of Breton's poem when they composed their own *blasons*. Of the ten poems collected by Aquaviva, the two that seem to me to be the closest to Breton's modernist *blason* are Jacqueline Cahen's "Poème d'amour physique" ("Poem of Physical Love") and Liliane Giraudon's "Extrait d'un alphabet morse" ("Excerpt from a Morse Alphabet"). Cahen's poem begins as follows:

Je t'aime
J'aime tes reins ta peau
ton foie tes boyaux
ta couleur tes cheveux ton cou
ton foie tes boyaux
tes odeurs tes boyaux
ta lymphe

J'aime ton foie ta rate
le pylore l'estomac
l'aorte
la jugulaire tous les capillaires
la jugulaire?

(I love you
I love your loins your skin
your liver your intestines
your colour your hair your neck
your liver your intestines
your odors your intestines
your lymph nodes

I love your liver your spleen
your pylorus the stomach
the aorta
the jugular all the capillaries
the jugular?)

Although this piece opens, like the most conventional of love poems, with the words "Je t'aime," it quickly subverts the usual conventions of the love lyric. By its anatomizing, medical language and its obsessive naming of a multiplicity of bones and organs inside the male body, Cahen's poem cleverly inverts the practice of the sixteenth-century male *blasonneurs*. As indicated earlier, Renaissance male poets such as Marot were preoccupied with listing the visible, surface attributes of a particular female body in order to emphasize the erotic pleasure it afforded the male poet's attentive gaze. Cahen, by contrast, surprises her reader by shifting the poem's emphasis to what is *not* seen. Thus, Cahen skilfully updates the tropes of the culture of dissection analysed by Jonathan Sawday in his study of early-modern culture.

Cahen then continues her anaphoric listing of parts of the male body, preceded by "j'aime." Woman becomes the agent of desire here. Her language, in its violence, disrupts the traditional notion of female passivity:

J'aime ta rate évidemment
les ombres des fosses sous-épineuses
et l'excessive douceur de la saignée
Ah! Comment résister à la tentation de la saignée.

(I love your spleen obviously
the shadows of the cavities under your spine
and the excessive sweetness of the bleeding
Ah! How to resist the temptation of the bleeding.)

Deliberately "scandalous" in its aggressive affirmation of women's right to voice their sexual fantasies openly, the language of Cahen's *blason* increases in intensity until it brings its speaker to orgasm in the end:

je sais nager entre les muscles et les nerfs
la brasse ou le papillon
je dédaigne le sang
j'aime nager entre muscles et nerfs

l'envie que j'ai de glisser mes doigts dans les
fentes sous-crâniennes effleurer la dure-mère prévoir
la faille et se distendre les phalanges dans l'entrelacs
des neurones

attraper disjoncter quelques synapses
les conduire jusqu'à l'orgasme.

(I know how to swim between the muscles and the nerves
The breast stroke or the butterfly
I feel disdain for blood
I like to swim between muscles and nerves

the desire I feel to slip my fingers into the
subcranial slots to touch the dura mater anticipate the fault and stretch out my fingerbones in the tracery
of the neurons
catch unjoin a few synapses
carry them to orgasm.)

Liliane Giraudon adopts an equally unorthodox approach to describing the male body while, like Cahen, assuming a subversive stance towards male-identified French poetic traditions. Here is Giraudon's *blason*:

Extrait d'un alphabet morse
"Je pisse du verre et du feu" – Théophile de Viau

Langue Epaules
Côte Orteil Reins Pied Sourcils
Torse Œil Urètre Tempes
Epiderme Nez Tête Index Encolure Regard.

(Excerpt from a Morse Alphabet
"I piss glass and fire" – Théophile de Viau

Tongue Shoulders
Rib Toe Kidneys Foot Eyebrows
Torso Eye Urethra Temples
Epidermis Nose Head Index Neck Gaze.)

Given that Marot's "Le Beau Tétin" has always been regarded as the paradigmatic *blason anatomique*, Giraudon's poem reads as a radically minimalist description of the male body. Giraudon simply lists a series of nouns corresponding to particular parts of the male body. No adjectives – or, even, articles – accompany these nouns. Moreover, she does not praise or blame these body parts; she presents them as they are. Her only aesthetic manipulation of the body parts is her arrangement of them in rows so that the capitalized first letter of each noun can be paired with the capitalized first letter of the other nouns in each line of the poem, to yield "LE CORPS TOUT ENTIER" ("THE ENTIRE BODY") as a hidden message. (The reference to Morse code in the poem's title alerts us to the coded message buried in the poem.)

Giraudon purposefully eschews the elaborate similes and the liberal use of adjectives typical of the Marotic *blason anatomique*. On the contrary, by a witty use of minimalist metonymy, she is able to evoke "LE CORPS TOUT ENTIER" in a few short, laconic lines lacking any overwrought poetic effects. Her claim to have captured "the entire (male) body" in words could have appeared excessively boastful. However, the deliberately understated use of language as well as her title, which implies that this poem is a mere "excerpt" from a longer work, suggest an attitude of modesty. Different as Giraudon's poem may seem when compared with its sixteenth-century model, one should note, nonetheless, that her poem still reproduces the two defining features of the Renaissance *blason*; the detailed description of a body and a self-conscious emphasis on the linguistic code through which the description takes place. The feminist significance of Giraudon's *blason* emerges less in her poem itself or in its title than in the odd quotation from Théophile de Viau: "Je pisse du verre et du feu." This quotation acts as a catalyst for a complex dialogue between "Extrait d'un alphabet morse" (and the nine other *blasons* in Aquaviva's book) and the long tradition of love poems written by male poets to and about women.

Giraudon's choice of Théophile de Viau's poetry as a foil or counter-example to her own poem is, at first glance, surprising, since Viau (1590–1626) was a famous poet of the *seventeenth* century. His work appeared long after the celebrated generation of Renaissance *blasonneurs* had written their poems on the female body. Giraudon offers no footnote explaining the reason for her selecting a quotation from Viau. One may speculate that what prompted her to view Viau as the representative male poet of sex and love is the ambivalent response to love and love poetry in his work. Many of Viau's love poems repeat the Petrarchan thematics of much Renaissance love poetry (such as the convention of the male lover's expression of his emotional suffering, caused by the cold indifference of the lady he loves). Yet, while reproducing many aspects of the Renaissance love lyric, Viau tended to critique this earlier tradition in order to set himself and his work apart from it, as Guido Saba notes in his study *Théophile de Viau: un poète rebelle* ("*Théophile de Viau: A Rebellious Poet*"): "naturellement enclin à l'expression de l'aspect sensuel de l'amour, Théophile reprend donc ces topoi (de la poésie de la Renaissance). [Cependant,] son langage direct et cru dévoile non seulement la recherche de la représentation concrète de l'intensité du plaisir onirique, mais aussi le refus de l'idéalisation pétrarquiste de la femme" ("naturally inclined to express the sensual aspect of love, Theophile takes up again those topoi (from Renaissance poetry). [Nevertheless], his direct and raw language reveals not only his search for the concrete representation of the intensity of dreamlike pleasure, but also his refusal to idealize woman as Petrarch had") (65).

Indeed, Viau became one of the most notorious libertine poets of the seventeenth century (one of his poems opened the 1621 anthology of erotic and obscene verse *Le Parnasse des poètes satyriques* [*The Satyr Poets' Parnassus*]). The line that Giraudon quotes as the epigraph to "Extrait d'un alphabet morse" is taken from a very crude, obscene poem by Viau entitled "Satire." The male speaker of this poem rages against his syphilis. These are the final four stanzas of the poem:

Je me fâche et me plains de tout,
Tout ce que je vois m'importune:
Ventre-bleu, le destin, me … ut,
J'enrage contre la fortune.

Je pisse le verre et le feu,
Je ne crache que de la colle;
Je n'ai presque un cheveu,
Ah, ventre-bleu, j'ai la vérole!

J'ai la gravelle dans les reins,
Je ne trouve plus qui je foute,
Et la sainte ampoule de Reims
Tarirait plutôt que ma goutte.

A cinquante ans un homme est mort,
Ce n'est plus rien que pourriture;
Morbleu, les destins nous font tort,
… tre d'eux et de la nature! (Viau, *Œuvres complètes, III* 138–9)

(I am angry and complain of everything,
All that I see bothers me:
Gadzooks, destiny ...s me,
I rage against fortune.

I piss glass and fire,
I cough up nothing but glue;
I have barely a hair left,
Ah, gadzooks, I have venereal disease!

I have gravel in my kidneys,
I find no one to fuck,
And Reims's holy phial
Would dry up sooner than my dripping;

At fifty a man is dead,
He's nothing more than rot;
'Sblood, our destinies wrong us,
...ck them and nature!]

Almost four centures before Giraudon, Théophile de Viau had already articulated a critique of the idealizing images of love and of the conventions of love poetry made famous by French Renaissance poets. Viau's earthy, shocking verse and his rebellious position within his culture provide Giraudon with a forceful precedent for her own critique of the Renaissance *blason*. The quoted line "Je pisse le verre et le feu" forces us to acknowledge the nasty reality of venereal disease – a reality omitted from the more decorous and abstract world of the *blasons*.

Viau's line "Je pisse le verre et le feu" helps us to clarify the significance of Giraudon's poem not only through a literal reference to a venereal disease, though. Viau's line is important here because it is a striking example of metaphor. As Giraudon has chosen metonymy as the trope by which she will present the male body, her quoting a *metaphor* about the male body is no accident. One could argue that Viau's line "Je pisse le verre et le feu" enacts a (con)fusion of the operations of the penis / phallus and the power of the male poetic imagination to generate arresting metaphors. The line unites the male body and the poetic imagination in a manner which a feminist critic today would certainly characterize as essentialist. Thus, Giraudon's poem may serve as a corrective to this phallic essentialism. In "Extrait d'un alphabet morse," the quotation from Viau finally sets up an ironic contrast between metaphor and metonymy, between male (poetry) and female (poetry), and between the penis as privileged body part versus a neutral laying out of the male body in words by Giraudon that do not privilege any one body part over the others. Thus, a multi-level politics of gender is implicit in Liliane Giraudon's apparently simple poem.

Frédérique Guétat-Liviani's "Blason du chromosome y" ("Blason of the Y Chromosome") is a text that unfolds as a series of witty picture-poems. Guétat-Liviani creates humorous rebuses in each poem in order to set up riddles for her reader. In each case, an envelope at the centre of the page has been opened to reveal an image or message. In the first example, the inside of the envelope shows the words "CHR O ME" and "OZ," followed by an image of a group of men – in French, "hommes." "CHR O ME" + "OZ" + "hommes" = "chromosome." A "y" appears in all four corners of the page as well. The next envelope in the series carries the message "puisque c'est une" ("since it is a [fem.]"), with an image of three girls (two smiling; one scowling and holding her folded arms against her chest), and the words "Nous l'appellerons X" ("We shall call her X"). An "x" stands in each of the four corners of the page. Then, the third opened envelope reveals a piece of paper covered in a grid pattern showing a large "Y" in the centre. Three of the four corners of this page state: "La Lettre Perdue" ("The Lost Letter"). The fourth envelope contains another piece of paper covered by a grid pattern. This time, the letters of the (French) alphabet fill the grid, *except* that the "y" has been omitted. The final image in Guétat-Liviani's rebus text presents the front of the envelope (which we have so far been studying from the back). There is a stamp in the upper right-hand corner. The address on the envelope reads "L'ETRE PERDU" ("THE LOST BEING"). Again, a "y" stands in each of the four corners of the page.

Guétat-Liviani's tongue-in-cheek postal allegory of sexual difference references Lacanian psychoanalytic theory and the sort of word-play around "la lettre" (letter of the alphabet, letter to be mailed to an addressee) for which Jacques Lacan is known. In his 1955 seminar exploring Edgar Allan Poe's story "The Purloined Letter," Lacan reads Poe's tale as an allegory for the functioning of desire and intersubjectivity.[7]

Poe's story – like psychoanalytic thought itself – centres on a curious enigma, on tangled interpersonal relations, and on the role of the detective / analyst, who is given the task of solving the mystery. "The Purloined Letter" of Poe's story is a letter stolen from a "royal personage" (whom Lacan refers to as "the Queen") by one of her royal ministers. It is urgent that this letter be recovered for, should the King learn of the existence of this letter and read it, the Queen will find herself hopelessly compromised. The police search the Minister's rooms with extreme scientific thoroughness, yet fail to discover the compromising letter there. So, the famous detective Dupin is called in to locate the letter and restore it to the Queen's possession. Dupin visits the Minister and quickly realizes that the stolen letter has been disguised with a new seal and hidden in plain view in a card rack hanging below the mantelpiece. Creating a diversion on his second visit to the Minister, Dupin successfully removes the purloined letter from the card rack and replaces it with a convincing copy – unseen by the Minister. Dupin turns the tables on the Minister, subjecting him to the same kind of trick that the Minister had played on the Queen. In the end, the letter (whose contents are never disclosed) is returned to its *proper* place.

Critic Jean-Michel Rabaté explains the importance of Lacan's reading of the Poe tale as follows: "In his analyses of Poe, Gide, and Joyce, Lacan identifies the structural function of a letter that never betrays its content but gives shape to the libidinal logic by which the subject is determined. Lacan's reading of Poe's 'Purloined Letter' remains emblematic of his entire strategy" because "the letter possesses a logic of its own, a logic fundamentally linked with the Unconscious, understood both as hidden knowledge and as writing machine" (28).

Guétat-Liviani's poem focuses on a particular facet of Lacan's discussion of "The Purloined Letter": the analyst's association of the letter, and of its appearances / disappearances and its mysteries, with women and the feminine. (The letter belongs to the Queen and conceals her secrets.) In Guétat-Liviani's rebus / allegory, "y," the signifier of men and masculinity, functions as a "lost letter" or a sign for "lost being," whereas Lacan had linked *women* and the feminine with lack. Thus, a deconstruction and mocking of masculine / male cultural authority is being rehearsed in Guétat-Liviani's series of image-poems.[8]

Michèle Métail's linguistic strategies for representing the male body in her *blason* derive from a quirky formalism. Métail is a member of the OuLiPo (Ouvroir de Littérature Potentielle [Workroom for Potential Literature]) group, which has included such luminaries as Roubaud, Raymond Queneau, and Georges Perec. To produce an Oulipian text, the poet must first select a formal constraint, which will then determine the structures of the poem. One well-known Oulipian constraint invented by Métail is the "Portrait-Robot," which OuLiPo's publication *Abrégé de littérature potentielle* (*Précis of Potential Literature*) (2002) defines in this way: "PORTRAIT-ROBOTS: Le principe de cette contrainte, introduite par Michèle Métail, est le suivant: à l'aide d'expressions toutes faites empruntées à un corpus donné (en prenant par exemple pour source un dictionnaire encyclopédique), faire le portrait descendant d'une personne, d'un corps de métier, etc." ("ROBOT-PORTRAITS": The principle of this constraint, introduced by Michèle Métail, is the following: using stock expressions taken from a given corpus (taking as a source, for example, an encyclopedic dictionary), make a portrait of a person, a profession, etc.").[9] To clarify how a "Portrait-Robot" works, the *Abrégé de literature potentielle* offers Métail's poem "Le Faussaire" ("The Forger"):

Faux visage
faux cils
faux nez
faux sens
faux bras
faux doigt
faux cul.

(False face
false eyelashes
false nose
false meaning
false arm(s)
false finger
false ass.)

In this poem, we may note, once again, an example of a parody of the Renaissance *blason*, transformed into a humorous, 'pataphysical genre.

The Métail poem included in Aquaviva's collection, "Blason poli pour Li Po" ("Polite Blason for Li Po") is constructed in a similar fashion to her "Portrait-Robot" quoted above. In it Métail presents a two-page list of lines of verse, each of which (with the exception of the final line) begins with the words "C'EST PARCE QU'IL EST" ("IT IS BECAUSE HE IS") followed by an adjective or a prepositional phrase in italics. The last line of the poem, "QU'IL S'EN EST FALLU D'UN POIL" ("THAT HE / IT WAS NEARLY") completes the unfinished sentence started in each of the other fifty-six lines. In a note at the bottom of the second page, Métail explains how the word game which inspired her poem works: "LI PO: poète chinois de la dynastie des Tang. Son nom dans le système de transcription phonétique appelé Pinyin est l'anagramme de POIL, ainsi que POLI" ("Li Po: Chinese poet of the T'ang dynasty. His name, in the phonetic system of transcription called Pinyin, is the anagram of POIL (body hair), and of POLI (polite)") (And – of course – it is identical to the last four letters of OULIPO!).

In keeping with standard Oulipian practice, Métail has based the creation of her poem upon abstract wordplay. An Oulipian text always refers, primarily, back to the language system which has produced it, as we saw in the case of Roubaud's ∈ in chapter 1. Hence, the title, "Poème poli ..." and the very last words, "...d'un poil," conceal anagrams that bring Li Po, as a body of writings, into the very texture of Métail's poem. Métail's choice of Li Po, one of the most famous classical Chinese poets, also reflects standard Oulipian practice, inasmuch as OuLiPo members have often employed their eccentric techniques for the production of "potential literature" to rewrite classic literary texts such as a sonnet by Baudelaire or a poem by Rimbaud or Mallarmé.

Through their highly skilful and entertaining plays on tradition in these very different poems, the nine contemporary *blasonneuses* have succeeded in creating a postmodern revision of Renaissance poetry. Their unusual takes on the male body unmask men's cultural assertions of their own power as arrogant posturing. The male body, in these poems, proves to be just as open to a dismantling, teasing, critical, or sceptical female gaze as the female body was for male poets of the sixteenth century.

The Art of Description Updated: Paul Louis Rossi's *Cose Naturali* and Tita Reut's *Vis Cachées*

1. *Paul Louis Rossi's* Cose Naturali

Paul Louis Rossi (b. 1930)'s collection of poems *Cose naturali* (*Natural Things*), written in 1978, was not published in its entirety in book form until 1991. Although the source of inspiration for *Cose naturali* was Rossi's contemplation of various Flemish and German still life paintings, the poems that he composed are not mere descriptions of the paintings that inspired them, as the poet explains: "Je glissais insensiblement des choses peintes à la surface lisse des toiles, aux phrases qui les décrivaient dans les catalogues pour enfin ne plus voir que les mots – ayant oublié les peintures – et d'oubli en oubli ne plus travailler que sur l'agacement de quelques vers, à l'infini ..." ("I slipped unawares from the things painted on the smooth surface of the paintings, to the sentences which described them in catalogues so that finally I could see only the words – having forgotten the paintings – and from forgetting to forgetting I came to work only on the setting on edge [agacement] of a few lines of verse, infinitely ...").

Cose naturali constitutes an homage to the still life as a genre, as well as a critical reflection on the cultural meaning of that genre. The poet makes the political significance of his collection most explicit in his brief forward and in his division of the book into three distinct sections: "L'homme" ("Man"), "Vanités" ("Vanities"), and "Les sens" ("The Senses"). The three sections are preceded by epigraphs taken from Ponge (Part I), Thomas Mann (Part II), and Joyce (Part III). Rossi's inclusion of quotations from these three great modernist writers signals his awareness of the historical authority of modernist writing and / or his sense of the distance between the time of the great modernists and our own, more sceptical and alienated literary moment. In any case, the connections between the modernists' example and Rossi's perspective must be explored if one is to appreciate the significance of his appropriation of art.

The first segment of *Cose naturali* bears the ironic title "L'homme." As Rossi himself acknowledges in his forward, the human figure – "man" – is almost completely absent from the world of the still life: "Et s'il paraît: l'homme, dans les scenes figées, c'est immobilisé à son tour comme objet parmi les objets, où comme la silhouette entrevue au seuil des portes et terrasses" ("And if he appears: man, in these immobile scenes, he also, in turn, is immobile like an object among objects, or like a silhouette glimpsed at the threshold of doors and sidewalk cafés [ter rasses]") (231). As these remarks indicate, the meaning of the still life depends on the radical deprivileging of anthropocentrism. The genre banishes "man" from its purview almost entirely.

The title *Cose naturali* is echoed in the quotation from Ponge that opens Part I: "tout risquerait de finir par une soif inextinguible de repos, de sommeil, de nuit, voire de sauvagerie et de mort, si n'intervenait, au fur et à mesure, quelque antidote de même niveau, qui ravisse et comble d'un seul coup l'homme entier, le trouble et le rassoie dans son milieu *naturel* ..." ("everything could well end in an inexhaustible thirst for rest, sleep, night, and even savagery and death, if some antidote did not gradually intervene, an antidote which might delight and overwhelm the entire man all at once, disturbing him and returning him to his *natural* milieu ...") (233, emphasis added).

One of the first poems in the collection, "l'été…" ("summer…"), appears to present only a brief evocation of a domestic scene:

Un vase
d'orfèvrerie avec
un bouquet
symétriquement
disposé

Un échiquier sur lequel
est versé un
gobelet de corne d'
où sont sortis deux dés

Derrière la table
pose de profil une
jeune femme portant
une corbeille de fruits. (237)

(A gold-plated
vase with
a bouquet
symmetrically
placed

A chessboard on which
is overturned a
goblet of horn from
which two dice have emerged

Behind a table
is posing in profile a
young girl carrying
a basket of fruit.)

The closely observed objects (a vase and a chessboard) remain in the foreground in the first three stanzas of this four-stanza picture / poem. The one human figure, a young woman, is not mentioned until the third stanza and, even then, she is subordinated to her function of carrying a third object – a basket of fruit. Through subtle emphases, without overt commentary, the poet shows us an estranged world, one not dominated by human figures.

In a longer poem from Part I, "Ode à Sébastien Stoskopff" ("Ode to Sébastien Stoskopff"), Rossi offers us a moral fable in which the artist Sébastien Stoskopff falls victim to the dangerous, illusory pleasures that still life paintings both tempt us with and warn us against. By overindulging in drink, Stoskopff ends up dead. Rossi's ode to Stoskopff recommends caution and moderation to the reader by invoking the *vanitas* motif of still life. Indeed, he incorporates the German title of a scholarly study on *vanitas* in the still life tradition directly into his poem.

The evocation of *vanitas* leads us into Part II of *Cose naturali*, "Vanités." In choosing this title, the poet ostensibly denounces the futility of the human pursuit of fleeting pleasures, either gastronomic or carnal. He alerts us to the inevitability of death, which must follow indulgence in earthly pleasures, in the end. The naive reader / viewer of still life may be seduced by the illusory delights that the paintings present, whereas a more perceptive reader / viewer will find the stern moral message hidden in the painting or poem, as in this still life text from "Vanités" (Vanities):

deux raies
trois poissons
un crabe
et quelques moules

le poisson éventré
(tâche rose)
laisse pendre ses viscères. (244)

(two skate [raies]
three fish
a crab
and a few mussels

the eviscerated fish
(a pink smear)
Has his entrails hanging out.)

At a superficial level, this picture simply shows us fishes, crabs, and mussels to be eaten as a delicious meal. At second glance, this is a shockingly graphic image of death. The smooth, shiny surface of the fish's body in the second stanza has been violated and torn open in order to force us to gaze upon the mess of an eviscerated skate before us. Here, Rossi discreetly sketches a verbal picture that, nevertheless, highlights the secret violence which traditional still life paintings have so often featured.

Two further poems from "Vanités" underscore the complexity of the poet's dialogue with the still life tradition. The first one is entitled "La Bécasse" ("The Woodcock"):

Bécasse   morte
    accrochée
par un fil

rouge
    passé
dans
le bec
contre
    un vieux
mur
à
    un
        clou. (245)

(Dead   woodcock
    hung
by a red
wire
    threaded
into
his bill
against
    an old
wall
to
    a
        nail.)

Rossi plays with the *trompe-l'oeil* aspect of the still life in this poem, as the painting / page itself imitates the wall where the dead woodcock has been nailed up temporarily. A metapoetic play upon illusion and reality, upon readerly insight or naivety, is on display here. The starkly minimalist presentation of the image renders it all the more arresting.

Another poem from "Vanités" features a compelling – but problematic – assimilation of poetry to painting by Rossi. In this poem, "Polychromie soutenue" ("Sustained Polychromaticity"), he attempts a fusion of the two art forms:

Sur une nappe blan
  che un grand verre
    de vin (blanc)

un verre de bière
  cylindrique pl
at portant un crabe
citron entamé à
  côté   un couteau
  manche de vermeil
émaillé
      en damier
  noir et blanc

petit bassin
      étain flû
  te de verre renversée
composition en
  diagonale sur
  fond gris. (246)

(On a white table
cloth a large glass
  of (white) wine
a glass of beer
  cylindrical pl
ate carrying a crab
lemon bitten into be
side a knife
vermillion handle
enameled
    in checkerboard pattern
black   and white

little basin, bowl, pan
        pewter gl
ass flute turned over

diagonal com
position on
  gray background.)

Despite the superficially banal enumeration of a series of objects on a white tablecloth in this poem, Rossi's choice of the title "Sustained Polychromaticity," as well as the metaesthetic flourish at the end of the poem "composition en / diagonale sur / fond gris" ("diagonal com / position on / gray background"), indicate that a serious reflection on the process of representation underlies this short poem. Rossi's curious, fussy placement of the words on the page – to mirror the placement of the objects on the table – reminds one of the still life painter's careful and methodical observation of his subject matter. Moreover, the poet's meticulous positioning of blank spaces between and around the words of his text echoes the painter's concern with space, line, and colour. Indeed, notations of colour assume primary importance in the poem: "nappe blanche," "vin (blanc)," "manche de vermeil," "damier / noir et blanc," "fond gris." The most unexpected innovation in the poem is, obviously, the unaccountable separation of certain words into two parts and Rossi's situating of these two parts in different lines of the poem: "blan / che," "pl / at," and "flû / te." Dividing these words up in this way creates an estranging effect. So, the poet intends to startle us for some reason. He wishes, I suspect, to force us to see that language is not – cannot be – an innocent or transparent medium of communication, even when it is ostensibly being used to describe objects on a table. Rossi's disconcerting and subtle manipulations of representation in *Cose naturali* reflect keen insights into the ideological consequences of the interpretation of art.

The third, and final, section of the book, "Les sens," opens with a quotation from Joyce: "Sa croyance se fortifiait, s'exagérait, du fait des ténèbres et du silence où réside l'invisible paraclet, celui dont les symboles sont la colombe et le vent puissant, envers qui tout péché est irrémissible …" ("He believed this all the more, and with trepidation, because of the divine gloom and silence wherein dwelt the unseen Paraclete, Whose symbols were a dove and a mighty wind, to sin against Whom was a sin beyond forgiveness") (125).[10] The quotation emphasizes spiritual purity as opposed to sin. By linking this particular quotation to the idea of the five senses' ability to mislead and corrupt us rather than lead us to true understanding, Rossi reiterates the ethical message which grounds *Cose naturali* as a whole. Once again, we are warned that, in the end, all is vanity. The poet makes this message explicit in a poem from Part III, "Et songeant à se rendre immobile": "Car les / cinq couleurs" dit le Sage "rendent l'homme / aveugle les cinq sons rendent ses / Oreilles sourdes" ("And thinking of making himself immobile": "for the / five colours" says the Wise man, "make man / blind the five sounds make his / Ears deaf") (250). Another poem from "Les sens," "quand les objets" ("when the objects") (252), presents an even harsher condemnation of overindulgence in sensual pleasures, as the poem intimates that, at the end of life, all that remains is cold, solitude, and an awareness of the impersonal passage of time.

In "quand les objets" – one of the last poems in the collection – Rossi evokes the figure of Adrian Leverkühn, the doomed hero of Thomas Mann's famous twentieth-century reworking of the Faust myth, *Doctor Faustus* (1948). Leverkühn is a gifted composer who, like Goethe's Faust, sells his soul to the devil in exchange for higher knowledge and fame. In his arrogance, Leverkühn places himself above the rest of humanity. At the end of the novel, he pays the price for his arrogance and his amoral world view by losing everything he cherishes and becoming a mere shadow of his former self. Rossi refers to Leverkühn's fate in these lines: "Et songerez au froid qui saisit Adrian Leverkühn comme ultime épreuve / Avant de vous trouver glacé à votre tour / n' / écoutant ..." ("And you will think of the cold which seized Adrian Leverkühn as a final test / Before you find yourself frozen in turn / not / listening ...") (252). Leverkühn's fate surely has a particular relevance in Rossi's text, which alludes constantly to the dangers of succumbing to the lure of aesthetic beauty and illusions. Since Leverkühn was a brilliant composer, one can infer that the susceptibility of the artist to being tricked and to having his or her view of the world perverted by a too single-minded commitment to art is the underlying theme of the lines from Rossi's poem evoking Leverkühn's fate.

In her book *History, Myth and Music: Thomas Mann's Timely Fiction*, Susan Von Rohr Scaff examines numerous connections between the Faust myth, German history during the Nazi period, and Mann's problematizing of the artist's role. "Reading *Doctor Faustus*," she writes, "we find that humankind, symbolized by the German nation, has fallen into perdition and that the highest human achievements, symbolized by art, may have been inspired in the depths of hell" (126). Although Rossi's evocations of the Faust myth and its relationship to the artist remain far more understated and ambiguous than those of Mann's novel, the figure of Faust is a significant presence in *Cose naturali*. The short poem "Exilium Melancholiae," near the beginning of the book, presents only "Une table / chargée de livres // un vieillard / accoudé" ("A table / loaded with books // an old man / leaning on his elbows") (236), an image that recalls the opening passage of Goethe's *Faust*, in which the hero expresses his sense of world-weariness and his disenchantment with books and knowledge.

References to Faust, Adrian Leverkühn, and Sébastien Stoskopff, and the moral allegories associated with these figures, draw one's attention to various ethical issues underpinning Rossi's exploration of still life. What, then, is ultimately at stake in Rossi's resignification of the art of description through his renewal of the genre? Poet and critic Yves di Manno offers a far-reaching assessment of the cultural importance of *Cose naturali* in a short, provocative essay, "chose qui gagne à être peinte" ("thing improved by being painted"). In this essay, di Manno rejects the view of some earlier readers of *Cose naturali* who had regarded Rossi's still life poems as minimalist, impersonal, and slight. Di Manno, on the contrary, asserts that these deceptively simple poems conceal a powerful critique of contemporary European culture and its consumerist, shallow values, even though the poems appear, on the surface, to be anachronistic and unrelated to the contemporary world.

Di Manno first reminds us that Rossi's intention in composing his still life poems is not to describe or copy any existing paintings. Rather, Rossi aims to work with language in a manner similar to a painter's working with line, colour, and shapes. Di Manno argues that Rossi's approach to his project is fundamentally anti-lyrical, anti-subjective, and anti-metaphoric:

> Car si le but est bien dans un certain sens de bannir la subjectivité, la métaphore, l'intimisme, la technique employée n'a plus grand'chose à voir avec la description neutre (superficielle) d'un décor imaginaire ou contemplé, type nouveau roman: "La cafetière est sur la table" etc. Il s'agit au contraire de composer un texte *en vers* dérivant d'une matrice *prosaïque*, dans tous les sens du terme. De modeler, de façonner le poème à partir d'un matériau extérieur, dont le choix n'a certes rien de fortuit, mais en restant dans les limites de cette mise en forme, c'est-à-dire en investissant toute l'énergie créatrice, jusqu'à sa perte, dans ce strict équarrissage

> formel. Geste absolument décisif, forme et sens ne faisant dès lors qu'un, *par ce seul choix.* (34)
>
> (For if the goal is certainly in some sense to banish subjectivity, metaphor, personal sentiment, the technique Rossi uses has nothing in common with the neutral (superficial) description of an imaginary or observed setting, as in the *nouveau roman*: 'The coffeepot is on the table' etc. On the contrary, what Rossi is doing is composing a text *in verse* derived from a prosaic source – prosaic in every sense. Modelling, fashioning the poem from the basis of an exterior building material [matériau], which was certainly not randomly chosen, but remaining within the limits of this giving form to the chosen source, that is, while investing all his creative energy, right up to its loss, in this strict formal cutting up. This is an absolutely decisive gesture, whereby form and meaning now become one, *by this choice alone.*)

Thus, concludes di Manno, "tout se ramène dans ces pages à l'évidement, à la trituration, au polissage d'une matière, comme dans les arts plastiques justement, où l'énergie s'absorbe dans la répartition des couleurs, des volumes, des plans. Matière étant ici langage" ("everything in these pages comes down to an emptying out, a grinding, to a polishing of a material [une matière], exactly as in the visual arts, where energy is absorbed into the distribution of colours, of volumes, and of planes. The artist's material in this case being language") (34–5). These remarks suggest that Rossi has succeeded in creating a hybridization of poetry and painting in *Cose naturali* by adopting techniques and modes of writing that permit him to use words and to use the space of the page much as a painter would manipulate colours and forms on a canvas.

However, di Manno finds that *Cose naturali* also encodes a thoroughgoing critique of European individualism and materialism: "Car ce qui est en cause dans les *Cose naturali* … c'est la notion même d'individualisme propre à l'ensemble de la culture européenne, la faillite ou du moins les failles de la pensée qui l'étaie, son échec face à un certain nombre de questions éthiques, quelles que soient par ailleurs (dans l'ordre des techniques) ses indéniables avancées. *Ces crimes étant liés*" ("For what is at stake in *Cose naturali* … is the very notion of individualism specific to European culture, the bankruptcy or at least the flaws in the thinking which underpins it, its failure with respect to a certain number of ethical questions, regardless of its undeniable advances in technique / technology. *These crimes are connected*") (36–7). From this point of view, Rossi's inclusion in *Cose naturali* of poems carrying explicit statements condemning all indulgence in sensual pleasures and emphasizing the *vanitas* and *trompe-l'oeil* aspects of the still life genre functions as a condemnation of contemporary European materialism, even as it repeats a motif proper to still life paintings of the seventeenth century. Just as seventeenth-century Dutch still lifes displayed deceptive images of glittering, rare, and expensive goods, so Rossi's poems may provide an equivalent of the current taste for virtual, televisual images of beauty and plenitude that lack any substance or reality. In di Manno's words: "Car c'est une sagesse ou une science que l'artiste [that is, Rossi] tente aussi de fixer, par-delà la fiction de son geste – leçon d'humilité qui résonne avec plus d'urgence aujourd'hui que jamais, si l'on songe à ces millions d'écrans vides multipliant à satiété le leurre des visages et des objets: *Oh, fous! Fuyez la vanité …*" ("For it is a wisdom or a knowledge which the artist [that is, Rossi] is also attempting to put in place, beyond the fiction of his aesthetic gesture – a lesson in humility that resonates with greater urgency than ever today, if one thinks of those millions of empty screens multiplying to satiation illusory faces and objects: *Oh, fools! Flee from vanity…*"). (39)

2. Tita Reut's Vis Cachées: *A Poet's Tools*

Vis
rêve de spirale insomniaque
Vocable d'une forme
Dans la résistance définie (*Vis cachées* 48)

(A screw
An insomniac spiral dream
The word for a form
Within definite resistance)

In the fourth essay of his book *Looking at the Overlooked*, Norman Bryson posits a close connection between the still life as a genre and the feminine. Many classic still life paintings, he argues, bear evidence of a male artist's ambivalent intrusion into domestic space, which is culturally coded as womanly / feminine. At the same time, he notes that still life has traditionally been one of the genres in which women painters have excelled: "Throughout its history still life has been a genre regarded as appropriate for women painters to work in. The paintings by Rachel Ruysch (1664–1750) and Margareta Haverman (d. 1772) are virtuoso performances on a par with those of Willem Kalf or de Heem" (174). He also observes, though, that a sexist underrating of the genre partly explains this historical trend: "If still life could be regarded as an appropriate channel for female talent, this was because it ranked as the lowest form of artistic life, of course below the painting of biblical, mythological and national subjects, but also below portraiture and landscape, even below animal painting" (175). Bryson adds that paintings of flowers (those metaphorical analogues of female beauty) have long been a favoured subjected to be assigned to women painters.

Given this traditional bias associating women artists with a subject matter that is delicate, pretty, and domestic via still life, Tita Reut's collection of poems, *Vis cachées*, comes as a surprise, if not a shock. In *Vis cachées*, Reut (b. 1951) presents forty-four poems, each describing a different tool. Appropriating characteristically masculine-male objects, she has produced a complete toolkit in words. Her method of describing these tools combines a careful scrutiny of their function and outward appearance (their shape, size, and so on) with a fanciful, clever metaphorization of each tool. Through these metaphorizations, Reut's poems transcend literal description in order to underscore each object's hidden meaning (hence the title, *Vis cachées*, which also signifies a hidden *flaw* in something).

Here is a representative poem from Reut's collection:

Crochet
Mettre la masse à l'étal
Vol vertical suspendu
Viol inerte
Pentecôte
entre la genèse et la chute
dans le bruit que les mouches font
Clé de la fa ouverte
sur l'ascensionnelle partita
Croc de volée dévorée
Bec de faucon accolant l'immobile
L'agrafe tient en sa serre
un rêve d'apesanteur
projeté. (22)

(Hook
To place the mass spread out in the butcher's stall
A vertical suspended flight
An inert violation
Pentecost
between Genesis and the Fall
in the noise made by flies
The key of F opened
onto the ascending partita
A hook devoured
Falcon's beak embracing immobility
The staple holds in its grip
a dream of weightlessness
projected.)

Reut moves back and forth between literal description and metaphysical conceits in this poem, as the hook's utilitarian function is replaced by a metaphorical invocation of Pentecost and a violent vision of spirituality. Similar in shape to a treble clef or a falcon's curved beak, the hook acquires the attributes of what it resembles. Flying through the air and holding objects suspended, the hook becomes a figure for a magical overcoming of gravity in the poem's final stanza.

As the example of "Crochet" demonstrates, Reut moves repeatedly from contemplation of a physical object to the consideration of a metaphysical problem. Mythological intertexts also surface in several of her poems, through references to the Phoenix, to Icarus, Jacob, and Saint Sebastian. In fact, one soon realizes in reading this collection that the poet aims to alter the objects before her, rather than simply render them in words. Thus, in describing an anvil, she quickly transforms it into a sacrificial altar: "Enclume / bel étal / sacrificiel autel de la forge / où fume et s'érige la chair de métal" ("An anvil / lovely butcher's stall / sacrificial altar of the forge / where the metal's flesh smokes and is erected") (38).

Reut's evocations of these objects activate a fusion of whimsy and violence, of literalness and *préciosité*. A spinning top, for example, becomes "Fraise d'un gâteau moulure / la toupie creuse le nerf de l'orbite" ("like the strawberry of a cake mould / the top digs into the orbit's nerve") (47). Elsewhere, a handsaw's dangerously sharp teeth bite into a piece of wood, leading the poet to an unexpected metaphor:

Egoine
Egoine
Scieuse
Archet d'écriture mutilante
dans la rengaine du sécable

Petite carnassière à main nue
battant les lames
d'un envol de poussière
chuintant des crocs
sous le piston qui scinde

Trancher la question
par oukase du désir. (45)

(Hand Saw
Hand saw
Mechanical saw [Scieuse]
A mutilating writing-bow
in the same old story of what can be cut

Little carnivore bare-handedly
beating the (wood)strips
with a cloud of dust
hissing from your fangs
under the splitting piston / plunger

Deciding the issue
by a ukase of desire.)

In this description, the poet plays with the handsaw's literal function of cutting and slicing, as she personifies the tool into a "little carnivore" with sawdust dripping from its "teeth"! An allegory of the poetic process is evident here as well. The artisan's labours resemble those of the poet, as Reut transforms the action of sawing through wood into a form of writing.

The link to the visual arts in *Vis cachées* is underscored and intensified by Reut's inclusion in the book of four drawings of tools, sketched by her friends Arman and César, both of whom are major artists of the postwar period in twentieth-century France. Both Arman and César have belonged to the group of artists known as the "Nouveaux réalistes" – a group organized by the art critic Pierre Restany in the early 1960s. César first attracted wide-spread attention in France through his "Compressions." Michele C. Cone describes the genesis of the "Compressions" as follows:

> By the end of the fifties, the automobile had entered the fray of art. César Baldaccini, known as César (1921–98), who had achieved success with expressionist sculpture in rusty, welded iron parts, such as *Torso* (1954) … changed direction when he discovered near Paris an arsenal of abandoned car carcasses, and the American-made machines that compressed them … At the Paris Salon de Mai of 1960, César displayed these large parallelepipeds of contorted metal, each weighing a ton, made from crushed car carcasses. (51)

The presentation of these cubes of crushed metal as *sculptures* at the 1960 Salon de Mai caused a huge scandal. Cone adds that "[t]he publicity engendered by the Salon de Mai event reached far beyond the usual coterie of art world aficionados. César became a celebrity" (51). César's "Compressions" were later followed by "Expansions."

The work of Arman has gone through several different phases, each featuring a distinct approach to the treatment of the object. His early "Cachets" ("Stampings") ("estampages de tampons encreurs sur papier" ("impressings of inkstamps on paper") –Pierre Restany) were followed by the "Allures" series (tracings of objects). Later, Arman created his "Poubelles" ("Wastebaskets"). He next worked on accumulations of objects created through the grouping together of multiples of the same object. He is also known for his "Colères" ("Tantrums") in which he exhibits the results of his violent smashing of an object – most often a musical instrument. In addition, Arman has practised "Coupes" ("Cuts"): the slicing up of an object and the presentation of it in sections.[11]

Like Follain's child whose adventures we retraced in *L'Epicerie d'enfance,* Arman was initiated into his fascination with objects via his interest in collecting objects during his childhood. Jan Van Der Marck reports that "[a]s a child Arman dreamed of finding a treasure trove behind the paneling of his room that would consist of many objects of the same kind: tin soldiers, marbles, and so forth. He collected everything from stones and shells to plants and postage stamps, and he still remembers today how much he enjoyed counting them. Store windows fascinated Arman to such a degree that he has compared the making of his accumulations to the re-creation of those displays he so admired as a child" (74–7).

One type of object which Arman has frequently selected for his "accumulations" is the hand-tool. Thus Tita Reut's portrait gallery of tools in *Vis cachées* serves not only as a general tribute to the works of Arman and César but also as a search for a verbal analogue to one highly specific facet of Arman's art. Her tools work as both a general and a particular homage to the object, as transformed in modern art.

Why is Arman so interested in tools? Van Der Marck notes that Arman has said "I work with tools because I see them as human extensions" (92). Van Der Marck explains the significance of this privileging of tools:

> [T]he objects [Arman] has used in his work have, with rare exceptions, all been some form of tool or instrument. They are meant to do work, to produce. Tools go back as far as man himself; through them man attained power over a hostile environment. Life cannot be sustained nor art created without tools. Nothing is more functional than a tool: its whole meaning is in its use ... It leaps to life in our hand the instant we touch it, and from experience we can anticipate its weight. Tools are every man's objects of first resort. (92–4)

Most decisively for the influence of Arman's art on Tita Reut, Van Der Marck states that "[i]n Arman's latest work [i.e., from the early 1980s] tools have returned with a vengeance":

> On each grouping of hand tools, mounted with great panache flat against the wall, Arman imposes the structural frame most expressive of that particular kind of object. It is as though the artist projects and then freezes the action one might expect from hammer or saw, wrench or crowbar, each in its most aggressive posture. A constellation emerges that brilliantly integrates actual form and potential action ... Uninhibited by the conventional regularity of picture space, these wrenches, saws, and hammers follow the turn, push, and swing of their imagined movement as they fan out and describe arcs against the wall. They defy gravity, and in their reiteration of one basic shape would look abstract were it not for the menace of their implied force and deadliness. (99–101)

Colour plates which Van Der Marck includes in his book on Arman offer examples of this beautiful but menacing art of tools: Plate 103, *Stream of Life*, 1981 (Welded steel vice grips, 59 × 44 ½ in.); Plate 104, *Canal Street Hardware*, 1982 (Welded metal wrenches, 57 × 3 in.); Plate 105, *School of Fish*, 1982 (Welded steel vice grips, 64 × 96 × 3 in.) (Van Der Marck 100–3). The whimsical titles of these works – which, as Van Der Marck recognizes, can be evocative of potential violence – link Arman's creative imagination to that of Tita Reut, who employs *préciosité* to describe her tools (Reut and Arman have, in fact, collaborated on several projects).

The four drawings in *Vis cachées* by Arman and César represent three of the tools evoked verbally by Reut: hammer, wrench, and pliers. Like her poems, the drawings remove these tools from the sphere of their everyday use in order to resituate them in a more abstract setting. The two artists play with tools in order to force us to re-examine our relationships to them, and to objects more generally. So, in both of César's sketches, a Giacometti-like human figure with thin arms and legs and two large, staring eyes holds a disproportionately large tool – a hammer and a wrench (13, 18). In each case, the tool is as tall as the person holding it. This distortion of scale seems absurd or comical, at first glance. However, the artist's making the tools as large as the person holding them may be interpreted as a caveat against human arrogance. We may believe that tools were made to serve us, but, in fact, we remain dependent upon them.

Arman's sketch of pliers (21) problematizes the relationship between language and the visual image. This relationship may be a conflictual one, the drawing implies. In the middle of the page, the nine letters of the French word for pliers, "T E N A I L L E S," are being grasped and pulled by ten long pairs of pliers. To signal the contrast and conflict between the letters and the drawn pliers, Arman leaves the letters white (not shaded in) while making each pair of pliers very dark. The anthropomorphic "legs" and "mouths" of the pliers create the impression that the letters are being grabbed and, perhaps, eaten. Arman's image can be regarded as humorous or terrifying, depending on one's personal perspective. In any case, the image does indicate a struggle between words and visual images in their relationship to things.

Although, for the most part, the question of gender politics is kept in the background in *Vis cachées*, a few poems in the collection focus our attention on gender directly. One such poem is "Dame":

Dame
Où est la demoiselle de plomb?
Tapant du pied le sol saumâtre
de l'irrégularité
Danseuse tellurique
foulant dans le trépignement
de l'obstinée
Hie germanique, sabot des pavés. (27)

(Rammer
Where is the young lady made of lead?
Tapping with her foot on the brackish floor
of irregularity
Telluric dancer
stamping with the step
of the obstinate woman
Germanic rammer, wooden shoe of the cobblestones.)

To understand the game that is taking place in these lines, the reader needs to know that, in French, a rammer (or beetle) is called a "dame" (or "lady"). With comic verve, Reut plays on this incongruity between the name and the thing it refers to. One could, indeed, assert that the humour underlying this particular poem, "Dame," in which a masculine object – a tool made of lead – has a feminine ladylike name, reflects a humour that is representative of Reut's entire collection of forty-four tool poems, not only because the poet is a woman describing "manly" tools, but, more relevantly, because of the self-consciously elegant and whimsical language that she favours in these descriptions. Reut's language feminizes "masculine" objects. The language of her poems connotes a hyper-refinement and an aesthetic sensitivity somewhat reminiscent of the seventeenth-century French *précieuses*. I would argue that this neo-*préciosité*, in generating a textual hybrid mixing masculine and feminine, functions quite similarly to drag, whose subversive cultural performativity Judith Butler has demonstrated in her influential study *Gender Trouble*. In her discussion of the complexities and forms of slippage that drag and cross-dressing perform upon conventional notions of "man" and "woman," "masculine" and "feminine," Butler quotes anthropologist Esther Newton's study of drag culture, *Mother Camp: Female Impersonators in America*, where Newton writes:

> At its most complex [drag] is a double inversion that says "my 'outside' appearance is feminine, but my essence 'inside' [the body] is masculine." At the same time it symbolizes the opposite inversion: "my appearance 'outside' [my body, my gender] is masculine but my essence 'inside' [myself] is feminine." (103)

Using "feminine" language to describe "masculine" objects, Reut subverts conventional gender codes. Her blending of masculine and feminine, literal and figural, enacts a dazzling metamorphosis not unlike a consummately executed drag performance in words.

Tita Reut's introduction of linguistic "gender trouble" into a supposedly neutral and impersonal genre like the still life forces us to look at the still life differently. Like Paul Louis Rossi, she has renewed the vitality and meaningfulness of this classic genre. Following the example of Reverdy, Ponge, and Follain before them, both poets have renewed the cultural relevance of the art of description as an ongoing motif within poetry and painting.[12]

Playing with Things: Nathalie Quintane's *Chaussure* and C. Tarkos's *Calligrammes*

Christopher Tarkos (1964–2004) entered the avant-garde poetry scene in France in the mid-1990s. He quickly because recognized as a major contemporary poet, as a (if not *the*) representative of a new poetics centred on a departure from existing avant-garde practices. By the early 2000s Tarkos had published about twenty books, had given one hundred performances, and was beginning to enjoy an international reputation. His premature death from a brain tumour in 2004, at the age of forty, cut short a brilliant poetic career. The loss of Tarkos, and its occurrence just at the time that he had gained so prominent a place in contemporary poetry and poetics, has led, in the years since his death, to an intense rereading and republishing of many of his works. The publication by P.O.L. in 2008 of his *Écrits poétiques* (*Poetic Writings*), with a preface by Christian Prigent, marks a significant step in the acknowledgment of Tarkos's contribution to the literature of our time.

Prigent, in his preface, asserts that the appearance of texts by Christophe Tarkos and Nathalie Quintane in the mid-1990s constituted the emergence of a palpably different kind of writing:

> Quelque chose a eu lieu dans l'invention poétique en France aux alentours de 1995: Après diverses publications en revues, Christophe Tarkos publie *Oui* en 1996, Nathalie Quintane *Chaussure* en 1997, Charles Pennequin *Dedans* en 1999 ... En 1996, Quintane et Tarkos sont au sommaire de la *Revue de littérature générale* (P.O.L., éditeur), qui aura été le pont de l'épée (lien ET coupure) entre la génération nouvelle et les immédiatement précédentes: celle de l'objectivisme ironique d'Olivier Cadiot, celles des formalistes oulipiens (Roubaud, Grangaud), celle des avant-gardistes des années 1970–1980. (11)

> (Something happened in the field of poetic invention in France around 1995: After publishing several texts in journals, Christophe Tarkos publishes *Oui* (*Yes*) in 1996, Nathalie Quintane publishes *Chaussure* (*Shoe*) in 1997, Charles Pennequin publishes *Dedans* (*Inside*) in 1999 ... In 1996, Quintane and Tarkos are in the table of contents of the *Revue de litérature générale* (*Review of General Literature*) (P.O.L., publisher), which will have been the link AND cut-off point between the new generation and those immediately preceding it: that of the ironic objectivism of Olivier Cadiot, those of the Oulipo formalists (Roubaud, Grangaud), that of the avant-garde writers of the 1970s and 1980s.)

If one looks at three of Tarkos's best-known texts (all of them collected in the 2008 *Écrits poétiques*), one is struck by the "strangeness" of the writing, by its apparent hypersimplicity and banality, its repetitiousness. The first, *Processe*, consists of roughly one hundred pages of blocks of prose, all focusing on separate topics, and juxtaposed to form a text. There seem to be no coherence or identifiable "themes" in *Processe*, which is structured by means of constant discontinuity. *Oui*, also about one hundred pages, is a text highly evocative of Gertrude Stein's art of rhythmic repetitions of a relatively small number of words extended over many pages. This art of repetition is especially evident in some of her earlier experimental works such as *The Making of Americans* (1925).

Here is a brief passage from *Oui*:

> Le texte est expressif. L'expressivité du texte
> est bonne. Le texte expressif est un texte bon.
> Le texte est expressément. Le texte est expressif,
> et intense. Le texte extirpe, est, intensément. Le

texte est d'une grande expressivité, est un texte.
L'expression du texte est bonne, le texte est bon,
L'expressivité du texte est bonne, le texte est bon.
Le texte est expressif … (230)

(The text is expressive. The expressivity of the text
is good. The expressive text is a good text. The
text is expressly. The text is
expressive, and intense. The text has a great
expressivity, is a text. The expression of the text is
good, the text is good. The text is expressive …)

Finally, *Donne* (*Give(s)*), which runs to thirty-two pages, is a dazzling example of the kind of writing now dismissed by its detractors and embraced by its practitioners and aficionados as "unreadable" ("illisible"), as the concluding passage shows:

je l'ai tu à donnes je personne vu entendu il donnes
il pas je pour entendu le tu donne je je me
je comme quand le à Je l'ai l'ai cœur le quand pris, le
tu tu donne il le l'ai à le le été qu'à passé. (349)

(I have it you to gives I no one saw heard it gives
it not I for heard the you give I I me
I like when the to I have it have it heart the when taken, the
you you give he the have it to the the been that to passed.)

Much of Tarkos's writing has a manifesto-like force. (His 1999 texte, *Le Signe* = (*The Sign* =), bears the subtitle "Manifeste" ("Manifesto"). The 2008 *Écrits poétiques* opens with a short piece entitled "Manifeste chou" ("Stupid Manifesto"):

Ça ne peut plus durer comme ça. Il y a quelque chose qui ne va pas. Dans l'utilisation faite du mot poésie, dans l'utilisation qui est faite du mot. Ce n'est pas possible. Il faut faire quelque chose. On se retrouve dans n'importe quoi, la divagation, on ne sait plus où on met les pieds, il y a tout et rien, personne ne sait plus ce qu'il fait, ça ne veut plus rien dire. La pensée créatrice, la beauté verbale, sont réduites à des frivolités municipales, à des claquements de mains, s'engluent dans la bande sonore du championnat américain de basket (43)

(It can't go on like this. There is something that's not right. In the use made of the word poetry, in the use which is made of the word. It's not possible. Something must be done. One finds oneself in nonsense, digression, one no longer knows where to put one's feet, there is everything and nothing, no one knows any longer what he is doing, it no longer has any meaning. Creative thought, verbal beauty are reduced to municipal frivolities, to applause, they get stuck in the soundtrack of the American basketball championship)

Tarkos's writing is based on a fundamentally unfamiliar and controversial view and use of language which sets his work apart from that of his predecessors. A basic concept of his poetics is the idea of language as "word-dough" ("pâte-mot"):

> Pâte-mot est la substance, est la substance de mots assez englués pour vouloir dire, on peut se déplacer dans pâte-mot comme dans une compote, pâte-mot est une substance dont on peut mettre à plat la substance, on peut aussi la mettre pas à plat en bosse, en faire de la neige et en faire des nuages, il y a un certain nombre de composés qui peuvent être mis en tas, la compote, la neige, les nuages, la merde, la confiture, et le mélange de ces composés entre eux, eux est pâte-mot, eux est heureux, eux voient, eux peuvent prendre place, il y en a tout un tas; il n'y a pas de loi (32)
>
> (Word-dough is the substance, is the substance of words stuck together enough to have meaning, one can move around in word-dough as in a stew, word-dough is a substance which can be flattened out, one can also lay it flat in a hump, make snow with it and make clouds with it, there are a certain number of compound elements which can be piled up, stew, snow, clouds, shit, jam, and the mixture of these elements with one another, them is word-dough, them is happy, them see, them can sit down, there is a whole pile of them; there is no law)

Critics note that Tarkos's writing is grounded in the material world and in description; yet, his approach to describing things has little connection to that of any earlier *poètes de l'objet*. As Renaud Ego notes in his essay "Poésie-infinie-réalité: à propos de Christophe Tarkos" ("Poetry-Infinity-Reality: About Christophe Tarkos") "[l]a plupart des livres de Christophe Tarkos naissent à ras de terre, dans le choix de quelques objets ou situations prosaïques. On trouve ainsi un balai, un ballon, le zinc, dans *Oui*, des nuages, le tuba, du bruit dans *Pan*, du lait, la passoire, une couverture, le coussin, le soleil, la fumée, le carton, la théière, etc. dans *Caisses*" ("[m]ost of Christophe Tarkos's books are born right at ground level, in the choice of a few objects or prosaic situations. Thus, one finds a broom, a balloon, zinc, in *Oui*, clouds, a tuba, noise in *Pan*, milk, a strainer, a blanket, a cushion, the sun, smoke, cardboard, a teapot, etc. in *Caisses*") (156). However, Ego immediately cautions that Tarkos's approach to transcribing materiality is oddly abstract:

> S'ils partent du monde, ces poèmes semblent aussitôt s'en abstraire, car jamais ils ne s'attachent à la singularité de tel objet *hic et nunc* ou de tel acte réalisé dans des conditions historiques et personnelles données. Au contraire, ils remontent le plus souvent en amont de toute singularité, jusqu'à la racine de leur impersonnalité – là où un objet n'est plus *donné*, mais *quelconque*, contenant tous les objets appartenant à la même classe; là où un acte n'est plus effectué par une personne, mais est l'infinie potentialité du 'manger', du 'parler' ou du 'dormir.' C'est pourquoi ces poèmes ne parlent pas d'*un* nuage, mais de toute possibilité de nuage en tout nuage; non d'*une* théière mais *de la* théière comme il y a *du* lait, *de la* fumée – autrement dit, de la matière. (156)
>
> (Even if they come from the everyday world, these poems seem immediately to be abstracted from it, for they never attach themselves to the singularity of a particular object *hic et nunc* or to a particular act realized in any given historical and personal facts. On the contrary, they most often shy away from any singularity, to the very root of their impersonality – where an object is no longer *given*, but *anything at all.* Containing all the objects belonging to the same class; where an act is no longer performed by a person, but is the infinite potentiality of 'eating,' 'speaking' or 'sleeping.' That is why these poems do not speak of *a* cloud, but of any possibility of a cloud in any cloud; not of *a* teapot but of *some* teapot just as there is *some* milk, *some* smoke – in other words, some matter.)

Tarkos's work has been relevantly compared to that of a number of other writers as his critics endeavour to place him within key trends in literary history. So, Prigent states that "[l]e projet [de Tarkos] a, si l'on veut, quelque chose de pongien (L'objectivité du cageot ou de l'huître plutôt que la subjectivité lyrique et le souci ontologique). De prévertien … On pense aussi à Gertrude Stein" ("Tarkos's project has something Pongian about it (The objectivity of the crate or the oyster rather than lyric subjectivity and ontological concerns). Something Prévertian …

One also thinks of Gertrude Stein") (15). Interestingly, Renaud Ego proposes a somewhat different genealogy: "Sa logorrhée rappelle les tentatives de suspendre le contrôle de la pensée, comme le tenta le premier surréalisme, celui des tentatives d'automatisme; elle évoque ainsi les emballements de *l'innommable* beckettien, la physique verbale de l'insubordination recherchée par Michaux dans les drogues, la matéralité du texte envisagée comme un corps en mouvement par Guyotat, etc." ("His logorrhea recalls the attempts to suspend the control over thought in early surrealism, that of the experiments in automatic writing; it thus evokes the runaway monologues of Beckett's *unnameable*, the verbal physicality of insubordination sought by Michaux in drugs, the materiality of the text considered as a body in movement by Guyotat, etc.") (159).

An intertext with Apollinaire's *Calligrammes* might seem surprising, given Tarkos's post-modern destabilizing of literalness and of description, and his apparent rejection of the idea that a relationship between language and the referential world remains basic to poetry. Nevertheless, Tarkos pays homage very openly to Apollinaire's example in the second of the three volumes of his omnibus text *Ma Langue* (*My Language/Tongue*) (2004). The first volume of the three presents a long series of Tarkos's *carrés* (blocks of poetic prose) and the third volume contains the text of *Donne*. Volume Two of *Ma Langue* is entitled *Calligrammes*. It features a series of strange, crudely drawn shapes – generally one per page – with a sort of one-line caption placed underneath them.

At first glance, the odd, blob-like shapes and the terse comments or labels accompanying them in Tarkos's *Calligrammes* would seem entirely unrelated to the shaped poems of Apollinaire's 1914–18 *Calligrammes* examined in chapter 1. As we saw, the opening section of Apollinaire's text, 'Ondes,' presents various types of innovative poems. In "Les Fenêtres" or "Lundi rue Christine" he is experimenting with what he called "simultanism" by bringing together multiple perspectives in a single moment of time, somewhat in the manner of the Cubist painters' fracturing an object into several spatial planes given within one moment. In other poems, he displays a virtuoso mastery of concrete poetry and visual poetics, as the shapes of the objects drawn with words on the page imitate the things which the words describe. It is this second type of poem to which Tarkos is giving homage in his own text. Although Tarkos's *Calligrammes* present only one drawn shape on each page in most cases, Apollinaire's concrete poems always work by the juxtaposition of two or more drawn objects. There, the poet's task is, in part, to explore the relationships among these various objects.

Today concrete poetry is a well-established poetic genre. It has had numerous celebrated practitioners over several decades. This was not the case in 1914, however. Apollinaire's collection featuring concrete poems was a highly innovative work for its time, as Willard Bohn notes: "Apollinaire was the first to use visual poetry for strictly lyrical purposes. Traditionally, this genre was reserved for religious or philosophical poets, and it is no accident that many of the early [concrete] works assume the form of altars, wings, and eggs" (49). Bohn underscores the differences between Apollinaire's visual poems and those of poets of earlier centuries:

> As [the poet] himself noted, the calligrams are more visually expressive than their antecedents ... [T]he flexibility and freshness of form [in Apollinaire's calligrams] is related to the new freedom of subject matter. Within the fairly rigid confines of the printer's art, the calligrams present an astonishing variety of shapes: from the simple lines of everyday objects to visual ballets of complicated counterpoint. Typically, the poems swirl into themselves, swoop into the air, or advance toward the reader. There is a surprising amount of movement, in direct opposition to traditional figurative poetry, which is entirely static. (49)

Initially dismissed as childish, these poems, as stated in chapter 1, are now seen as a keywork in the modernist canon, closely related to the Italian Futurists' experiments with visual poetry and continuing the experimental writing of Mallarmé in his *Un coup de dés* (although Apollinaire had not yet read *Un coup de dés* when he was inventing his calligrams).

The two Apollinaire poems studied in chapter 1 – "La Cravate et la montre" and "Coeur, couronne et miroir" – demonstrate the high degree of complexity and the multiple levels of interaction between visual and verbal codes at work in the calligrams. To cite another example here, which I will contrast with Tarkos's idiosyncratic use of the calligram, let us now consider "Éventail des saveurs". This calligram presents a still-life-like grouping of several separate drawn objects. Reading the words of each individual poem and gazing at each drawing in "Éventail des saveurs," the reader is gradually able to decipher the messages which the poem contains while discerning the image of a woman's face hidden in the combination of the objects arranged down the page. Her eye, nose, and mouth are fairly easy to spot; her other features are perhaps less obvious or noticeable. Reading the five objects from the top of the page downward, we discover the following messages left for us by Apollinaire: first, the gun reads "Attols singuliers de brownings quel goût de vivre Ah!" ("strange atolls made of brownings such joy in life Ah!"); the eye reads "Des lacs versicolores Dans les glaciers solaires" ("Multicoloured lakes In solar glaciers"); the nose reads "1 tout petit oiseau qui n'a pas de queue et qui s'envole quand on lui en met une" ("1 very small bird who has no tail and who flies off when one sticks one on him"); the mouth reads "ouis ouis le cri les pas le phoNOGRAPHE ouis ouis L'ALOES éclater et le petit mirliton" ("yeses yeses the cry the steps the phoNOGRAPH yeses yeses THE ALOE exploding and the little kazoo"); the final object reads "Mes tapis de la saveur moussons des sons obscures et ta bouche au soufflé azur" ("My taste carpets monsoons of obscure sounds and your mouth with its azure breathing"). This poem could be considered a sort of *blason*, as it praises the various features of a female beloved by separating her into individual parts on the page. This is, obviously, a love poem, yet its placement in the later sections of *Calligrammes*, which focus on poems of war rather than peacetime, adds a darker undertone, as does the presence of the gun placed towards the top of the page. The poem seems simple, like "Coeur, couronne et miroir." However, both of these poems – and this is the case generally with the calligrams – conceal layers of ambiguity and complexity.

Readers who admire Apollinaire's calligrams are bound to be confused, even annoyed, by Tarkos's neo-calligrams. Tarkos's calligrams are very crudely drawn; they lack the visual appeal and aesthetic sophistication of Apollinaire's calligrams. Moreover, where Apollinaire offered his readers an actual poem to be read along with the image he had drawn, Tarkos uses words in a much more limited way in his text, where words appear in one-line captions or titles given at the bottom of each page. Apollinaire retains traditional lyric themes, fusing innovation and tradition in his *Calligrammes*. By contrast, Tarkos's clumsily drawn shapes and banal titles or captions for his poems avoid any sense of lyricism.

A listing of many of these titles or captions may help us to grasp the purpose behind Tarkos's text: "la petite étoile," "ce que je vois," "mon sourire," "il s'est écrasé," "le dessin ne ment pas," "un auto collant," "un sac," "un endroit," "parler, parler à quelqu'un," "un bonhomme," "le gonflement," "le dégonflement," "mes couilles," "l'opération," "une chemise," "une robe," "la une serviette," "un drap housse," "l'éponge," "une limace," "avec la volonté d'aimer," "un milieu," "un cheveu de mes cheveux," "le nez du surhomme," "un mon nez," "une tête penchée," "le sac à patates," "mon nombril," "mon genou," "ma tête," "huit sacs," "des objets," "un petit sac," "un grand sac," "une surprise," "ma langue," "un plongeon," "la lune," "le soleil," "l'étoile," "la lune loin," "la liberté" ("the little star," "what I see," "my smile," "he got run over," "the drawing does not lie," "a decal," "a handbag," "a place," "to talk, to talk with someone," "a guy," "the inflation," "the deflation," "my balls," "the operation," "a shirt," "a dress," "the a towel," "a shaum," "the sponge," "a slug," "with the will to love," "a middle," "a hair of my hairs," "the superman's nose," "a my nose," "a head leaving," "the bag of potatoes," "my navel," "my knee," "my head," "eight bags," "some objects," "a little bag," "a big bag," "a surprise," "my tongue," "a loon," "the moon," "the sun," "the star," "the moon far off," "freedom").

The nouns in this list can be fairly readily broken down into a few categories: parts of the body (ma langue, ma bite, ma tête, and so on) or objects (un sac, un drap housse, l'éponge, …) and places or elements in a landscape (un endroit, la lune, le soleil) as well as abstract nouns drawn into concrete shapes (une surprise, la liberté). Yet even as one attempts to find, and succeeds in finding, some kind of hidden order in this strange text, one still feels a nagging suspicion that Tarkos is really only making fun of his readers and / or of Apollinaire and / or of literary and art history. Are Tarkos's calligrams a put-on? Or can we taken them seriously?

In rereading Penelope Sacks-Galey's introduction to her 1988 study *Calligramme ou écriture figurée: Apollinaire inventeur de formes* (*Calligram or Figured Writing: Apollinaire as an Inventor of Forms*), I am struck by the number of statements she makes concerning the innovativeness of Apollinaire's calligrams which could apply equally well to Tarkos's poetry. Sacks-Galey writes, for instance: "Depuis son arrivée dans la littérature contemporaine, le calligramme désoriente, renverse les perspectives, déconstruit les cadres habituels des rapports logiques et affectifs. Il est une provocation, un calembour plastique … une écriture éclatée" ("From the time of its arrival in contemporary literature, the calligram disorients, reverses perspectives, deconstructs the usual frameworks of logical and affective relationships. It is a provocation, a visual pun … a shattered writing") (5). She adds that "[a]vec le calligramme, le verbe lire lui-même se trouve mis en question. Lire un calligramme de la même manière qu'un poème conventionnel est impossible" ("[w]ith the calligram, the verb to read itself is questionable. To read a calligram in the same way as a conventional poem is impossible") (7). Such statements about Apollinaire's ground-breaking and provocative poetics do, I think, also define the importance of Tarkos's experimental writing here. It is, after all, significant that the 'thematic' categories into which Tarkos's calligrams may be grouped recall the types of subject matter into which Apollinaire's calligrams were grouped: still lifes, portraits, landscapes.

Tarkos's project could be understood – or dismissed – as ironic, but he himself, in an interview, denied that his work was intended to be ironic (or formalist): "Les gens qui me parlent de formalisme, je ne comprends pas ce qu'ils disent; pour l'ironie, c'est un peu pareil. Est-ce que la télé, les séries B, c'est de l'ironie?" ("People talk to me of formalism, I don't understand what they are saying; concerning irony, it's a bit similar. Are television and B movies ironic?")[13]

In the end, Tarkos's calligrams may best be likened to literary Rorschach blots: they are on the page waiting for us to project onto them our own view of the poetic image: "c'est de l'ironie?" ("is this ironic?").

Nathalie Quintane's *Chaussure* (1997)

Nathalie Quintane (b. 1964), like Christophe Tarkos, became acknowledged as a forceful and distinctive new voice in French poetry in the 1990s, when her first texts appeared: *Remarques* (*Remarks*), *Chaussure* (*Shoe*), and *Jeanne Darc* (*Joan of Arc*). The latter two books were published by P.O.L., who has continued to publish most of Quintane's works to date. On P.O.L.'s webpage, Quintane states: "My style is simple but sometimes complicated." Indeed, a deceptive 'simplicity' does mark her writing – especially in her early texts. Quintane became associated with such contemporary avant-garde journals as *Nioques*, *Java*, and *Action poétique*. She was close to Christophe Tarkos and for many readers this association defined her place in the development of recent French poetry.

Discussing her work at a 2008 conference on *L'Illisible* (*The Unreadable*) which took place in San Diego, Quintane indicated how profoundly she was influenced by reading André Breton's *Anthologie de l'humour noir* (*Anthology of Black Humour*) and Lichtenberg's aphorisms as a teenager. In these two works, she found "une prose qui produit un effet violent" ("a prose that produces a violent effect"). She was also influenced by classical Japanese writer Sei Shonagon's *Pillow Book*, in which

Shonagon notes ephemeral phenomena of everyday life, working with what one could call "l'infra-ordinaire."

Because of Quintane's focus on the things of everyday life – especially in *Chaussure*, discussed below – she has often been read as a writer following the example of Francis Ponge. Although she acknowledges her respect for his work, she does insist, though, that "si j'ai commencé à écrire, ce n'était pas pour être assimilée à une 'famille'" ("if I began writing [literature], it was not in order to be assimilated into a 'family'"). Thus, she rejects the view taken by some critics that "Nathalie Quintane est la petite-fille de Francis Ponge" ("Nathlie Quintaine is Francis Ponge's granddaughter"). Humour plays a central role in her poetics; she admires Swift and Lewis Carroll. She adopts the position that "la poésie, c'est la distance" ("poetry is distance"). Thus she compares poetry to "une douche écossaise" ("a cold shower").

At the same 2008 conference, Agnès Disson presented a paper on Quintane's work in which she argued that Quintane's texts display "une transparence qui mène à l'opacité" ("a transparency that leads to opacity"). Quintane foregrounds banality, using "une langue sans affect et sans nostalgie" ("a language without affect and without nostalgia"). Her writing proceeds from "une mise en parenthèse de l'expérience subjective et de la subjectivité" ("a bracketing off of subjective experience and subjectivity"), in Disson's words. Rather than attacking language head-on in the manner of Artaud or Guyotat, Quintane adopts the method of "filouter, trafiquer avec la langue, éponger" ("stealing, trafficking in language, mopping up"), Disson argued. The goal of her writing, in Disson's view, is "non éliminer ou épurer quoi ce que soit, mais ajouter une couche supplémentaire" ("not to eliminate or purify anything, but to add a supplementary layer [to language]").[14]

"There is a bit of Imelda Marcos in many women," writes Valerie Steele in the introduction to her book *Shoes: A Lexicon of Style*, "How many pairs do you own? … Research indicates that the average American woman has twelve pairs of shoes in her closet, more than twice as many as the average man. However, there are many women who have over 100 pairs of shoes … and counting" (8). Steele begins her study of shoes and fashion by immediately acknowledging the spicy, erotic appeal that shoes – especially women's shoes – can convey:

> Shoes are better than sex, claims cartoonist Mimi Pond. "Shoes are totems of Disembodied Lust. They are candy for the eyes, poetry for the feet …

> They stand for everything you've ever wanted. Buying shoes, she added, is "the highest form of shopping." Shoes, or at least certain shoes, also exert an almost Pavlovian influence on men. "Women may scour the world for the shoes of their heart's desire, but it's men who swoon at their feet," writes Jody Shields. (8)

Steele concludes that "shoes have an apparently obvious function – to protect the feet. In reality, of course, shoes serve a variety of other functions as well, from conveying status and enhancing sex appeal to indicating membership in a particular 'style tribe'" (8).

In 1997, Nathalie Quintane published a text entitled *Chaussure*. Given the contemporary fascination with the symbolism and styles of shoes in our fashion- and media-saturated world, her choice of subject matter and title would, at first glance, seem trendy and, perhaps, provocative. The description of Quintane's project in *Chaussure* presented on the book's back cover, however, absolutely undercuts any such assumption:

> *Chaussure* n'est pas un livre qui, sous couvert de chaussure, parle de bateaux, de boudin, de darwinisme, ou de nos amours enfantines. *Chaussure* parle vraiment de chaussure. *Chaussure* ne résulte pas d'un pari; il ne présente aucune prouesse technique, ou rhétorique. Il n'est pas particulièrement pauvre, ni précisément riche, ni modeste, ni même banal … *Chaussure* s'est gorgé de tout ce qu'il a croisé sur son parcours: des patins, des chaussons d'escalade, un homme avançant en palmes sur la plage, Socrate nu-pied dans Athènes, Caligula, Imelda Marcos (bien sûr), la Transcaucasie, l'invention de la chaussure, le squelette du pied, la terre qu'on foule, etc, et il l'a rendu. Bref, c'est un livre de poésie pas spécialement poétique, de celle (la poésie) qui ne se force pas.

> (*Shoe* is not a book which, using shoes as a pretext, speaks of boats, blood sausage, Darwinism, or our childhood loves. *Shoe* really talks about shoes. *Shoe* is not the result of a bet; it presents no technical feats, or rhetorical feats. It is not particularly poor, nor exactly rich, neither modest, nor even banal … *Shoe* has gorged on everything that it has encountered in its path: skates, climbing shoes, a man walking on palm leaves on the beach, Socrates barefoot in Athens, Caligula, Imelda Marcos (of course), Transcaucasia, the invention of the shoe, the skeleton of the foot, the earth which one stomps on, etc., and it has rendered all of this. In short, it is a not especially poetic book of poetry, the sort of poetry which is not forced.)

So, far from having written a titillating or style-conscious descriptive guide to the worlds of shoes (as did Valerie Steele), Quintane has deliberately downplayed, even nullified, the erotic or fashion-oriented side of shoes. Instead, she chose the shoe as a focus for her text because of its association with the banality of everyday life. In *Chaussure,* the shoe has no higher metaphoric appeal for the reader's imagination. It remains – always, only – a shoe. It is a metonym for ordinariness, an object that refuses to be romanticized. The opening section of *Chaussure* presents a series of flat statements about shoes – either general facts or personal experience regarding shoes:

> Dans les vitres des magasins, les chaussures ont les lacets noués.
> Dans leur boîte, les chaussures sont protégés par une feuille de papier de soie pliée en deux.
> A l'intérieur de chaque chaussure, l'étiquette du fabricant se déplace parfois, sans se décoller.
> Dans leur boîte, les chaussures sont disposés tête-bêche. (11)
>
> (In the department store display windows, the shoes have their laces tied.
> In their box, shoes are protected by a piece of silk paper folded in two.
> Inside each shoe, the manufacturer's label sometimes shifts without coming unglued.
> In their box, the shoes are placed head-to-toe.)
>
> Parfois, dans une forêt, au bord d'un chemin, je vois une chaussure abandonnée.
> Une chaussure me paraît plus grande, quand je suis à plat ventre devant elle. (52)
>
> (Sometimes, in a forest, at the edge of a path, I find an abandoned shoe.
> A shoe seems bigger to me when I am flat on my stomach in front of it.)

Although the back cover description designates this text as "un livre de poésie," the writing throughout is resolutely, relentlessly prosaic, as sentence follows sentence while the speaker accumulates an ever-longer series of factual statements about shoes. Such a writing technique could, superficially considered, come across as merely a game or an exercise. Nevertheless, as Agnès Disson notes in an article on Quintane, on Anne Portugal, and on Pascale Monnier, there is much more at stake in Quintane's anti-poetic treatment of her topic: "Nathalie Quintane …

pousse dans les derniers retranchements les frontières habituelles de la poésie: par un brouillage délibéré avec la prose, par le choix d'une sorte de distanciation, d'une neutralisation peu associée d'ordinaire à l'écriture poétique; et enfin par l'utilisation d'un matériau quotidien mais inattendu" ("Nathalie Quintaine … pushes the usual limits of poetry to their furthest extreme: by a deliberate mixing of poetry with prose, by the choice of a certain distancing, a neutralization not often ordinarily associated with poetic writing; and finally by the use of subject matter which is everyday but unexpected") (215). (The publication of Quintane's book with P.O.L., a press specializing in innovative contemporary writing which subversively challenges poetry-prose distinctions, in itself suggests a desire to contest the boundaries and definitions that have traditionally marked poetry as a genre.)

In the second section of *Chaussure*, Quintane extends her catalogue of facts about shoes to earlier historical periods and a broader geographic area:

> Les sandales des anciens Egyptiens étaient fabriquées en papyrus
>
> …
>
> Quand Jason perdit une sandale, quelle fut sa honte? (73)
>
> (The ancient Egyptians' sandals were made of papyrus
>
> …
>
> When Jason lost a sandal, how ashamed was he?)

She mentions anecdotes about the shoes of Socrates, Caligula, Khrushchev, and (as one might expect) Imelda Marcos.

This more "historical" section of the book is followed by a short thematic section ("L'invention de la chaussure," 89–92; "L'usure de la chaussure," 93–5; "Fin de la chaussure?" 96–7) ("The invention of the shoe," "The wearing out of the shoe," "The end of the shoe?") which encapsulates the "life" of shoes, from their "birth" to their "death," one could say. Quintane thus reaches the logical limit in the literary representation of the object, in a sense. In her text, lyric subjectivity is entirely absent; in its place, the object – and "objective" facts – assume centre stage. Her evocation of the three stages of a shoe's *existence* reflects a crucial leitmotiv of the French tradition of *la poésie de l'objet*, then.

In a fourth and final section, Quintane resumes her inventory of facts about shoes. Yet, almost at the end, she seems to incorporate poetry back into this exceedingly prosaic text. First, she proposes a comparison of the shoe to a rose (that most poetic of flowers!) (140). Then, she actually inserts a verse poem into the text (143). However, this "poem" makes only flatly prosaic remarks on shoes:

> La chaussure s'appelle chaussure,
> Même quand le vent tourne
> La chaussure s'appelle chaussure. (143)
>
> (The shoe is called shoe,
> Even when the wind turns
> The shoe is called shoe.)

At the end of the book, one page after her own text has come to a halt ("Tous les lieux, et toutes les fois, où je n'étais pas chaussée. // Toutes les chaussures que je n'ai pas portées") ("All the places, and all the times, when I was not wearing shoes. // All the shoes which I have not worn") (157), Quintane slyly adds a quote from Jaques Lacan at the bottom of the next page, like a coda: "Le principal est la chaussure" ("The main thing is the shoe").[15]

This final quotation performs the role of an after-thought or teaser to Quintane's deadpan recital of facts about shoes. With it, she coyly gestures towards psychoanalysis, the theoretical sphere where shoes have assumed a certain importance since the late nineteenth-century. With the nineteenth-century sexologists' inclusion of fetishism within the category of sexual perversions, shoes and shoe fetishists have not infrequently attracted the attention of psychoanalysis (beginning with Freud's 1905 *Three Essays on the Theory of Sexuality*). Psychoanalytically influenced literary critics, such as Emily Apter or Naomi Schor, have also focused on the fetish in some of their best-known work. In a discussion of the sexuality of things in late-twentieth-century commodity culture, Apter observes how, in that culture, "[o]bjects are revealed as provocations to desire and possession. The objectified female anatomy is sexually domesticated through sartorial masquerades, just as the household fetishes of cars, TVs, and swimming pools are shown to be sites of displaced lack, dream surrogates for better values".[16] Apter explains that, originally, "the word *fetisso* came into parlance as a Portuguese trading term associated with 'small wares' and 'magic charms' used for barter between blacks and whites. White merchants, compromising both their religion and their 'rational' economic principles, took oaths on fetishes in order to seal commercial agreements" (5).

The psychoanalytic appropriation of this term emphasizes the intense erotic fascination that certain objects (usually clothing or shoes) hold for some men.[17] The fetish object replaces the person who wears it and acquires a quasi-magical erotic appeal (hence the theoretical adoption of a term that had signified a "magic charm"). What was – literally – a banal object thus becomes a powerful conveyor of sexual mystique. According to Freud, the fetish has the ability to fascinate certain men because it acts as a substitute for a phantasized maternal phallus. If Woman has, literally, no penis, certain items of her clothing can, nonetheless, assume phallic associations: the shape of a shoe or its heel, or the panties, with their proximity to the genital region, for example. As a substitute for something which does not actually exist, the fetish both reveals and conceals castration anxieties. Paradoxically, through the agency of the fetish, lack (of a maternal phallus) generates sexual fantasies and obsessive erotic response.

In closing her text with a quotation from Lacan, Quintane is acknowledging her awareness of the possible associations of shoes with fetishism (although she does not include this point about fetishism in the catalogue of "facts" on shoes presented in the four sections of *Chaussure*). What is the significance of the Lacan quotation, then? Why acknowledge the role of the shoe as fetish *outside* the boundaries of *Chaussure* itself? My interpretation of this use of the Lacan quotation is that, once again, Quintane is playing with the reader, engaging but frustrating his or her expectations. She piques the reader's curiosity but, ultimately, the Lacan quotation – like the interest in shoes as metaphors or fashion signifiers that Valerie Steele's book on shoes encourages – leads nowhere beyond itself. Quintane utilizes the literal against the metaphoric; for her, the object is (only) what it is. If she *plays* with an object in *Chaussure*, she remains committed to an unadorned, unpoetic approach that resonates with Jean-Marie Gleize's designation of contemporary experimental poetry as "la poésie après la poésie."

Conclusion: Two Traditions

Throughout this study we have observed how twentieth-century French and American poets have appealed to the object as privileged subject matter for a variety of reasons. A focus on the object enables an aesthetic of impersonality, as the human observer remains at the margins of the poem. Eschewing an emphasis on lyrical subjectivity, the object poet avoids emotion. Like the still life painter, the object poet chooses a modest and neutral subject matter. Behind this choice of an apparently banal subject matter, the poet and the painter explore aesthetic problems. An unobtrusive content allows the verbal and the visual artist a unique freedom.

As I noted in chapter 1, the concerns of French and American poets of the object closely parallel each other during the years of high modernism between 1910 and 1930. Imagist, Objectivist, Cubist, and Surrealist poets all foreground the place of the object in their works as they develop a boldly different aesthetic. After 1930, however, these two poetic traditions diverge significantly from each other. In France, in the 1940s, 1950s, and 1960s, the object remains central to a range of poetic projects, from Ponge's playful "definitions-descriptions" of things and words, to the revitalizing of realism by Follain and Guillevic. Tortel, in his fascination with ocular poetics and the relationship between textuality and reality in his garden poetry, continues the tradition which Follain, Guillevic, and Ponge had advanced. Tortel's assimilation of the object to woman in his appropriation of Scève's *Délie* as a model extends the interesting but politically troubling association between the object and the feminine which so strongly emerged in the work of earlier poets like Ponge and Williams. From the 1970s onward, as seen in chapter 7, the object inspires a number of post-modern poetries, including Tortel's later collections written in proximity to *la modernité négative*, as well as some Oulipo texts such as *Signe d'appartenance* and the anti-poetic experimental writing of Tarkos and Quintane.

By contrast, in the United States, the place of the object in poetry changes dramatically after 1930. Poets such as Pound, Williams, and Zukofsky, who had initially developed a complex poetics via a manipulation of the object, moved to a very different aesthetic stance. All three poets became occupied with the project of elaborating a new twentieth-century epic: Williams's *Paterson*, Pound's *The Cantos*, Zukofsky's *A*. Oppen, for his part, was silent for two decades after publishing *Discrete Series*.

If one considers the work of American poets who began publishing their work after 1945, their relationship to the object is much more muted, even ambivalent, than that of their great precursors (and their French counterparts). Post-war American poets have not forgotten the object; however, they are rarely willing to grant it the sort of pride of place which their major precursors did. Along with this diminished focus on the object, a general turning away from linguistic and formal experimentation also characterizes the writing of several mid-century American poets, such as Elizabeth Bishop, Richard Wilbur, and Theodore Roethke, all of whom are yet consciously indebted to, and in dialogue with, modernist precursors such as Williams, Moore, and Stevens. The downplaying of the role of the object in the work of these poets can be interpreted as a sign of their desire to differentiate themselves from their modernist precursors' achievement.

Elizabeth Bishop's first two collections of poetry, *North & South* (1946) and *A Cold Spring* (1955), seem to me to be her strongest. In several poems in these collections, such as "The Fish," "The Map," "The Imaginary Iceberg," "Cirque d'hiver," and "The Manmoth," she takes familiar objects and reveals their uncanny quality through careful description, or else examines odd, fanciful creatures and things. The strange and compelling atmosphere of her poems may partly be accounted for by their closeness to the example set by Bishop's precursors, especially Moore and Stevens. Moore was for many years a mentor to Bishop, after the two met during Bishop's senior year at Vassar. The two poets carried on a long correspondence and a deep friendship. They shared a love of describing things, a taste for exotic animals, a concern with exactitude, and a predilection for impersonality. Nonetheless, Moore's stance as a poet is much more didactic than Bishop's. Some of Bishop's critics find Stevens's example to be even more decisive than Moore's. Harold

Bloom states that "[t]he influence of Wallace Stevens on her work rendered Bishop rather uneasy … But poets are chosen by their precursors: They do not choose. Stevens's greatest poetry gives what he called 'the hum of thoughts evaded in the mind,' and so does Bishop's. Moore, endlessly curious about *things*, created a mosaic of impressions, brilliantly vivid. With Stevens and Bishop, we are in a cosmos of imagined things, things taken up into the mind. Stevens's massive aesthetic broodings are scaled down and somewhat ironized in Bishop, but her mode of reflection essentially is his" (Bloom 2011, 39–40). In coming more and more in time to reject Stevens's idealism while continuing to admire his work, Bishop finds herself in the characteristic position of the mid-century American poet.

Richard Wilbur, like Bishop, came of age reading the poetry of the modernists, yet his work is less formally and thematically ambitious than theirs. His use of traditional poetic forms and his preoccupation with craftsmanship make his poetry appear rather conservative. Critics often discuss the influence of Marianne Moore on Wilbur. William Carlos Williams, with his concern for things, has also been a significant influence.[1] Wilbur's relationship to Wallace Stevens is complicated. In an interview with Paul F. Cummins, he commented:

> I'm sure that my enthusiasm for Stevens, circa 1948–52, has affected my own work, although I can't say just where. Of late I have found his work too undramatic, connoisseural, and inconclusively ruminative, but still pick it up with pleasure and may have another spell of enchantment, in time. For all his stress on the *ding an sich*, I find him too hothouse subjective right now. (Butts 43–4)

A strong impulse towards recording and celebrating our link to things runs through Wilbur's work, and his third collection of poems is entitled *Things of This World* (1956). He values the imagination for its ability to capture and represent an "energy" which runs through the world and things: "To me, the imagination is a faculty which fuses things, takes hold of the physical and ideal worlds and makes them one, provisionally" (Butts 185). The poem "Love Calls us to the Things of This World," from his third collection, showcases his sense of the imagination's dynamic interactions with everyday reality. In this poem, seeing the sheets hanging on a clothesline summons up the image of angels floating in the air. By the end of the poem, though, following this initial flight of fancy, the poet takes us back to everyday reality: "The soul descends once more in bitter love / To accept the waking body." Adopting a gesture common to the poet of objects here, Wilbur returns the gaze and the imagination to the world of concrete particulars that grounds human consciousness.

Theodore Roethke dedicated his breakthrough 1948 collection of poems, *The Lost Son*, to William Carlos Williams. However, Roethke's relationship to Williams and his poetics is complicated, even contradictory, as Jerome Mazzaro reports: "In objecting to a comment in *100 American Poems* (1948) that he 'derived his undressed and deceptively simple style from the cross-grained imagist, William Carlos Williams,' Roethke told Selden Rodman: 'I do owe him a debt for jibing me in conversation and by letter to get out of small forms; but his own work I don't know as well as I should … His (Wms.) rhythms are more staccato, more broken, seems to me.' Yet, in a letter to Williams (1944), he had acknowledged some affinity: 'Anything with images equals Imagism equals Old Hat. Oh well, you know all that better than I; have seen it, have been fighting it.' And in a letter to [Kenneth] Burke (1946), he admitted to a Williams-like literalness" (55). Roethke, with his concern for memory and the unconscious and his tendency towards a species of mysticism, remains fundamentally different from Williams, regardless of their several affinities, Mazzaro concludes: "Williams' view of language as 'bricklaying' where words are solidified against translucency and connotation much in the way pigment was solidified by the cubists is different from Roethke's Yeatsian view of words as a means for the evocation of memory" (56).[2]

In both of these great modern traditions in poetry and poetics, seeing through things and with things has provided a strong stimulus to aesthetic renewal. Observing objects has led poets in many directions, producing a multiplicity of works which deepen, or challenge, our sense of lyric poetry.[3]

Notes

Introduction

1 See Schneider, *Still Life*, 7.

2 Although Brown's articulation of the distinction between "objects" and "things" is indebted to Martin Heidegger's essay "What is a Thing?," Brown nevertheless is not adopting Heidegger's ideas uncritically. In a discussion of the uses of the object in Pop Art, for example, he writes that "Heidegger taxonomizes things into mere things (such as pebbles), equipment and work (such as art). Much of pop art, of course, works to elide such distinctions" (Brown, *Things*, 15).

1 The Object in Modernism in the United States and France

1 "Imagisme," in Pound, *Early Writings*, ed. Nadel, 209–10.

2 Altieri, *The Art of Twentieth-century American Poetry*, 20.

3 Zukofsky, *Prepositions*, 12.

4 See Axelrod and Deese, eds., *Critical Essays on William Carlos Williams*, 1–48.

5 Moore quoted in Costello, *Marianne Moore*, 94.

6 DeKoven, "Gertrude Stein and Modern Painting: Beyond Literary Criticism," in Hoffmann, ed., 171–83.

7 See Harryette Mullen's *Trimmings* and Steve McCaffery's *Any Way Oakly*. Both texts are bold rewritings of *Tender Buttons*.

8 Zukofsky, *Prepositions*, 12.

9 Oppen, "The Mind's Own Place," in Cope, ed., 29–37.

10 Oppen, quoted by Noble 256.

11 Mallarmé, "Magie," *Œuvres complètes II* 251.

12 I have used Jean-Louis Camille's critical edition, *L'Épitre du voyant: Alcide Bava/Arthur Rimbaud (avril-août 1871): Étude* (*The Seer's Epistle: Alcide Bava/Arthur Rimbaud (April-August 1871): A Study*) (Amsterdam: Rodopi, 1997). For an insightful discussion of the history of the term "voyance" before Rimbaud, see Eigeldinger, "La Voyance avant Rimbaud" ("Clairvoyance Before Rimbaud") in Schaeffer, ed., 9–107.

13 See Bohn's discussion of these early critical responses to the *Calligrammes* in his *Aesthetics of Visual Poetry*, 46.

14 See their introduction to their edition of *Calligrams.*

15 Jacob quoted by Jean-François Louette, *Sans protocole* (*Without Protocol*), 154.

16 Jacob quoted in Robert Guiette, *Vie de Max Jacob* (*Life of Max Jacob*), 130–1.

17 See McEvilley, "Basic Dichotomies in Meret Oppenheim's Work," in Burckhardt and Curiger, eds., 44–53.

18 José Pierre interprets this object as conveying a veiled reference to Breton's text *Le Revolver à cheveux blancs* (*The White-Haired Revolver*). Making this connection would then invite us to "suivre une piste où la fumée, synonyme de la blancheur, rapprocherait la fumée de la détonation [du revolver] de la fumée de la cigarette par l'intermédiaire, sans doute, de l'écume des vagues" ("follow a trail where smoke, a synonym of whiteness, would bring together the smoke of [the revolver's] detonation and the smoke of a cigarette through the intermediary, probably, of the foam of waves") (137).

19 Segalen quoted in Hsieh 26.

20 Lawrence Ryan, "*Neue Gedichte* – New Poems," in Metzger and Metzger, eds., 133.

21 William Waters, "The *New Poems*," in Leeder and Vilain, eds., 65.

2 Cubism and the Poetry of the Object: Pierre Reverdy's Aesthetics of Impersonality

1 Although Reverdy himself rejected the term "Cubist poetry," many critics have used this term to describe his work. (See, for example, Jean Rousselot and Jean Cassou.) I shall be following this established critical practice in referring to his work up to, and including, the 1930 collection *Pierres blanches*, as "Cubist."

2 See Rothwell, *Textual Spaces*, 107–39.

3 For a detailed discussion of the circumstances surrounding the creation of *Au Soleil du plafond*, see Rothwell, "Cubism and the Avant-garde Prose Poem," and Hattendorf, "The Aesthetics of the Visual and the Verbal."

4 It would be appropriate at this point to remember how often the subject matter of still-life paintings has been regarded as a "non-subject." Christopher Green remarks of Cubist still life that "[i]f it was possible in the Cubist milieu to treat the figure in Cubist figure-painting as if it could simply be discounted, this was even more the case with still-life, especially after 1916. Still-life, not unlike the costume of Harlequin, came to be taken as the sign for the *disappearance* of all subject-matter from painting, except as pretext" (148).

5 Reverdy, quoted in Bocholier, *Pierre Reverdy*, 150.

6 Reverdy, *Lettres à Jean Rousselot*, 33.

7 Reverdy, *Lettres à Jean Rousselot*, 36.

8 Reverdy, quoted in Rousselot, "Pierre Reverdy," 77.

9 In my book *Antonin Artaud's Alternate Genealogies: Self-portraits and Family Romance* (Waterloo, ON: Wilfred Laurier University Press, 1996), I explore Artaud's strategies for pursuing the rewriting of his own family romance through rewriting or translating the life-stories of others (such as Heliogabalus, the Cenci family or Ambrosio, the protagonist of Matthew Lewis's Gothic novel *The Monk*). Reverdy's continual rewriting of an Oedipal fantasy through the images of sunset and nightfall, as interpreted by Collot, may have served a psychosexual goal or need comparable to that which provides part of the coherence of Artaud's *œuvre*.

10 Reverdy, *Lettres à Jean Rousselot*, 33.

3 The Text as Object: Francis Ponge's Verbal Still Lifes

1 Although Ponge has very often been read primarily as a poet of things, some critics contest, or even reject, the notion that objects constitute the main focus of his work. For instance, in his critical study *Poétique de Francis Ponge* (*Francis Ponge's Poetics*), Bernard Beugnot, one of the best-known Ponge specialists and general editor of the Pleiade edition of his *Œuvres complètes* (2002), all but dismisses the view of Ponge as a verbal still-life artist: "'... le poète botaniste et zoologue, le descripteur de l'objet sur lequel trébuchent toutes les paraphrases' (J.-P. Aron, 1952), 'le ciseleur de natures mortes' (Jean Cau), ces formules séduisantes méconnaissent bien des aspects de l'œuvre, et des plus essentiels" ("'... the poet as botanist and zoologist, the describer of objects which all the paraphrases of Ponge's texts stumble over' (J.-P. Aron, 1952), 'the maker of still lifes' (Jean Cau), these seductive formulas misread many aspects of Ponge's œuvre, including come of the most essential aspects") (17). If Ponge is

read in a superficial and literal-minded way, as a realist merely describing the outward appearance of objects, plants and animals, then I would agree with Beugnot's rejection of *that* reading of his work. However, as I argue in this chapter, a much more nuanced, metapoetic interpretation of Ponge's use of objects and of the still-life tradition does, in fact, enhance and deepen one's understanding of his achievement as a poet. As Ponge himself wrote, discussing the art of Chardin, "la moindre nature morte est un paysage métaphysique" ("even the most modest still life is a metaphysical landscape") ("De la nature morte et de Chardin," *Œuvres complètes* Vol. II, 665).

2 See Richard, "Francis Ponge," in his *Onze études sur la poésie moderne* (*Eleven Studies of Modern Poetry*), 161–81.

3 Robert W. Greene, for instance, counters Sartre's "nécrologique" ("obituary-like") (as Greene puts it) reading of *Le Parti pris des choses* by asserting that "what is perhaps the central image in Ponge's œuvre [is] that of birth." Greene, *Books Abroad* (Autumn 1974): 665.

4 A critique of Cartesianism is implied in Ponge's use of the term "avec méthode" (echoing Descartes's title *Le Discours de la méthode*). This possibility is all the more likely when one notes that Ponge begins "My Creative Method" by stating, tongue-in-cheek, "Les idées ne sont pas mon fort" ("Ideas are not my forte") (OC Vol. I, 515).

5 See *Le Peintre à l'étude* in OC Vol. I (87–161) and *L'Atelier contemporain* in OC Vol. II, 563–758.

6 For a detailed discussion of Ponge's movement away from "textes clos" towards open-ended explorations of things, see Gleize and Veck, *Francis Ponge*. Early on in their study, Gleize and Veck quote Ponge, who writes that "[l]a poésie se trouve dans les brouillons acharnés de ceux qui espèrent, qui militent pour une nouvelle étreinte de la réalité" ("[p]oetry is found in the stubborn rough drafts of those who hope, who struggle for a new kind of embracing of reality") (21).

7 For an excellent discussion of the political significance of *Le Savon*, see Rachlin, "Francis Ponge, *Le Savon* and the Occupation."

8 See "De l'eau," OC Vol. I, 31–2.

9 Some of the most interesting studies on Ponge and the visual arts are Jordan, *Art Criticism of Francis Ponge*; Sears, "Bracketing Painting: Ponge's Criticism of Braque"; and Pap, "From Ekphrasis to 'Movement'."

10 Oldenburg is, of course, not the only contemporary visual artist to have altered and revitalized the traditional still life, although his is arguably the boldest contemporary reworking of the genre. Other particularly notable contributors to this project of transforming and rethinking still life are the American artist Barnet Rubenstein and the Canadian artist Gathie Falk.

These artists have made use of unusual subject matter or provocative aesthetic strategies for the placement of their objects in the gallery space. Rubenstein, for instance, has assembled piles of objects in his studio in order to create still-life works that some consider to be as imposing as landscape paintings. (One is reminded of Ponge's remark that "la moindre nature morte est un paysage métaphysique.") David Carbone describes one of Rubenstein's "landscape-table paintings": "For his key form [Rubenstein] took an object that had appeared in the work of a student he was then mentoring. It was a Chinese restaurant take-out container, known as an oyster pail. Every box was carefully drawn life-size and initially seemed free of all formal associations. Their apparent emptiness was essential, even a bit absurd … In these magnificent paintings, folded and closed oyster pails are stacked from front to back, from side to side, filling almost the entire picture-space. Shifted and rotated in every ordinary way, these cardboard containers become almost musical units of form … In these most unlikely images, take-out containers are re-imagined as internal forms. Here, with his 'subject matter in view,' Rubenstein moves instinctively from the realist imagination to the poetic" (81–2).

Gathie Falk's manipulations of the object are equally clever and ambiguous, gently humorous but disturbing. In one case, she has placed a series of ceramic objects that look like real shoes inside small display cabinets. In another, she has placed ceramic *trompe-l'oeil* sculptures of men's shirts on individual pedestals in a gallery. Each shirt stands up by itself, with no head or body to support it. Falk assigns a man's name to each "shirt," heightening the effect of distancing and uneasiness, as well as the humour of her project.

4 Description as Transfiguration: Jean Follain's (Meta)Poetics of the Object

1 See Calderon, "Jean Follain: Objects in Time," 137.
2 Follain, "Compte Rendu de la soirée-rencontre de *Io*" (1965). Quoted in Debreuille, *Jean Follain*, 191.
3 In the final chapter of her excellent study *Jean Follain: Le même, autrement* (*Jean Follain: the Same, Otherwise*), Françoise Rouffiat offers a very helpful overview of the critical pieces and poems written by these and other poets on Follain's œuvre.
4 Follain, "Formes de la poésie" ("Poetic Forms") (1960) in Debreuille, 188.
5 Follain, "Formes de la poésie," 184.
6 Follain, "Formes de la poésie," 187.
7 Follain, "Le Langage de la poésie" ("The Language of Poetry"), 16.

8 Frénaud, quoted in Rouffiat, 218.
9 See Conisbee, *Chardin*, 9–10.
10 See Pearce, *Collecting in Contemporary Practice*.
11 This is one possible meaning of Rouffiat's characterization of Follain's œuvre as "le même, autrement."

5 The Object as (M)Other: Guillevic's Poetry and Object-Relations Theory

1 See Popovic, "Les Morts et le pain" ("The Dead and the Bread").
2 In appealing to Klein's theories I am not proposing that one undertake a biographical approach to reading Guillevic's poetry. A psychoanalytic interpretation of the poet's *personality* is not my aim. Rather, I am arguing that a Kleinian theoretical perspective provides a useful tool for following the development of tropes and images linked to the maternal in his poetry. This will make possible a reorientation of critical interpretations of the place of the object in these poems, I believe. In discussing the role of the maternal figures here, I will not take the facts of Guillevic's biography as a sure source of "truth" which his poems merely reproduce *telle quelle*. On the contrary, I consider these biographical elements themselves as a sort of *text* whose meanings are continually shifting over time.
3 As far as I know, Harvey is the only other critic writing on Guillevic's poetry to have discussed the relevance of Klein's theories for a reading of Guillevic's texts.

6 Jean Tortel's Poetics of the Desiring Gaze

1 The title of Suzanne Nash's excellent 1989 article "Living Transcription: the Poetry of Jean Tortel" reflects the poet's own goal of a transparent writing out of what he sees before him.
2 G. Jouanard and J. Tortel, "Quelques pierres blanches..." ("A Few White Stones... ") 206.
3 G. Jouanard and J. Tortel, "Quelques pierres blanches," 218.
4 This line has a quasi-religious resonance because of the significance of the "host" as the body of Christ in the Catholic Mass.
5 A contemporary critical perspective on the Délie sharply different from those of Guild and Frelick is given by Jerry C. Nash in *The Love Aesthetics of Maurice Scève*. Nash asserts that "[o]ut of the very negativity and darkness viewed by many of Scève's readers to be the essence of the *Délie* emerges a radiance which is that of the poetic imagination and the poems themselves … [T]he *Délie* as poetic construct is a setting in which the

questions raised by disorder and melancholy may be answered, ultimately leading to release and recovering and new-found unity. ... *Délie* is the celebration of life, the fragmentation of the self and its reconstruction through art, the achievement of a reconstruction and healing of self through the construction of the poem wherein the finding of living, unified form coincides with the defeat of anguish and melancholy and obscurity" (146). Although his reading of *Délie* is thoughtful and serious, one could object that Nash settles for a somewhat one-sided and excessively rosy view of this text, which other critics read as dark, ambivalent, and plagued by negativity.

7 *L'Objet après L'Objet*: Contemporary French Poetry

1 Quoted in Consenstein, "Asian Influences," 56.
2 Another – and equally fascinating – example of a recent *poème-objet* is presented in Lettrist poet Maurice Lemaître's quirky text *Canaille* (*Rabble*), in which Lemaître uses the rebus form to tell a story. As drawings of objects represent various sounds in *Canaille I*, for example, the reader is able to piece together a series of events. Lemaître's combining objects into a puzzle / game / experimental text this way is as daring and impressive as Roubaud's revitalization of the *poème-objet* in ∈.
3 See, for example, Judith Butler's *Bodies That Matter* (New York: Routledge, 1993).
4 Thomas Sebillet, "Art poétique françoys," quoted in Tomarken, 139.
5 Aquaviva, "Ouvrage," in *Blasons du corps masculin*. As this book is unpaginated, no page numbers will follow quotations from *Blasons du corps masculin*.
6 Katherine Conley makes this point cogently in her *Automatic Woman*.
7 See Lacan, "Séminaire sur 'La lettre volée'," *Écrits*, 19–75.
8 One should also note that rebus texts were very popular among the *grands rhétoriqueurs* poets at the beginning of the sixteenth century, including Clément Marot's father, Jean.
9 Métail in *Abrégé de littérature potentielle.*
10 This passage occurs midway through Joyce's *A Portrait of the Artist as a Young Man* in a long passage in which the protagonist, Stephen Dedalus, has listened to a priest's imprecations against sin and Stephen's thoughts replay these ideas.
11 See Restany and Cabanne, 66–9.
12 Marina Warner points out in a discussion of the gender of nouns in French that the names for tools in French are often feminine. She regards this

assigning of feminine gender to tools as manifesting sexist attitudes underlying linguistic practice. The assigning of the feminine to tools suggests that they serve as "feminine" helpers, subservient to their male users. The "feminine" tools fit into a man's hand and are manipulated by him, as they obey his will. If Warner's argument about the unstated attitudes of masculine arrogance underpinning linguistic usage in French here are correct, then her insights add a further twist – or (I cannot resist the irony!) a further *turn of the screw* – to the play of, and with, gender pursued by Reut in *Vis cachées.*

13 "Entretien de Bertrand Verdier avec Christophe Tarkos" in Tarkos, *Écrits poétiques*, 353.

14 The proceedings of the 2008 San Diego conference were published as *L'Illisibilité poétique en question* (*Poetic Unreadability at Issue*), ed. Gorrillot and Lescart.

15 Lacan, *Le Séminaire Livre IV*, 42.

16 Apter, "Introduction" to Apter and Pietz, 2.

17 According to (orthodox) psychoanalysis, fetishism is an exclusively male perversion. Feminist critics like Apter, Schor, and Elizabeth Grosz have contested this view, offering their own models of female fetishism. See Apter, *Feminizing the Fetish*, Schor, "Georges Sand and Fetishism," and Grosz, "Lesbian Fetishism?"

Conclusion

1 See *Conversations with Richard Wilbur*, 32.

2 Another significant figure who should be acknowledged here is May Swenson. Swenson's poems, particularly those presented in her first two collections, *Another Animal* (1954) and *A Cage of Spines* (1958), show the influence of Marianne Moore. The collections include a number of animal poems. The animals are described with a careful precision and impersonality. *A Cage of Spines* includes several poems such as "Fountain Piece I" (73–4) and "The Charm Box" (78–9) which are evocative of Rilke's *Dinggedichte*. "Fountain Piece II" (122–3) closely resembles Conrad Ferdinand Meyer's "Römische Brunnen" ("Roman Fountain"), a famous *Dinggedicht* preceding Rilke's. Swenson's 1970 collection *Iconographs* follows the tradition of Apollinaire's *Calligrammes*, with numerous concrete poems imitating the things they describe through their shape on the page.

3 Another odd set of object poems from contemporary France should be mentioned here. In his 2016 book *Paul Celan, les jours et les nuits* (*Paul*

Celan, Days and Nights), poet Jean Daive proposes a provocative and intriguing parallel between Stein's *Tender Buttons* and Romanian-French poet Ghérasim Luca's *Le Vampire passif* (*The Passive Vampire*) in their eccentric treatment of the object. Daive writes that "ces deux livres mettent en équations narratives et théoriques, d'un côté un monde d'objets (Gertrude Stein) qui impose un protocole de la nature morte et d'un autre un théâtre d'objets (Ghérasim Luca), lequel est une présentation de notre vacuité et de notre décor et il en émerge comme d'un chapeau l'O.O.O., c'est-à-dire l'Objet Objectivement Offert. Cet objet inspire un autre protocole de la nature morte dont les effets indésirables entraînent instabilité de pensée, dépossession, persécution, circulation, vol consenti, apocalypse. Ces deux livres consacrent le délire, le dérèglement, la vie du rêve, ils manipulent exemplairement la perspective en trompe-l'oeil. L'objet perd sa chance visuelle, parce qu'il appartient à la vie d'un rêveur" ("these two books create a narrative and theoretical equation of, on the one hand, a world of objects (Gertrude Stein) which imposes a still life perspective and, on the other, a theatre of objects (Ghérasim Luca), which presents our vacuousness and our décor and from out of this comes as if from out of a hat the O.O.O., that is the Object Objectively Offered. This object inspires another perspective on the still life whose undesirable effects bring on instability of thought, dispossession, persecution, circulation, a theft which is consented to, an apocalypse. These two books consecrate delirium, disorder, the life of dreams, they manipulate perspective into trompe-l'oeil in an exemplary way. The object loses its visual advantage, because it belongs to the life of a dreamer") (121–2).

Bibliography

Works by Individual Poets

Apollinaire, Guillaume. *Calligrammes* (1918). In Apollinaire, *Œuvres complètes*, texte établi et annoté par Marcel Adéma et Michel Décaudin. Paris: Gallimard, 1956.

Aquaviva, Constance, ed. *Blasons du corps masculin*. Marseille: Nèpe & Spectres Familiers, 1990.

Bishop, Elizabeth. *Poems*. New York: Farrar, Straus and Giroux, 2011.

Breton, André. *Œuvres complètes*. Vols. I–IV. Marguerite Bonnet, general editor. Paris: Gallimard, 1988–2008.

Follain, Jean. *Agendas 1926–1971*. Paris: Seghers, 1999.

– *Canisy*. Paris: Gallimard, 1942.

– *Chef-lieu*. Paris: Gallimard, 1950.

– *D'après tout*. Paris: Gallimard, 1967.

– *Des Heures*. Paris: Gallimard, 1960.

– *L'Épicerie d'enfance*. Paris: Corrêa, 1938.

– *Espaces d'instants*. Paris: Gallimard, 1971.

– *Exister*. Paris: Gallimard, 1947.

– *Exister, suivi de Territoires*. Paris: Gallimard, 1969.

– "Formes de la poésie". In *Lire Follain*, edited by Serge Gaubert, 183–90. Lyon: Presses universitaires de Lyon, 1981.

– "Le langage de la poésie." *Revue des Sciences Humaines* 265 (Spring 2002): 13–31.

– *La Main chaude*. Paris: Corrêa, 1933.

– *Objets*. Limoges: Rougerie, 1955.

– *Ordre terrestre*. Montpellier: Fata Morgana, 1986.

– *Territoires*. Paris: Gallimard, 1953.

– *Tout instant*. Paris: Gallimard, 1957.
– *Usage du temps*. Paris: Gallimard, 1943.
Guillevic, Eugène. *Art poétique*. Paris: Gallimard, 1989.
– *Autres*. Paris: Gallimard, 1980.
– *Avec*. Paris: Gallimard, 1966.
– *Carnac*. Paris: Gallimard, 1961.
– *Le Chant*. Paris: Gallimard, 1990.
– *Creusement*. Paris: Gallimard, 1987.
– *Du Domaine*. Paris: Gallimard, 1977.
– *Du Domaine, suivi de Euclidiennes*. Paris: Gallimard, 1985.
– *Étier*. Paris: Gallimard, 1979.
– *Euclidiennes*. Paris: Gallimard, 1967.
– *Exécutoire* Paris: Gallimard, 1947.
– *Inclus*. Paris: Gallimard, 1977.
– *Maintenant*. Paris: Gallimard, 1993.
– *Motifs*. Paris: Gallimard, 1987.
– *Paroi*. Paris: Gallimard, 1970.
– *Requiem*. Paris: Tschann, 1938.
– *Requis*. Paris: Gallimard, 1983.
– *Sphère*. Paris: Gallimard, 1963.
– *Sphère, suivi de Carnac*. Paris: Gallimard, 1977.
– *Terraqué*. Paris: Gallimard, 1942.
– *Terraqué, suivi de Exécutoire*. Paris: Gallimard, 1968.
– *Trente et un sonnets*. Paris: Gallimard, 1954.
– *Trouées*. Paris: Gallimard, 1981.
– *Ville*. Paris: Gallimard, 1969.
Jacob, Max. *Le Cornet à dés* (1916). In Max Jacob, *Œuvres*, edited by Antonio Rodriguez. Paris: Gallimard, 2012.
Mallarmé, Stéphane. *Œuvres*. Edited by Yves-Alain Favre. Paris: Garnier, 1985.
– *Œuvres complètes*. Edited by Henri Mondor and G. Jean-Aubry. Paris: Gallimard, 1945.
– *Œuvres complètes II*. Édition présentée, établie et annotée par Bertrand Marchal. Paris: Gallimard, 2003.
Moore, Marianne. *The Complete Poems of Marianne Moore*. New York: Macmillan, 1967.
– *Predilections*. London: Faber and Faber, 1956.
Oppen, George. *New Collected Poems*. New York: New Directions, 2008.
– *Selected Letters*. Durham: Duke University Press, 1990.
– *Selected Prose, Daybooks, and Papers*. Edited by Stephen Cope. Berkeley: University of California Press, 2007.

Ponge, Francis. *Œuvres complètes tome I.* Édition publiée sous la direction de Bernard Beugnot. Paris: Gallimard, 1999.
– *Œuvres complètes tome II.* Édition publiée sous la direction de Bernard Beugnot. Paris: Gallimard, 2002.
Pound, Ezra. *Selected Poems.* New York: New Directions, 1957.
– *Early Writings.* Edited by Ira Nadel. Harmondsworth: Penguin, 2005.
Quintane, Nathalie. *Chaussure.* Paris: P.O.L., 1997.
Reut, Tita. *Vis cachées.* Marseille: La Différence, 1993.
Reverdy, Pierre. *Cette émotion appelée poésie, écrits sur la poésie.* Paris: Flammarion, 1974.
– *Lettres à Jean Rousselot, suivies de Pierre Reverdy romancier, ou quand le poète se dédouble par Jean Rousselot.* Mortemart: Rougerie, 1973.
– *Note éternelle du présent, écrits sur l'art 1923–1960.* Paris: Flammarion, 1973.
– *Œuvres complètes Tome I.* Paris: Flammarion, 2010.
– *Œuvres complètes Tome II.* Paris: Flammarion, 2010.
Rilke, Rainer Maria. *New Poems.* Translated and edited by Joseph Cadora (1907, 1908). Port Townsend: Copper Canyon Press, 2014.
Rimbaud, Arthur. *Lettres du voyant* (1871). Genève: Droz, 1975.
Roethke, Theodore. *Collected Poems.* New York: Anchor, 1974.
Rossi, Paul Louis. *Cose naturali* (in *Quand Anna murmurait*) Paris: Flammarion, 1995.
Roubaud, Jacques. ∈. Paris: Gallimard, 1967.
– "J'ai choisi le sonnet." *La Quinzaine littéraire* 42 (1 to 15 January 1968): 6.
Segalen, Victor. *Briques et tuiles.* Montpellier: Fata Morgana, 1987.
– *Trahison fidèle. Victor Segalen, Henry Manceron, Correspondance 1907–1918.* Paris: Le Seuil, 1985.
– *Stèles* (1912). Édition critique, commentée et augmentée de plusieurs inédits, établie Par Henry Bouillier. Paris: Mercure de France, 1982.
Stein, Gertrude. *Tender Buttons* (1914). The Corrected Centennial Edition. Edited by Seth Perlow. San Francisco: City Lights, 2014.
Stevens, Wallace. *The Collected Poems* (1954). New York: Vintage Books, 1990.
Swenson, May. *Collected Poems.* New York: Library of America, 2013.
Tarkos, Christophe. *Ma Langue.* Paris: Al Dante, 2000.
Tortel, Jean. *Arbitraires espaces.* Paris: Flammarion, 1986.
– *De mon vivant.* Marseille: Cahiers du Sud, 1942.
– *Des corps attaqués.* Paris: Flammarion, 1979.
– *Le Discours des yeux.* Marseille: Ryôan-Ji, 1982.
– *Explications ou bien regard.* Lausanne: Mermod, 1960.
– *Feuilles, tombées d'un discours.* Marseille: Ryôan-Ji, 1984.
– *Instants qualifiés.* Paris: Gallimard, 1973.

– *Limites du corps*. Paris: Gallimard, 1993.
– *Limites du regard*. Paris: Gallimard, 1971.
– "Montpellier 24.04.78." In *Jean Tortel: l'œuvre ou vert*, edited by Catherine Soulier. Montpellier: Université Paul Valéry Montpellier III, 2001.
– *Naissances de l'objet*. Paris: Cahiers du Sud, 1955.
– *Passés recomposés*. Marseille: Ryôan-Ji, 1988.
– *Précarités du jour*. Paris: Flammarion, 1990.
– *Relations*. Paris: Gallimard, 1968.
– *Les Solutions aléatoires*. Marseille: Ryôan-Ji, 1983.
– *Les Saisons en cause*. Marseille: Ryôan-Ji, 1987.
– *Les Villes ouvertes*. Paris: Gallimard, 1965.
Wilbur, Richard. *Collected Poems 1943–2004*. Orlando: Harcourt, 2004.
Williams, William Carlos. *The Collected Poems of William Carlos Williams Volume I 1909–1939*. New York: New Directions, 1986.
– *Selected Essays*. New York: New Directions, 1954.

Other Works Consulted

Abrégé de littérature potentielle. Paris: Mille et une nuits, 2002.
Ades, Dawn. *Dalí* (1982). London: Thames and Hudson, 1995.
Adrian, Dennis. "Georges Braque's Monumental Still Lifes." *Art News* 71.1 (November 1972): 30–3.
Albertini, Lucie, and Alain Vircondelet. *Vivre en poésie: Entretien avec Lucie Albertini et Alain Vircondelet*. Paris: Stock, 1980.
Alexandre, Didier, and Catherine Mayaux, eds. *Lectures d'une œuvre: Stèles et Équipée: Victor Segalen*. Paris: Éditions du Temps, 1999.
Allix, Guy. "À l'entour de Guillevic / Guillevic à l'entour." In *Guillevic: Les chemins du poème*, edited by Serge Gaubert (Marseille: Sud, 1987), 219–30.
Altieri, Charles. *The Art of Twentieth-century American Poetry: Modernism and After*. Oxford: Blackwell, 2006.
– "The Objectivist Tradition." *Chicago Review* 30. 3 (Winter 1979): 5–22.
Apter, Emily, and William Pietz, eds. *Fetishism as Cultural Discourse*. Ithaca: Cornell University Press, 1993.
Arland, Marcel. "Saluer un vrai poète." In *Lire Guillevic*, edited by Serge Gaubert, 17–18.
Arséguel, Gérard. "L'expérience originelle chez Jean Tortel." *Critique* 224 (janvier 1966): 60–7.
– "Jean Tortel: le regard écrit." *Critique* 426 (novembre 1982): 977–80.
Attal, Jean-Pierre. "Sens et valeur du mot *main* dans l'œuvre de Pierre Reverdy." *Critique* 179 (April 1962): 306–28.

Axelrod, Steven Gould, and Helen Deese, eds. *Critical Essays on William Carlos Williams*. New York: G.K. Hall, 1995.

– *Critical Essays on Wallace Stevens*. Boston: G.K. Hall, 1988.

Bachelard, Gaston. *La Poétique de la rêverie* (1960). Paris: PUF, 1965.

Bancquart, Marie-Claire. "Poésie: Leçon de choses, mythologie." In *La Poésie Française au tournant des années 80*, edited by Philippe Delaveau, 139–47. Paris: Corti, 1988.

Baudrillard, Jean. *Le Système des objets*. Paris: Gallimard, 1968.

Beauvoir, Simone de. *Le Deuxième sexe*. Paris: Gallimard, 1949.

Béguin, Albert. *Poésie de la présence*. Neuchâtel: Éditions de la Baconnière, 1957.

Bellos, David. *Georges Perec: A Life in Words: A Biography*. Boston: D.R. Godine, 1993.

Benoît, Monique. "Guillevic: Une géométrie obsessionnelle." *Études littéraires* 5.2 (August 1972): 291–308.

Beugnot, Bernard. *Poétique de Francis Ponge: le palais diaphane*. Paris: PUF, 1990.

Bishop, Michael. "Marie-Claire Bancquart: Énigme et clarté." *Dalhousie French Studies* 38 (Spring 1997): 135–41.

Blanchard, Eli. "On Still Life." *Yale French Studies* 61 (1981): 276–98.

Blanchot, Maurice. *La Part du feu*. Paris: Gallimard, 1949.

Blau du Plessis, Rachel. "'Uncannily in the Open': In Light of Oppen." In *Thinking Poetics: Essays on George Oppen*, edited by Steve Shoemaker, 203–27. Tuscaloosa: University of Alabama Press, 2009.

Bloom, Harold. *American Modernist Poets*. New York: Infobase Publishing, 2011.

– *The Anxiety of Influence: A Theory of Poetry*. New York: Oxford University Press, 1973.

– ed. *Gertrude Stein*. New York: Chelsea House, 1986.

– ed. *Marianne Moore*. New York: Chelsea House, 1987.

– ed. *Wallace Stevens*. New York: Chelsea House, 1985.

Bocholier, Gérard. *Pierre Reverdy: le phare obscur.* Seyssel: Champ Vallon, 1984.

Bohn, Willard. *The Aesthetics of Visual Poetry 1914–1928*. Cambridge: Cambridge University Press, 1986.

Bol, Victor P. *Lecture de Stèles de Victor Segalen*. Paris: Lettres Modernes Minard, 1972.

Bouillier, Henri. *Vistor Segalen: Stèles*. Édition critique établie par Henri Bouillier. Paris: Mercure de France, 1982.

Bowd, Gavin. "Guillevic's *Carnac*: From *La Révolution* to *Le Rivage*." *Dalhousie French Studies* 22 (Spring–Summer 1992): 97–110.

Bozon-Scalzotti, Yvette. "Francis Ponge: Parti pris des choses ou misogynie?" *The French Review* 67.2 (December 1993): 230–42.

Bradley, Fiona. *Surrealism*. London: Tate Gallery Publishing, 1997.

Breslin, James E. *William Carlos Williams: An American Artist*. New York: Oxford University Press, 1970.

Broda, Martine. "Tortel au-delà de la transparence." *Critique* 37.404 (January 1981): 31–9.

Brophy, Michael. *Eugène Guillevic*. Amsterdam: Rodopi, 1993.

– "Le Fragment et le réseau." *Europe* 734–5 (June–July 1990): 117–24.

Brown, Bill, ed. *Things*. Chicago: University of Chicago Press, 2004.

Bryson, Norman. *Looking at the Overlooked: Four Essays on Still Life Painting*. Cambridge: Harvard University Press, 1990.

Burl, Aubrey. *Megalithic Brittany: A Guide to Over 350 Ancient Sites and Monnuments*. London: Thames And Hudson, 1985.

Burt, Ellen S. "Mallarmé's 'Sonnet en yx': The Ambiguities of Speculation." In *Stéphane Mallarmé*, edited by Harold Bloom, 97–120. New York: Chelsea House, 1987.

Butts, William, ed. *Conversations with Richard Wilbur*. Jackson: University Press of Mississippi, 1990.

Calderon, Pierre. "Jean Follain: Objects in Time." In *Sensibility and Creation*, edited by Roger Cardinal, 136–48. London: Croom Helm, 1977.

Carbone, David. "The Subject Matter in View." *Modern Painters* (Autumn 1997): 81–2.

Cardinal, Roger. *Sensibility and Creation*. London: Croom Helm, 1977.

Carlson, Celia. "Compelling Objects: Form and Emotion in Williams's Lyric Poetry." *William Carlos Williams Review* 26.1 (Spring 2006): 27–49.

Chol, Isabelle. *Pierre Reverdy: Poésie plastique: Formes composées et dialogue des arts (1913–1960)*. Genève: Droz, 2006.

Cleghorn, Angus, and Jonathan Ellis, eds. *The Cambridge Companion to Elizabeth Bishop*. Cambridge: Cambridge University Press, 2014.

Collot, Michel. *Horizon de Reverdy*. Paris: PENS, 1981.

Cohen, Francis. "La Chute renversée." *Critique* 555–6 (August–September 1993): 537–45.

Cone, Michèle C. "Pierre Restany and the Nouveaux Réalistes." *Yale French Studies* 98 (2000): 50–65.

Conisbee, Philip. *Chardin*. Oxford: Phaidon, 1986.

Conley, Katherine. *Automatic Woman: The Representation of Woman in Surrealism*. Lincoln: University of Nebraska Press, 1996.

Consenstein, Peter. "Asian Influences in the Poetry of Raymond Queneau and Jacques Roubaud." *Philological Papers* 40 (1994): 56–63.

Costello, Bonnie. *Elizabeth Bishop: Questions of Mastery*. Cambridge: Harvard University Press, 1991.

– *Marianne Moore: Imaginary Possessions*. Cambridge: Harvard University Press, 1981.

Dagognet, François. *Éloge de l'objet: pour une philosophie de la marchandise*. Paris: J. Vrin, 1989.

D'Angelo, Kathleen. "'The Sequence of Disclosure': The Truth Hidden in Things in George Oppen's *Discrete Series*" *Paideuma* 40 (2013): 157–89.

Daive, Jean. *Paul Celan, les jours et les nuits*. Caen: Nous, 2016.

Davidson, Michael. "Dismantling 'Mantis': Reification and Objectivist Poetics." *American Literary History* 3.3 (Fall 1991): 521–41.

Debreuille, Jean-Yves. *Jean Follain: Un monde peuplé d'attente*. Paris: Autres Temps, 1995.

Decaunes, Luc. *Poésie au grand jour*. Seyssel: Champ Vallon, 1982.

DeKoven, Marianne. *A Different Language: Gertrude Stein's Experimental Writing*. Madison: University of Wisconsin Press, 1983.

Démoris, René. *Chardin, la chair et l'objet*. Paris: Adam Biro, 1991.

Derrida, Jacques. *Signéponge/Signsponge* (1977). Translated by Richard Rand. New York: Columbia University Press, 1984.

Diehl, Joanne Feit. *Elizabeth Bishop and Marianne Moore: The Psychodynamics of Creativity*. Princeton: Princeton University Press, 1993.

Diggory, Terence. *William Carlos Williams and the Ethics of Painting*. Princeton: Princeton University Press, 1991.

Dijkstra, Bram. *The Hieroglyphics of a New Speech: Cubism, Stieglitz, and the Early Poetry of William Carlos Williams*. Princeton: Princeton University Press, 1969.

Di Manno, Yves. *endquote: digressions*. Paris: Flammarion, 1999.

Disson, Agnès. "L'Altérité au féminin: Anne Portugal, Pascale Monnier, Nathalie Quintane." In *Écritures contemporaines 4: figures du poème dans la poésie contemporaine de langue française*, edited by Anne Struve-Debeaux, 207–20. Paris: Lettres Modernes Minard, 2004.

Dolle, Marie, ed. *Lectures de Segalen: Stèles et Équipée*. Rennes: Presses Universitaires de Rennes, 1999.

Doumet, Christian. "Stèles ou la lecture inscrite." *Littérature* 59 (October 1985): 31–47.

Driscoll, Kerry. *William Carlos Williams and the Maternal Muse*. Ann Arbor: UMI Research Press, 1987.

Ego, Renaud. "Poésie-infini-réalité: à propos de Christophe Tarkos." In *Quatorze poètes: Anthologie critique et poétique*, edited by Lionel Destremau and Emmanuel Laugier, 155–61. Paris: Prétexte, 2004.

Eigeldinger, Marc. "La Voyance avant Rimbaud." In *Arthur Rimbaud: Lettres du Voyant*, edited by Gérald Schaeffer, 9–107. Geneva: Droz, 1975.

Fairbairn, John. *Invitation to Go*. Oxford: Oxford University Press, 1977.
Finkelstein, Haim N. *Surrealism and the Crisis of the Object*. Ann Arbor: UMI Research Press, 1979.
Fischer, Luke. *The Poet as Phenomenologist: Rilke and the New Poems*. New York: Bloomsbury, 2015.
Fisher, Tom. "A Political Poetics: George Oppen and the Essential Life of the Poem." *Arizona Quarterly* 65.2 (Summer 2009): 83–98.
Formentelli, Éliane. "Présences du blanc, figures du moins." *L'Espace et la lettre: Cahiers Jussieu 3* 10 / 18 (1977): 257–94.
Frelick, Nancy M. *Délie as Other: Toward a Poetics of Desire in Scève's Délie*. Lexington: French Forum Publishers, 1994.
Freund, Thatcher. *Objects of Desire: The Lives of Antiques and Those Who Pursue Them*. New York: Pantheon, 1993.
Gardner, Belinda Grace. "From 'Breakfast in Fur' and Back Again: The Conflation of Images, Language and Objects in Meret Oppenheim's 'Applied Poetry'." In *Meret Oppenheim*, edited by Thomas Levy, 7–23. Bielefeld: Kerber Verlag, 2003.
Garrigue, Jean. *Marianne Moore*. Minneapolis: University of Minnesota Press, 1965.
Gaubert, Serge, "À plus d'un titre." In *Guillevic: Les chemins du poème*, edited by Serge Gaubert, 207–18.
– ed. *Lire Follain*. Lyon: Presses Universitaires de Lyon, 1981.
– ed. *Lire Guillevic*. Lyon: Presses Universitaires de Lyon, 1983.
Gelpi, Albert, ed. *Wallace Stevens: The Poetics of Modernism*. Cambridge: Cambridge University Press, 1985.
Giordan, Claudine. "Ponge et la nomination." *Poétique* 28 (1976): 484–95.
Giudici, Enzo. *Maurice Scève: Bucolico e "Blasonneur."* Naples: Liguori Editore, 1965.
Gleize, Jean-Marie, and Bernard Veck. *Francis Ponge: "Actes ou textes."* Villeneuve d'Ascq: Presses Universitaires de Lille, 1984.
– "Guillevic, Lettre, L'étang." *Littérature* 35 (October 1979): 75–88.
– "Je ne sais situer." In *Jean Tortel: L'œuvre ou vert*, edited by C. Soulier, 15–25.
Godel, Vahé. "La Navigation immobile de Jean Follain." *Critique* 34 (November 1978): 1090–2.
Goldenstein, Jean-Pierre. "Pour une sémiologie du calligramme." *Que Vlo-ve?* 1.29–30 (July–October 1981): 1–8.
Goldenstein, Lorrie. *Elizabeth Bishop: The Biography of a Poetry*. New York: Columbia University Press, 1992.
Gombrich, E.H. "Tradition and Expression in Western Still Life." *The Burlington Magazine* 103.698 (May 1961): 175–80.

Gorrillot, Bénédicte, and Alain Lescart, eds. *L'Illisibilité poétique en question.* Villeneuve d'Ascq: Presses Universitaires du Septentrion, 2014.
Green, Christopher. *Juan Gris.* London: Whitechapel Art Gallery, 1992.
Greene, Robert W. "Encomium for Ponge." *Books Abroad* 48 (1974): 659–68.
Guéron, Jacqueline. "Lecture de Jacques Roubaud." *Critique* 26 (1970): 724–40.
Guiette, Robert. *Vie de Max Jacob.* Paris: Nizet, 1976.
Guild, Elisabeth. "Writing and Drawing in Scève's *Délie.*" In *French Poetry: The Renaissance Through 1915,* edited by Harold Bloom, 59–73. New York: Chelsea House, 1990.
Guillevic. "Un Poète majeur." In *Lire Follain,* edited by Serge Gaubert, 17–21.
Halter, Peter. *The Revolution in the Visual Arts and the Poetry of William Carlos Williams.* Cambridge: Cambridge University Press, 1994.
Harel, Simon. *L'Écriture réparatrice: Le défaut autobiographique (Leiris, Crevel, Artaud).* Montréal: XYZ, 1994.
Harrison, Victoria. *Elizabeth Bishop's Poetics of Intimacy.* Cambridge: Cambridge University Press, 1993.
Harrow, Susan. *The Material, the Real, and the Fractured Self: Subjectivity and Representation from Rimbaud to Réda.* Toronto: University of Toronto Press, 2004.
Harvey, Stella. *Myth and the Sacred in the Poetry of Guillevic.* Amsterdam: Rodopi, 1997.
Haskell, Barbara. *Claes Oldenburg: Object into Monument.* Pasadena: Pasadena Art Museum, 1971.
Hattendorf, Richard. "The Aesthetics of the Visual and the Verbal: Successful Interference in Pierre Reverdy's and Juan Gris's *Au Soleil du plafond.*" *Symposium* 48.2 (Summer 1994): 91–104.
Heidegger, Martin. "The Thing." In Martin Heidegger, *Poetry, Language, Thought,* translated by Albert Hofstadter. New York: Harper Perennial Classics, 2001.
Heller, Michael. *Conviction's Net of Branches: Essays on the Objectivist Poets and Poetry.* Carbondale: Southern Illinois University Press, 1985.
Hermans, Theo. *The Structure of Modernist Poetry.* London: Croom Helm, 1982.
Hinshelwood, R.D. *A Dictionary of Kleinian Thought.* London: Free Association Books, 1989.
Hoffmann, Michael J., ed. *Critical Essays on Gertrude Stein.* Boston: G.K. Hall, 1986.
Hollier, Denis. "L'Opinion changée quant à Ponge." *Tel Quel* 28 (Winter 1967): 90–3.
Hsieh, Yvonne. *Victor Segalen's Literary Encounter with China: Chinese Moulds, Western Thoughts.* Toronto: University of Toronto Press, 1988.

Husson, Julia. "Pierre Reverdy and the 'poème-objet'." *Australian Journal of French Studies* 5:1 (January–April 1968): 21–34.

Hutchinson, Ben. *Rilke's Poetics of Becoming*. London: Maney Publishing, 2006.

Jean, Raymond. *Jean Tortel*. Paris: Seghers, 1984.

Jennison, Ruth. *The Zukofsky Era: Modernity, Margins, and the Avant-garde.* Baltimore: Johns Hopkins University Press, 2012.

Johnson, Ellen H. *Modern Art and the Object: A Century of Changing Attitudes.* 1976. New York: HarperCollins, 1995.

Jordan, Shirley. *The Art Criticism of Francis Ponge*. London: W.S. Maney & Son / Modern Humanities Research Association, 1994.

– "The Construction of the Female in the Texts of Francis Ponge." *Modern Language Review* 94.I (January 1999): 33–45.

Jouanard, Gil, and Jean Tortel. "Quelques pierres blanches dans le jardin de Jean Tortel." In *Colloques Poésie–Cerisy Tome I: Clancier, Guillevic, Tortel,* edited by Georges-Emmanuel Clancier, 201–18. Marseille: Sud, 1983.

Jourdan, Pierre-Albert. "Un goût très fin d'éternel." *Sud* (1979): 108–12.

Joyce, James. *A Portrait of the Artist as a Young Man.* 1917. Oxford: Oxford University Press, 2000.

Kalstone, David. *Becoming a Poet: Elizabeth Bishop with Marianne Moore and Robert Lowell.* New York: Farrar, Straus, Giroux, 1989.

Kamber, Gerald. *Max Jacob and the Poetics of Cubism*. Baltimore: Johns Hopkins University Press, 1971.

Kenny, Robert. "Le Nom effacé." *Nottingham French Studies* 28.2 (Autumn 1989): 4–25.

Kepes, Gyorgy, ed. *The Man-made Object*. New York: Braziller, 1966.

Kinnahan, Linda A. *Poetics of the Feminine: Authority and Literary Tradition in William Carlos Williams, Mina Loy, Denise Levertov, and Kathleen Fraser*. Cambridge: Cambridge University Press, 1994.

Kittay, Jeffrey. "Introduction." *Yale French Studies* 61 (1981): i–v.

Klein, Melanie. *Envy and Gratitude and Other Works, 1946–1945.* London: Hogarth Press and the Institute of Psychoanalysis, 1975.

– *Love, Guilt and Reparations, and Other Works, 1921–1945*. London: Hogarth Press, 1975.

Lacan, Jacques. *Écrits*. Paris: Seuil, 1966.

Lapacherie, Jean-Gérard. "Écriture et lecture du calligramme." *Poétique* 50 (avril 1982): 194–206.

Laszlo, Pierre. "*La Leçon de choses*, or Lessons from Things." *Sub-Stance* 71 / 72 (1993): 274–88.

Laude, Jean. "Jean Tortel: La parole et l'objet." *Critique* (August–September 1961): 697–709.

Leclerc, Yvon, ed. *Lire Reverdy*. Lyon: Presses Universitaires de Lyon, 1990.

Leeder, Karen, and Robert Vilain, eds. *The Cambridge Companion to Rilke*. Cambridge: Cambridge University Press, 2010.

Leggett, B.J. *Wallace Stevens and Poetic Theory: Concerning the Supreme Fiction*. Chapel Hill: University of North Carolina Press, 1987.

Leiris, Michel. Introduction to *Le Cornet à dés* (1917) by Max Jacob, 9–13. Paris: Gallimard, 1945.

Lemichez, Jean-Luc. "Origines inscrites." *Revue des Sciences Humaines* 38.151 (July–September 1973): 411–33.

Lesko Baker, Deborah. *Narcissus and the Lover: Mythic Recovery and Reinvention in Scève's Délie*. Saratoga: Anma Libri, 1986.

Leuwers, Daniel. *L'Accompagnateur: Essais sur la poésie contemporaine*. Marseille: Sud, 1989.

Lévêque, Alain. "Au pays de mémoire." *Sud* (1979): 113–27.

Lock, Peter. "Mutilation and Reparation: Writing in Melanie Klein." *Sub-Stance* 22 (1979): 17–27.

Lockerbie, S.I. Introduction to *Calligrammes: Poems of Peace and War (1913–1916)* by Guillaume Apollinaire, 1–20. Translated by Anne Hyde Greet. Berkeley: University of California Press, 1980.

Longenbach, James. *Modern Poetry after Modernism*. New York: Oxford University Press, 1997.

Lorho, Robert. "Les 'insidieux moments' de Follain." *Europe* 513–14 (January–February 1972): 206–12.

Louette, Jean-François. *Sans protocole: Apollinaire, Segalen, Max Jacob, Michaux*. Paris: Belin, 2003.

Lowry, Glen D. Foreword to *Objects of Desire: The Modern Still Life* by Margit Rowell. New York: Museum of Modern Art / Harry N. Abrams, 1997.

Luca, Gherasim. *Le Vampire passif*. Paris: José Corti, 2001.

MacGowan, Christopher J. *William Carlos Williams's Early Poetry: The Visual Arts Background*. Ann Arbor: UMI Research Press, 1984.

Mao, Douglas. *Solid Objects: Modernism and the Test of Production*. Princeton: Princeton University Press, 1998.

Maulpoix, Jean-Michel. "Les 80 ans de Jean Tortel." *La Quinzaine littéraire* 428 (6 November 1984): 17.

– "Un simple souffle d'éventail." In *Les Poésies de Stéphane Mallarmé: "Une rose des ténèbres,"* edited by José-Luiz Diaz, 23–30. Paris: SEDES, 1998.

Mazzaro, Jerome. "Theodore Roethke and the Failures of Language." In *Profile of Theodore Roethke*, edited by William Heyen, 47–64. Columbus: Charles E. Merrill, 1971.

McEvilly, Thomas. "Basic Dichotomies in Meret Oppenheim's Work." In *Meret Oppenheim: Beyond the Teacup*, edited by Jacqueline Burckhardt and Bice Curiger, 44–53. New York: Independent Curators, 1996.

Merleau-Ponty, Maurice. *L'Oeil et l'esprit*. Paris: Gallimard, 1964.
Metzger, Erika A., and Michael M. Metzger, eds. *A Companion to the Works of Rainer Maria Rilke*. Rochester: Camden House, 2001.
Miller, J. Hillis. *Poets of Reality: Six Twentieth-century Writers*. Cambridge: Harvard University Press, 1965.
– ed. *William Carlos Williams*. Englewood Cliffs: Prentice-Hall, 1966.
Minahen, Charles D. "From 'vers de circonstance' to 'circonstance des vers': Intimations of a Mallarmé Fan." *Dalhousie French Studies* 25 (Fall–Winter 1993): 27–33.
Monroe, Jonathan. *A Poverty of Objects: The Prose Poem and the Politics of Genre*. Ithaca: Cornell University Press, 1987.
Muensterberger, Werner. *Collecting: An Unruly Passion*. 1994. San Diego: Harcourt Brace, 1995.
Müller, Wolfgang. *Rainer Maria Rilkes "Neue Gedichte": Vielfältigkeit eines Gedichttypus*. Meisen-Heim am Glan: Anton Hain, 1971.
– "Rilkes *Neue Gedichte* und der Imagismus." *Blätter der Rilke-Gesellschaft 30* (2010): 231–44.
Nadel, Ira B., and Shirley Neuman, eds. *Gertrude Stein and the Making of Literature*. London: Macmillan, 1988.
Nash, Jerry C. *The Love Aesthetics of Maurice Scève: Poetry and Struggle*. Cambridge: Cambridge University Press, 1991.
Nash, Suzanne. "Entretien de Jean Tortel avec Suzanne Nash." *PO&SIE* 29 (1984): 90–106.
– "Living Transcription: The Poetry of Jean Tortel." *Studies in Twentieth-Century Literature* 13.1 (Winter 1989): 27–42.
Neugebauer, Jörg. "'Auch Noch das Entzücken ein Ding auszusagen': Was Sagt einem Heutigen Lyriker Rilkes Poetik in der *Neuen Gedichte*?" *Blätter der Rilke-Gesellschaft* 30 (2010): 175–84.
Newton, Esther. *Mother Camp: Female Impersonators in America*. Englewood Cliffs: Prentice-Hall, 1972.
Nicholls, Peter. *George Oppen and the Fate of Modernism*. Oxford: Oxford University Press, 2007.
Noël, Bernard. "Le Discours des yeux." *Action poétique* 89–90 (1982): 124–37.
Nykrog, Per. "À la veille du grand adieu: Sur les 'idéogrammes lyriques' d'Apollinaire." *Romanic Review* 80.1 (January 1989): 109–23.
Olscamp, Marcel. "Guillevic ou la folie lucide." *Écrits du Canada français* 62 (1988): 95–104.
Orange, Tom. "William Carlos Williams Between Image and Object." In *William Carlos Williams and the Language of Poetry*, edited by Burton Hatlen and Demetres P. Tryphonopoulos, 127–56. Orono: National Poetry Foundation, 2002.

Paillier, Alain. "Figures d'un monde végétal (Approches de Jean Tortel)." Thèse de doctorat de troisième cycle, Université Paul Valéry, Montpellier III, 1975.

Pap, Jennifer. "From Ekphrasis to 'Moviment': Ponge's 'Nuage … Informe'." *Dalhousie French Studies* 55 (Summer 2001): 95–119.

Patterson, Jennifer. "Reading States of Climax: Masculine Expression and the Language of Orgasm in the Writing of Surrealist Philosopher and Poet André Breton." In *Textuality and Sexuality: Reading Theories and Practice*, edited by Judith Still and Michael Worton, 148–9. Manchester: Manchester University Press, 1993.

Pearce, Susan M. *Collecting in Contemporary Practice*. London: Sage Publications, 1998.

Pearson, Roger. *Mallarmé and Circumstance: The Translation of Silence*. Oxford: Oxford University Press, 2004.

Pickard, Zachariah. *Elizabeth Bishop's Poetics of Description*. Montreal and Kingston: McGill-Queen's University Press, 2009.

Pierre, José. "Breton et le poème-objet." In *L'Objet au défi*, edited by Marie-Claire Dumas and Jacqueline Chénieux-Gendron, 131–42. Paris: PUF, 1987.

Pierrot, Jean. *Guillevic ou la sérénité gagnée*. Seyssel: Champ Vallon, 1984.

Pike, Robert E. "The 'Blasons' in French Literature of the Sixteenth Century." *Romanic Review* 27 (1936): 223–42.

Popovic, Pierre. "Les Morts et le pain: Lecture sociocritique de *Terraqué*." In *Lectures de Guillevic: approches critiques*, edited by Sergio Villani, Pascal Michelucci, and Paul Perron, 315–30. New York: Legas, 2002.

Postel, Philippe. "De la pierre au poème: la forme stèle." In *Lectures d'une œuvre: Stèles et Équipée: Victor Segalen*, edited by Catherine Mayaux and Didier Alexandre, 43–74. Paris: Éditions du Temps, 1999.

Poucel, Jean-Jacques. *Jacques Roubaud and the Invention of Memory*. Chapel Hill: University of North Carolina Press, 2006.

Poulet, Georges. *Études sur le temps humain III: Le point de départ*. Paris: Plon, 1964.

Rabaté, Jean-Michel. *Jacques Lacan and the Subject of Literature*. Houndmills: Palgrave, 2001.

Rachlin, Nathalie. "Francis Ponge, *Le Savon* and the Occupation." *Sub-Stance* 87.27.3 (1998), 85–106.

Ragg, Edward. *Wallace Stevens and the Aesthetics of Abstraction*. Cambridge: Cambridge University Press, 2010.

Ray, William. *Literary Meaning*. London: Basil Blackwell, 1984.

Réda, Jacques. "Note sur Jean Follain." *Cahiers du Sud* 44 (1956): 122–7.

Restany, Pierre, and Pierre Cabanne. *L'Avant-garde au XXe siècle*. Paris: Balland, 1969.

Rheims, Maurice. *La Vie étrange des objets: histoire de la curiosité*. Paris: Plon, 1959.

Richard, Jean-Pierre. *Onze études sur la poésie moderne*. Paris: Seuil, 1964.

Riffaterre, Michael. *Semiotics of Poetry*. Bloomington: Indiana University Press, 1979.

Riggs, Sarah. *Word Sightings: Poetry and Visual Media in Stevens, Bishop, and O'Hara*. New York: Routledge, 2002.

Risset, Jacqueline. *L'Anagramme du désir: sur la Délie de Maurice Scève*. Paris: Fourbis, 1995.

Robinson, Lynn. "L'Objet et le mystère de l'existence dans l'œuvre de Jean Follain." Thèse de doctorat de troisième cycle, Université de Nice, 1976.

Rodriguez, Antonio. *Modernité et paradoxe lyrique: Max Jacob, Francis Ponge*. Paris: Jean-Michel Place, 2006.

Romer, Stephen. Introduction to *Carnac* by Eugène Guillevic, 9–23. Translated by John Montague. Newcastle Upon Tyne: Bloodaxe, 1999.

Rose, Barbara. *Claes Oldenburg*. Stuttgart: Edition Hansjörg Mayer, 1976.

Rosenberg, Pierre, ed. *Chardin*. Paris: Éditions de la Réunion des Musées Nationaux, 1999.

Rosenblum, Robert. *Cubism and Twentieth-century Art*. New York: Abrams, 1966.

Rosset, Clément. *L'Objet singulier*. Paris: Minuit, 1979.

Rothwell, Andrew. *Textual Spaces: The Poetry of Pierre Reverdy*. Amsterdam: Rodopi, 1989.

– "Cubism and the Avant-garde Prose Poem: Figural Space in Pierre Reverdy's *Au Soleil du plafond*." *French Studies* 42.3 (July 1988): 302–19.

Rouffiat, Françoise. *Jean Follain: le même, autrement*. Seyssel: Champ Vallon, 1996.

Rouget, François, and John Stout, eds. *Poétiques de l'objet: l'objet dans la poésie française du Moyen Âge jusqu'à nos jours*. Paris: Champion, 2001.

Rousselot, Jean. "Jean Follain sur son orbite." In *Lire Follain* edited by Serge Gaubert. Lyon: Presses Universitaires de Lyon, 1981. 11–16.

– "Pierre Reverdy, romancier; ou, quand le poète se dédouble." In *Lettres à Jean Rousselot* by Pierre Reverdy, 59–83. Mortemart: Rougerie, 1973.

Rowell, Margit. *Objects of Desire: The Modern Still Life*. New York: Museum of Modern Art / Harry N. Abrams, 1997.

Rustan, Marie-Josèphe. "Reverdy ou la poésie du poète." *Cahiers du Sud* 319 (1953): 464–76.

Ryan, Judith. *Rilke, Modernism and Poetic Tradition*. Cambridge: Cambridge University Press, 1999.

Saba, Guido. *Théophile de Viau: un poète rebelle*. Paris: PUF, 1999.

Sacks-Galey, Penelope. *Calligramme ou écriture figurée: Apollinaire inventeur de formes*. Paris: Lettres Modernes Minard, 1988.

Salinger, Wendy, ed. *Richard Wilbur's Creation*. Ann Arbor: University of Michigan Press, 1983.

Samuels, Peggy. *Deep Skin: Elizabeth Bishop and Visual Art*. Ithaca: Cornell University Press, 2010.

Sartre, Jean-Paul. "L'Homme et les choses." In *Situations I* by Jean-Paul Sartre. Paris: Gallimard, 1948. 226–70.

Saunders, Alison. *The Sixteenth-century Blason Poétique*. Bern: Peter Lang, 1981.

Sawday, Jonathan. *The Body Emblazoned: Dissection and the Human Body in Renaissance Culture*. London: Routledge, 1995.

Scepi, Henri. "Suggestion et abstraction: les objets de l'écriture." In *Mallarmé*, edited by André Guyaux, 53–67. Paris: Presses Universitaires de Paris-Sorbonne, 1998.

Schapiro, Meyer. *Modern Art: 19th and 20th Centuries: Selected Papers*. London: Chatto and Windus, 1978.

Schmidt, Albert-Marie, ed. *Poètes du XVIe siècle*. Paris: Gallimard, 1969.

Schneider, Norbert. *Still Life: Still Life Painting in the Early Modern Period*. Köln: Taschen, 1994.

Schwartz, Lloyd, and Sybil P. Estess, eds. *Elizabeth Bishop and Her Art*. Ann Arbor: University of Michigan Press, 1983.

Scott, David. *Pictorialist Poetics: Poetry and the Visual Arts in 19th-century France*. Cambridge: Cambridge University Press, 1998.

Scroggins, Mark, ed. *Upper Limit Music: The Writing of Louis Zukofsky*. Tuscaloosa: University of Alabama Press, 1997.

Sears, Dianne. "Bracketing Painting: Ponge's Criticism of Braque." *Dalhousie French Studies* 21 (Fall–Winter 1991): 1–13.

Shoemaker, Steve, ed. *Thinking Poetics: Essays on George Oppen*. Tuscaloosa: University of Alabama Press, 2009.

Soulier, Catherine, ed. *Jean Tortel: l'œuvre ou vert*. Montpellier: Université Paul Valéry Montpellier III, 2001.

Stamelman, Richard. "From Muteness to Speech: The Drama of Expression in Francis Ponge's Poetry." *Books Abroad* 48.4 (Autumn 1974): 688–94.

Stanley, Sandra Kumamoto. *Louis Zukofsky and the Transformation of a Modern American Poetics*. Berkeley: University of California Press, 1994.

Stapleton, Laurence. *Marianne Moore: The Poet's Advance*. Princeton: Princeton University Press, 1978.

St Aubyn, F.C. *Stéphane Mallarmé (Updated Edition)*. Boston: Twayne, 1989.

Steele, Valerie. *Shoes: A Lexicon of Style*. New York: Rizzoli, 1999.

Steinmetz, Jean-Luc. "Écarts." In *Lire Reverdy*, 63–72.

Sterling, Charles. *La Nature morte de l'antiquité à nos jours*. Paris: Pierre Tisné, 1952.

Strathausen, Carsten. *The Look of Things: Poetry and Vision around 1900*. Chapel Hill: University of North Carolina Press, 2003.

Terry, Patricia. "Introduction." In *Roof Slates and Other Poems of Pierre Reverdy*, translated by Patricia Terry and Mary Ann Caws. Boston: Northeastern University Press, 1981: 3–13.

Thomas, Henri. "Follain: ciel appris, ciel vivant" *NRF* 34 (1969): 427–31.

– Preface to Jean Follain. In *Exister, suivi de Territoires*, 7–12. Paris: Gallimard, 1969.

Tixier, Jean-Max. "Jean Tortel ou l'écriture différentielle." *Courrier du Centre International d'études Poétiques* 121–2 (November–December 1977): 3–10.

Tomarken, Annette and Edward. "The Rise and Fall of the Sixteenth-century French Blason." *Symposium* 29.1–2 (Spring–Summer 1975): 139–63.

Tomlinson, Charles, ed. *Marianne Moore: A Collection of Critical Essays*. Englewood Cliffs: Prentice-Hall, 1969.

Tortel, Jean. *Le Préclassicisme français*. Paris: Les Cahiers du Sud, 1952.

– "Jean Follain: Appareil de la terre." *NRF* 151 (July 1965): 138–40.

– *Guillevic*. Paris: Seghers, 1971.

– "Lecture première." In *Guillevic: Les chemins du poème*, edited by Serge Gaubert, 9–20.

– "Ponge qui n'a de cesse." In *Ponge inventeur et classique*, edited by Philippe Bonnefis and Pierre Oster, 16–33. Paris: U.G.E., 1977.

– *Francis Ponge cinq fois*. Marseille: Fata Morgana, 1984.

Valette, Bernard. "Le point de vue du linguiste." In *Analyses et réflexions sur Ponge: Pièces: les mots et les choses*, edited by Paul-Laurent Assoun. Paris: Ellipses, 1988. 23–8.

Van Der Marck, Jan. *Arman*. New York: Abbeville Press, 1984.

Van Gijseghem, Hubert. *La Quête de l'objet: pour une psychologie du chercheur de trésor*. Québec: Hurtubise HMH, 1985.

Vendler, Helen. *Wallace Stevens: Words Chosen Out of Desire*. Knoxville: University of Tennessee Press, 1984.

Viau, Théophile de. *Œuvres complètes III*. Édition de Guido Saba. Paris: Champion, 1999.

Visser, Margaret. *Much Depends on Dinner: The Extraordinary History, Mythology, Allure and Obsessions, Perils and Taboos of an Ordinary Meal*. 1986. Toronto: HarperPerennial, 1992.

Warehime, Marja. "Manifestoes and Still Life: Chardin and Ponge" *French Forum* (January 1984): 59–68.

Webster, Michael. *Reading Visual Poetry after Futurism: Marinetti, Apollinaire, Schwitters, Cummings*. New York: Peter Lang, 1995.

Willis, Patricia C., ed. *Marianne Moore: Woman and Poet*. Orono: National Poetry Foundation, 1990.

Wilson, D.B. *Descriptive Poetry in France from Blason to Baroque*. Manchester: Manchester University Press, 1967.

Woods, Roy. *Rilke Through a Glass Darkly: Poetry of R.M. Rilke and its English Translations: A Critical Comparison*. Trier: Wissenschaftlicher Verlag Trier, 1996.

York, R.A. "Some Semantic Structures in the Verse of Jean Follain." *Romanic Review* 70.4 (November 1979): 384–98.

Zukofsky, Louis. *Prepositions: The Collected Critical Essays*. 1967. Berkeley: University of California Press, 1981.

Index

www.ingramcontent.com/pod-product-compliance
Lightning Source LLC
LaVergne TN
LVHW090150080826
844660LV00013B/751/J

* 9 7 8 1 4 8 7 5 0 1 5 7 0 *